NATURE RESERVES
of GREAT BRITAIN

Dennis Furnell

Bishopsgate Press Limited
37 Union Street, London SE1 1SE

To Ann and Robin

A Catalogue record of this book is available from the British Library.

ISBN   1 85219 033 7

All enquiries and requests relevant to this title should be sent to the publisher, Bishopsgate Press Ltd., 37 Union Street, London SE1 1SE.

Printed in Hong Kong through GlobalCom Pte Ltd

Two asterisks ** denotes reserves that can be visited by permit only.

One asterisk * denotes reserve where a permit is required for hides or access off the main area.

The recommendation given as to when to visit the reserves indicates the best season in which to see the most flora and fauna, but it should be noted that all the reserves are interesting at any time of year.

Contents

THE WAY THROUGH THE WOODS

by

Rudyard Kipling

They shut the road through the woods
Seventy years ago.
Weather and rain have undone it again,
And now you would never know
There was once a road through the woods
Before they planted the trees.
It is underneath the coppice and heath,
And the thin anemones.
Only the keeper sees
That, where the ring-dove broods,
And the badgers roll at ease,
There was once a road through the woods.

Yet, if you enter the woods
Of a summer evening late,
When the night-air cools on the trout-ringed pools
Where the otter whistles his mate,
(They fear not men in the woods,
Because they see so few)
You will hear the beat of a horse's feet
And the swish of a skirt in the dew,
Steadily cantering through
The misty solitudes,
As though they perfectly knew
The old lost road through the woods. . . .
But there is no road through the woods.

Bluebell Wood

INTRODUCTION

In this, the last quarter of the 20th century, the country-side is no longer the workplace of the mass of people, it has become a place in which to relax, to enjoy the natural things of life and to find a sense of peace; but it has always provided inspiration for poets and writers. Environmentally the British Isles occupy a unique position in the northern hemisphere, not only are they protected from the extremes of weather that afflict other countries situated on the same line of latitude, by the waters of the Atlantic Ocean and North Sea, but the mighty gulf stream brings water warmed by the equatorial sun to temper the winds.

It is not possible to look at the natural history of Britain today without taking into account the passage of time. In the same way that one cannot truly appreciate the beautifully illuminated Lindisfarne Gospels as solely a work of art out of context with their spiritual significance. Even as those patient monks worked at their brilliant illuminations the rock on which their monastery was founded was recovering millimetre by millimetre from the downward pressure of thousands of millions of tonnes of ice that had moved across the landscape during the last Ice Age reforming hills and mountains originally created from ancient sediments. Above and below the thin skin of cool stable rock constituting our world powerful forces are at work dictating the variety of plant and animal species to be found, but climatic events too play a major part as does altitude and prevailing winds.

The Ice Age was instrumental in redistributing the fertility of the British Isles, stripping and scouring the softer rocks from northern regions and depositing them in the form of boulder clay or gravel in the valleys of the Midlands and south east England leaving an exposed granite shield which took a great many thousands of years of peat deposit and Caledonian pine forest to heal and cover with a bandage of green plants.

We live in a countryside of great diversity. Man's work, his roads, towns and cities occupy less than ten per cent of the total surface and much of the concentration of habitation and industrial exploitation occurs for sound economic and social reasons along river valleys and on the inland flood plains associated with many lowland rivers. Wildlife too finds the living easy in this lowland countryside. Ample water, high soil fertility and a mild micro-climate constitutes the richest combination for plant productivity, the very reason man has colonised such places and cultivated them for arable crops and livestock production.

Natural events may have provided the basal material of the British Isles the rocks, hills, valleys, lakes and streams but man has so modified the landscape over the centuries that little that is truly wild or natural remains. Plants, animals, insects and birds have adapted or vanished as the countryside has altered; tiny creatures like butterflies and moths have become extinct as well as the more obvious sea eagle, wolf and wild boar as man has destroyed the habitat or killed the creatures themselves through ignorance or because of competition for food. But even as the carnage of the Great War ripped the very soil of Europe and claimed the sacrifice of millions of people plans were afoot to designate areas of the British Isles where birds and animals could live in safety, and from those seeds of conservation have grown a network of nature reserves from Land's End to John O'Groats funded by public and private money, encompassing hundreds of thousands of hectares and ranging in size from the huge Loch Leven reserve, more than 1500 hectares of Tayside in Scotland and maintained by the Nature Conservancy Council, to the tiny urban Brook-mill Road reserve tucked away in London's Lewisham a mere quarter hectare of recreated coppice and chalk grassland on a disued railway line.

As a species man needs to commune with nature and recent surveys have shown that country walks are now the most popular outdoor leisure activity in the land.

Peacock on Ragwort

For such a small country we have produced a large number of poets, writers and artists who have drawn upon the countryside and the people who live and work there as their raw material. Some names and counties spring instantly to mind. Northamptonshire and the poet John Clare, William Barnes and Thomas Hardy who both found inspiration in the lanes and coombes and wild heaths of Dorset; and where would the neat villas and sandy conifer plantations of suburban Surrey rank in literature had it not been for .the brilliance and gentle irony of John Betjemen. Betjemen's more popular works would appear to be entrenched in suburbia on the cricket fields and tennis courts, but he drew also on his close association with Cornwall, a county where I too spent part of my childhood, for many of his more intense and moving poems of the sea and childhood memories.

The dry cold plains, open skies and coastal marshes of the wild fowl-rich county of Suffolk fascinated George Crabbe as well as the watercolour painters of the Norwich School, but Crabbe would find it hard nowadays to "Wander in the winding glade" as in his poem "Late Wisdom", for the tractor is king here now and the land has been subjugated by the economics of modern agriculture.

A long association between shepherd and downland created rolling waves of flower-rich chalk hills that in summer shimmer with butterflies and it was to this landscape that Rudyard Kipling was attracted. He is perhaps best known for his stories about India and the Raj yet the Sussex countryside lit a spark in his creative mind that echoes in many of his poems. His early days were spent in the quiet wooded valleys of the west country and he used the United Services College in North Devon as the setting for his novel "Stalky and Co".

Wordsworth and the lakeland poets immortalised Cumbria where lakes lie in ancient ice-scoured valley bottoms reflecting deep green oakwoods and bracken covered hillsides, and ever changing skyscapes where buzzards and ravens mew and croak and where the few remaining pairs of golden eagles hunt over the shattered rocks of the high fells.

The harsh economic reality of mining in the Welsh valleys obscured their natural beauty, but today the principality is one of the least developed parts of our islands and because of this red kites and rare mammals are still found where oakwoods cling to the hills and fast flowing rivers tumble from the folded landscape. The wildness of the Welsh scenery was well matched by the talent of Dylan Thomas whose eye for place was as clear as his vision of the characters he created in "Under Milk Wood". Off the Welsh coast, like an Atlantic seal in deep water, lies Anglesea where the last of the Celtic druids confronted the Roman armies of Agricola two thousand years ago and where dune orchids bloom on Newborough Warren National Nature Reserve.

Sir Walter Scott found the subject matter for his poetry and novels in the rugged border country. Here the healing bandage of herbage is thin over the scars of the last great glaciation when hard rocks welled up from deep within the core to form a wild and beautiful landscape. Little is left of the old forest of Scots pine and birch that once covered the highlands before the "clearances" but you can still find remnant populations of the birds and mammals formerly common in England when it was more heavily wooded; now many of these very special creatures, wild cat, osprey and crested tit to name a few, survive only in the wild fastness of Scotland. The Scots national poet Robert Burns never wrote specifically of the osprey yet he drew much on the Scottish landscape and its wild inhabitants for his verse.

During the 20th century Britain's landscape has changed dramatically. We can no longer wander at will for our laws of land ownership mean than much of the countryside is closed to public access. More than half our broadleaved woodlands have been felled and the land on which they grow converted to arable farming; also many areas of downland, heath and moor have been "improved" so that no longer are they safe for wildlife or open to walkers.

The losses are staggering, witness the demise of hundreds of square miles of open Dorset heathlands, world famous as the setting for several of Thomas Hardy's novels. Sand quarrying, army exercise ranges, farming and conifer plantations have whittled away the wilderness home of the smooth snake and sand lizard, nightjar, hobby and the Dartford warbler. A few isolated acres remain outside the umbrella of conservation bodies and of course the RSPB reserve at Arne and one or two other places under the control of the Nature Conservancy Council provide a stable refuge and some degree of ecological continuity.

Even the primaeval wilderness of the flow country of Caithness is under threat from commercial forestation with conifer plantations marching across the land like so many battalions of troops marshalled in straight lines for maximum tax advantage. Here, where birds have nested undisturbed for millennia, where the red-throated diver calls like a soul in torment, nature should be king, yet even in this quiet place man has encroached for profit and nature has had to give way.

To my mind reserves are a contradiction of the conservation ethic. That we need them at all means the conservation movement has in some way failed to get its message across. Instead of the whole of the country being

Redshank

capable of supporting a wealth of wildlife side by side with the works of mankind in peaceful coexistence, nature is confined within the strict limits of reserves and a few pockets of undeveloped land. Fortunately conservation has become fashionable, but even so more land is "preserved" to produce game for shooting than is made available for wildlife, and despite undoubted public desire to protect our environment the diversity of habitat continues to decline as do numbers of species of wild plants and animals.

In this book you will discover those places where many of our best-loved poets found their inspiration. Needless to say some of them are greatly altered. Time itself wreaks changes. Trees mature and are felled by the elements, or by man. The loss of elms through Dutch elm disease so altered the landscape of Northamptonshire that were John Clare to return today to his home village of Helpstone he wouldn't recognise it. The lacy pattern of winter elms against a wide sky is now only a memory, but nevertheless the modern landscape is still full of beauty, still a source of inspiration ·and wonder, and nature reserves have encapsulated habitats that once existed over large parts of the British Isles. Many of these reserves have unrestricted access, others can only be visited by permit or prior arrangement. All are well worth a visit. Your interest may be birds or botany or simply the freedom to walk in pleasant surroundings, and few countries can offer such a range of differing landscapes within such a small area as the British Isles. Quite simply they are the most beautiful group of islands on earth.

With this book as your guide may you also find that deep sense of pleasure and wonderment which shines so clearly from the lines of our favourite poems.

I meant to do my work today —
But a brown bird sang in the apple tree,
And a buttefly flitted across the field,
And all the leaves were calling me.

And the wind went sighing over the land,
Tossing the grasses to and fro,
And a rainbow held out its shining hand —
So what could I do but laugh and go?

Richard le Gallienne

AVON & SOMERSET

The ancient county of Somerset, and its new addition Avon, makes a complex environmental and geological mix. The contours and river systems created a desirable place for man and wildlife over many millennia, and evidence of human occupation can be seen in the pre-historic timber and wattle roadways that cross the once extensive peat lands and marshes of the Somerset Levels; they were formed when the seas rose after the last Pleistocene Ice Age flooding the delta system of three rivers creating a natural horseshoe-shaped depression bounded by the Quantock Hills and the gentle sloping Mendips. When the sea meandered into this depression, it conspired with reed and moss and water plants to produce a varied natural habitat of reed swamp and marsh and over a period of 7000 years a peat layer built up — in places four metres thick. When man ceased his wanderings as a hunter gatherer he settled down to farm the easily tilled fertile soil. Good fishing, plenty of fowl and the proximity of the nearby hills in time of flood or warfare, were an added bonus.

In order to farm the Levels more than 8000 kilometres of field ditches and drainage channels had to be dug, mainly by hand, to ease the water out of the peat. As in so many other places man's activity has drastically altered the habitat, nevertheless, until relatively recently, long established farming methods helped to provide a rich and varied wildlife, but post war agricultural schemes, sub-sidised by central government and latterly by the EEC to maximise food production have, in many cases, brought with them an unacceptable cost to the environment. Even the richest, ostensibly protected areas, are being degraded making them less suitable for breeding waders, so much a feature of springtime in this area.

On quiet winter evenings the atmosphere invites the mind to wander into realms of myth and magic; it's easy to see why medieval chroniclers set the Isle of Avalon, the court of King Arthur and his Queen, the fair Guinevere, on the knoll at Glastonbury. It is said that the bones of Arthur and his Queen were found in the 12th century by the monks of the Abbey and subsequently re-interred close to the site of the Lady Chapel. When Alfred Lord Tennyson read the tales set down by Geoffrey of Monmouth and Malory, he was inspired to write "Idylls of the King", and also "The Lady of Shalott". In verse two — part one, he sets a scene that could only be found around the Mound of Glastonbury:-

"Willows whiten, aspens quiver,
Little breezes dusk and shiver
Thro' the wave that runs forever
By the island in the river
          Flowing down to Camelot.

Four gray walls, and four gray towers,
Overlook a space of flowers,
And the silent isle imbowers
          The Lady of Shalott.

This whole poem echoes the quiet solemnity of the Somerset Levels when the wind is off the sea, and the scent of waves and salt water through the leaning pollard willows mingles with the sound of wintering waders and wildfowl. Few places are so steeped in history. It's almost a race memory, invoked by simple events such as the sensation when your hands grip the textured surface of binoculars, to watch the teal and mallard burst upward at the sight of a hunting peregrine. So, in far off times, other hands would tighten upon the warmth of a yew wood long bow taking the strain as the sinew string nocked tight over the goose feather-fletched arrow.

On the seaward side of the Levels is Bridgwater Bay. The rivers that drain from the surrounding hills and fertile vale of Taunton Dene seek their eventual outfall near Burnham-on-Sea. Here the mudflats are a mecca for birdwatchers and birds alike, with great congregations of shelduck feeding on the tiny snails and invertebrates in the wide expanse of rich mud exposed twice daily by the tide. The bay is most exciting in spring when whimbrel and curlew pause in their northward migration to rest and feed.

The Somerset and Avon region is rich in contrasts. From the hard reef limestone of the Mendip hills, where the historic river-cut Cheddar Gorge provides a special habitat for rare limestone flora like the Cheddar Pink, to the equally harsh and uncompromising coastal habitat afforded by the desert-like environment of the Barrow Dunes, held in check only by marram grass, and the rich farmland, ridge and furrowed, rolling towards Yeovil, Crewkerne and the Blackdown Hills. The M5 motorway runs through the region like an artery, its unsprayed, unpeopled banks patrolled by kestrels at a ratio of one pair every three kilometres or so, hovering in wait for small mammals and insects over the verges.

The road is both a blessing and a curse. In the main the very ease and speed of travel along this trunk route has left quiet villages and woods relatively undisturbed, the traffic rushing straight through pell mell either to the industrial centres of the north and midlands, or south to the Devon and Cornish summer holidays resorts; but the very existence of the road has exerted pressure to develop formerly inaccessible areas, and has made large projects

like the proposed Severn tidal barrage attractive to planners in order to feed the energy needs of the growing City of Bristol, and the county town of Taunton. The problem of development, and the needs of man, are often dealt with at the expense of the environment, but Bristol's need for drinking water created the twin lakes of Blagdon and Chew valley now naturalised into the landscape, and a prime stopover point for wintering flocks of wildfowl and swans.

Most of Somerset and Avon is dominated by the Bristol Channel, even that part of Exmoor within Somerset's boundary is so influenced; watered by moist winds off the sea, the frequent rains run off the catchment as small swift streams conspiring to produce wet wooded valleys, thick with oaks and ringing in spring with birdsong. The green and gold moorland enhanced by the calls of buzzard and curlew is protected from the harshest winter weather by the tempering effect of the westerlies.

The twin fingers of Brean Down and Sand Point reach out into the Bristol Channel towards the islands of Flat Holm and Steep Holm, relics of a land mass long ago eroded. Steep Holm is a nature reserve and a monument to the environmentalist and broadcaster Kenneth Allsop. Its fellow rocky islet Flat Holm lies almost central to the stream of the channel and is a reminder of a time when Wales and Somerset were closer than brothers.

AISHOLT RING WALK (Somerset TfNC) — *All year*

Aisholt Ring Walk has spectacular views from the highest point in the Quantock Hills. On a clear day you can see Devon, Somerset and the blue hills of Wales. Buzzards share the solitude, although this is fast disappearing due to increasing public pressure.
Circular trail 9km – Map ref: ST 182338.

ASHAM WOOD (Somerset TfNC)** — *Spring, summer*

Asham Wood is an interesting piece of ancient woodland that has been coppiced to increase its wildlife diversity.

Exmoor ponies   *Avon and Somerset*

The plant cover reflects this regime and many unusual plants are present in some numbers. For instance meadow saffron, rare over most of the county, blooms here prolifically; this plant of the lily family has the unusual habit of the flower spike, without its leaves, appearing from the soil in early September.
33.4ha

AVON GORGE (NCC) — *Spring, summer*

Much of the reserve has been quarried and the otherwise steep rock faces shaped into a series of steps and ledges where plants and trees can find a root-hold. There are a number of species here that hark back to a distant past such as very old oak trees, large ash trees and small-leaved lime, a relic of a time when much of the country was covered by a mighty forest. The site is of outstanding botanical importance with Bristol whitebeam, the rare spiked speedwell and Bristol rock cress. This type of limestone habitat is superb for all forms of wildlife, the diversity of plants encourages a wealth of insects and on these insects depends a healthy population of birds. Predatory birds at the top of the food chain are well represented with tawny owls hunting the substantial small mammal population, and sparrowhawks taking advantage of the many small birds.

In Britain the term "balanced habitat" is something of a contradiction, but here there is perhaps a sign of natural checks and balances operating on the inhabitants of the Gorge.
105ha – Map ref: ST 553731

BREAN DOWN SANCTUARY (NT) — *All year*

The limestone rock that forms much of Brean Down was probably much bigger, but during the last Ice Age powerful glacial action removed large quantities of this rock. Brean Down is a relic of these ancient times, a limestone ridge jutting into the Severn estuary.
The site is one of outstanding importance because of its position on the edge of a major bird flyway, and each year huge numbers of birds of many different species pass by the point, or stop to rest and feed before moving on. The increasing population of peregrines in the west of England and Wales habitually visits this sanctuary and on a winter's day it is unusual not to see at least one of these fast flying falcons on the wing.
64ha – Map ref: ST 296586.

BRIDGWATER BAY (NCC) — *All year*
especially migration times

The outflow of water from the Somerset Levels provides immense fertility to the muddy shoreline of this bay used by vast numbers of waders and duck in winter to feed and to roost. Shelduck find a safe haven here when moulting, and these colourful birds can be seen for much of the year. In hard weather herons, driven in by the frost-covered dykes and waterways, find the flounders and small fish a life saver, especially when the winter freeze is prolonged.

The area also supports a fascinating salt marsh flora, and seeds from the maritime plants provide a food source for the many migrant finches that sweep in from the continent of Europe. Long walks along the sea-wall show an ever changing natural history vista whether in winter or in spring and early summer when the migrants are on the move.
2400ha – Map ref: ST 278464

BROWN'S FOLLY (Avon WT) — *Spring, summer*

A series of Bath stone quarry terraces full of downland plants and looking over mixed woodland. Brown's Folly is superb for woodland birds, and the mine-shafts harbour bat colonies, especially greater horseshoe bats.
12.8ha – Map ref: ST 798664

CATCOTT (Somerset TfNC)** — *Spring, summer*

Fen and heath wetland on either side of an alder path provides a marvellous habitat for dragonflies, and typical birds of the Somerset Levels breed here including willow-tits. The meadows are outstanding with a flora reminiscent of old flood meadows before drainage and peat extraction spoiled so much; marsh bedstraw, marsh marigold, yellow loosestrife and a host of other grassland plants are part of the rich sward. The Somerset Levels are remarkable for the numbers and species of dragonflies and Catcott is no exception.
14ha

CHEDDAR CLIFFS (NT)** — *Spring, summer*

Rare Cheddar pinks and green-winged orchids bloom here on their native limestone cliffs. Collecting and heavy public pressure once threatened this very fragile ecosystem, but now it is protected and hopefully will continue to provide a unique series of rare ecological niches for plants.
80ha

CHEW VALLEY & BLAGDON RESERVOIRS*
(Bristol Waterworks Co) — *All year*

These drinking water reservoirs are renowned for waterfowl and terns, and form a vital link in the chain of large inland waterways dotted across the country. Blagdon is deeper than Chew Valley and both are trout fisheries of some note, but Chew Valley attracts diving duck because they can reach the weed growth in the shallow water. In spring and autumn there is a passage of common, arctic, sandwich and black terns, as well as a substantial variety and number of waders while wildfowl counts in winter on both lakes can run into many hundreds of birds; the appearance of whooper and Bewick swans in hard weather is a bonus for regular birdwatchers.

The presence of such large numbers of birds is bound to attract predators, peregrines are regular visitors in winter, and there is a resident population of sparrowhawks. In autumn young osprey can be seen fishing as they stop and feed on the long journey that will eventually take them to Africa. Breeding birds include many of the common passerines, and waterfowl that nest on the lakeside margins. Increasing numbers of gadwall, ruddy duck and shoveller can be seen.
Chew Valley 656ha – Map ref: ST 570615
Blagdon 178ha – Map ref: ST 516596

CLEEVE HERONRY (Avon WT)** — *Spring, summer*

One of the most important heronries in the south west, in excess of 40 pairs. The adult birds arrive in late winter to begin the process of repairing and refurbishing the nests, and the turmoil and squawking that goes on as birds try to steal sticks from each other leads to endless activity. While the birds are incubating things quieten down, but the uproar begins again as the reptilian chicks demand food from their elegant but hard pressed parents.
3.2ha

CONEY WOOD (Woodland Trust) — *Spring, summer*

Standing on the banks of a tributary of the river Alham, Coney Wood is small and at its best in late spring when the trees are in full leaf and birds in full song. There is a substantial badger sett which is increasing in population density as the wood receives full protection.
1.2ha – Map ref: ST 692389

EBBOR GORGE (NCC)* — *Spring through autumn*

This immense landscape feature was cut through by water and the debris from ancient glaciations. Once the watercourse ran over a flat limestone plain now part of the Mendip plateau, but where is the great river that used to flow along the bottom of this valley? Limestone is soluble and rainwater, being slightly acidic, dissolves the alkaline rock. Deep underground are fissures and caves where water has found its way through, and the Axe which once used this valley as its course to the sea is now deep underground emerging at Wookey Hole.

The rivers that wore away the gorge also deposited soil, and time and the growth of tens of millions of plants and micro-organisms has produced conditions where trees can find enough soil to take root clothing the sides of the gorge where the inclination is not too steep; their roots adding to the erosion by cracking the fragile limestone as they search for food and anchorage. On the plateau above are remnants of limestone grassland and heath and, where the trees have not invaded, orchids bloom.

There is some evidence that the hazel and ash have been coppiced since the Bronze Age and a great deal of the material used for the old trackways across the Levels is thought to have been cut from Ebor. There was a long period of time when coppicing was not employed on the valley bottom, but pastoralism needed small timber and in time the woods were coppiced again. It is a regime of woodland management that provides the maximum wildlife potential. Some of the fertile soil on the valley bottom has been cultivated, often used as pasture, and the plant life of these small fields is very varied.

Small mammals include colonies of bats who roost in the caves and rock crevices; the very rare greater horse-shoe bat roosts here as well as less rare species like long-eared and noctule bats. The bird life of this fascinating landscape is very rich indeed, many birds that sing and breed here spend their winters in Africa and when they return in spring the dawn chorus is dramatic. Peregrines, sparrowhawks, kestrels and buzzards are regularly seen; peregrines don't nest in the gorge, but in time they may colonise some of the more inaccessible crags, after all they have bred in the gorge at Symonds Yat which is a similar habitat with a similar food potential.
46ha

EXMOOR NATIONAL PARK (ENPC) — *All year*

Straddling north Devon and the Somerset coast the moor still retains some of its ancient character although incursion by agriculture has led to a marked diminution of the area's wildlife potential. The moor is a very special place, there's still a trace of the wild landscape that has existed for a 1000 years or more, since it was stripped of trees by early man. Red grouse thrive here and, of course, the unique wild Exmoor ponies with their mealy muzzles and hardy constitutions are able to exist where other animals would die. The Exmoor pony is part of the wild ecosystem, their busy jaws keep the turf short and prevent regeneration of trees, as do the sheep and the few cattle that share this wild area.

The woods that fill the coombes and valleys often show evidence of having been coppiced for centuries, the broad mossy stools of oak are sometimes 5ft. across and bear many trunks. These trees may be 1000 years old and some are past their prime and rotting, but where they have been restored by proper coppice management they take on a new lease of life. The woods and valleys are full of birds and mammals and small herds of red deer kept viable mainly for stag hunting, can also be found in the woods and on the moorland slopes.

An enormous amount of human traffic passes over the moor and holidays are spent in the tiny hamlets, but most people tend not to wander far from their cars, and the unique wild quality of Lorna Doone's Exmoor eludes them.

The region is at its best in April and May when the birdsong is dramatic and buzzards can be seen circling over the blue-green hillsides looking for rabbits, the heather and Dorset heath is quite lovely on a fine day. The weather comes mainly from the west with frequent rain, and many of Devon's most famous rivers are born on this boggy plateau fed by the wet west wind.
68,635ha

FROME VALLEY NATURE TRAIL
(Bristol Naturalists' Society) — *Spring through autumn*

Swift clear water is a perfect habitat for arrowhead and water-crowfoot and both are found here in the water-meadows. The whole reserve is very peaceful and when the migrant warblers return to the woods and their traditional nesting sites in early spring, the atmosphere is magical; the descending song phrase of the willow warbler can be heard all along the riverside. Birds feature strongly here, over 70 species have been recorded including kingfishers. The springtime butterfly population is enhanced by orange tip butterflies.
4.5km – Map ref: ST 622765

FYNE COURT (Somerset TfNC Headquarters) —
Spring through autumn

Lake, beech woodland, an old quarry and an arboretum provide enormous variety. The Somerset Trust for Nature

Conservation have their headquarters here, and Fyne Court also houses the Interpretive Centre for the Quantocks. In spring and early summer the area is alive with birds and insects.
9ha – Map ref: ST 223321

GOBLIN COMBE (Avon WT)** — *Spring, summer*

This attractive reserve lives up to its name for there is a decidedly magical air about the deep-cut wooded valley worn down through the limestone rocks by thousands of years of wear from torrential rivers; now much of the water is gone — deep underground — and woodland has colonised with ash, yew, beech and sycamore over hazel and box. The area is enhanced by scree and shallow limestone and turf thick with dwarf varieties of downland flowers; where the sun strikes the slopes you'll find butterflies galore, common blues are here and so are small copper butterflies whose food plant, sheep's sorrel, grows profusely.

Bird life ranges from spotted flycatchers in the woodland to an immense diversity of songbirds in the more open scrubby coppiced areas. Owls and small birds of prey thrive on this ample supply and the large numbers of small mammals that live in this sheltered environment. Foxes and badgers can be seen, and there are several bat colonies.
9ha

HORNER WOOD (NT)* — *All year*

Unique ancient woodland on the edge of Exmoor showing how man can positively affect the ecosystem. Coppice was the norm here for many hundreds of years with little change, a fact indicated by the presence of plants such as lesser scull-cap, ivy-leaved bellflower, bilberry and golden-rod. The upper slopes are affected by the harsh weather that afflicts this area in winter, the wind stunting the trees, while lower down the ancient coppice stools are reverting to climax woodland which is changing the plant and insect population. However, coppice is a system of woodland management that can easily be reinstated and the subsequent opening of the canopy would reinvigorate the ground flora and dependant insect life. The wood is extremely rich in mammals, both large and small, and is a wintering site for red deer.
405ha – Map ref: SS 897454

MENDIP CONSERVATION AREA (Somerset TfNC) — *All year*

This Conservation Area encompasses a multitude of habitats. Quarrying for stone and lead mining have greatly altered the flora and fauna and the wooded areas support ancient plants such as herb-Paris while a coppice regime in Long Wood has enhanced the variety of birds. Mining and lead streaming in the pleasantly named Velvet Bottom has so contaminated the soil it is unfit for grazing but plants growing here have adapted to heavy metal contamination; the site has been worked for lead since pre Roman times only becoming uneconomic in the late 19th century. The whole area is fascinating and the flora and fauna wide ranging.
586ha – Map ref: ST 482545

NORTH HILL NATURE TRAIL (ENPC) — *All year*

Circular walk climbing from the harbour at Minehead giving walkers a fine view of different habitats from the shoreline to gorse moorland and, as the path runs through woodland, a fine series of environments for birds and insects; butterflies and moths are abundant as are spring-time birds.
5km – Map ref: SS 968474

SHAPWICK HEATH (NCC)** — *Spring, summer*

Part of the old Somerset Levels, the type of remnant Fen at Shapwick Heath is becoming rarer as drainage and peat cutting continues. The reserve is maintained only by close attention to water levels and the moisture content of the soil so vital to the unique bird, insect and plant communities, but it remains rich in unusual fenland plants and insects.
221ha

SOMERSET & NORTH DEVON COAST PATH (CC) — *All year*

From County Gate to Minehead the path covers a wide variety of habitats from farmland and heather to moors and woodland; especially interesting are the high rolling hills looking out over the Bristol Channel. Kestrels hover over the short wind-cropped turf searching for voles, stonechats call from twigs of hawthorn and blackthorn trimmed by salt breezes and the occasional peregrine sweeps by on the wind; there is a small breeding population in the west country. Fulmars and gulls also play on the wind, and on fine days when the sun is hot the turf is alive with butterflies; especially common blues and the grass feeding species of browns such as small heath and meadow brown; bumble bees are a feature of this wind-grazed landscape.
25km – Map ref: SS 793487 - 971467

STEEP HOLM (Kenneth Allsop Memorial Trust Reserve) — *April through October (Day trips Saturdays)*

Steep Holm is a superb limestone island reserve dedicated to the memory of Kenneth Allsop, one of the stalwarts of the modern, media led conservation movement that has achieved so much over the past ten years in making the general public aware of the many threats to the environment.

Somerset Levels   *West Sedgemoor*

The island, lying in the middle of the Bristol Channel, has a number of particularly fascinating natural features from rarities like the wild leek and wild peony to the island race of slow worms that are far larger than the mainland species. The herring gull colonies are important and lesser and greater black-backed gulls breed here. There is also a large healthy population of hedgehogs and muntjac deer which were introduced some years ago. Most exciting is the return of the peregrine falcon as a breeding species, a fact that would have been much appreciated by Kenneth Allsop.

20ha

WEST SEDGEMOOR (RSPB)** — *All year*

An extremely important wetland site renowned for breeding and migrant waders and huge gatherings in spring of whimbrel; The flooded marsh can be filled with flocks of golden plover, lapwing and duck. These grazing marshes are maintained by the Society in the traditional way, but one or two features have been added to cater for the thousands of birdwatchers who visit this wonderful area; a pool has been created and a hide built.

At this point the Levels are bounded by wooded hillside. Fivehead Wood which looks down onto the Levels is superb in spring with migrant songbirds, nightingales, and many woodland plants; the ridge provides updraughts where buzzards and breeding rooks play and circle. In winter the levels show another face for the water that gives them life floods the surface providing a refuge for thousands of wildfowl; sadly only a remnant of this fascinating and precious environment remains to give a flavour of the many hundreds of acres that used to exist up to Victorian times.

200ha

BEDFORDSHIRE

&

HUNTINGDONSHIRE

There, interspersed in lawns and opening glades,
Thin trees arise, that shun each other's shades.

— Pope

The first of many contacts with this county came when, as a new national serviceman I was taken to the gates of RAF Cardington. It was a depressing experience for although the immense hangars, which still stand like cathedrals on the Bedfordshire skyline, were home to some of the most impressive airships the world has ever seen, to me the huge slightly faded camouflaged green hulks were uninspiring, and I was being inducted into a way of life that, though subsequently most enjoyable, was causing me considerable trepidation.

Since then I have spent a great deal of my working life in the county, although I actually live next door in Hertfordshire. I started a natural history programme on the commercial radio station Chiltern Radio covering Bedfordshire, Buckinghamshire, Hertfordshire and Northampton and then moved to BBC Radio Bedfordshire where I now broadcast a regular weekly programme called "Country Seen".

In my library is an old book on the counties in England; written before the Second World War which tells of a Bedfordshire very different from the county today, of a system of farming that was based more upon cattle and hay than grain and oil seed rape. It also tells of a system of agriculture in the doldrums such as we are beginning to see again in this last decade of the 20th century as land is taken out of production and returned to nature.

The Bedfordshire of pre-war England is more or less extinct. The county's proximity to London has meant that tiny rural communities with their decorated plaster cottages and extensive woodlands have been turned into commuter dormitories, only coming to life at weekends when the "incomers" come together to enjoy "rural" life. Like so much of the southern Midlands region the county has a dual personality; the chalk and limestone of the

Totternhoe Knolls　　　　　　　　　　　　　*Beds & Hunts*

Chilterns rises and falls from Dunstable Downs to the hills on the eastern edge of Luton, and away to where former sheep walks, now cultivated, stretch into north Hertfordshire. These downlands were once alive with butterflies and awash with rare orchids.

There is a definite sense of open country, especially where man has taken the clay for making bricks and has created huge holes since filled with water. In some parts of the county the brick pits have been used for dumping household refuse and where this has happened wildlife has suffered from pollution. In other places the pits have been opened for chalk or for gravel. Looked at from the point of view of a traveller from another country, it would appear that a great deal of Bedfordshire has been taken away on the back of lorries and trains to build towns and cities in other counties. Even the chalk hills that run through Luton and on to East Anglia have been excavated for the cement industry. However, many of the open cast workings, abandoned for several decades, are now very rich in wildlife with stands of orchids and rare plants, the steep faces of the quarries providing safe nest sites for kestrels.

The river Great Ouse, and its flood plain, dominate the central part of the county running through Bedford where the local Naturalist's Trust has its headquarters in Priory Park. The river valley is bounded by fertile farmland as it heads towards the fens and the wildfowl productive Washes and in many places the river banks have been colonised by wildlife. Elsewhere intensive agriculture on the deep clay soils tends to reduce the wildlife potential.

The river wanders across the flat plain of Huntingdonshire with a series of lakes and bows where sand and gravel has been worked, the county is based mainly on clay and gravels the remnants of a time when the north sea regularly inundated this low lying region to form part of the East Anglian fenlands. Only a morsel of this spectacular landscape now remains; Wood Walton Fen is a prime example where an attempt is being made to establish a tiny population of large copper butterflies reintroduced from Holland — the original English large copper butterfly became extinct in the 19th century through fen drainage and heavy collecting.

The geology of Bedfordshire differs from the low fenland soils of Huntingdonshire mainly because of the presence of the greensand ridge, a series of low hills covered in conifer plantations, the most famous of which is at Sandy, surely the most familiar address in conservation — The headquarters of the RSPB at The Lodge, Sandy, Bedfordshire. The greensand imparts a heathy flavour to the grounds of the Lodge with many heathland and woodland plants: animals and of course, birds to be seen in the grounds.

The future of the county depends upon industry and the road network feeding the developing towns of Bedford, Stevenage, Luton and the huge new city of Milton Keynes on the Beds/Bucks border. The roads, especially motorways, support a very good population of small mammals and kestrels along their banks, and larger mammals like foxes, badgers and muntjac deer use them as highways to colonise; but the roads bring people and demands on land for housing and industrial development which in turn requires water and the man-made asset of the immense reservoir at Grafham Water has one of the highest wildlife populations anywhere in the southern Midlands. Yet man can be a limiting factor to the county's potential for it is a region of contrasts and conflict man with his environment! Bedfordshire's most famous son, and author of "The Pilgrim's Progress" would find a more tolerant community and greater freedom to preach than in his day, but I doubt he would be able to recognise in today's county the peacefulness and quiet of the 17th century countryside.

And after April, when May follows,
And the whitethroat builds, and all the swallows,
Hark! where my blossomed pear tree in the hedge,
Leans to the field and scatters on the clover
Blossoms and dewdrops — at the bent spray's edge -
That's the wise thrush; he sings each song twice over,
Lest you should think he never could recapture
The first fine careless rapture.

ARLESEY OLD MOAT ** (Beds & Hunts WT) — *Spring, summer*

Encompassing an ancient moat dating from the 12th to 14th centuries and the protective arm of the Manor of Arlesey Bury which is separated from the river Hiz by a step bank, this reserve is based on land formerly cultivated. The moat is silted, and has a rampant growth of reed sweet grass, geat pond sedge and reed mace. In consequence there are ample nesting sites for reed and sedge warblers, reed buntings and redpolls; and the water itself is excellent for amphibians and dragonflies.
2.4ha

ARTHURS MEADOW (Beds & Hunts WT) — *Spring, summer*

Arthurs Meadow is a small reserve, dedicated to Arthur Oswald, an amateur orchid specialist. Ridge and furrow are maintained to retain the grassland diversity with four species of orchids and a host of other grassland plants.
1.8 acres – Map ref: TL 291693

BANKSIDE ** (Beds & Hunts WT) — *Spring, summer*

A memorial to its former owners, Mr & Mrs Angel, Bankside is an interesting mixture of wet and dry hay

meadows, ponds and marginal wetland. The hay is traditionally cut annually and the flora reflects this with a wide variety of hay meadow flowers including introduced fritillaries. Several small brick pits, connected to the river Great Ouse, provide excellent marginal vegetation for breeding birds, and also for the very rare dragonfly (Libellula fulva.)
2ha

COLLEGE LAKE NATURE RESERVE
(Berks, Bucks & Oxon NT) — *Spring, summer*

Part of Castle Cement's Pitstone quarrying operation, this new reserve opened in 1988, shows the transition from open chalk pit to lakes, and eventually to a varied calcareous grassland habitat. Its proximity to the nearby wildfowl-rich waters of Tring reservoirs is bound to attract a wide range of duck and other waterbirds as the habitat develops.

FERRY MEADOWS COUNTRY PARK (Peterborough Development Corporation) — *All year*

A pleasant way to use an exploited countryside for the benefit of both human and natural inhabitants. Once a huge area of gravel workings, Peterborough Council have planned this country park containing a series of lakes and habitats on the banks of the river Nene. There is still much development required, but the concept will bear fruit and the resulting natural colonisation of the workings and banks by different plants, insects and birds over the years will produce an ever changing scene of natural history interest. Already the shingle banks along the pits have attracted breeding pairs of little ringed plover.
200ha – Map ref: TL 145975

FLITWICK MOOR (Beds & Hunts WT) — *Spring, summer*

Just after the Romans left, Flitwick Moor was no more than a bend in the river Flit; a natural dam impounded the water, and the reed swamp that resulted gradually built up a considerable peat deposit so that by this century it has grown to 4ft thick in places and ripe for exploitation as fuel by the local gas works where it was used to purify town coal gas. The combination of acid peat and lime-rich ground water produces an interesting variety of plant and insect life, and the woodland that has grown up where the peat has been mined provides a series of productive habitats for birds; 90 species have been seen, including rarities like grasshopper warbler, and water rail have bred here. Management aims to slow down the spread of woodland and raise the water table to prevent too great a change in the flora and fauna of the moor.
28ha – Map ref: TL 046354

GAMSEY WOOD (Beds & Hunts WT)** — *Spring, summer*

Gamsey Wood is part of a much larger stand of timber that has been felled over the centuries, and thought to be part of the great wood that edged the fenlands in medieval times. There are many plants present that indicate age, particularly primroses, bluebells, wood anemones and enchanter's nightshade. Now coppiced, the site is rich in migrant warblers.
4ha

GRAFHAM WATER (Beds & Hunts WT) — *All year*

A huge lake, some 640 hectares, was formed when the valley was dammed in the 1960s. Not only is it used as a drinking water supply, for which it was originally intended, it also supports sailing, wind surfing and an active trout fishery. The natural inhabitants include large flocks of wildfowl that use the water to roost and feed in spite of human pressure; occasionally an osprey will stop over on passage.
148ha – Map ref: TL 143672

HOLYWELL MARSH (Beds & Hunts WT) — *Spring, summer*

The presence of a spring in the churchyard at Holywell has led to the development of a small marsh with an immense stand of butterburr.
0.2ha – Map ref: SP 991536

KING'S WOOD (BCG-Beds & Hunts WT) — *Spring, summer*

One of the best remaining examples of original forest cover in the county, superb for songbirds and bluebells. It was subjected to extreme pressure because of a plan to sell off small plots for leisure projects, but the resulting degradation is being overcome with the County Council and the Trust purchasing these plots as they become available.
29ha – Map ref: TL 037393

THE LODGE (RSPB) — *All year*

The Lodge at Sandy is the headquarters of the RSPB, Europe's foremost bird conservation charity. Sitting on a block of sandstone that juts into the featureless floodpain of the river Great Ouse, Sandy has a wide variety of habitats, many of which are man-made, and every feathered visitor is scrutinised most avidly; consequently the list of visiting birds reads like a potted handbook. A hide at the front of the main house overlooks a small man-made lake full of carp and constantly visited by birds of all kinds from sparrowhawks to swallows and the occasional kingfisher.

The grounds are not only rich in birds, they are also scenically beautiful, and visitors leave feeling the Society could not have chosen a better place for its headquarters. Much of the woodland is conifer with some magnificent specimen trees from the arboretum surrounding the house. The number of feeding stations encourages a wide range of birds to the trees and outside the offices, to a person the staff are all avid birders. There are large numbers of Scots pine and stands of commercial forestry with no access to the general public, but this affords a little solitude to resident breeding species.

An attempt has been made to strengthen the colony of natterjack toads that lives in the bracken and underbrush; and there are a number of mammal species, including muntjak deer and innumerable grey squirrels, who avail themselves of the ample food put out for the birds. There are some unusual insects, including the pine hawk moth, uncommon in south east England. It's an interesting place with heath woodland and grassland in close proximity to one another.
41.6ha – Map ref: TL 188478

MARSTON THRIFT (Beds & Hunts WT)** — *Spring, summer*

Mixed deciduous coppiced woodland, part of a larger block of forest, supporting a wide range of bird life; garden and willow warblers are extremely common. Also the site of a rare species of woodrush (Luzula forsteri) which does not occur anywhere else in the county.
5.2ha

MONKS WOOD (NCC)** — *Spring, summer*

This must be one of the most carefully studied woods in the country. At the beginning of the century it was clear felled. Then as the woodland regenerated, it was coppiced, encouraging a wide range of plants, many symptomatic of ancient woodland. The variety of soil types allows for plenty of woodland plants; cowslips and primroses inter-bred to form an oxlip-like hybrid.

Over a thousand species of beetles have been recorded here, and the butterfly fauna, for which Monk's Wood is justly famous, is particularised by the presence of the black hairstreak, and both the brown and white letter hairstreak are here in smaller numbers.

The woodland is noted for its nightingales, although these birds have declined dramatically throughout the Midlands and south east England through changes in forest management; and for the wild service tree, re-latively common here, but rare elsewhere. Midland and common hawthorn grow in the woods, and there is an intermediate hybrid of both species. The richness of plants, animals, birds and small mammals at Monk's Wood gives an indication of the variety that would have been found in the true woodland of this country before man intervened.
156.8ha

MOWSBURY HILL (Beds & Hunts WT) — *Spring, summer*

A medieval moated site within an Iron Age fortification, and a scheduled ancient monument, the grassland supports a wide variety of calcareous species including adder's tongue fern and bee orchid.
6.8 acres – Map ref: TL 066532

OLD WARDEN TUNNEL (Beds & Hunts WT)** — *Spring, summer*

A remnant of Beeching's railway cuts in the 1960s; the flora in this railway cutting is similar to the old hay meadow flora now so rare. The Trust have maintained a regime of grassland management on the banks outside the tunnel by mowing twice yearly to promote smaller grass species and the original flowering plants of old lime-rich grassland; the range of birds and butterflies is extensive.

In the past the banks would have been scythed, and the dead grass and plant material removed, to prevent sparks from the old coal-fired steam locomotives causing a fire. When the cutting was abandoned, and the rails removed, rank grasses and scrub invaded; but the declaration of this site as a nature reserve in the early 1970s reversed the process and restored the old plant communities. The tunnel itself is being supplied with boarded bat roosts.
2ha

RAVELEY WOOD (Beds & Hunts WT)** — *Spring, summer*

Raveley Wood is thought to be on the site of an ancient woodland, considerable clearance and regeneration has taken place over the years and the rookery is a particularly important feature.
5.7ha

SAPLEY SPINNEYS (Beds & Hunts WT) — *Spring, summer*

Once an outlier of the Royal forest of Sapley, the remains of which have been cleared over the last 300 years, the spinneys consist of a number of elms grown from suckers. There is a growth of turkey oak and ash, sycamore and hornbeam with a ground flora which indicates the wood's ancient origins. Thirty species of birds have been recorded.
7.33ha – Map ref: TL 246743

SUTTON WASH (Beds & Hunts WT) — *All year*

Given to the Trust by an anonymous donor in 1972 Sutton Wash is part of the Bedford river flood relief scheme. Adjacent to several other reserves run by the RSPB, Cambs WT and the Wildfowl and Wetlands Trust it has an interesting mixture of grasses and wild plants able to withstand periods of immersion. The seeds of many of these grasses and docks form the food supply for the wildfowl in winter.
8.53ha – Map ref: TL 415779

TOTTERNHOE KNOLLS (Beds & Hunts WT/BCC) — *Spring, summer*

This SSSI is justly famous for its orchids and originally was the site of a Norman castle. Beneath the turf is a hard fine white chalk known locally as Clunch or Totternhoe Clunch Stone which was mined, and faces many local buildings; the site is now extensively quarried for chalk for the nearby cement works.

The thin turf is a veritable flower garden in season with many species of orchid, including man, bee, frog and the very rare musk orchid, more than fifty-five species of flowers have been recorded such as clustered bellflower, carline thistle, wild thyme and yellow rattle. The butter-flies too reflect the downland habitat with chalkhill blues and small blues common in late summer.

This is one of the best vantage points in the Vale of Aylesbury to see hobbys hawking for insects in the late summer evenings prior to their migration, and their presence is often indicated by the metallic alarm calls of swallows and martins. More than thirty species of birds breed on or near the reserve, and many more are resident at different times of the year.

13.6ha – Map ref: SP 980220

WARESLEY & GRANSDEN WOODS (Beds & Hunts WT)** — *Spring, summer*

Thought to be a remnant of the prehistoric forest that once clothed this part of the country, these woods have a fascinating range of soil types and flora. Greensand and wet clay provide a contrast in the flora, the beautiful oxlips with their clusters of lime-yellow flowers on long stems enjoy the wetter clay, while primroses prefer the better drained greensand; where the two species overlap some interesting hybrids develop.

Coppiced for centuries there's a variety of rather large coppice stools, many past their prime because of lack of cropping before the area became a nature reserve. Now the regime of coppicing is being reintroduced and the results are startling. In spring the woods ring with birdsong and the ground is a carpet of flowers and from May to late September birds take advantage of the insect food. Large numbers of birds nest here, including all three species of woodpecker. Mammals include badgers, foxes, weasels, stoats, hares and woodmice in abundance. The long term plan for the future of these woods is as exciting as was their ancient past.

28.7ha

WOODWALTON FEN (NCC)** — *Spring, summer*

A tiny remnant of the old east Anglia peat fenland which holds a colony of the large copper butterfly (Lycaena dispar batavus) a beautiful creature that feeds on water dock; the original British large copper (Lycaena dispar dispar) was extinguished in the late Victorian era. The fens are·constantly under threat of drainage as the surrounding farmland is eroded. The peat in the fields adjoining the reserve shows signs of the bog oak forest that once covered this region before the sea flooded in.

The area gives us a view into the landscape of Hereward the Wake and the Fen Tigers who made a living fishing for eels and fowling long before the fens were drained. It's a hard and difficult place, alive with mosquitos and biting insects in summer, but magical none the less. The wet heathland is home to a wide variety of insects, especially dragonflies who find the conditions perfect for both larval and adult stages. Fen violet and wood fen rush are two specialities, the former being very rare.

Without doubt this reserve is one of the most important in east Anglia, with agricultural degradation of the fenland landscape, and soil structure, proceeding at an alarming rate. By the year 2000 it may be the only oasis of fertility and natural diversity in an otherwise sterile landscape.

208ha

BERKSHIRE

The Royal County of Berkshire is drained by several fine clear streams; that is until they reach the busy commuter belt when, the Thames especially, changes its face. In their upper reaches the Kennet, Loddon and Pang are renowned for the purity of their waters and the size of their trout, dancing with insects where swallows hawk and dragonflies patrol thick banks of waterside vegetation; and what can be more pleasurable than to watch a large wild speckled brown trout sip a mayfly off the surface film.

These clear rivers encourage water voles like 'Ratty' in "Wind in the Willows"; it takes only the smallest flight of imagination to be aware of a bright eye looking at you from a hole in the opposite bank and hear a squeaky, but cultured voice, extol the virtues of the river. When Kenneth Grahame's Mole and Water Rat first meet, Ratty initiates Mole into the pleasure of boating:-

"The Rat said nothing, but stooped and unfastened a rope and hauled on it; then lightly stepped into a little boat which the Mole has not observed. It was painted blue outside and white within, and was just the size for two animals; and the Mole's whole heart went out to it at once, even though he did not yet fully understand its uses.

The Rat sculled smartly across and made fast. Then he held up his fore-paw as the Mole stepped gingerly down.

Water Vole "Ratty"   *Berkshire*

"Lean on that!" he said, "Now then step lively!" and the Mole to his surprise and rapture found himself actually seated in the stern of a real boat.

"This has been a wonderful day!" said he, as the Rat shoved off and took the sculls again. "Do you know, I've never been in a boat before in all my life". "What?" cried the Rat, open-mouthed. "Never been in a — you never — well, I — what have you been doing, then?"

"Is it so nice as all that?" asked the Mole shyly, though he was quite prepared to believe it as he leant back in his seat and surveyed the cushions, the oars, the rowlocks, and all the fascinating fittings, and felt the boat sway lightly under him.

"Nice? It's the only thing," said the Water Rat solemnly, as he leant forward for his stroke. "Believe me, my young friend, there is nothing — absolutely nothing — half so much worth doing as simply messing about in boats".

The Thames has been revitalised by a cleaning up operation and salmon fry released into the river have begun to return to the lower reaches, and what a pleasure it will be to see them fight the weir races as they did in Queen Elizabeth I reign. Then the salmon were so prolific that the London apprentices insisted on a clause in their articles of indenture stating they were not to be fed salmon more than twice a week. I think it will be many years before the fish are that numerous again, if indeed such a thing ever happens.

The Thames has such an influence upon the region, almost everything that occurs either to do with it or its many tributaries, affects the wildlife. Mute swans, once so common here, have suffered in recent years from lead poisoning from a number of sources, foremost of which is the split lead shot used by coarse anglers to weight their lines against the current. This small soft shot is lost in tons, the metal is slow to degrade and stays in the gravel margins where it is ingested by the birds along with small stones and gravel, used in conjunction with the swan's muscular crop to grind up plant material; the lead enters the bird's bloodstream and they die.

Cnanges have been implemented to end the use of lead shot, but it will be some time before the river is completely lead free and the swans begin to recover their numbers. There is better news for kingfishers. These beautiful birds are on the increase as there are many reserves where they can breed in clear streams fishing for the minnows, sticklebacks and bull heads for their young.

Three predominant soil types dictate the trees and plants that clothe those parts of the county not yet developed. Heavy London clay rises to an arm of chalk known as the Berkshire Downs and this clay, with its acid infertility, contrasts with the Downs, equally as impoverished, but with a well adapted alkaline flora and fauna; and here and there gravels from ancient glaciers and acid well-drained greensand overlay the clay.

At the heart of the county lies the huge Royal estate of Windsor Great Park. Once the centre of a mighty chase known as the Royal Forest of Windsor, now home to some of the largest and most ancient oaks in the country. A ridge of sandy acid soil in the park has been planted with straight rows of commercial conifers, and this type of sandy soil is also apparent in the flora and fauna at Wokingham.

Reading has the doubtful distinction of being the fastest growing town in the southern half of Britain, its position in the Thames valley is ideal for communication and the ready supply of gravel for constructing houses, offices and roads. The gravel workings that edge the M4 motorway have filled with ground water and quickly become naturalised, and despite heavy public pressure from leisure persuits like windsurfing and water ski-ing on these massive man-made lakes there's a healthy growing population of waterfowl.

The countryside surrounding Reading is very much one of cereals and oil seeds, but after the cereal fields have been cut, and before they are ploughed for next year's crop, huge skeins of feral Canada geese, often numbering over 100 individuals, fly in to rest and feed on the stubble. They seem oblivious to the sound and fury of the traffic rushing past.

Berkshire has a reputation for affluence, and perhaps this prosperity has been beneficial for wildlife, with more people having the leisure time to enjoy the countryside, and exhibiting a greater awareness of the threats hanging over the county's wild places.

DINTON PASTURES COUNTRY PARK (Wokingham DC) – *All year*

The council has taken the initiative here and created a considerable recreation area out of the dereliction that is the result of mineral extraction on a large scale. The pits have been allowed to fill with water, and have been landscaped so that a wide range of birds and animals can benefit, as well as man. Plenty of fish in the lakes has meant good fishing for herons and cormorants, inevitable and interesting visitors to these inland waters which also hold increasing flocks of wintering wildfowl.
111ha – Map ref: SU 785718

EDGBARROW WOODS (Bracknell DC) — *Spring, summer*

In parts Edgbarrow Woods resemble the Dorset heaths, with a wide range of sandy habitats that encourages Scots

pine and silver birch in clumps and coppices. In the past much of this heath would have been burned to keep the heathery areas open, but in recent times fewer fires have meant that self-seeded trees have grown much larger. Heather and cross-leaved heath are typical plants of wet and dry heathland habitats, and the emperor moth and delicate silver-studded blue butterfly occur here in summer. Slow worms and adders are also found in small numbers.
31.2ha – Map ref: SU 837632

INKPEN COMMON (Berks, Bucks & Oxon NT) — *Spring, summer*

Acid heathlands support their own special type of plant and animal communities. This reserve is particularly rich in plants that prefer wet acidic soils — bog bean, bog asphodel, and cross-leaved heath flowers by the bogs with their feet in the water. Where the sandy soil is deeper, the drier land plants predominate, bell heather and common heather with clumps of gorse, its roots deep into the soil searching for moisture. Fire damage is always a problem with heathland, and Inkpen has suffered badly in the past, but heather and gorse and broom soon reclaim the land, which is often temporarily filled by the fireweed, rosebay willow-herb.
10.4ha – Map ref: SU 382641

RIDGEWAY PATH (Berkshire CC) — *Spring, summer*
Possibly a Neolithic track in some places, it's a strange feeling treading in the footsteps of Celtic shepherds of past ages. The passage of thousands of feet over the centuries has worn a deep cutting into the soft chalk soil with banks clothed in chalk downland plants. The views are spectacular.
15km – Map ref: SU 464848 – SU 595807

THATCHAM REEDBEDS (Newbury DC) — *All year*
One of the largest areas of common reed beds in the country, Thatcham is a mecca for birds and birdwatchers alike, the sheer numbers of swallows and martins in spring and autumn indicate its feeding potential. In spring and summer the reeds are alive with reed and sedge warblers, all requiring an ample supply of insect food; especially if their nests have been taken over by a young cuckoo, a bird much in evidence here.

Reed beds are a busy habitat. The cuckoos add their voices to the jangly jarring spring chorus of warblers, the strange cries of water rails and the whinny of little grebes; all this activity attracts predatory birds, and sparrow-hawks and hobby falcons hunt over the reserve; the latter with wide powerful stoops, sometimes taking the newly-fledged swallows and martins, but more often their objective is one of the many large dragonflies that hawk over the marshes and open water. Sparrowhawks hunt warblers and reed buntings, using the cover of the reed beds to hide their approach and diving over the top of the banks to ambush their unsuspecting prey.

The plant life is extremely rich with a range of wetland plants that includes hemp agrimony, comfrey and yellow loosestrife; and wet woodland that consists mainly of specially adapted species like alder and willow with a considerable bird population. The presence of alder trees

and their seed cones are a magnet for wintering flocks of siskins.
12.8ha – Map ref: SU 501673

WELLINGTON COUNTRY PARK (Wellington Enterprises — Stratfield Saye Estate Offices, Reading Berks RG7 2BT

A beautiful area of woodland, parkland and lake Wellington Country Park has a great deal of natural history interest to offer. The lake has its own population of full-winged Canada geese and in winter these are joined by a variety of wildfowl. It is one of the few places where the elusive purple Emperor butterfly is relatively common; its larvae, which looks like slugs, feed on sallow leaves. When the insect emerges it is quite superb; the brown-winged female has a dusting of the iridescent violet scales, but the smaller male has the most beautiful reflective violet purple wings.

In the same mixed oak woodland an equally beautiful, but smaller butterfly, the white admiral also flies in July, and as well as these lovely insects the reserve had fallow deer, medium-sized deer who forms small herds — the stags have palmate antlers, and roe deer, smaller shy creatures of open woods, dark rusty brown in colour with short sharply tined antlers.
244ha – Map ref: SU 724626

WINDSOR GREAT PARK (Crown Estate Commissioners) — *All year*

The regime of pollarding for poles and firewood has prolonged the life of many of the great park oaks beyond their natural span, some are reputed to be 700 or 800 years old, and the majority have been growing here for 500 years.

The importance of this area to the Royal family is just as strong today as ever it was, but now the land is employed more democratically than when it was a private hunting forest simply for the benefit of the sovereign; a great many people derive pleasure from the wildlife within the oak woods. Part of the estate has been planted with conifers, fast reaching maturity, which provide a variety of nesting sites for birds, although these commercial plantations are of less natural history interest than the ancient forest where the flora and fauna has been allowed to remain and develop.

Within the park there is a large forest nature reserve where the original structure of an ancient forest with its attendant wildlife has been allowed to remain undisturbed. This particular nature reserve is of international importance.

In the park as a whole the predominance of oak and beech woodland, coppice, pollards and mighty standard trees, encourages the widest range of habitats and the richest natural food source for birds and small mammals and, together with heath, wetland and the lakeside habitats of Virginia Water, allows a breeding bird population almost unique so close to a major connurbation. Here nightjars can still be heard, stonechats, woodlarks and linnets breed on the heath and gorse, and the mandarin duck, first introduced as an ornamental waterfowl, has adapted so well it is a regular breeding member of the British waterfowl community.

Leaf warblers and other insect eating birds find ample food supplies in the oak canopy, and the number of old trees with soft tissue allows woodpeckers to nest; all three species are regularly encountered. Little owls and tawny owls have also taken advantage of the abundant nest holes and sparrowhawks and kestrels are increasing. There are more sightings of buzzards, and each year hobbys rear young in the mature conifer plantations; you can enjoy their superb mastery of flight in late August as they hunt for summer chafers in the early evening.

Such an ancient, relatively uncultivated habitat, encourages a balance of organisms within its soil structure, evidence of which is seen in the huge variety of fungi that appears in autumn, a number of which are very rare. Needless to say there are the insect janitors and predators, some 2000 species of beetles live within the park's boundaries.

This is one of the best places to see the silver-studded blue and white admiral, two butterflies with totally different habitat requirements. The former a denizen of heathy places, the latter a creature of deep woodlands and sunny rides.

Several deer species thrive here. Muntjac have crept in almost unseen and are doing remarkably well, while roe deer keep to the cover of the conifer woods, and although shy fallow deer are present, as is the red deer, the largest of our native species, they are not often seen. A large area of the park is designated a deer preserve.

Although there is adequate public access with a main road cutting right through, you can still detect the wilderness despite its proximity to Heathrow airport. On spring mornings you can enjoy the birdsong, and savour a feeling of peace and timelessness.

6000ha – Map ref: SU 953735

BUCKINGHAMSHIRE

From time immemorial man had trodden the hills and vales of this county. From the affluent valley of the upper Thames, to the sprawling new city of Milton Keynes, and the quiet backwaters and beautiful water meadows of the river Great Ouse in the north; embracing a swathe of habitats and an extremely varied range of soil types which give rise to a wealth of wildlife.

Across the county from west to east strides the Ridgeway, a highway since Neolithic times for shepherds and travellers; the passage of their feet has cut down through the chalk so deeply that in places it runs between steep banks; banks rich in orchids and other chalk downland flowers. It's a beautiful scene where wheatears flirt their tails as they sit on top of the ancient anthills, while kestrels hover on the updraughts scanning the flowery sheep-nibbled turf for short-tailed field voles or grasshoppers.

John Betjemen was unkind to Slough, even before it took on its new role as a vital polyglot suburb at the forefront of modern communications. Were he alive today I doubt he would recind his evocation to the bombs to "come fall on Slough"; but perhaps he might have felt less ill disposed towards the area had he explored the surrounding countryside where there's much natural history interest in the parklands and flat farmland, especially in winter.

Further north the chalk soil supports the remnants of the once massive Chiltern beechwoods, planted to fill the requirements of generations of High Wycombe furniture 'bodgers' (particularly Windsor chairs.) The beech tree is king here, although many of the tall columnar boles, past their prime, were tumbled in the high winds that struck southern England in the hurricane of October 1987. Yew and wild cherry grows in these woods, also planted as a source of raw materials for the furniture trade.

These days High Wycombe depends mainly upon high technology for its prosperity. The woods are overblown and need rejuvenating; nevertheless they are still beautiful and on a spring day, when the sun slants down through pale green leaves, and the dry woodland floor glows as if lit by fires, the atmosphere within their bounds is a delight.

Such woodlands would have been a familiar sight to John Milton, who escaped from the plague in London to the village of Chalfont St Giles. His poem "O Nightingale" indicates that this bird was a common songster in his day, now they are few and far between, heard only rarely in the woods of Buckinghamshire. However, the local naturalist Trust (BBONT) is a powerful force in the county and many of the reserves within their care would have gladdened Milton's heart.

The soft contours of the Chilterns fall away to one of the most beautiful and typical of all British landscape features, the flat plain of the Vale of Aylesbury. The high fertility of the plain has meant heavy agricultural use, but enough of the old Vale is left to see what it must have been like in its hey-day. Off the beaten track many tiny villages still exist, their original inhabitants replaced by wealthy commuters and weekenders, but it must be said this has allowed these villages to retain much of their original charm.

Between Aylesbury and Buckingham is some of the least developed countryside in south east England, deep woodlands and open farmland form a landscape that would be familiar to the Victorians. On the Northampton and Buckingham border parts of the once extensive Salsey forest remain, an area of woodland that formed part of the primeaval forest cover that was England's normal habitat until Elizabeth I. The flat plain continues, undulating slightly, to the edge of the urban sprawl of Milton Keynes. Here fertile farmland and old flower-rich meadows have vanished beneath factories, offices and housing developments.

Leonard Clark's poem "Country and Town" evokes Buckinghamshire to perfection. The woodlands, farms and fields are loud with birdsong and contrast with the new urgency of transplanted communities:-

"Country and Town".

When the first celandine
opens pale eyes and fox cubs play
in the thin light
all the brisk day,
the land is green
and all the pools are bright.
Small birds in bold blocks
flit from sun into shadow,
a long-legged calf
staggers into life, an ox
bellows for company in the long meadow,
a tree-top chiffchaff
happily calls his name
over and over
as if it were some game
or other, early bees
raid the crops of clover.
In my town garden
two wild cherry trees
come bravely out
as if begging my pardon
that they should flower at all
where cars scream at the roundabout
and no chiffchaffs call.

The Tove, the Great Ouse and Ouzel, drain the surrounding landscape towards the oxbows and floodplain of the adjoining county of Bedfordshire, and the Grand Union Canal wends its way south to the Thames across the eastern flank of the county, forming a natural flyway for migrating birds: goshawks and osprey, geese and duck, waders and terns, and small migrant songbirds all use the course of the canal as a guide and a place to rest and feed on their immense annual world-wide journeys.

BERNWOOD FOREST (NCC — FC)** — *Spring, summer*

Bernwood Forest is a mixture of conifer interspersed with remnants of the original forest of oak, ash, goat willow or sallow and silver birch. It is worthy of recommendation for its invertebrates, but there are also many birds and in spring the trees are alive with willow and garden warblers, blackcaps and whitethroats.

Recent change in the management of farmland and forest has made life easier for the resident sparrowhawks who find ample nesting in the conifer plantations, and perfect hunting in the ride system employed by the Forestry Commission for fire control. In early summer these rides are often heavily overgrown with grass, and fallow and roe deer enjoy the fresh tender shoots and drink the water where it collects in deep wheel-cut ruts.

In the fire control pools insects find shelter, and the dragonfly fauna is excellent. It's a well known site for the beautiful purple Emperor butterfly, once these lovely insects were lured within the reach of the Edwardian lepidopterists nets by baiting the rides and clearings with stinking meat or fish. The Emperor has a taste for things gamey and will come down to dead rabbits that have succumbed to myxomatosis. Sometimes the white admiral butterflies will have a good year, then they too can be seen drinking water from puddles or from the bramble flowers, jostling beside the bees to get at the nectar. Another small butterfly whose larvae feed on blackthorn is the black hairstreak, these attractive insects sometimes form the bulk of the butterfly population of a small area of the forest where their food plant grows.
409ha

BOARSTALL DECOY (Berks Bucks & Oxon NT)* — *Spring, summer*

A traditional dog-lure duck decoy, used in the past to trap birds for the table. The decoy with its tapering net pipe is operated by a decoy-man with a dog traditionally called piper and trained to appear and reappear from behind reed screens along the length of the pipe, the fowl follow the dog out of curiosity and eventually are frightened, by the decoy-man, into flying towards the end of the tapering net enclosure, where they are captured, ringed and released.
7.2ha – Map ref: SP 623151

BUCKINGHAM CANAL (Berks Bucks & Oxon NT) — *Spring, summer*

A disused arm of the Buckingham canal with the usual plant and insect communities of slow moving water. Insect life is very rich, especially diving beetles, dragonflies and damselflies; and the larvae of the elephant hawk moth, which has large eyespots on its body which are exposed when it's threatened, feeds on the succulent

supply of willow-herb until it's ready to pupate.
0.5km – Map ref: SP 728357

CHESHAM BOIS WOOD (Woodland Trust) — *Spring, summer*

Chesham Bois wood has an ancient lineage, but now much of the reserve is commercially planted with single age beech forest for the furniture industry. Situated on an attractive hillside overlooking Chesham the wood is reaching maturity. The Woodland Trust have carried out a great deal of much needed management thinning the beeches and removing conifers, and this has allowed more light to reach the woodland floor, even so relatively few plant species are capable of growing in the shade afforded by the beech canopy, although bluebells make a beautiful show in spring, and there's a developing shrub layer which attracts warblers.
16ha – Map ref: SP 960003

CHURCH WOOD (RSPB) — *Spring, summer*

An attractive woodland full of birds, especially hole nesters. All three species of woodpeckers nest in Church Wood as do nuthatches and the tit species who take advantage of the holes made by others. There's also a well represented mammal population with muntjac deer, stoat, fox, woodmice and bank voles.

The wood harbours an interesting plant life; green hellebore and butcher's broom are lime-rich indictor plants of ancient lineage. Over 200 plants have been identified and the addition of a pond has improved the bird and insect potential. Butterflies are a speciality with woodland species like white admiral that lay their eggs singly on honeysuckle leaves and the oak dependant purple hairstreak butterflies that fly high over the canopy in July.
14ha – Map ref: SU 973873

COOMBE HILL NATURE TRAIL (NT) — *Spring, summer*

A most attractive escarpment. The monument at Coombe Hill was built here especially so that it could be viewed from a wide area. The path across the hills shows marked differences in the flora as the cap of clay with flints over chalk produces both acid and neutral soil. Where the clay ends and the chalk begins the hills show all the flora of calcareous grassland. It's an excellent site for juniper, a chalk grassland speciality, which provides song posts for whitethroats in spring and early summer. The Wendover side of the hill is carpeted with harebells, some of which are extremely pale. On a clear day this reserve provides one of the best vantage points on the entire Chiltern range. Earthworks on adjacent hilltops show man's association with the region for thousands of years.
2km – Map ref: SP 853063

IVINGHOE BEACON (NT) — *Spring, summer*

One of the oldest fortified hilltops in the country, the beacon has long fertile chalk slopes degrading to a thinner soil composed almost entirely of chalk rubble which encourages horseshoe vetch and carline and stemless thistle. In spring the slopes are covered with cowslips, and Duke of Burgundy fritillary butterflies lay their pearly eggs on

Badger Cubs   *Millfield Wood*

the underside of the leaves. Later on in the year burnet moths join the chalkhill blues, common and small blue butterflies to flit about in the sunshine.

The variety of orchids has declined, less sheep grazing and fewer rabbits have allowed scrub and rank grasses to invade some areas; but bee, fragrant and spotted orchids are still here to delight the eye. Occasionally near the paths, where the grass is short, you may see a frog orchid, so small and insignificant it might pass unnoticed.

On the other side of the beacon, away from the apalling sight of the cement works at Pitstone, is a beautiful vista of the Vale of Aylesbury with Totternhoe Knolls in the middle distance.
400ha – Map ref: SP 961168

MILLFIELD WOOD (Berks Bucks & Oxon NT) — *All year, (especially spring)*

Millfield Wood is an SSSI and contains several indicator plants of ancient woodland. Bluebells and dog's mercury are abundant, and coral root and herb paris occur in sufficient numbers to be notable. The beech trees appear to be self-seeded, although it's likely that man has intervened as the timber was used extensively for the furniture industry. Below the wood is a bank of chalk grassland rich in flowers, and in July small blue and marbled white butterflies can be seen.

There's also a badger sett which has been 'watched' for over 20 years, and other mammals include muntjac, rabbits and foxes who, at certain times of the year, reside in the badger sett.
19 acres – Map ref: SU 870954

RIDGEWAY PATH (CC) — *Spring, summer*

Part of a longer trail, this ancient sheep walk runs across the Chiltern scarp taking in some of the most beautiful insect-rich chalk grassland. In places the passage of feet have worn down the chalky soil to such an extent that now the path is at the bottom of a dry gully with flower-rich banks on either side. The bullseye-striped snails of chalk grassland are extremely common here, in past times they were a food source for glow-worms, once very common, but now very rare.

Kestrels hang on the wind, and it's not uncommon for walkers to encounter a buzzard soaring on the up-

draughts. There's a primeval feeling about this pathway.
30km – Map ref: SP 770013 – 961168

SALCEY FOREST (Berks, Bucks & Oxon NT — Northants WT)** — *Spring, summer*

Salcey Forest is a small part of the great relict Midland Forest of the Middle Ages found at the northern tip of the county. This was the old wild wood familiar to people of the Bronze Age before pastoralisation. The flora reflects the management of the trees and understory which for centuries has been substantially cropped for poles, firewood and building timber. These products have largely been superseded, but the woodland's value as a natural reservoir of wildlife is undisputed. The bulk of the forest lies in Northamptonshire.
13.2ha

STONY STRATFORD WILDLIFE CONSERVATION AREA (Berks, Bucks & Oxon NT) — *All year*

Created from the gravel extractions to build Milton Keynes, this area is naturalising well, as many of these gravel inspired wetlands do if managed sympathetically. A wide range of birds, including waders, have begun to take advantage of the many breeding sites, one of the first being redshank followed by little ringed plover and ringed plover. An attempt has been made to encourage kingfishers and other hole nesters such as sand martins to nest in artificially constructed sandbanks on islands in the flooded workings, and there's a good growth of sallow and willow scrub and some hawthorn that make excellent breeding sites for small songbirds.

The lakes are well weeded, and the availability of food for dabbling and diving ducks is encouraging a growing winter wildfowl population which can be viewed from hides on the banks; the increasing insect life includes a growing population of dragonflies. The area probably won't develop its full potential for some years.
22.3ha – Map ref: SP 785412

CAMBRIDGESHIRE

"Bedford Level" — John Dyer.
Yet much may be performed, to check the force
Of nature's rigour: the high heath, by trees
Warm-sheltered, may despise the rage of storms:
Moors, bogs, and weeping fens, may learn to smile,
And leaves in dykes their soon-forgotten tears.

From north to south, east to west, man has reshaped the countryside of Cambridgeshire and greatly affected the flora and fauna.

In the north the great flood plain and fenlands of the Nene and the old Bedford river drains the water from the fertile silt and peat farmland. In the heartland, around the ancient city of Ely with its imposing cathedral, lies the flat landscape and wide open skies of an area that was marshy fen until the Middle Ages.

In the south the county is equally contrived, little remains of the once extensive forests that clothed the clay, and the rolling downland in the west has all but vanished under the plough. However, where pockets of the original habitats remain there is still considerable wildlife diversity. The use of agricultural pesticides has largely removed the common frog and many of the insects from the drains that criss-cross the fenland. Nevertheless there

are dragonflies and moorhens and plots of wild fen hiding in the most industrialised farming landscape.

The fenlands have their own special atmosphere, largely due to the fact that the past can be read so clearly in the cultivated fields; there are distinct traces of events that happened between 7000 to 8000 years ago.

When the ice age finally relaxed its grip on this region the process of healing was startlingly rapid; the warm wet regime of the post-glacial period allowed dense forests to grow far out beyond the county's boundaries, beyond the Norfolk and Suffolk coastline onto the low lying land of the North Sea basin. The region's rivers flowed into a mighty estuary with the Thames and the Rhine forming the great Magelmosian bog where wildfowl from the whole of Europe and Asia wintered. As the glaciers retreated their melt waters flooded the North Sea basin, and within five thousand years the rising sea had also flooded the low lying land of East Anglia.

The forests that covered the landscape were soon overwhelmed and drowned, their timber either rotted to swell the rising blanket of peat that began to fill the shallow brackish inland sea, or fell into the oxygen-free mud to be preserved. Some of the root systems of these trees are still embedded in the silt protected from decay by sterile peat.

In the 17th century a Dutch engineer call Vermuden was employed to drain the fens, and carried out this commission with astonishing success building a series of barriers, sea defences, washes and drainage channels that allowed farming to take place on the deep organic fen soil. Peat can continue to thrive only in wet anoxic conditions so when the windmill pumps began to drain the water away, the turning sails rang the death-knell for the fenland soil. As the land dried out and crops were planted the peat oxidised and blew away on the east wind. These fenland blows cause havoc even today, and in places the soil has completely disappeared, the bog oak root systems mute evidence to how drastically an environment can be altered.

The sandy infertile silt fields are enclosed by banks two or three metres high, and roads and houses stand on top of these banks that once were level with the rest of the land. Only careful control of the pumping regime prevents these areas from re-flooding, and re-flooding may be the only way of rejuvenating the fens, although the process would take centuries to reproduce a protective usable blanket of peat from moss and reeds.

The county may have relatively few natural habitats, but those that remain are of particular importance because they represent a microcosm of one of the most diverse ecosystems in response to period flooding.

ARCHERS WOOD (Woodland Trust) — *Spring, summer*

Close to Sawtrey, lying on a ridge of land bordering the fens, this wood is a remnant of a much larger belt of woodland, 17 miles long, that ran across the county in Saxon times. Archers wood and nearby Aversley wood formed part of the same wild wood complex and exhibits all the features that typify old managed woodland. It's a perfect nesting site for warblers and songbirds, and its proximity to ample food supplies on nearby fenland makes it a prime site for woodcock. The remains of Sawtrey Grange, once the home of an order of white-robed friars is covered by the woodland.
43.6 acres - Map ref: TL 174810

AVERSLEY WOOD (Woodland Trust) — *Spring, summer*

One of the largest woods in Cambridgeshire and an SSSI. Aversley forms part of the same Saxon wood system as nearby Archers wood. It has been coppiced for centuries, the tall standard trees providing building timbers and the coppice being used for poles and firewood. Extremely rich in butterflies and songbirds, even nightingales have been heard on numerous occasions, and the woodland flora includes bugle, early purple orchid, bluebells, cowslips and meadowsweet, while the understory shrubs include blackthorn which attracts black hairstreak butterflies. This is one of the best sites in the county for examples of the comparatively rare mature wild service or chequer tree.
152 acres - Map ref: TL 158815

BEECHWOOD (Cambs WT) — *All year*

Few beech woods are left in the county, so this reserve has a particular role to play in providing a diversity of wildlife habitats. Beech woods have a dense canopy and the dimly lit woodland floor is suitable for the delicate white helleborine; the lack of ground cover does restrict the number of nesting birds but in good 'mast' years, when the beech trees produce a superabundance of seeds, bramblings and other finches take advantage of the bonanza.
4.8ha - Map ref: TL 486548

CHIPPENHAM FEN (NCC)** — *Spring, summer*

Chippenham Fen is a microcosm of Cambridgeshire habitats with fen woodland and meadowland. Where peat digging has taken place a superb wetland habitat has formed with great fen sedge, bog bean and bog violet or common butterwort, this latter plant of impoverished acid marsh was endowed with special powers — it was believed that cows that grazed these marshy meadows and ate this plant were supposed to yield milk particularly beneficial to new born infants.

The marsh helleborine grows here, a rare and tender member of the orchid family; more robust and widespread is the southern marsh orchid which flowers in late spring and early summer. It's a breeding site for many of the warblers including grasshopper warblers, blackcap, willow warbler and garden warbler.
105ha

DEVIL'S DYKE (Cambs WT—CCC) — *Spring, summer*

Devil's Dyke is a Saxon earth work, a monument to the fear which drove these highly organised people to erect a barrier between themselves and their neighbours. The Dyke is still impressive — more than 30 miles long it encapsulates a linear nature reserve. Plants of a past age, such as the Easter flowering pasque flower grow on dry chalk slopes that later on support a number of summer flowering orchids. Where the Dyke has overgrown with blackthorn and hawthorn scrub small songbirds nest, but scrub encroachment needs to be controlled or the varied flora and insect life will vanish. Sheep and rabbits kept the Dyke open for centuries, but now arable farming is the norm in this area, and management has to be carried out by the Trust.
34ha - Map ref: TL 570660 – 654585

ELY ROSWELL PITS (AWA) — *All year*

Rosswell Pits owe their existence to the need to keep the banks of the river Great Ouse high enough to prevent flooding; the resulting hollows have produced a wide ranging series of wetland habitats that complement the wildlife potential of a nearby river. Summer birds are attracted to the abundant waterplants edging the lakes, and sedge and reed warblers, great-crested and little grebe breed regularly as do redpoll and blackcap, birds of less aquatic tastes. The pits are popular with wintering wildfowl and the variety attracted to the water is extensive. Waders and terns on passage stop over to feed and rest on the margins and shallows.
32ha - Map ref: TL 547805

FOWLMERE (RSPB) — *All year*

Once a thriving watercress farm, the springs and beds of Fowlmere are now overgrown with common reed, and literally alive with birds at all seasons. A series of public hides allows visitors to observe reed and sedge warblers at their nests, and in winter the sight of bearded tits may be your reward for patience.

The great willow herb and purple loosestrife which form dense colourful stands shield the little grebe and coot on the ponds in front of the main hide; and in spring cuckoos parasitise the reed warblers and you can watch the female cuckoo dip down into the reed warbler's nest to deposit an egg while the real parent is away.

Kingfishers are regulars, and the reserve is full of surprises, a chance sighting of an osprey on passage to or from Loch Garten, a hen harrier quartering the reeds for an unwary moorhen, or a sparrowhawk dashing from cover to snatch a reed bunting, and bittern sometimes appear in hard weather as do considerable flocks of fieldfares and redwings.
26ha – Map ref: TL 407462

HAYLEY WOOD (Cambs WT)** — *Spring, summer*

Ancient woodland standing on boulder clay and chalk and managed as coppice with standards. The resulting habitat is unusually rich in spring with nightingales, willow, garden and wood warblers. There's a medieval lane called Hayley Lane, of particular interest to birds as it provides ample feeding, and whitethroats can be heard singing along its edge.

The rotational system of coppicing is highly developed to produce a range of woodland blocks containing much interest. The coppice is dated which allows you to see the rate of development of the coppice stools and ground flora. In excess of 275 flowering plants thrive here, including one of the largest displays of oxlips in Great Britain. Crested cow wheat is another indicator of ancient woods as is wood millet; both grow in abundance. Early purple orchids and bluebells bloom together in the rides, and the sight of unusual plants like herb paris delight the eye. The autumn display of fungal fruiting bodies is incredible, some 370 have been recorded. If you visit the wood in May you'll be entranced as it's like a journey in a time capsule, back to the England of the Middle Ages.
48.8ha

NENE WASHES (RSPB)** — *All year*

These washes are the result of drainage and flood relief work begun by the Dutchman Vermuden. A three mile stretch of meadowland is embanked to form a flood meadow to take water from the Nene/Ouse river systems in winter, or in times of exceptional summer rains. It's an almost perfect habitat for many birds; the naturally enriched pasture produces a huge crop of wild plants and grass seeds which feed the winter wildfowl.

In spring and summer the flood meadows dry out, leaving short grass just perfect for breeding waders like snipe and redshank; larks and wagtails also find ample food on the grasslands for their broods in late summer. Insect eaters and specialists like sand martins and swallows and the swift-flying hobby thrive here, and rarities such as black-tailed godwit and marsh harrier are also seen in summer.

The surrounding washes are gradually collecting into reserves, a vital haven for wildfowl, as a considerable amount of wildfowl shooting still takes place.
582 acres

OUSE WASHES (Cambs WT/RSPB) — *Winter*

The sloping profile from one embankment to the other of the old and new Bedford drains, with the flood meadows between, could hardly have been better designed for maximum wildlife interest. It was a master stroke of ecological engineering and ensured that the flood waters of the Bedford river should inundate the washes.

Vermuden's work has stood the test of 200 years, and during this time birds and mammals have come to depend upon the annual inundation of the washes for their livelihood. In summer the ditches that surround the washes are full of common reed, frog bit, purple and yellow loosestrife and a host of other water plants; the washes themselves are ablaze with grasses and wet meadow flowers, marsh ragwort, docks and reed canary grass, and alive with insects and mammals.

The numbers and variety of summer breeding birds is immense and includes the rare ruff and black-tailed godwit that breed on the meadows, as do snipe, redshank, lapwing, teal, mallard, tufted duck, garganey, gadwall, shelduck and shoveller duck. The reed beds that edge the washes and ditches are home to a great number of breeding pairs of reed and sedge warblers, reed buntings and yellow and pied wagtails find abundant insect food here. Another rarity that finds the ample insect life to its liking is the black tern; and some pairs have attempted to breed in recent years.

Winter migrants depend on the summer's activity, and it is in winter that the greatest interest is aroused in the hearts and minds of birdwatchers as vast flocks of wildfowl arrive from their arctic and northern European breeding sites to winter on this safe marshy food rich reserve. In excess of 55,000 wildfowl can be seen here in hard weather, the vast majority being inmense gatherings of wigeon; but other dabbling ducks such as mallard and shoveller, pintail and teal provide a dramatic spectacle when a passing peregrine disturbs the resting flocks as they rise with a roar of wings and wild music in their alarm calls.

The Wildfowl Trust observation point attracts massive numbers of whooper and Bewick swans (as many as 3000 Bewick's have been counted) and they can be seen at close quarters from the hides feeding on potatoes and grain donated by local farmers and put out for the birds by Trust staff. This food brings down a wide variety of rare and unusual wildfowl, and there's also a chance that these gathering birds will attract a bird of prey, a merlin or the day flying short-eared owl.
1747 acres – Map ref: TL 471861

ROMAN ROAD (CCC) — *Spring, summer*

An ancient Celtic, later Roman road, that has survived into the modern world. Its verges are clothed with many flowers that reflect the past herb-rich landscape; perennial flax is among several plants once common in

the surrounding fields, but now restricted to the pathside vegetation.
8km – Map ref: TL 494547 – 560498

SOHAM MEADOWS (Cambs WT)** Spring, summer

Ridge and furrow was the old system of land management here, the wet and dry undulations produce a series of habitats once common in the area, but now increasingly rare. The wide variety of meadow plants include the strange adder's tongue fern found in the damp ditches, and plants of the drier landscape include autumn gentian and bee orchid. A variety of ponds and scrubby areas with hedges provide plenty of nesting sites in spring for song birds such as willow warblers and whitethroats. Snipe and redshank are also found on the reserve.
32ha

THRIPLOW MEADOWS (Cambs WT)** — *Spring, summer*

An exceedingly important area of old wet pastureland and meadows; large colonies of marsh orchids thrive in the undisturbed unimproved marshy turf.
4.4ha

WANDLEBURY (Cambridge Preservation Society) — *Spring, summer*

Known for its Iron Age fort, this area of former chalk pastureland in the Gog-Magog Hills is now covered with a wide range of trees and shrubs with only a small amount of the original chalk downland turf remaining. Excellent for spring birdsong.
44ha – Map ref: TL 493533

WICKEN FEN (NT) — *Spring, summer*

One of the oldest nature reserves in the county, Wicken Fen is a huge natural laboratory where the study of wetland and fen management has been taken to a high level. The original fenland was managed for thatching reeds, but this died out nearly a century ago when a process of colonisation by reed scrub and trees began that

Ouse Washes   *Cambs.*

would ultimately have ended in full-blown wet oak woodland. That the wood survived at all in this sea of agriculture is something of a minor miracle and its existance speaks to us of a time when the fens covered many hundreds of miles and were full of life.

The pumps once required to drain the fen now maintain the integrity of the water table. Surrounding farmland is drained so effectively that without constant care and management of the water the wetland reserve areas would dry out. Here, in a state of equilibrium, you can find all the stages of development of open water and reed and sedge beds, through the invasion of woody shrubs to climax woodland. The fen contains a microcosm of the plant, insect and bird life once found all over this area prior to drainage. Huge numbers of southern marsh orchids and wetland species such as hemp agrimony, wild angelica, meadowsweet and yellow loosestrife encourage a wonderful butterfly fauna, and the dragonflies and damsels are a delight.

The birds vary dramatically with the season, there are ample nest sites for both migrants and resident breeding birds and the open water provides food and refuge for winter wildfowl in large numbers. There are several hides, including a tower overlooking the mere and the surrounding fenland.
272ha – Map ref: TL 563705

CHESHIRE

The beautiful river Dee forms part of the boundary between Wales and England and runs into the most superb estuary which, together with the Mersey peninsula, creates an area of international importance for wildfowl and waders. Unfortunately amid a highly populated landscape with its attendant industries and roads the wildlife is not entirely safe, even in this haven, for plans are afoot to build tidal barrages across the narrow estuary to produce power. It is the fate of estuaries to be developed by man, but we tend to forget that as ecosystems they are already very highly developed with a number of plants, animals and birds directly dependant upon them; even the smallest alteration in water level or salinity will have far reaching effects upon the natural inhabitants in the mud, in the water, and in the air.

The county has only become highly populated over the past 300 years, prior to the industrial revolution woodland stretched almost from border to border; sessile and pedunculate oak woods rang with birdsong in spring and supported wild boar and deer. Now the woods are all but gone, cut down by the demands of charcoal burning and agricultural improvement, and the boar is long extinct.

It would be hard for Lewis Carroll to find inspiration now in the fields where once the vicarage stood in which he spent the first eleven years of his life (the vicarage was burned to the ground in 1883 and was not rebuilt) — A pillar marks the spot and carries a quotation from one of Carroll's poems.

"The Three Sunsets":-
An island farm, mid seas of corn
Swayed by the wandering breath of morn
the happy spot where I was born.

A place of childhood revisited is an experience we can all enjoy, it reminds us of a time when we were different people — when the pages of our life were almost empty, ready to be written upon in letters large or small depending upon talent, ambition and expectation.

Carroll's childhood imagination must have been stirred by events in that Victorian vicarage. Was it a Cheshire countryside populated by weird animals, grinning cats and white rabbits? Did family picnics in the quiet fields and woods inspire his classic story? One of the wonders of childhood is a certain clarity of imagination. Children have few preconceptions so for the Queen in a pack of cards to possess a real personality is quite logical, especially on a hot, rather uneventful, summer's afternoon when adults are being pious and all you want to do is play in the sun.

We know a great deal about well-heeled, middle class people and their way of life during the Victorian era, but of the lives of the mass of men and women who toiled to make this prosperity possible we know little. Perhaps the working conditions in the forests, fields and factories of Cheshire was less harsh than in the nearby city of Liverpool. The salt extraction which formed a major part of the county's economy since Roman times had little dramatic effect upon the landscape, unlike iron, lead or coal mining. The brine springs that rise to the surface from the rich deposits deep underground require no slag heaps or dark satanic mills, and the treatment of this mineral resource is less destructive.

From Northwich to Sandbach there are huge deposits of salt, some of which rise to the surface and create areas reminiscent of salt marsh rather than the inland flora one would expect. Past exploitation of the salt deposits has led to some slumping of the land's surface forming the phenomenon known as flashes; however, the influence of the last ice age, and the flow of glacial drift, also caused some of these flashes.

Natural underground erosion by water also lead to the formation of water-filled depressions which in turn have become the famous peat mosses of Cheshire. Again ice helped to create this wild and interesting landscape as the retreating glaciers left behind thick beds of impervious clay overlaid with a variety of soils. Where blocks of ice were separated from the main body of the glacier their weight depressed the ground producing a phenomenon called "kettle holes", which in time developed into meres and mosses.

This is not a county of extremes, the rainfall, though influenced by the prevailing westerly winds from the Irish Sea and the Atlantic is usually held by the clouds until they rise onto the uplands of the Pennine chain or the Welsh mountains to the west. In this way Cheshire is the beneficiary of the water supply, without being deluged by it. The farmland, and the many streams and rivers that flow through the county gently water, rather than soak, the rich soils of the Cheshire Plain where herds of cattle produce the milk to make the famous Cheshire cheese.

Many of the woodlands left after the great clearances of the last four centuries grow on steep inaccessible land unsuitable for agriculture, nevertheless they are important because they hold a microcosm of the wealth of life that once was found all over the region from Wales to the Pennines and south to the Midlands. Now only the Forestry Commission woodlands of the Delamere forest give a flavour of the past vast tree cover and the spring birdsong.

ALDERLEY EDGE (NT) — *Spring, summer*

The sandstone hills at Alderley Edge, with their cover of sessile and pedunculate oak hybirds give an indication of the past richness of the county. On a fine day the views over the Cheshire Plain to the Pennines are superb.
88.4ha – Map ref: SJ 860776

BLACK LAKE (Cheshire CT)** — *Spring, summer*

The lake lies within the Delamere Forest and shows the transition between open water and floating bog. There is an area of sphagnum moss raft where other plants are colonising the surface and beginning the inevitable progression to dry land.
0.4ha

DIBBINSDALE (Wirral BC) — *Spring, summer*

Based on a variety of habitats Dibbinsdale includes an area of ancient woodland composed of wyche elm and ash on the sides of the valley; the indications are that this woodland may date back more than 4000 years. Consequently the bird population is abundant with many different species including tawny owl; the damper grassland and reed beds attract grasshopper warblers.
47ha – Map ref: SJ 345827

GAYTON SANDS (RSPB) — *Autumn, winter*

One of the most important wildfowl and wader refuges in the country, the sands and the spartina salt marsh are among the richest in the whole of the Dee estuary. In winter there is a constant passage of waders and duck as the tide opens and closes the feeding stations, and the area is in a state of constant change as plants such as spartina reclaim the mud and turn it to dry land.

The plants that grow on the salt marshes are prolific and produce huge crops of seeds that stay the hunger of the winter visitors. Finches in large numbers, including twite, are seen here every year, and that other wintering finch, the brambling, also appears when the weather becomes hard.

The mud and water provide a perfect habitat for the hundreds of pintail, shelduck, wigeon, mallard and teal that gather here as well as the thousands of waders that throng the mud and leave for the safe roost of the saltings at high tide. Grey plover, knot, dunlin and bar-tailed godwit occupy most niches in the estuarine ecosystem and their needs are well catered for here.

With such an assemblage of birds, predators are bound to be common, and peregrine, hen harrier and small hunters like the merlin are often seen in winter along with short-eared owl, the latter hunting the huge population of small mammals, particularly short-tailed field voles that feed on the seeds and vegetation.
5040ha – Map ref: SJ 274789

HILBRE ISLAND (Wirral BC)** — *Autumn, winter*

There are three islands in all — Little Eye, Little Hilbre and Hilbre Island all three combine to provide an important winter refuge for waders; the sea that surrounds them is also important as a gathering place for

sea duck and divers; huge numbers of knot, dunlin, sandpipers, godwits, sanderling, greenshank and spotted and common redshank feed on invertebrates in the mud.

In spring and autumn thousands of birds stream through on passage with common and arctic terns, little and sandwich terns a regular sight. The population of gulls is enhanced by rarities and vagrants appearing virtually every season. The bird observatory on Hilbre Island is a valuable guide to seabird movements, and the variety of species make these islands a mecca for birdwatchers.
6ha

LITTLE BUDWORTH COUNTRY PARK (CCC) — *Spring, summer*

During the last ice age this area was the meeting point for the Welsh and Irish ice fields, and when they melted they left behind huge quantities of sands and gravels. This particular reserve is a sand deposit with a typical heathland flora and fauna; birch woodland is beginning to invade, control of which must form part of the future management plan. Small pools of standing water are developing into mosses, and the reserve is a popular site for entomologists.
33ha – Map ref: SJ 590655

MARBURY COUNTRY PARK (CCC)* — *Spring, summer*

The Cheshire Trust for Nature Conservation have their headquarters here and control the 6ha site at Marbury reed bed. The park itself is open to the public and there are a number of attractive nature walks, however it is necessary to have a permit from the Trust to visit the reed beds.
76ha – Map ref: SJ 651763

RED ROCKS MARSH (Cheshire CT) — *Spring, summer*

A small area of sand dunes and a dune slack fringed with lime-rich grassland which supports many plants typical of a fertile alkaline dune system. The reserve's main claim to fame is its small colony of breeding natterjack toads whose success is enhanced by the warm sunlit water.
4ha – Map ref: SJ 204884

RISLEY MOSS (Warrington New Town Development Corporation) — *Spring, summer*

This remnant of peat moss in the Mersey valley is being allowed to reconstitute its former condition by judicious use of water levels controlled by a sluice. The raised centre of the moss is not open to the public, but there are adequate vantage points, and a tower hide. The dragonflies here are fascinating, and the presence of birds like barn owls and wintering short-eared owls and kestrels indicates how productive are the small mammals, especially voles. Sparrowhawks, buzzards, and the occasional hen harrier hunt the many small birds, and several pools encourage wintering wildfowl and passing waders to stop over.
81ha – Map ref: SJ 663921

ROSTHERNE MERE (NCC)** — *Autumn, winter*

Natural subsidence and "kettle Hole" development are thought to have created this mere, the largest in Cheshire. (A kettle hole is created by a mass of ice and the associated drift of glacial clays and material which collect in depressions left when the vast inland icebergs slowly melted.) This mere is unusually deep, indicating that a combination of factors led to its formation.

At its deepest point the water is nearly ninety feet, too deep for many species of water birds to feed, but it has become popular with wildfowl as a daytime roost, particularly as the other meres in the area have become subject to human pressure. Duck may include wigeon, teal, shoveller, mallard, goosander, goldeneye and ruddy duck, an introduced stiff-tailed duck that has been increasing in numbers and distribution over the past decade. Thousands of wildfowl shelter here in hard weather, and when they flight out in the evening to feed their place is taken by vast numbers of gulls. In fact the gull's droppings have led to a change in the quality of the water in the lake, the de-oxygenating effect of so much guano has rendered much of the deep water virtually lifeless.

The birds, and their constant movement, provide an unfailing source of interest for birdwatchers, and in spring and early summer migrant songbirds from Europe and Africa fill the reserve which takes on a totally different aspect as the water margins bloom and the birds fly over the lake to collect insect food for their young.
150ha

SANDBACH FLASHES (Cheshire CT) — *All Year*

Not so deep as Rostherne Mere, these ponds, or flashes, have less to do with ice and more to do with the extraction of the salt deposits that underlay this part of the county, remnants of an ancient inland sea which dried out 200 million years ago leaving salt hundreds of metres thick in some places.

The reaction of ground water on these deposits produced brine which rises as brine springs, and these too have been exploited for salt by the local inhabitants since prehistoric times. However, the extraction of salt from the deeper levels, either by man or naturally, has led to subsidence, and it is this subsidence which has created the flashes. Elton Hall railway flashes and Watch Lane flash have a high salt content in their water and plants like sea aster and sea spurrey occur, although these are plants more associated with a marine environment.

The variety of birds breeding on the reserve indicates the ample food supply; and a large number of wintering wildfowl gather here. There is no public access to the flashes, but adequate vantage points from which to observe the water's surface are available.
51ha – Map ref: SJ 725595 / SJ 727607

SHEMMY & SOUTH MOSSES (Cheshire CT)** — *Spring through autumn*

Evidence of glacial action can be found in the soils surrounding this pair of connected basin mires thought to be the result of Kettle Hole formation, though on a smaller scale than Rostherne. They show how mosses eventually become dry land as the sphagnum moss, with its own particular related series of plants, closes the surface of the glacial lake or pool and begins the long process of infill with dead and saturated acid plant material. In time, and it may take thousands of years, the lack of nutrients and oxygen in the water leads to peat forming and filling in the hole when the surface takes on the typical dome shape of a blanket bog.

These two are in the transition state of valley mires, where the surface has been overlayed with a floating blanket of peat and its associated plants. This floating blanket gradually thickens and forms a textured green carpet that belies the danger beneath, at present it is exceedingly dangerous with less than a metre of peat in some places and, obviously it is extremely sensitive to trampling and disturbance.

Later on in their development the mosses will begin to grow trees upon their floating surface, these trees will continue until their weight exceeds the holding capacity of the peat blanket when they will sink through the surface and die to form part of the mass of naturally preserved plant material collecting at the bottom of the pool. This is history in action and the site has to be protected from mankind and his depredations.
6ha

TATTON PARK COUNTRY PARK (CCC) — *Spring, summer*

Close to the busy conurbation of Manchester, the park has to contend with a considerable amount of public pressure in late spring and summer, nevertheless the woodland is at its best for birds in April and May; the bird life in autumn and winter on Melchett Mere makes a visit well worth while. Summer also brings a large number of dragonflies out over the scrubby land, and in the woodland butterflies flit about the rides.
400ha – Map ref: SJ 745816

WIRRAL COUNTRY PARK (Wirral BC) — *All year*

A disused railway with its embankments and cuttings is at the heart of this reserve, and provides an excellent opportunity to study some of the varied geology of the area and to see how the rock affects the wildlife which is dependant upon soil conditions. The railway used to link up to the RAF training camp at West Kirby, and many a raw recruit travelled along this line on his way to suffer the rigours of "square bashing". Now the line is returning to nature, and perhaps will serve the region better in this role than formerly.
43ha – Map ref: SJ 237834

CORNWALL

"When the east wind blows up Helford river the shining waters become troubled and disturbed and the little waves beat angrily upon the sandy shores. The short seas break above the bar at ebb-tide, and the waders fly inland to the mud-flats, their wings skimming the surface, and calling to one another as they go. Only the gulls remain, wheeling and crying above the foam, diving now and again in search of food, their grey feathers glistening with the salt spray.

The long rollers of the Channel, travelling from beyond Lizard point, follow hard upon the steep seas at the river mouth, and mingling with the surge and wash of deep sea water comes the brown tide, swollen with the last rains and brackish from the mud, bearing upon its face dead twigs and straws, and strange forgotton things, leaves too early fallen, young birds, and the buds of flowers."

Lovers of the works of that brilliant writer Daphne Du Maurier will recognise these introductory paragraphs to her novel "Frenchman's Creek" as she decribes the running tide and the east wind off the sea on the Helston river where it fingers inland from the south west Cornish coast. Her words light a candle in my memory, not specifically for Frenchman's Creek, but for the river Gannel just around the headland from the holiday resort of Newquay. These days the miles of golden sands are a bustle with summer visitors for half the year, and even the winter storms and cold cannot deter the hardy surf riders who wait for the gales to bring the long Atlantic rollers.

I remember my childhood on Towan and Tolcarn, in the austere post war quiet, when the impression of my bare feet on the sand was the only human sign, when the only sounds above the cannonade of bursting surf were the piping and squabbling of oyster-catchers resplendent in their morning suits of black and white, and the deep bass voices of the greater black-backed gulls as they scavenged the sea creatures torn from their element by the ferocious winds.

Happily the Gannel is still much the same, the elegant Brunel designed arches of the Trennance viaduct forming a backdrop to the wide sandy estuary. Here you can spend hours watching the tide ebb and flow, and the flickering wings of sanderling, knot and turnstone, and listen to the music of curlew and redshank as the rising tide pushes them further up the strand, and when the tide ebbs, search for shells and pieces of wood carved by the sea, and smell the sea air and taste the salt upon it.

From the soft south coast to the high hard cliffs of Bude and Morwenstow where the county melds into Devon the landscape is rarely far from the sea's influence, even the hedgerow trees bow in homage before the 'westerlies'.

The land has played host to man for thousands of years. Tin and copper, silver and lead have been won by hard labour and skill from the ancient strata, and the county is littered with spoil tips, streaming tips, engine houses and long abandoned shafts where bats find peace and refuge. The Romans, the Phonecians and the Gallic Celts traded tin and copper with the Cornish Celts; now only two mines remain working to crack the granitic ores, and the air, scrubbed clean over 3000 miles of Atlantic ocean, is so pure that rare lichens encrust the north coast cliffs.

Mining has been part of the culture of Cornwall as well as the mainstay of its economy for eons, agriculture was merely subsistence, but there was wealth to be had in the silver shoals of pilchard, small herring-like fish that swarmed along the coast at certain times of year. Commercial overfishing and changes in deep sea currents robbed the Cornish of their pilchards and caused famine and mass migration from the peninsula in the 18th and early 19th century, even now the pilchards apear only infrequently. The result of this sudden loss of a staple food can still be seen in the abandoned homesteads and small stone-walled fields left to the wild flowers and the butterflies. Such events may also have occurred in the very distant past for at sites such as Chysauster the stone dwellings of bronze age man are mute evidence of a change in circumstances and eventual abandonment.

On the north coast the sea has etched the soft strata of deeply folded rock, creating crevices where seabirds can find places aplenty to lay their eggs and rear their young. Here on this rugged rocky coastline a few pairs of Cornish choughs provide a tenuous link with the recent past when their fingered primaries could be seen hanging on the updraughts all along the crags of the western seaboard. Here too the peregrine falcon is recovering and each year their breeding success increases as the effects of persistent insecticides decline and old eyries, abandoned since the 1950s, once again provide a nursery for the fluffy peregrine eyasses.

The return of the peregrines spells trouble for the rock doves that clatter from the roofs of sea caves like those at Pentargen, made famous by H.G. Wells in his fascinating novel, "The Sleeper Awakes" — it was here that the man who was to become the sleeper in the story is first encountered by the reader. The sleeper and his long life were a work of fiction, not so the doves, they are the mainstay of the hunting falcons and although the purity of their lineage may have been diluted by genes from racing pigeons 'gone native' these birds still have a turn of speed to make any falcon work hard for its supper.

The softer southern coastline provides anchorages ideally suited to maritime trade. Here the estuaries are wider and less scoured by the sea, and the mud provides a haven for the invertebrates upon which the fish and waterbirds depend. The warm wet winds of the Atlantic insulate the whole county from all but the harshest winters, even the cold easterly winds from the continent are modified by their passage over the wide expanse of the south western approaches, but though the warm waters of the gulf stream may temper the cold blast of the winds that batter the south Cornish coast they do not modify their force. It is this combination of warm, but violent winds that has provided conditions where relict populations of plants can survive in deep secret valleys.

BENSKINS WOOD (Woodland Trust) — *Spring, summer*

Benskins wood looks across the Tamar to Devon, and constitutes a fascinating area of developing maritine woodland.
1.1ha – Map ref: SX 409539

BUDE MARSHES (North Cornwall DC) — *All year*

Close to a busy holiday area this reserve offers peace and natural variety. Views from the hide in winter consist of waders and migrants; and in spring and summer the marshland and reed beds are home to reed and sedge warblers.
3.2ha – Map ref: SS 207062

CAMEL ESTUARY (Various bodies) — *All year*

Unusual for a major river estuary the river Camel runs out to the sea through sand bars rather than mud, enhancing the wildlife potential of this very beautiful estuary. In spring and summer the waterside walk that runs from Padstow to Wadebridge is a delight, with the banks and rocky walls that once formed cuttings along Brunel's Great Western Railway now ringing to the sound of birds and alive with butterflies and a colourful variety of wild-flowers.

This same walk in winter and early spring is a mecca for bird-watchers. Herons gather in large numbers to fish for small dabs and flounders, and the curlew add background music to a truly magical scene. The gentle slope of the hills on either side of the estuary reflects the ever changing sky as clouds race across on the Atlantic winds, and winter flocks of white-fronted geese are a generous bonus. These geese would have rushed away at the approach of the wreckers of the Cornish coast as depicted in Sabine Bearing-Gould's novel "In the Roar of the Sea", when this area was the setting for his stirring tale. The opening chapter describes so well the wind blown sand "Burying the 15th century church at which Peter Trevisa was the rector"; but the church has now been rescued from the driving sands.
800ha – Map ref: SW 980735

CHAPEL PORTH NATURE TRAIL (CCC) — *All year*

Part of the Atlantic coast nature trail system, this reserve is extremely varied; a deep stream-cut valley, coastal heathland and rocky cliffs provide habitats for stonechats, ravens and buzzards. Sea birds such as kittiwake, guillemot and gannet can be seen from the cliffs.
3.2km – Map ref: SX 697495

COOMBE VALLEY NATURE TRAIL (Cornwall TfNC) — *Spring, summer*

A Nature Trail with excellent access running through a variety of woodland types; unfortunately large blocks of conifers detract from an otherwise very exciting area. Remnants of a laid beech hedge can still be seen, now grown into mature trees. Excellent for woodpeckers, butterflies and unusual plants.
2.5km – Map ref: SS 203116

FAL-RUAN ESTUARY (Cornwall TfNC)** — *All year*

One of the most beautiful estuaries in the United Kingdom, the mud flats, enriched with the overflow from China clay workings inland, are massed with waders in winter. Black-tailed godwit probe the mud along with curlew, greenshank and redshank; and both grey and golden plover search the tideline for worms and small crustaceans. The Cecil Stevens Memorial Hide (RSPB) overlooks the estuary providing incredible views of the wader population.

The sea shore, salt marsh and woodland all mirror Cornwall's ancient past, for the untouched nature of this estuary shows the natural plant succession very clearly; and Fal-Ruan, though largely restricted, is reowned for its rare species. Perhaps there is a message here! When we restrict certain areas purely for nature, the benefits are manifold.
100ha

HAYLE ESTUARY (Various bodies) — *All year*

Within the confines of the town of Hayle the estuary has an industrial feel about it, yet all along the southern edge are huge areas of sandy tidal flats. The river drains into a salt marsh, and below the head of the estuary is an embanked pool known as the Carnsew Basin, a deep water area providing excellent roosting and fishing for a number of birds. There's a trackway along the eastern arm of the estuary and at low water the mud flats and reed marsh are filled with feeding waders and a considerable variety of duck and grebe.
100ha – Map ref: SW 553373

KYNANCE CLIFFS (Cornwall TfNC) — *Spring, summer*

Serpentine rocks create the perfect habitat for plants normally found on the Lizard peninsula; and the combination of coastal grassland, heath and cliffs provides many nesting sites for birds.
26ha – Map ref: SW 688132

THE LIZARD — *All year*

The complex geology has given rise to a very specialised series of plant communities because the warm southwesterly climate encourages a long growing season of a variety of heathland plants, including Cornish heath, as well as a number of unusual dwarf and pygmy rush

species. Dorset heath also grows here and the April display of spring squill is famous. Chives and dog-violet thrive, and small acid bogs support round-leaved sun dew and bog asphodel. On the Gabbro the Cornish heath gives way to bell heather, cross-leaved heath, grass and purple moor, a strange grass-like fern called pillwort and the very rare heath Erica Williamsii, a hybrid between Cornish and cross-leaved heath.
400ha – Map ref: SW 701140

LOE POOL NATURE WALKS (NT) — *All year*

Almost in the centre of Mount's Bay this freshwater lake, behind a shingle bank, provides an all year round habitat for a variety of waterbirds; and the woodland that surrounds the lake on the three sides is a magnet for songbirds.
Various lengths – Map ref: SW 639259

LOWER PREDANNACK CLIFFS (Cornwall TfNC) — *Spring, summer*

The heath that occurs here is similar to that found on the Lizard, and filled with an incredible variety of lichens and heaths; but the plants are smaller for the wind, a feature of the Cornish coast, checks their growth.
16ha – Map ref: SW 660163

PETER'S WOOD (Cornwall TfNC) — *Spring, summer*

An ancient forest of oak and ash rises on one side of the deep-cut river valley that runs down to meet the sea at Boscastle. Tall oaks swarm up the hillside, their canopy forming a food-rich habitat for insects and birds from resident tit mice to the migrant songsters that appear in early April. Thomas Hardy used Boscastle as the model for Castle Boterel in his novel "A Pair of Blue Eyes" and there's little doubt that he knew these woodlands very well for his wife was sister-in-law to the rector of St Juliot Church which Hardy helped to restore. One can imagine him walking under the overhanging trees that line the footpath through the valley bottom, listerning to buzzards mewing as they played on the sea breezes.
10ha – Map ref: SX 113910

RED MOOR (Cornwall TfNC) — *Spring, summer*

Red Moor is so natural it's difficult to imagine that the whole site was once a tin streaming area where the soft silver metal was extracted from surface deposits. The landscape that has resulted from all this activity is one of moorland pools, woods and reed beds and marshy ground hummocked and ditched as if by some past glaciation rather than the picks and shovels of Cornish miners. It's very peaceful and the variety of breeding birds and insects is outstanding, as are the plants that thrive in the many different habitats from wet willow woodland to low oak copse; the scene is ever changing and provides a feast for the naturalist. Dragonfly species are many and varied and can be seen at close quarters as they search for food or a mate over the many small pools. The surrounding countryside is superb, for buzzards tend to congregate on sunny days riding upwards on the thermals that bubble up

from the dark surface of the land.
24ha – Map ref: SX 077622

ST ANTHONY-IN-ROSELAND NATURE WALK (NT) — *Spring, summer*

The beautiful Roseland Peninsula is the setting for this nature walk which takes you through a wide range of habitats from high sea cliffs to woodland and eventually a creek. It's an excellent place for migrant butterflies and moths in mid summer with red admiral and painted lady and the occasional clouded and pale clouded yellow. When the wind is from the south east humming bird hawk moths and other more exotic hawk moths are blown across from France to feed on the many lovely wild flowers.
6.4km – Map ref: SW 868329

SOUTH WEST PENINSULA COASTAL PATH (CC) —*All year*

From high plateau to wader-rich estuaries this must be one of the most exciting coastlines in the country. The range of rock types, from very ancient to comparatively young sediments, provides a series of habitats for birds like the peregrine falcon and chough and the many sea birds that throng this superb wild coastline. Here and there signs of man's enterprise can be seen in the crumbling 19th century chimneys of tin mine pumping and winding houses clinging to rock ledges above the boil and backwash of the sea. It is the sea and the fierce salty Atlantic winds that have moulded Cornwall's natural history backdrop trimming the trees and bushes as though a master topiarist had been at work.

On the north coast the last remnants of the large blue butterfly colonies struggled in vain to survive in the face of changing agriculture and the reduction in sheep-grazed or rabbit-cropped turf on the seaward facing slopes. However, this area is still home to many interesting insects, and hopefully one day the large blue will be re-introduced here. Nevertheless this is one coastal path where the range of habitats and species and the magnificent scenery will leave you enthralled from beginning to end, and the possibility of good weather and bright, but usually windy days, encourages long stretches to be planned in advance. I have to warn you there are so many distractions on the way that the walk is bound to take far longer than its distance would lead you to believe.
475km – Map ref: SS 212174 / SX 455534

Red Moor   *Cornwall*

Kestrel

mudflats the waders call across the entire estuary. The site is open to threat from shoreline development such as a marina, but as the number of wetland sites available to wintering wildfowl and waders decreases in the country as a whole, protection of this very important estuarine habitat will become even more vital. On a winter's day, when the tide is on the make, the range of waders is astonishing — godwits and even the odd party of avocets can be seen when conditions are right.
400ha

TRELISSICK NATURE WALK (NT) — *Spring, summer*

Part of this trail runs through ancient woodland along the slopes above the beautiful river Fal. Birds to be seen include buzzard and heron, and in spring the woodland is a prime site for migrant warblers, they arrive here prior to fanning out over the rest of the country.
3.2km – Map ref: SW 837396

VENTONGIMPS MOOR (Cornwall TfNC)** — *Spring, summer*

One of the few remaining rich south western heathlands, the delightfully named Ventongimps Moor is rich in plants and insects, particularly dragonflies. The range of wet and dry heath with deep pools and marshy stream-sides adds to a unique series of habitats that were formerly common in the county, but now reduced to mere remnants. The dry heaths are mainly composed of Dorset heath, heather, bell heather and common and western gorse creating a variety of nesting and breeding sites for birds, mammals and reptiles; the wet areas contain a healthy amphibian population.
8ha

TAMAR ESTUARY (Cornwall TfNC)** — *All year*

The Tamar forms the boundary between Devon and Cornwall and comes at last to the sea between Torpoint and Plymouth. The estuary, once far more industrialised than today, is developing a huge head of wildlife, especially herons and wading birds and from the wide

CUMBRIA

For oft, when on my couch I lie
In vacant or in pensive mood,
They flash upon that inward eye
Which is the bliss of solitude;
And then my heart with pleasure fills,
And dances with the daffodils.

— William Wordsworth.

Cumbria is the land of the Lakeland poet — who has not heard of Wordsworth's golden daffodils; but perhaps one person in particular will be seen to have had a more far-reaching effect upon the environment of fells and lakes than all the refined wordsmiths. Beatrix Potter with her world of small creatures and superb watercolours of mice and rabbits, geese and foxes typical of the fell country, earned a great deal of money from her children's books and with it bought land which she bequeathed to the nation so that the Lakeland countryside she so loved should be preserved. In later life Beatrix Potter became almost a recluse, giving up writing and devoting her skills to farming at Hill Farm, Hawkshead, especially breeding the hardy, grey-fleeced herdwick sheep thought to have been brought to the Lakelands by the invading Vikings.

Most people think of Cumbria only in terms of the lakes and fells, but in truth there is a greal deal more to this county — the Solway Firth is a mecca of geese, Morecombe Bay attracts immense numbers of waders, the red sandstone cliffs at St Bees Head provide excellent breeding ledges for sea birds and the dunes at Ravenglass present a fascinating spectacle of the inter-relationship between plants and the gull colony.

Perhaps one of the most exciting things to happen in the latter part of the 20th century has been the re-establishment of the golden eagle as a breeding species in the newly acquired RSPB reserve at Haweswater reservoir. These majestic birds have begun to breed regularly and foretell of a population increase which may be a renaissance for birds of prey after a century of destruction. Peregrine and merlin are already breeding regularly and success-fully on Cumbria's high ground, though the latter is more susceptible to man's encroachment of its remote breeding grounds, and though protected they are still declining in numbers.

The glaciers that crept inexorably over the Cumbrian landscape with unimaginable force smoothing the hill tops and carving out the valleys, left one or two living remnants of their passing; where debris from the dying glaciers settled creating barriers and natural dams at the head of ice-worn gorges, deep lakes formed and in these ice cold waters arctic char and whitefish flourished; isolated in this way they developed into separate sub species. However, such deep water is not so attractive to wildfowl, even in winter relatively few birds feed on the open water, although where the margins are less deep, goosander and red-breasted merganser, fish-eating sawbill ducks, hunt small trout in the pebbly shallows.

The whole area bears many ice inflicted scars and in places they look as if they had happened only yesterday. Where carboniferous limestone strata was exposed by glaciation it has formed pavements, smooth grey tables of rock interlaced with deep cracks called clints or grykes. These have come about because the naturally occurring carbonic acid present in normal rain water dissolves its way into faults in the limestone; time and weather do the rest. These grikes provide miniature canyons where plants and insects can grow in a protected environment away from the cold fierce winds that often threaten the high ground. In the period since the last world war much of this limestone pavement has been mined for garden ornaments and building stone, fortunately this is now controlled and the pavement is less at risk than formerly. The preservation of this type of specialised habitat and its rare plants and insects is of vital importance.

Most of this very beautiful county is subject to heavy pressures from recreational interests. Walkers and climbers flock to the rugged peaks and the long distance ways in summer, but in doing so they subject the natural world to immense disturbance. Many of the birds that breed here like the merlin and raven are losing out because they must have larger, remote territories in order to survive. However, the corollary to this is that while walkers and climbers are putting pressure upon the wild creatures, their combined voice, together with that of organised conservation bodies, is helping to stop many excesses in the form of shooting and poisoning that has brought these birds to the very brink of oblivion.

A balance is very necessary here between the requirements of man and the needs of the natural world or Beatrix Potter's magical countryside will be greatly impoverished.

ARNSIDE KNOT NATURE WALK (PC/NT) — *Spring, summer*

The limestone grassland and woodland along the walk holds a wealth of natural history surprises, red squirrels are but one of the features; there are many woodland butterflies in the high summer sunshine, and the area is rich in mammals which tawny owls take advantage of under cover of darkness.
1-5km – Map ref: SD 451773

ASBY SCAR (NNC) — *Spring, summer*

High above the M6 is a unique, almost desert-like, geological environment where the great ice sheets of the last glaciation scraped and ground away the sharp edges; they also levelled areas of fossil-rich limestone sweeping them clear of soil or any organic matter, creating platforms of stone known as limestone pavement. Asby Scar is one of these limestone exposures and the combination of prevalent climatic conditions, naturally acidic rain water and wind have shaped the flat pavement into a maze of fissures called "grikes" miniature valleys, and "clints" loose slabs of undercut limestone created as the acid rain water dissolved the alkaline rock. The same process continues today as minute quantities of rock are dissolved away with every rainfall.

Organic matter collects in these grikes forming a roothold for mosses and simple plants, and over thou-

The Langdales   *Cumbria*

sands of years soils have formed enabling higher plants to grow, protected from harsh winds and frost. The humidity and warmth of these naturally occurring propagation units produces a habitat resembling a miniature canyon.
160ha – Map ref: NY 648103

BRANTWOOD NATURE TRAIL (Brantwood Estate — Coniston water) — *Spring, summer*

Running beside one of the most beautiful of lakes, Brantwood Nature Trail takes in a great deal of typical lakeland habitat. Oak woodland is kept open by sheep grazing and on the side of the lake, where relatively little natural regeneration is taking place, there are spectacular views; and the possibility of seeing a red squirrel feeding on the ground is a reminder of Beatrix Potter who bequeathed so much of this landscape to the nation.
4km – Map ref: SD 313958

CLAIFE NATURE WALK (NT) — *Spring, summer*

Windermere is probably one of the best known inland waters in the country. Created by melt water after the last ice age the deep lake exhibits thermocline currents that make its waters unpredictable, nevertheless there is a constant flow of boat traffic, even in winter.

The extreme depth means that relatively few fish-eating birds are found in the centre of the lake, but on the margins the bird life is extensive and varied. Throughout the year mergansers breed along the banks between exposed tree roots, and can be seen turning stones to get at small trout and bullheads. Dippers too find ample feeding and common sandpipers nest in quiet sandy bays where human traffic is minimal and water bistort flowers stand above the surface like pink sentinels. The predominance of hardwood forest is attractive to redstarts and pied flycatchers returning to nest after wintering in Africa.

The Forestry Commission has carried out some blanket afforestation which has provided a home for red squirrels, and the occasional pine marten; and in winter the lake is dotted with wildfowl and small flocks of Bewick and whooper swans.
2.4km – Map ref: SD 388954

CLAWTHORPE FELL (NCC)** — *Spring, summer*

Clawthorpe Fell is an area of limestone pavement providing variety and interest from the very rare and exotic dark red helleborine, a plant of the orchid family associated with this type of habitat, to bloody cranesbill and lily-of-the-valley. The limestone grikes often carry a wide range of rare or unusual ferns and rigid buckler-fern and polypody are found here in some numbers.
14ha

FRIARS CRAG NATURE WALK (NT) — *Spring, summer*

Friars Crag Nature Walk trails around beautiful Derwent Water, it's particularly attractive with a wide range of waterside and woodland creatures, plants and insects; and on a clear fine day in summer the scenery is quite superb.
2.4km – Map ref: NY 264227

GELTSDALE (RSPB)** — *All year*

Geltsdale contains a number of Cumbrian habitats from the high moorland of the northern Pennines rising to 2000ft at Coldfell to hillsides, woodland and the Tarn at Gelt Woods. The range of birds is dramatic and red grouse, lapwing, golden plover and ring ouzel nest on the high ground while in the woodland pied flycatchers and redstarts, wood warblers and sparrowhawks breed.

The streams and Tarn support dippers, goosander and common sandpipers and in winter whooper swans are seen with wintering wildfowl, including goldeneye. The woodlands harbour foxes, red squirrels and roe deer. By its very nature the plant life is rather limited, but extremely interesting for all that.
12,300 acres

No access to moorland, but views from bridleways:-
Tindale — Map ref: NY 616593
Jockey Shield — Map ref: NY 561557

Riverside walk through lower Gelt Woods starts at:-
Gelt Bridge — Map ref: NY 520592

HAWESWATER (RSPB) (by arrangement with North West Water Authority) — *All year*

The aquisition of this immense reserve in July 1988 was particularly important as the agreement included a management plan for the unique Naddle Low Woods. This area encompasses many vital breeding sites for endangered birds of prey, including the eyrie of the sole English breeding pair of golden eagles, as well as a high population density of peregrine falcons, sparrowhawks and buzzards. The woodland also contains some very ancient hollies that provide food and nesting sites for woodpeckers and other hole nesters like redstarts and pied flycatchers.

There is a considerable population of pied wagtails, and from the road that runs beside the flooded valley that constitutes the reservior there are ample opportunities to see wheatears and whinchats; high ground birds such as ring ousels, are in evidence too.

This is superb walking country, and access to the reserve is relatively unlimited. The lake itself has several islands, once small hillocks, but now black-headed gull colonies. In spring the hillsides are bright with spring flowers, and in summer the roadsides are flanked with tall foxgloves which is no wonder when you consider the fellsides and woodlands have been allowed to develop over the centuries until now there is a wide variety of plant and animal and insect species.
25,000 acres Approximately

HERVEY (Cumbria WT)** — *Spring, summer*

This reserve comprises a progression of limestone pavement habitats, from the wide open scoured areas of Asby Scar to the limestone woodland at Hervey itself; this is the intermediate stage with some soil having been deposited thereby allowing a richer and more diverse limestone flora to develop. The steep western slopes encourage high altitude species woodland with smaller specimens of yew and juniper bushes, ash and birch. Where there is more shelter and deeper soil the trees grow taller; and where the fragile pavement has been overlaid with grassland the

bird life is richer, especially skylarks, meadow and tree pipits; and, over the margins of the marshy pool, pied wagtails hunt for flies.
100ha

LAKE DISTRICT NATIONAL PARK (LDSPB) — Spring, summer

The Lake District is the largest national park in the country and can also boast the highest point. The immense variety of habitats, birds, plants, insects and mammals and the superb scenery draws summer tourists like bees to the honey pot, but the area is also very beautiful in winter. The westerly winds off the Atlantic modify the climate, though there's usually plenty of snow on the high tops, but rain rather than frost is the norm, and the plant life reflects these gentler conditions.

Juniper bushes are common, although in places they are stunted to low growing shrubs by the force of the wind, but where there is shelter they can reach quite normal proportions. Woodland is as much a feature of the Cumbrian landscape as are lakes and fells. The provision of blocks of conifers by the Forestry Commission and private forestry companies has done little to improve an already beautiful landscape, but until forestry policy is changed at government level the dark green rectangles will continue to mar the hillsides.

Red squirrels and the few pine martens left prefer the deep darkness of the conifers, but the majority of native birds and mammals naturally gravitate towards the more open native broadleaved woodlands with their ample food supply and good access, and even the red squirrels can be seen in some numbers in most of the broadleaved woods.

Cumbria is large on sheep, unfortunately sheep and woodlands don't really go together, the sheep nibble the regenerating seedlings and in time the woods take on a single-age aspect, any dramatic event can remove whole areas of woodland cover within a few years leaving no saplings; soon all that is left is rock strewn grassland. Happily over the past decade this threat to Cumbria's woods has been recognised, areas are being fenced against sheep and the regeneration has been astounding.

The park's very long coastline, from the Solway Firth to Ravenglass and Morecombe Bay takes in some of the most beautiful bird-rich areas; there are dunes and cliffs and every kind of wildlife and bird habitat. A visit here is a must on the itinerary of any naturalist.
224,300ha

LANCELOT CLARK STORTH (Cumbria WT)** — *Spring, summer*

At Lancelot Clark Storth the limestone pavement is seen at its most productive with six steps of varying degrees of development on view. The reserve climbs from a rich, almost impenetrable, woodland to open heather and bracken covered platforms. At the lower levels, where the grikes have been well filled with organic material and the soil is rich, there's a profusion of lady's bedstraw, ox-eye daisies, common spotted orchid and fly orchids, and carpets of wild thyme. It is considered the richest area of limestone pavement in the whole of the British Isles.
56.2ha

Coniston Water   *Lake District Nat. Park*

MOOR HOUSE (NCC) — *Early summer*

Moor House is a particularly rich area of blanket bog built upon glacial drift; the bog and its associated peat layer is up to eight metres thick in places. The climate is typical of high ground and anyone unprepared can be caught out by snow, mist or freezing rain. However, the conditions that make life difficult for humans suit the plants and animals which are well adapted to live and breed here; low growing bog plants and the breeding birds such as snipe, curlew, red grouse, the native ring ouzel and dipper all find this area very much to their liking. An occasional peregrine may hunt here, and although the population of birds is relatively low the falcons can find enough to more than satisfy their appetite.
4000ha – Map ref: NY 730325

NETHER WASDALE NATURE TRAIL (Cumbria WT) — *Spring, summer*

Running beside the reservoir and nature reserve of Wastwater, the scenery is splendid and there's always a chance of seeing a peregrine or even a golden eagle hunting the high ground; the latter can be confused at a distance with a buzzard. The woodland and open grassland supports wheatear, pied flycatchers, redstart, wood warbler and tree pipit in spring.
5.5km – Map ref: NY 147048

PENNINE WAY (CC) — *Spring, summer*

Fifty kilometres of high moorland and fell, starting from Alston, and with some of the finest views to be seen anywhere in the country. The amount of foot traffic has driven away much of the wildlife from the proximity of the track though grouse can still be seen, and the Way runs through a large part of the NCC reserve of Moor House where golden plover, curlew and lapwing breed.

The sound of the high upland birds in spring is a delight and there's often a chance to see the dashing flight of a hunting peregrine falcon, or the slow measured quartering of a patrolling golden eagle.

This area was once a rich source of lead, and the lead workings have created sheltered habitats where ring ouzels and rock pipits can find nest sites. Many altitude or cold-adapted plants are found along the course of this path from saxifrage and sandwort of the sandstone exposures to cotton and deergrass where the water has provided a habitat for mosses. Past the deep valley of Dufton Ghyll Wood the path turns east through dramatic countryside before it enters County Durham and meets the huge entrapment of Cow Green reservoir.

50km – Map ref: NY 698489 – 815286

RAVENGLASS (CCC)** — *Spring, summer*

The sand dune system on the peninsula at Ravenglass is perhaps best known for its gull colony and the fact that four species of terns breed here, including little and sandwich terns, as well as several species of waders and duck. The presence of so many birds affects the vegetation as their droppings allow for a rich flora on an otherwise rather infertile soil; there are a number of unusual plants on the dunes including field gentian and carline thistle and the abundance of plants in turn provides cover for incubating parent birds. Amphibians breed here and six species have been recorded, including a good colony of natterjack toads; adders are also found in many of the sheltered places.

383ha

ST BEES HEAD (RSPB) — *Spring, summer*

The majestic sandstone cliffs of the promontory at St Bees Head are ridged and weathered, and the platforms created by the elements harbour an exciting breeding colony of seabirds; one of the few breeding sites in the UK for black guillemots, although they are few in number. Other auks, however, are well represented with as many as 2000 pairs of common guillemots and almost 1000 razorbills.

The cliffs are sheer and dangerous, but the cliff top walk is spectacular with flora as varied as the soils. Some acid soils are clothed in heath and gorse and heath spotted orchid, while others sport a carpet of kidney vetch and cushions of bloody cranesbill; and in the spring early purple orchid. The cliffs overlooking the sea make an exciting look-out point to watch the passage of seabirds, terns and skuas, and the updraught of air from the Irish sea provides a playground for many birds. Among the gulls and fulmar petrels, you might see a raven or a hunting peregrine.

5km – Map ref: NX 959118

SOUTH WALNEY (Cumbria WT) — *All year*

South Walney is in fact attached to the peninsula on the north western tip of Morecombe Bay. The "island" is shaped like an ice axe which is apt for the shingle and gravel from which the dunes were built are remnants of a glacier which melted here leaving its cargo of spoil. The region is best known for its birds with the most southerly breeding colony of eider and almost the largest colonies of herring gulls and lesser black-backed gulls in the country. Their success spells disaster for other breeding birds, but a number of species do in fact manage to bring off broods in spite of the hordes of hungry predatory gulls in the skies above.

Gravel extraction has been considerable allowing plants to colonise, and the gullery imparts its own fertility to the dune system; many plants grow here that would never find sufficient nutrients on other sea facing dunes. The proximity to the fertile flats of Morecombe Bay brings immense numbers of duck and waders, and up to 1000 oyster-catchers regularly use the foreshore at high tide.

92ha – Map ref: SD 215620

DERBYSHIRE

"The Waterfall" — James Thompson

Smooth to the shelving brink a copious flood
Rolls fair, and placid; where collected all,
In one impetuous torrent, down the steep
It thundering shoots, and shakes the country round.
At first, an azure sheet, it rushes broad;
Then whitening by degrees as prone it falls,

And from the loud resounding rocks below
Dash'd in a cloud of foam, it sends aloft
A hoary mist, and forms a ceaseless shower.

And falling fast from gradual slope to slope,
With wild infracted course, and lessened roar,
It gains a safer bed; and steals, at last,
Along the mazes of the quiet vale.

Thompson's waterfall typifies this landscape shaped by ancient ice and running water. To most people Derbyshire means the Peak District and the beautiful Dales and rivers, and the landscape used by the novelist George Elliot. She transposed several of the local towns and villages in "Adam Bede" she turned Dovedale into Eagledale; and Charlotte Brontë took her heroine's name from a family living in Hathersage — the town itself was "Jane Eyre's" Morton.

The region itself has two faces — two distinct areas with contrasting rock types, each giving their own particular character. The gritstones of the Dark Peaks impart an acid ring to the soil and plant cover, at one time these hills were densely wooded with sessile oak and rowan and a few birch trees, but since the Neolithic Age, man has exploited the high ground, developing special breeds of sheep, such as the shaggy Derbyshire gritstone, to weather the harsh conditions, and which have kept the hills free of trees and scrub. The erosion that follows loss of tree cover can take thousands of years to rectify and, it is unlikely that the primeval forest that once clothed the area, now so popular with hill walkers, could ever be re-established. There's a strange contrast here for undoubtedly the area would be less popular with walkers if they had to tramp the hills with no view other than the twisted trunks of stunted oaks.

The soft rounding of the hills gives this part of Derbyshire much of its charm. The high ground is wild, but safe for birds of prey like peregrine and merlin and breeding waders such as golden plover and curlew.

On the other hand, the White Peaks form a series of gentle fertile habitats rich in minerals; they have the creamy texture of limestone and in places are deep cut with some of the most beautiful limestone rivers. The Lathkill, for instance, has the interesting habit of vanishing into its bed in the upper reaches to appear further downstream after a brief subterranean excursion, a particular feature of limestone rivers.

This limestone region was popular with man long before the tourist boom. There are caves aplenty and many holes in the county's crust caused by the action of water as well as mankind. Stone Age man took advantage of many of the cave systems for living accomodation, and relics of his presence abound. Between Edale and Castleton are a number of caves including one where Blue John, an attractive mineral used for jewellery and small turned decorative items was mined, and Bagshaw Caverns and the cave system at Pool's Cavern at Matlock give an indication of the power of water to dissolve rock and create caves.

Derbyshire was also popular with the Romans because of the ample stocks of lead and other minerals. Lead was important to them, they used it for many everyday utensils, but it may have undermined their health through lead poisoning. Disused Roman lead mines litter the region, and a particularly good example can be seen on the hill above Matlock Bath, and the metal was mined around this area on a commercial scale until recent times.

Caves and lead mines are not the only holes in the ground in Derbyshire. Industry has long been dependant on the coal measures that lie deep beneath the ground in a wide band. But now many of the mines are closing for economic reasons, and their associated spoil heaps have begun to return to nature; in time they will become part of the green landscape. Some of them, those with a considerable coal content, have been known to ignite spontaneously and burn for many years creating a micro climate on certain parts of their surface that allows plants to thrive, even in periods of quite cold weather. However, modern methods of dealing with such fires is becoming more sophisticated, and they are now soon brought under control.

As the spoil heaps grow their coat of plants and begin to support populations of animals, the engine sheds and other buildings are taken over by birds and bats as breeding sites and roosts. There is a possibility that given time, and a reduction in exploitive industry, Derbyshire may again become a quiet place where birds sing and lambs gambol in a seemingly natural landscape. The landscape is certainly beautiful and dramatic, and there's no reason why, with careful planning, it could not become one of the loveliest of England's counties.

BUXTON COUNTRY PARK (Buxton & District Civic Association) — *Spring, summer*

Based on the caves at Pool's Cavern, the park also boasts a considerable area of woodland with beech, ash and sycamore.
40ha – Map ref: SK 050727

CROMFORD CANAL (Derbyshire WT) — *Spring, summer*

One of a network of canals once vital for supplying mineral wealth for the industrial revolution, Cromford has fallen into disuse by man, but not by nature. In summer dragonflies and damselflies patrol the water, and the plants, fish and amphibians make it particularly interesting; the water is often clear, allowing for better observation of fish and aquatic insects. Moorhens cluck and scurry in the reedy edges, and the occasional kingfisher sprints from one fishing post to another. In early spring warblers fresh from Africa proclaim their territories. Canals are always used as natural flyaways, and it's not at all uncommon to see sparrowhawks hunting the linear woodland that grows along the canal banks; very often the alarm call of a wren or robin will tell you there's an aerial marauder about.
3km – Map ref: SK 333544 / 350520

DERBYSHIRE DALES (NCC) — *Spring, summer*

Few landscape features indicate so clearly the nature of their beginnings. The Dales were formed through erosion of the solid limestone rock by the flood waters of a melting glacier over ten thousand years ago; the immense ice cap that had lain over the land for nearly a million years had already begun the process by wearing channels in the softer rock strata, carving gullies that would become watersheds during the thaw. The agent for this erosion was the mass of boulders and grit carried along at the base of the glacier as it progressed, inch by inch, over the centuries.

The last ice age was not one single period of intense cold, it consisted of a series of ice ages with interstadials (periods) of warm weather between. It is thought that our own time is merely an interstadial between glaciations, and in time the ice will return and the Dales will be shaped anew. But for now we can marvel in the beauty of these water-worn gorges and limestone valleys with their cream and silver stone, and the intensity of life that depends upon the prevailing soil and moisture conditions.

The original flora passed through stages of foliation from lichen to birch scrub and, ultimately, high ash woodland with guelder rose, hazel, rowan, field maple and wyche elm. Evidence of this special forest is found in trees like the rock whitebeam, which occurs in very few other places. Since the primeval woodland yielded to man and his sheep, there have been successive replantings over parts of the Dales, some of conifer and sycamore, fast maturing timber. The ground flora is typical of limestone woodland with water avens in the valley bottoms and on the slopes, where the sun's power is stronger, the variety is greater with nettle-leaved bellflower, yellow star of Bethlehem and the purple red flowers of mezereon, a rare member of the Daphne family. The plant most commonly associated with ancient woodland on limestone or chalk is dog's mercury, which is found in abundance. The variety increases on south facing slopes where the grassland may hold in excess of 50 species to the square metre, similar to that found on old chalk downland.

In the valleys, where the rivers have worn themselves beds of pebbles and smooth limestone, dippers and pied and yellow wagtails breed. The birds in the Dales vary from warblers and seed eaters in the sheltered wooded parts to wheatears on the high ground, while the hillsides provide plenty of upcurrents for soaring buzzards and ravens, though the latter have declined rapidly over the past decade. Other predatory birds include sparrowhawk and kestrel and the occasional peregrine — the whole area is a delight at any time of year, but it's especially good in spring and early summer.
234ha – Map ref: Lathkill Dale SK 203662
Monk's Dale – SK 141725

ELVASTON CASTLE COUNTRY PARK NATURE TRAIL (DCC) — *Spring, summer*

This nature trail runs through woodland and past a lake with a feeder stream. The rhododendron has impoverished the ground flora, but there are bluebells, primroses and the strong garlic smell of the white flowers of ransomes. The availability of plenty of nest sites for woodland birds attracts blackcap, willow and garden warblers and the difficult to spot lesser spotted woodpecker. The lake and stream harbour water birds and kingfishers and grey wagtails.
1.5km – Map ref: SK 413332

KINDER-BLEAKLOW UPLANDS (PPJPB) — *Summer*

These are the high hard uplands of the Dark Peak country, a millstone grit cap of acid rock that encourages the growth of peat and heather moorland. It's a landscape of golden plover, merlin, red grouse and ring ouzel, and in spring the wide open, bronzy green heather and cloud-berry sward echoes with the wild music of curlew. It's walking country, and the Penine Way passes through. It's also the beginning of many streams, some of which are destined not to see the light of day after they plunge into the softer limestone on the southern edge of the Dark Peak.

Kinder Scout stands high and majestic at 2088 feet above sea level, its waters falling through the Kinder Down Fall to run towards the sea. The high ground intercepts the westerly winds and wrings the moisture from them, it's not a place to venture unprepared, even in mid summer, for the temperatures and drenching rain can soon fall, and it's easy to succumb to exposure. The Dark Peak was once an area of blanket mire practically unequalled in England, but the peat has eroded cutting the land into deep furrows, and the blanket mire that formed this unique ecosystem is in the process of breaking down, largely due to industrial pollution.
4500ha – Map ref: SK 090929

OGSTON WOODLANDS (Derbyshire WT)** — *Spring, summer*

Ogston is one of the largest areas of woodland in lowland Derbyshire, a small part of which is recognised as being of great age, probably a remnant of the type of woodland that colonised the countryside after the last ice age. These valley woods have been planted with a variety of trees such as beech and larch, and there's a hide in a clearing to make it easier to watch the birds. For some time the understory has been dominated by rhododendron which may have been introduced as cover for pheasant shooting; for whatever reason it is a considerable pest in woodland as it tends to overshadow the bluebells and other interesting woodland plants.

The rich variety of trees encourages a larger than normal bird population, over 70 species have been recorded, and in spring the wood is a delight. Wood, garden and willow warblers nest here, and the beautiful blackcap can be heard singing in late spring. Resident birds include titmice, chaffinch, greater spotted woodpecker, and tawny owl and sparrowhawk breed in the wood.
32ha

THE PEAK NATIONAL PARK (PPJPB) — *Spring, summer*

The Peak National Park was the first of its kind to be opened to the public, and here lies the problem. We all have a perfect right to use the park for recreation, although access is not unlimited, and in the area of the White Peak district, where the greater fertility of the limestone encourages a more restricted land use with hay meadows and sheep in fields bounded by dry limestone walls, the right to wander is constrained.

The Dark Peak is a monument to man's misuse of the environment. The peat hags and blanket bogs that once thrived on this gritstone plateau with its steep craggy cliffs and waterfalls were a unique, self supporting, ecosystem; now that ecosystem is in decline the moss that made up the bulk of the peat has been killed by industrial pollution, gradually the moorland is eroding as the peat dries out and oxidises. The even undulating blanket of peat moorland has been cut through, sometimes to the height of a man, to the rock beneath. In 100 years if nothing is done to arrest the degradation of the Peak's peatlands little will be left.

On the southern edge of the park the White Peak, with its glass clear rivers and woodlands of ash and oak is more fertile, and to some, less forbidding. They stand lower than the Dark Peak, their softer rock having eroded under the ice blanket more dramatically than the gritstone cap of the Dark Peak. It's an area where walkers predominate, though it can be dangerous if you're not prepared. Winds from the Irish Sea and storm systems from the Atlantic empty their rain onto the high ground.

One section of the Penine Way terminates at Edale and as anyone who has completed it will know, the sights along the way can elate even the most tired walker. The buzzard is the bird of prey of the uplands here, though the tiny merlin, becoming more and more rare as pressure on the high ground increases, is still seen.

In the valley woods the spring song of warblers, tits and finches can be stilled by the menacing shape of a hunting sparrowhawk, fortunately these birds are on the increase following the reduction in persistent insecticides in the environment; and it is to be hoped that some way may be found to preserve and enhance the peatlands of the Dark Peak before they erode altogether.
140,378ha

PENNINE WAY (CC) — *Spring, summer*

This section of the Pennine Way rises to cross the highest point of the Peak National Park at Kinder Scout before it terminates in the limestone valley of Edale.
30km – Map ref: SE 078047 / SK 124857

SHIPLEY COUNTRY PARK (DCC) — *All year*

Shipley Country Park is an extensive reserve with Mapperly reservoir at its heart, and there is a hide at the reservoir where visitors can watch the wintering wildfowl which might include goldeneye. The variety of woodland birds is excellent because of the many different environments afforded by this park, and the small mammal population includes wood mouse and short-tailed field vole which form the bulk of the diet of the tawny owls and kestrels that breed here. Foxes are relatively common, and a small herd of fallow deer find ample grazing on the grasslands. The lake encourages dragonflies to breed and there are several common species including brown hawker.
400ha – Map ref: SK 426458

DEVON

Devon is a county of little streams. They fissure the complex geology and emerge through the soft shales and slates, marls and chalks in myriad ways. Along the south coast the broad muddy estuaries at Exmouth and Salcombe provide a winter refuge for a multitude of wildfowl and waders; and only a few miles out to sea the gulf stream warms the incoming winds. A fall of snow or a hard frost, other than on the moors, is rare and it's this mild climate that allows for rich grass, fat cattle and cream.

On the north coast the Taw and Torridge rivers provided the author Henry Williamson with settings for his stories "Tarka the Otter", and "Salar the Salmon". In his introductory chapter to the tale of Tarka which he entitled "The Gentleman's River", he describes finding the source of the Taw and Torridge:-

"Leaving the village one morning, with staff and knapsack, I climbed to the watershed of the Taw and Torridge, to enter a region of mist and dead and dying heather. There I discovered Taw head, where the smallest trickle cried faintly in the mossy channel of its granite bed, and crossed the bog by leaping and hopping from peat-hag to peat-hag, fearful of sinking into the black unknown, to where sister Torridge began her life. While curlews cried wildly above dragging clouds I made notes and a sketch of how little brother Taw, four inches in width from bank to bank, moved out of Cranmere tarn, to run bright at his beginning, while sister Torridge hardly stirred out of the silence and mystery of the peat. Soon the two parted, to run their different ways, each collecting tribute water from every smaller combe and valley until they met again in the estuary below the monk's bridges of Barnstaple and Bideford, where their waters pound with salt waves on the grey pebbly-ridge of Westward Ho!"

It was on the north west rise of Dartmoor that my earliest impressions about the environment were formed and have influenced my life and work as a naturalist ever since.

The county slopes like a wedge of gently maturing cheese from the high harsh cliffs at Hartland Point where fulmars glide stiff-winged on the wind, where the heather tops of Exmoor soak up the moist westerlies in their peaty crowns releasing it, sometimes as a moderate trickle and sometimes as a rushing spate, to form the Exe, Devon's longest river, easing out on the south coast in a gentle broad estuary protected from the force of the easterlies off the sea by the dunes of Dawlish Warren.

Inland the high hard ancient shield of Dartmoor with its granite tors and peat covered plateau rises dramatically, 1216 feet above sea level. This moorland, the source of many of Devon's streams, also gives birth to the river Dart, arguably one of the most beautiful rivers in England, running as it does through wooded gorges past the village of Holne where Charles Kingsley, author of "The Water Babies" and "Westward Ho!" was born in the Vicarage in 1819. On through banks of wild daffodils and wood anemones the river tumbles and glides, its unruly power now largely unused by the many historic water-mills that once tapped its strength for crushing ore and fulling cloth. It reaches the salt taste of the tideaway at Totnes then on to the open sea through the glorious oak-wooded hillsides that flank the estuary behind the town of Dartmouth on one side and Kingswear on the other.

Dartmoor is a relic of volcanic activity six million years ago; the tors and the gigantic granite boulders that surround them are the remains of eroded plugs left standing like ancient sculptures. Large parts of the moor are used for military exercises and public access is restricted; but this restriction has actually assisted the conservation of the moor, preserving the natural wildlife from massive human disturbance.

Man has lived on the moor since very early times. Stone Age and Iron Age hut circles and tiny stone walled field systems are clearly visible on many of the southerly hillsides, and man's effect upon nature over the years has helped the open moorland to spread. Tin, copper and iron mining, granite quarrying, and the subsequent smelting of ores with charcoal in the 'Stannary' towns of Tavistock and Ashburton hastened the clearance of the oak forest from many of the moorland slopes, a process that has accelerated alarmingly since the Second World War. In the last 40 odd years Devon has lost nearly 50 per cent of its ancient woods, converted to conifer plantations and farmland, and as they have been cut down and altered so the wild flowers, such a feature of these damp maritime lichen-hung coppice forests, have also disappeared.

Many of the rich hedgegrows date back to before the birth of Christ, the lanes and tracks that run between them are etched deep, forming a network of miniature sheltered valleys where ferns and wild flowers grow, and where common lizards bask in the warm summer sunshine. These historic hedges and sunken lanes provide excellent thoroughfares for foxes and badgers and other mammals as well as safe nesting sites for songbirds.

The true wealth of the county lies in its rich red soil composed of sands and minerals laid down in a hot dry desert 300 million years ago in the "Devonian" period, when giant amphibians and primitive reptiles ruled the world. The red Devonian rocks are particularly evident along the coastline from Torquay to the Exe estuary. South from Torbay is an amazing variety of ancient and

unusual rock types some, like the grey Devonian limestone outcrop at Berry Head, support rare and unusual flora and fauna more at home in the Mediterranean than south Devon. From Berry Head to Dartmouth the bewildering array of rocks range from hardened volcanic ash to shales, mudstones and iron ores; a record in stone of Devon's turbulent geological past. The coastal path along this stretch of the south west peninsula is one of the loveliest in the country.

Indeed Devon is twice blessed, its twin coastlines being unique and providing a wealth of nest sites for birds, especially seabirds, and off the north coast, in splendid isolation, lies the seemingly inhospitable island of Lundy enhancing the variety of Devon's wildlife with its puffins and manx shearwaters, and the unique Lundy cabbage.

Most human visitors know Devon in summer when the county is in bloom, and the air full of birdsong; yet it's mild aspect encourages many migrant birds to stay late, others to arrive early and some, like the chiff chaff and blackcap, remain all year.

ARLINGTON COURT NATURE WALK (NT) — *Spring, summer*

This nature walk between Barnstable and the slopes of Exmoor runs through a wide range of habitats, some of them excellent for birds and insects, the heronry in particular is very special, and the herons can be seen for much of the year fishing on the nearby river, the banks of which are wooded and support buzzards, ravens and sparrowhawks. The spring birdsong is quite powerful and varied and in mild weather chiff chaffs can be heard in very early spring.
2.4km – Map ref: SS 611405

AXMOUTH-LYME UNDERCLIFFS (NCC) — *Spring, summer*

If ever there was an enchanted place, this is it! Created by an accident of nature when an immense segment of the cliffs slipped towards the sea on a winter's night in 1839 following a prolonged period of heavy rain; the chasm left behind was infilled by several smaller slippages creating a series of hidden valleys and combes with marshy areas growing on mud composed largely of chalk and organic material supporting a rare flora, including fen orchid; the undercliffs are known for ferns and liverworts.

Water, the cause of the original landslip, still percolates through the soft rock causing small landslips and creating yet more sheltered places where humidity and warmth are trapped, and an almost jungle-like atmosphere has developed. The area is excellent for breeding birds, there is such a variety of trees and scrub that nightingales and common warblers nest here in some numbers. There are also many species of moth and the delicate wood white butterfly which thrives in the calm air and dense vegetation.

When viewed from the surrounding seasides meadows, the "slipped" area resembles typical Devon woodland and birds like buzzard hunt rabbits and small mammals, although the many nooks and crannies provide perfect hiding places from prying eyes; badgers, foxes and roe deer can live their lives free from human interference. The

site can be dangerous, the 1839 slippage was not the only one to have occurred during the past 1000 years and there's little doubt that given similar conditions there would be further substantial slides. Despite its secret beauty the undercliff must be treated with care.
320ha – Map ref: SY 268896 – 329916

AYLESBEARE COMMON (RSPB) — *Spring, summer*

Aylesbeare Common is reminiscent of the Dorset heaths and shares many similar flora and fauna. Part of the Devon pebble-bed heaths with a variety of habitats from dry heath to ponds, open scrubby woodland, streams and bogs, the reserve is renowned for being the principle site in Devon for breeding Dartford warblers, a bird whose fortunes fluctuate wildly depending upon the frequency or otherwise of hard winters and heath fires, the latter would appear to be the main controlling factor and warblers have often vanished completely after a fire not to return for several seasons. However, they are close to the Dorset breeding population and hopefully they will spread. Nightjars and curlew also breed at Aylesbeare as do tree pipit and marsh tit in the wooded areas. The plant cover is typical of the heaths and harbours reptiles that thrive in the dry conditions. Dragonflies and damselflies are common in the marshy areas.
180ha – Map ref: SY 057898

BERRY HEAD COUNTRY PARK (Torbay BC) — *All year*

Though damaged by limestone quarrying the bluff of Berry Head has a special grandeur. Sheltering the fishing town of Brixham and sporting the ruins of a Napoleonic Fort, the head is composed of one of the largest blocks of Devonian limestone in the country and harbours a wealth of unique plants and animals such as the white rock rose that blooms here in summer. Limestone is wonderful for orchids, and bee, fly, common spotted, pyramidal and autumn lady's tresses are common.

When the Head was more open and sheep-grazed large blue butterflies thrived on the wild thyme in July, and although the large blue is extinct there are still a great many other butterflies to be enjoyed here, including common blues. They are rather strange in that a number of the females have a great deal of blue scaling on the wings, an aberration known as semi syngrapha when it occurs in chalkhill blue butterflies.

The birds in this fascinating country park are frequently swelled by migrants and vagrants from the continent. I've seen Dartford warblers on the gorse bushes, and Greenland gyr falcon on the cliffs. The presence of such a superb nesting site encourages auks and there is a thriving guillemot and razorbill colony on the ledges with a considerable number of kittiwakes and fulmars. This colony is gradually extending along the cliffs. In times past there was a peregrine eyrie on the steepest face of the Head and recently these birds have been attempting to nest on nearby cliffs. (The RSPB have installed a video camera to observe the auks and peregrines from the comfort and safety of the visitor centre). There are frequent sightings of kestrel and buzzard and

Berry Head Country Park

sparrowhawk, and wintering merlin are regular visitors.
43ha – Map ref: SX 943564

BLACK TOR COPSE (Duchy of Cornwall/NCC) — *Summer*

This reserve is not far from the place where I spent my childhood, and the stunted lichen covered oaks, seemingly as old as the mossy rocks from which they spring, have always fascinated me. The wood is high up on the moors, but sheltered from the worst of the Dartmoor weather by its position in a valley. It's a quiet place where the fluty notes of a ring ouzel sound in spring, and the gaunt shape of a wintering great grey shrike provides a highlight for naturalists. Foxes are common here, but have learned to avoid mankind so are difficult to see.
28.9ha – Map ref: SX 567890

BOVEY VALLEY WOODLANDS (NCC) — *Spring, summer*

Bovey Valley woods are old, there's evidence of coppicing, and the abundant mosses and lichens indicate the purity of the air. There's also a wealth of birds in spring, including redstart, pied flycatcher and the occasional dipper, and it's a good site for wood warblers. Butterflies are common though difficult to see in the canopy, but the speckled wood butterfly is always in evidence from early spring to late summer.
71.2ha – Map ref: SX 789801

BRAUNTON BURROWS (NCC) — *Spring, summer*

The sand dunes at Braunton Burrows were formed from wave-washed, wind-blown sand pounded in the mill of the Atlantic Ocean and deposited in Bideford Bay at the outfall of the Taw and Torridge rivers. The whole area is immensely rich at all times of year, though in spring the dunes come alive with flowering plants, and orchids and the speciality of the reserve, water germander, draws botanists from far afield.

The fertility of the slacks and dunes depend upon two factors, the availability of water and the presence of lime in the form of shell fragments. The marram grass holds and stabilises the dunes and an impervious layer beneath the sand encourages open pools where dragonflies breed and many plants came to fruition. In the drier slacks a rabbit-nibbled turf has developed which is attractive to butterflies, and where rain has leached the lime from the sand, the powerful root systems of gorse ramify the loose ground acting as anchors to dense bushes that in turn provide superb nest sites for linnets. Elsewhere hawthorn and privet form nesting sites for many birds that breed here.

This is a superb area and fortunately public pressure is alleviated somewhat by the presence of an army range which restricts access at certain times, an inhibition which may be a little irritating for humans, but is excellent for wildlife.

604ha – Map ref: SS 464326

CHUDLEIGH KNIGHTON HEATH (Devon WT) — *Spring, summer*

Tragically the immense Bovey Basin heathlands have been destroyed by mining for lignite and by building and roads, now only Chudleigh Knighton Heath remains relatively untouched. The heath is superb for a wealth of dragonflies and butterflies and adders. In spring large numbers of breeding warblers and yellowhammers frequent the reserve, and it's rare not to see a buzzard circling overhead. Kestrels and sparrowhawks are common, and tawny owls and the occasional long-eared and barn owl are seen here. The sandy ground is rather impoverished, but many specialised species manage to retain a root-hold.

74ha – Map ref: SX 838776

DARTMOOR NATIONAL PARK (DNPA) — *Spring, summer*

As a child I spent a great deal of time on the moor. An area of magic and myth, of rapidly changing moods from brilliant sun with sub-tropical temperatures to a wet mist off the sea soaking and chilling to the bone anyone unwary enough to venture out unprepared. Sheep, cattle and ponies have helped to shape the harsh terrain, their busy jaws preventing tree regeneration, keeping the turf short and restricting the plants to those that can withstand heavy grazing pressure.

The moor was formed many millions of years ago when volcanic activity forced pipes and bosses of lava up through the underlying carboniferous rocks, these up-wellings changed the nature of the sedimentary rocks on the moorland edge, firing them into many differing rock types. The millions of years that have elapsed since the volcanism ceased has seen erosion and the movement of immense glaciations and shattering cold, and the softer sedimentary rocks have been worn away leaving the tors standing like so many sculptures on the hilltops surrounded by the frost-shattered remnents of the plug known as clitter.

For those who know it the majesty of the moor is tempered by the bogs and mires, the most dangerous being Fox Tor Mires where animals and men can vanish through the semi-liquid surface leaving no trace. Elsewhere on Dartmoor the bogs are less menacing and more beautiful, like emerald green velvet where the mosses grow on the wet surface. The Dart is born from one of these mosses high up on the moor and soon swells to a powerful river of exquisite beauty where salmon and sea trout struggle to spawn in gravels that may hint at a glint of gold or silver or the glitter of mica. The trout of the moorland streams have a tough time, they run the gauntlet of dippers and kingfishers and when they reach a reasonable size form a target for herons and the occasional otter. There are still a number of otters, such charming creatures, in the quieter backwaters, but public pressure and pollution has them doomed in Devon. The same cannot be said for the more aggressive, catholic-feeding mink which have filled the otter's previous niches with surprising rapidity. It would be hard for Tarka to find a mink-free holt today.

The tree cover ranges from the stunted, lichen-hung oaks of Wistman's Wood and Black Tor Copse to the lush coppiced oakwood of the moorland valleys ringing with birdsong from a thousand throats; pied flycatchers, redstarts and wood warblers arrive in some numbers from Africa in early spring as the windflowers blow and the wild daffodils nod in gentle coombes. This is a wonderful place, and although the level of public pressure exerted upon it threatens some of the habitats and species it is still a very rich natural wilderness. Certain areas of the moor are restricted by the military and this may be the salvation of some of the moorland habitats.

94.500ha

DART VALLEY (DNPA/Devon WT) — *Spring, summer*

In my biased opinion the Dart valley is the most beautiful river valley in England, and one of the richest natural habitats. The river forms a warm sheltered environment even in the harshest weather, and many creatures and plants thrive in or near its whisky-coloured water. It's a spate river, able to rise within an hour to a raging torrent and often catching out unwary animals. Rain water on Dartmoor is held in the peat, like water in a sponge, until a certain point is reached where the sodden vegetable matter can hold no more, then it is released in a steady flood into the narrow rocky watercourse where its speed and power increases. Tiny golden trout and armoured caddis and rock-clinging fresh water limpets are able to survive these perodic inundations and consequently have colonised every niche and cranny and mossy boulder in the stream. The bankside is where you will see dippers, kingfishers and a large number of wagtails of all three species.

364ha – Map ref: SX 672733 / 704704

EXE ESTUARY (Various bodies) — *All year*
DAWLISH WARREN (Teignbridge DC) — *All year*

The Exe estuary and The Warren at Dawlish form part of one of the most productive habitats in the west country. In winter the two reserves are alive with birds and bird-watchers. Bar-tailed and black-tailed godwits, avocet, greenshank, curlew, oystercatchers and a host of small waders throng the mudflats, but it is the estuary's flock of dark-bellied brent geese that draws the visitors. There may be bigger flocks in other parts of the country, especially in Sussex, Hampshire and along the east coast, but they are not set among such romantic scenery as in the beautiful Exe estuary.

The area is also rich in wintering duck and the numbers are increasing as other sites become over developed for industrial use or as marinas or barrages. The dunes at Dawlish protect the estuary and at high tide form a roost for thousands of grey plover and other waders, especially oystercatchers; and the hides at the back of the dunes, beyond the golf course, can be very productive at high tide. There are many vantage points all round the estuary, though the prime sites are at Powderham along the sea wall and at Exmouth and the public house garden at Topsham. What could be more pleasurable on a winter's day than eating a pub lunch while watching black-tailed godwits and avocets on the nearby shoreline.

Recently the RSPB have purchased the water meadows below Topsham and the canal (*Map ref: SX 958875*) and the brent geese and waders can gather in peace away from wildfowlers, for there is still a great deal of shooting on the Exe estuary, and even though the geese are protected, as are many of the other birds that winter here, the disturbance caused by shooting is damaging for conservation of both species and habitat.
Exe Estuary 12sq km – Map ref: SX 980785
Dawlish Warren 70ha – Map ref: SX 981787

LUNDY ISLAND (NT) — *Spring, summer*

It was an important milestone in conservation history when the sea floor and the waters around this granite island were designated the first of Britain's marine nature reserves. Many people think of Lundy as the Island of Puffins, but the puffin colony is in severe decline for a variety of reasons. The fate of other sea birds though is more satisfactory, and there are plenty of guillemots, razorbills and other rock nesting species including fulmars and kittiwakes, on the ledges and in the rock crevices.

Lundy is well known for the rare migrants that stop and rest after traumatic, and often one way, migrations; over 400 species of birds have been recorded since records were started. The Lundy cabbage grows here and nowhere else, highlighting the special nature of island sub-species and their vulnerability to change. Fortunately this particular plant appears to have a reasonably secure future.

Lundy is a relic of a turbulent past, a piece of long extinct volcano that was active shortly after the age of the dinosaurs. The softer rocks of the cone have eroded leaving this plug of extremely hard rock as a haven in the midst of a hostile sea. The marine life around the island is extremely varied and reflects the protection from trawl

Puffins   *Lundy Island*

fishing and dredging for shellfish that has so altered the sea bed fauna and the weed growth on much of the nearby continental shelf.
450ha – Map ref: SS 143437

NORTHAM BURROWS (DCC) — *All year*

Here at the north of the Taw and Torridge the elvers come inshore from their long sea voyage, and during Henry Williamson's time otters would have gathered on moonlit nights to harvest them as they moved from the ocean to the river. This is a beautiful part of Barnstable Bay with the long Atlantic rollers bringing a cargo of pulverised sand and sea shells to form wind blown dunes, and sweep sand and shingle from the rocks filling the rock pools creating microcosms of the ocean.

The sea brings food to the shore, and the rivers pour their nutrient-filled silt into the estuary. Here and there, where marshy saltings develop, the dusty grey spiny leaves of sea holly trap and hold the sand and the nutrients with their complex root systems, and shelduck use old rabbit burrows for their nests. In winter a host of waders can be seen racing the tide for morsels, or roosting above the tideline.
263ha – Map ref: SS 444298

SLAPTON LEY (FSC) — *All year*

The freshwater lake at Slapton Ley is entrapped behind a steeply shelving shingle bank built up by the sea and separated from it by only a few hundred yards, and the juxtaposition of the two environments is highly productive of wildlife. The lake is thickly fringed with common reed and the hide, at the Torcross end, looks out over a lily bed which is popular with coot. The water is not particularly deep, but extremely productive of fish, especially roach, perch and rudd and on these fish prey large pike. The pike will take ducklings in spring, but the waterfowl are used to this natural predation and try to avoid it by moving the ducklings away from the most hazardous spots by reeds and lily beds.

The reeds form a broad band around the Ley but at the opposite end to Torcross, where the road to Dartmouth winds up a steep hair-pin bend, the reed bed is a dense blanket with carr woodland developing where Cettis warblers sing explosively, and otter are seen, though this is very unusual; however, it is thought that at least one is permanently in residence here. Otters can be confused with mink, which are relatively common on Devon's rivers and have certainly been recorded here in winter. The Ley itself is a haven for wildfowl and many species are seen, including sea duck. In late summer large numbers of dragonflies throng the water's side and huge gatherings of swallows and house martins congregate in the reeds, prior to migration, and are chased by hobby falcons. It's a superb area for migrant butterflies and clouded yellows and Queen of Spain fritillaries appear here most years along with humming bird hawk moths.

The shingle bank, composed of pebbles from a considerable range of geological formations, is the most south westerly of its kind in Britain. A large number of salt tolerant plants grow on the narrow strip of land between the top of the shingle slope and the road dividing the beach from the Ley, but pressure from holiday-makers and fishermen precludes any shingle nesting birds. Nevertheless there is always something of interest to see here at all times of year, be it sea duck and divers in winter, migrants passing through, terns in autumn and spring, or even an osprey fishing in the sea or the shallow waters of the Ley.

190ha – Map ref: SX 826431

SOUTH WEST PENINSULA COAST PATH (CC) —
Spring through autumn

Devon has two coastlines, each beautiful and rich in wildlife, but quite different in character. The southern coastal path runs over rolling countryside with the sea cliffs on one side and farmland and gentle slopes full of plants and butterflies on the other. Blackthorn bushes grow in profusion supporting a wealth of bird life and the seascape is ever changing as the clouds race each other across the horizon and buzzards and kestrels hang on the updraughts.

On the northern coast wind is the pervasive force, the Atlantic gales cut the trees down to size and shape the blackthorn and buckthorn bushes into natural topiary, and trim the turf to a lawn-like consistency, helped by the rabbits. It's a seabird coast; and the path follows the stark, magnificent cliffs; its also the land of the peregrine the rock pipit, and wide horizons filled with thrift turf and Lady's tresses orchids on south facing slopes. There may be longer paths in Britain, but I doubt many can boast such a variety to the mile, and such beauty.

256km – Map ref: North Devon SS 213174 / SS 793487
South Devon SX 493531 / SY 332916

WEMBURY MARINE CONSERVATION AREA
(WMCA Advisory Group) — *Spring, summer*

A combination of geological and marine coincidences make Wembury a reserve of great importance. Close by Plymouth and one of the busiest ports in the west country and a short stretch of superb coast and shoreline, the area is of intense educational interest and used by diving parties. The point at Wembury is also important as a resting site for seabirds on passage, and waders too find shelter and food on the beaches.

6km – Map ref: SX 507484

WISTMAN'S WOOD (Duchy of Cornwall/NCC) — *All year*

Wistman's Wood is often cited as being typical of ancient oak woodland, and it's a miracle it has managed to survive into the 20th century, the stunted oaks struggle through the rocky Dartmoor terrain, cut and shaped by wind and cold and grazing pressure. Perhaps this is the very reason why it has remained, its position made it too difficult and too unproductive to remove. The wood gives an indication of the type of open oak woodland that once covered much of Dartmoor before man and his animals cleared it for agriculture and pastoralism. There's a quality of timelessness here, perhaps because the lichens and mosses that cling to the contorted branches resemble so many grey beards.

24ha – Map ref: SX 612772

Slapton Ley

DORSET

Dorset has the good fortune to be poorly served by motorways and this has probably saved it from the worst ravages of tourism; you can still find, albeit fast disappearing, meadows and woods maintained by a regime of agriculture unchanged since the Middle Ages and small villages nestling in the folded landscape where the Dorset poets William Barnes and Thomas Hardy would have felt at home.

Though inspired by the same county Barnes and Hardy came from different social classes. Barnes was born into a 'downstart' family of small farmers on Bagber Heath, and in his younger labouring days could have passed muster as a character in a Hardy novel cutting furze for the fire and bracken for bedding, and joining in the rumbustious rural life in a way that the more taciturn Hardy could never have contemplated. Barnes had the countryman's love of water and the gentle river Stour hard by the village of Hinton drew him like a magnet. In his day the mill on the river would have been a bustling place; now its water wheel is still although the buildings are sometimes used by film companies as a backdrop. Barnes appears to have had a particularly soft spot for mills, something I share, and his following lines express the rightness of these timeless structures in the rural landscape:-

And yonder down beneath us crawls
The Stour towards the Eastern Hills,
To drive by many foaming falls
The mossy wheels of many mills.

Hardy too was a fan of mills and water and though his style was more sombre there's no doubt he enjoyed immensely the Dorsetshire countryside, especially the timelessness of this area where man has lived for centuries, and the hill forts dotted over the downland facing the sea, particularly the hill fort at Eggardon, high above Powerstock Forest, which featured heavily in his work. Hardy knew Eggardon and its moods well and celebrated his friend and fellow poet Barnes in one of his poems about the hill.

"The Last Signal"
Silently I footed by an uphill road
That led from my abode to a spot yew-boughed;
Yellowly the sun sloped down to westward,
And dark was the east with cloud.

Then, amid the shadow of that livid sad east,
Where the light was least, and a gate stood wide,
Something flashed the fire of the sun that was facing it,
Like as brief blaze on that side.

These words remind me of a visit I made to Dorset with a friend, the painter Gordon Beningfield, standing in the late evening in a layby on the seaward side of Eggardon looking down towards Shipton Hill. Quite suddenly as the sun sank low on the horizon its light reflected off the sea like a golden mirror "a brief blaze on that side", indeed the sight was so dramatic that Gordon later painted a picture of the scene which captured the feeling exactly.

For 14 years Gordon and I have been making regular visits to the area, often for a particular reason such as giving fund-raising talks for the Dorset Naturalist's Trust to buy land such as Lower Kingcombe Farm, but mostly to soak up the atmosphere and explore the lovely countryside.

Dorset is excellent for butterflies, the variety and numbers are amazing. The silver-washed fritillaries that fill the oak woods of Powerstock Common have been flying in August for millennia.

The county's geology is one of the reasons why it is so blessed; deep rolling folded chalk hills topped with fuller's earth leading to tall but unstable cliffs of deep grey marl full of fossils or biscuit coloured limestone. The lack of development of the county's sea-shore is due in part to the use by the military of Lyme Bay and the Lulworth ranges for gunnery practice. This contradiction has meant that large tracts of land which might otherwise have been farmed or turned over to caravan parks and holiday developments, have been allowed to revert to natural landscape.

Lower Kingcombe

It is something of a shame that the heathlands inland were not also treated in this way, for much of the classic heath has been spoiled by forestry, mined for minerals and farmed so that now the Dartford warbler, the smooth snake, the hobby and the dragonflies on which it feeds have been driven into mere pockets. But times are always changing, and the county has been developing a tourist industry based in part upon its native poets and writers, partly on its archaeological interest, and also on its undoubted natural history interests, beauty and peace.

ARNE (RSPB) — *All year*

Arne is a vital link in the chain of heathland reserves around Poole harbour and comprises a varied habitat from creeks and saltmarsh to wet valley bogs and heathland covered with clumps of gorse where Dartford warblers nest. The spring "parachute-song" of the meadow pipit is an attractive feature, and they nest here as do yellowhammers and linnets.

The ground covering plants mainly consist of cross-leaved heath, common heather and bell heather and in places, the speciality of the region, Dorset heath, a heather-like plant which in summer and early autumn buzzes with insects and honey bees. Butterflies such as the silver-studded blue abound in summer and you can see as many as 22 dragonfly species. The woodlands are home to sparrowhawks, and hobby falcons that breed in nearby pines hunt dragonflies and swallows over the pools.

The strange, uncommn bog bush cricket makes its home here and the proximity of the mudflats in the huge, almost land-locked basin of Poole harbour, makes it a very special place for winter bird-watching with huge numbers of wildfowl and waders, including Brent geese and black-tailed godwit, and the bouyant flight of the marsh harrier is a common sight.
525ha – Map ref: SY 984885 / 972877

BROWNSEA ISLAND (Dorset TfNC/NT) — *Spring through autumn*

Brownsea Island is regularly in the news, being under threat from oil exploration. It is a haven for a number of species, including red squirrel, and the lagoon is a particular feature of the site with excellent feeding places for a huge range of water birds. The area is very well supplied with waders in autumn and spring, and Poole Harbour is one of the best places on the south coast for waterfowl. The island is almost an extension of the nearby heathland with sandy gravelly terrain and a clay-lined valley between the two higher parts of the island. The main value of such a site is the fact that birds can rest and feed in the middle of an area which can be busy with recreational traffic for much of the year.
100ha – Map ref: SZ 032877

CRANBORNE COMMON (Dorset TfNC) — *All year*

This is an excellent site for nightjars and Dartford warblers, the common consists of an area of Dorset heathland which is of immense ecological importance for the flora and fauna it harbours. Some smooth snakes are found on the dry heathland.
42.8ha – Map ref: ST 103112

Dartford Warbler   *Arne*

DORSET COASTAL PATH (DCC) — *Spring, summer*

The Dorset coastal path is a fascinating walk. It begins on the fossil-rich blue-grey marl cliffs of Lyme Regis where the scenery and herbage ranges from chalk grassland in the west to dry sandy heath, and moves on across the heathy wildness of Studland to end at Poole Harbour. The path runs over some dramatic scenery with a vast range of wildlife, and summer butterflies include chalkhill blues on the cliffs above the strange formations of Durdle Dor and Lulworth Cove.
(Booklet by HMSO obtainable from the bookshop adjoining Dorchester museum.)
116km – Map ref: SY 344928 (Lyme Regis)
Map ref: SZ 042860 (Poole Harbour)

DURLSTONE COUNTRY PARK (DCC) — *Spring, summer*

The park is situated on the south west peninsula coastal path where it swings around the limestone mass of Durlstone Head. Its dramatic coastline, with marvellous sea views to the Isle of Wight, attracts a large number of visitors which from the wildlife point of view does limit its value as a nature reserve.

The limestone substrate dictates the flora and fauna and supports a large range of lime-loving plants from pyramidal and spotted orchids to yellow rattle, quaking grass, carline thistle and horseshoe vetch, as well as some long established ant hills that provide an ideal habitat for butterflies. The chalkhill blue is common in July and August and the beautiful, but scarce, adonis blue will sometimes produce two generations, one in spring and another late in summer to coincide with the emergence of the chalkhill blues; burnet moths in their brilliant red and violet-shot black jostle on scabious flowers and greater knapweed with small blues, Lulworth skippers and marbled whites.

The prevailing wind determines how tall the hawthorn and blackthorn shrubs will grow, the salt breeze snips them down until they cling to the lower slopes like well-manicured hedges. These winds also helped to shape the rugged limestone cliffs perfect for seabirds, especially fulmar petrels, where they can be seen riding the wind and playing in the upcurrents. The cliffs are superb for watching the comings and goings of many seabirds and not infrequently puffins fish and bathe in the water far below. Situated as it is on a natural flyway from the continent of Europe, in spring and autumn migrants shelter in the low growing scrub on the hillsides and on the plateau where quarrying operations have provided handy hollows.
104.4ha – Map ref: SZ 032773

Eggardon Hill

EGGARDON HILL (Part NT) — *Spring, summer*

Hardy immortalised this Iron Age hill fort, using it as his model for Haggerdown in "Far from the Madding Crowd". It was built by Celtic war Lords in the 2nd century BC, and I discovered it many years ago when exploring Powerstock Common and the oakwoods there. The great hill with its mulit-vallate ramparts enjoys ever changing moods depending on the season. On winter days it lowers over its butt-ended valley and the purple oaks of the forest below, yet as spring flushes the carpet of ancient gnarled trees with green it positively beams and as autumn dyes the canopy with reds and golds the hill looks on contentedly. Updraughts from the hill provide soaring for buzzards and sparrowhawks and in summer hobbys chase the plentiful insects over the ramparts.
Map ref: SY 540963

THE FLEET & CHESIL BANK* (Strangeways Estate) — *All year*

Behind the protective bulwark of Chesil Bank, lies this botanically rich reserve with eelgrass and other water plants providing ample food for waterfowl. It's closed to the public during the swan breeding season, and there's also a sanctuary, with no public access at any time. At the end of the West Fleet, the area supports rare breeding terns and waders in spring and early summer. The tidal Fleet is marvellous for waders in autumn, and the spring migration brings a regular flow of rare species; it's also a winter haven for wildfowl and with the sea on the other side of the shingle bank attracts large numbers of winter migrants. From time to time otters visit the reserve but they are rarely seen by casual visitors.

The seaward side of Chesil Bank is a perfect vantage point for watching dolphins and seals and occasional schools of pilot whales. In winter the seabirds may include skuas, and in early spring and summer colonies of little and common terns fish for sandeel in the surf close inshore. It's not uncommon to see the very rare little tern's nuptial display when the male offers a small fish to the female.

The Swannery, situated at the end of the West Fleet is part of this diverse habitat; Abbotsbury was Hardy's Abbotsea and supports one of the largest breeding colonies of mute swans in Europe.
800ha – Map ref: SY 568840 – 668754

FONTMELL DOWN (Dorset TfNC)** — *Spring, summer*

Fontmell Down is one of the best areas of Dorset downland left in the county. For centuries it was grazed by sheep and the short turf was full of plants and butterflies. There has been a certain amount of conifer planting in the area, but plans to replace the conifers with broadleaved native species are under consideration. In the main the reserve has retained much of the short turf so typical of sheep-grazed downs with some yew and hawthorn scrub, which adds to the wildlife potential. Butterflies and orchids are the particular specialities here.
57.2ha

HARTLAND MOOR (NCC)** — *Spring, summer*

One of the best areas of the remaining southern heathland is found at Hartland moor; the variety of habitats from dry heath to wet heath grading to saltmarsh provides a rich setting for dragonflies and reptiles, and hobbys are frequent visitors.
258ha

HENGISTBURY HEAD (BC) — *Spring through autumn*

An ancient hill fort, Hengistbury looks out over the sea, and inland to the lagoon and rivermouth of the Stour. It is one of the most atmospheric spots on the coastline and superb for watching seabirds and terns on passage. In winter there's an immense gull roost and large numbers of oystercatchers.
100ha – Map ref: SZ 175907

HOD HILL & HAMBLEDON HILL (NT/Dorset TfNC) — *Spring, summer*

Barnes went to school in the lovely town of Sturminster Newton, once the capital of the Blackmoor Vale and wrote of these hills, both places of great antiquity where iron age man built complex fortresses, now they harbour pockets of open sheep-grazed downland.

The insect fauna is spectacular in late July early August with chalkhill and Adonis blue butterflies, and in early spring cowslips grow in profusion on south facing slopes providing food for the larvae of Duke of Burgundy fritillary butterflies, an attractive species found mainly in chalk grassland. The hilltops have been designated sites of special scientific interest being rich in chalk grassland flowering plants such as horseshoe vetch and carline thistle; quaking grass and bird's foot trefoil form an integral part of the sward as do the several species of orchids that bloom in June and July to enjoy the summer sun and light breezes.

The two hills are very steep. General Woolfe trained his soldiers, later to storm the Heights of Abraham in 1759 during the Canadian war against the French, on Hambledon Hill which gives you some idea of the inclination, but the climb is worth the effort as the view is spectacular.

Hod Hill   – *2.6ha* – *Map ref: ST 857106*
Hambledon Hill – *12ha* – *Map ref: ST 845126*

THE ISLE OF PORTLAND (Various bodies) — *Spring, summer*

Portland stands high above the long shingle bar of Chesil Beach forming an isolated knob of fossiliferous limestone. The town itself has been devastated by quarrying for stone, although the chalkhill blue butterfly still inhabits the grasslands at the seaward side of Southwest. The Bill is primarily of importance for migrating birds, and it's a fossil hunter's paradise where huge ammonites, sea creatures that lived in the age of the dinosaurs, can be picked up from virtually every pile of quarrying spoil. The view is spectacular, looking over the town from above West Cliff and out along the shingle beach towards the Swannery at Abbotsbury.

1050ha – Map ref: SY 682738

LODMOOR COUNTRY PARK (RSPB) — *Spring, summer*

Lodmoor comprises salt marsh and freshwater marsh with pools, reeds and scrub supporting similar birdlife to nearby Radipole. Redshank and yellow wagtail nest on the marshy ground and it's a major staging post for migrating yellow wagtails. In autumn, waders congregate to feed and rest, and in winter many species of wildfowl, including Brent geese from Poole Harbour, feed together with flocks of wigeon, teal and shoveller. The occasional pintail up end in the pools along with shelduck.

60.7ha – Map ref: SY 687807

LOWER KINGCOMBE ESTATE *(Dorset TfNC/Various bodies)*

In 1987 there was a flurry of excitement in the conservation movement when Lower Kingcombe Farm came onto the market. Through the efforts of a number of people, myself included, money was raised to buy the farm at auction in conjunction with a private Charitable Trust. The land is unique in that its field patterns have remained unchanged since a land survey in the early 19th century, and farming had been carried on without any input of fertilisers or sprays. Such a sympathetic regime had led to a wonderful variety of naturally occurring habitats, from the damp woodland bordering the river Hook which flows through the site, to the drier hay meadows and woodlands on the upper slopes of the valley.

The butterfly and dragonfly population, the birds and the flowers all combine to make Lower Kingcombe a very special area of outstanding interest; the sale marked a turning point in the way natural habitats are viewed, in terms of monetary value. The acquisition of this estate, which adjoins the reserve at Powerstock Common, has begun a series of purchases that should lead to the whole of this superb area being saved for wildlife.

600acres

LULWORTH RANGE WALKS (MoD Coastal downland) — *Spring, summer/open days*

There might appear to be a conflict of interests here as the ranges are owned by the Ministry of Defence and used for artillery and small arms practice, yet among this array of potentially death dealing ordnance is a wealth of wildlife and habitat almost unique in southern England. You'll find vistas of open downland and more than 10km of coastline with plant and animal communities virtually untouched by man's hand. Where firing has taken place the pits and scars of long spent explosives provide a spur for those plants that need disturbed ground to gain roothold, and for a few short years shell craters are ringed with nettles or reddened with rosebay willow-herb before the nutrients are used up and the peacock butterflies and elephant hawk moths go elsewhere to lay their eggs.

Were it not for those ranges it would be hard to imagine what the sea-facing downs of Dorset once looked like as most of the coastal fields outside the range area are now under barley or rape or have been "improved". The price of maintaining this rare and endangered habitat is restricted public access, but times and dates when the range is open to visitors can be obtained from the Dorset TfNC.

Various lengths – Map ref: SY 882804

POWERSTOCK COMMON FOREST (Dorset TfNC) — *Spring, summer*

The forest is part of the ancient chase of King John of Magna Carta fame. The soil that lines the valley and covers the slopes is heavy clay, damp and of poor quality, but perfect for ash trees, and the wonderful gnarled oaks that have been coppiced for timber and firewood for centuries until now they resemble modern sculptures. The deep shade of the summer woods is home for common dormice and a host of small mammals, and the woodland flora contains such rarities as herb paris growing among the hazel coppice stools. The forest had been badly damaged by the Forestry Commission, but recently Dorset TfNC have acquired the whole common and with help from the Countryside Commission and Conservation Volunteers the conifers are gradually being cleared and the oakwoods and ash stands re-established.

The higher slopes are clothed with bracken and hazel coppice and at the upper limit a strata of coarse fuller's earth provides an ideal situation for badgers to dig extensive setts into the hillside.

The forest is a marvellous place for warblers, nightingales and other woodland songbirds in spring and summer, and buzzards frequent the valley soaring round and round in the upwelling air against the hillside. Sparrow-hawks nest in the oak trees and hobby falcons and the occasional peregrine falcon can be seen from the higher road across Eggardon hill.
49.2ha – Map ref: SY 540963

PURBECK MARINE RESERVE & KIMMERIDGE BAY
(Dorset TfNC) — *Spring, summer*

On the coastal path near Vane Farm is the first and most productive oil well on the British mainland, and on the beach at Kimmeridge Bay the slightly greasy oil shales, mined by the Romans as a precious stone, indicate the presence of oil. But these shales constitute a far more valuable jewel in the crown of modern conservation because they are found at the landward boundary of Britain's first mainland marine reserve the foundation of which marked the beginning of co-operation between conservation bodies and commercial fishing interests.

The reserve encompassess the cliff-top and foreshore and, of course, offshore for a distance of one kilometre. There's an excellent interpretive centre on the cliff-top and a constant stream of visitors from all over the world. The Kimmeridge ledges, rocky platforms of fossil-rich limestone, hold a wealth of sea life both above and below the tide line. This diversity is enhanced by the proximity of two marine habitats, the east and west channel basins; and a number of rare seaweeds and marine creatures can be found in the waters off shore.
650ha – Map ref: SY 909788

RADIPOLE LAKE (RSPB) — *All year*

Shielded from the worst of the sea's fury by Portland Bill and Weymouth Bay this fascinating habitat is situated almost in the heart of the town. Mainly a wetland reserve comprising rough pasture, reed beds, natural lakes and man-made lagoons, it's an SSSI and a statutory bird sanctuary and also has the virtue of being easily accessible with a superb observation centre.

There are migrants in spring and autumn as well as a varied selection of nesting species such as reed, sedge, Cetti's and grasshopper warblers, kingfishers, bearded tits and great crested grebes. Swallows, martins, yellow wagtails and small warblers congregate here in autumn prior to migration, and in winter huge numbers of mute swans fly in to moult and join the wintering duck. Terns are frequent visitors in spring and autumn and in winter some rare gulls appear on the lakes.

The insect life includes dragonflies, especially the emperor, and there are plenty of migrant butterflies such as painted lady and clouded yellow.
78ha – Map ref: SY 676796

STUDLAND (NCC) — *Spring, summer*

The land here shades from chalk turf to southern heath, arguably the most rare habitat in the British Isles; and the land-locked Isle of Purbeck with its diverse geology once had at its heart the largest stretch of undeveloped acid heath in Europe, 40,000 hectares of untamed heath lay in a broad band across the countryside reaching almost to Dorchester, now only about 2000 hectares are left.

Heathlands have evolved a community of plants and animals, birds and insects perfectly adapted to a harsh infertile environment. They were laid down in the Tertiary period, 20 to 25 million years ago, when the first horses and primitive elephants and rhinoceros-like mammals roamed the land. Major geological upheavals left behind a landscape of coarse pale sands and in some places, where impervious clay formed in valley bottoms, wet heath and bogs developed.

Where the heath is dry, heather and the special plant, Dorset heath, predominate, binding the sand and enabling gorse and broom to take root. Normally stands of silver birch would begin the process of converting open heath to woodland, that this never happened is due in part to the inflammability of the plant cover in summer. Heath fires, together with man's intervention, conspired to maintain the special character of this area until the 20th century. Now only fragments remain, the Forestry Commission and private forestry groups have encroached on the heath, planting serried ranks of conifers and draining bogs by deep ploughing. Agriculture too has reclaimed and developed the sandy soil for crops. Here and there industrial estates have eaten into the remaining wild places and sand quarrying has removed whole hillsides — and the unique plant and animal communities are losing out. The smooth snake, a creature found only on southern heaths is being driven to the brink of extinction — reserves like Studland have been created in an attempt to maintain its numbers.

On the promontory that projects into Poole harbour is The Little Sea, a freshwater lagoon, formed over centuries. In winter vast numbers of duck gather for food and to roost; you can watch them from the hide which is open on Sundays. Dragonflies and damselflies abound near the

Slow Worm   *Studland*

pools of peaty water, and there are more species of heathland dragonflies on the margins of The Little Sea than anywhere else in England.

However, it is in summer that Studland really comes into its own with a large variety of heathland flora and fauna. The shy Dartford warbler has its stronghold here, and the area is renowned for sand lizards, common lizards, slow-worms and grass snakes. Adders sun themselves on south facing slopes. The marshland plant communities are interesting too with bog myrtle and cross-leaved heath and other characteristic plants like greater sundew a carnivorous bog dweller that has adapted to a paucity of nitrogen in the soil by catching its own supply in the form of insects on its sticky leaves.
631ha – Map ref: SZ 034836

WHITENOTHE UNDERCLIFF (NT/Dorset TfNC) — *Spring, summer*

The white chalk slopes and natural architecture of Durdle Dor and the bays and coves of West Lulworth are spectacular. The south Dorset downs come hard against the sea here, and erosion has produced a landscape of soft sheltered valleys with a gentle micro-climate where chalk downland plants such as rock rose and rare downland orchids bloom, while adders sun themselves undisturbed on the dry spoil heaps of rabbit warrens. Scrub fills the hollows, and bramble provides nesting sites for linnets and yellowhammers. The phenomenon of "slumping" (where a softer less stable rock strata collapses outwards and downwards) has created wet hollows where horsetail, stinking iris, reeds and rushes, grow in profusion.

Such a variety of habitats provides for many creatures. Peregrine falcons regularly hunt the cliffs, and kestrels use the updraughts to aid their hovering skills while searching for short-tailed field voles in the rabbit-nibbled turf. In summer the cliffs are alive with butterflies, particularly chalkland species; and in June and July you'll see the speciality of the area, the Lulworth skipper.

Out at sea the fertile shallow waters provide a food source for puffin and other small auks, and in spring and autumn terns and skuas migrate along the coast.
46ha – Map ref: SY 765813

DURHAM, CLEVELAND, TYNE AND WEAR

The geology of this region is a record of a time when the earth was undergoing cataclysmic upheavals. In the Carboniferous and Permian periods the land mass was one vast continent, which paleontologists call Gondwana. This immense supercontinent was to see the beginnings of many of the precursors of the creatures with which we are familiar today, including the reptile ancestors of our own order, the mammals.

This area is based on carboniferous deposits that have provided much of the industrial impetus of the past 200 years; it was the coal dug from the Durham coalfields that drove the ships of the late Victorian battle fleets that patrolled the largest Empire the earth has ever seen. And all this power had been stored up during a time when huge dragonflies and primitive reptile-like amphibians were the dominant life forms, when the growth of ferns and club mosses almost exceeded imagination, growing in enormous swampy coal forests 350 million years ago.

Today the ground is pock marked with both open cast and deep mines that have been dug in search of the black gold, but the industry itself is in decline, and only a handful of the mines are still active; even the spoil heaps have been sculpted back into the landscape. In this place, where the land has been turned inside out, normality and nature are once again holding sway.

The surface of Gondwana was still intact, though upheavals were daily shaking the land, when under the surface of the sea deep limestone beds were being built up from the mortal remains of minute marine creatures. This graveyard of countless billions of shelly skeletons was compressed by the movement of time and rocks into hard magnesian limestone, holding fossils from 280 million years ago when the first egg-laying reptiles were developing, and massive crocodilians were catching fish in warm shallow fresh water seas. On land the iron-rich red rocks of the Permian deserts roasted under a brilliant sky, and mammal-like reptiles, as big as a Hereford bull, stalked their prey on stumpy legs.

The vast deposits of magnesian limestones of the Permian seas now form the coastline of this region. The hard pale rock has been eroded by weather and time into cracks and fissures providing nesting sites for seabirds, eventually it decomposes into lime-rich soil and calcareous grassland; in places this limestone is overlaid with the gravels and clays of the last ice age.

Inland, where the high ground of Cumbria rears towards the sky, is the Whin Sill, a ridge of intruded volcanic rock which the Emperor Hadrian used as the basis for his famous wall built as a defence against the northern barbarians. This was as far north as Roman culture was permitted to penetrate. At that time the area would have been heavily forested with oak and ash, small-leaved lime and field maple. Now only a few remnants remain of those great deep dark woods in places where agriculture could not, or would not venture, and where charcoal burning was uneconomical.

A little over a decade ago this region was heavily industrialised, now the changes that have affected so much of northern England have settled on this trio of counties, the industry here is more sophisticated and based less and less on the extraction of fossil deposits. There is a new wave of light industry and where the hills and coast have been recovered from man's onslaught tourism is taking over, encouraging us to examine the beauties of a much neglected landscape. This is not a part of the country that immediately springs to mind as one of intense natural history interest, but the reclamation of valleys, hills and moorland, and the rich sea cliffs between the Tyne Estuary and Sunderland, shows there is plenty to enjoy. Indeed Sir Walter Scott visited the county often staying with friends at Rokeby; he wrote many of his poems here, particularly "Brignall Banks" of which the chorus would seem to impart the idea of a rural scene in spite of the county's industrialisation:-

Yet Brignall banks are fesh and fair,
And Great woods are green,
And you may gather flowers there,
Would grace a summer queen.

The climate is less wet than nearby Cumbria, the westerly winds having been wrung dry over the Lake District; it is the weather from the east that affects the region most, the cold easterly winds blow in bringing sea fog, but on days when the sun's rays warm the land the weather is more reminiscent of a southern county.

Our past knowledge of the area owes much to the monks who came here from Lindesfarne, driven out by the ruthless Danes. For seven years they wandered carrying with them the "incorruptible" body of St Cuthbert until they found a haven at Chester-Le-Street, but in 995 they were again put to flight eventually settling at Dunholme and on a bold headland in a loop of the river Wear a little "bough church" was raised, the forerunner of the most magnificently situated of English cathedrals. We also owe a special debt of gratitude to one particular monk, the Venerable Bede who died in 735 and was reinterred in 1020 in the Lady Chapel of the beautiful cathedral at Durham. Bede had a keen interest in the politics of the Dark Ages, and it is due to him that we know so much of our country's past. He was a latter day reporter allowing us to understand many of the events of those turbulent times.

The river Wear beside which Durham's cathedral stands begins turbulently on the Pennines, roaring and tumbling through fern clad valleys, past fields and towns and finally meandering out into the North Sea at Sunderland. It carries with it the spirit of the county, and a countryside reborn out of its industrial past.

BIG WATERS (NWT) — *All year*

As its name suggests this relic of mining, where the ground has subsided allowing water to fill the depression, has had ample time to naturalise. The breeding bird population includes moorhen, great crested and little grebe, mallard and tufted duck with shoveller and teal among the wintering wildfowl.
15ha – Map ref: NZ 227734

BLACKHALL (Durham WT)** — *Spring, summer*

The mixture of rock and soil types found along these cliffs of magnesian limestone overlaid with clay helps to produce an interesting flora and fauna; and in the gulleys and hollows where the clay is thick typical wetland plants like iris thrive.

Where the limestone habitat predominates there is a wide range of plants such as bloody cranesbill and common rock rose, several unique insects dependant upon this latter plant. One, the cistus forester is a small green-winged day flying moth with a fascinating life cycle, spending its first instars inside the leaves of rock rose eating the soft parts of the leaf until the caterpillar is seen, as if in a transparent envelope. This uncommon moth can be confused with the larger forester which feeds on trefoil and both are similar in shape to the burnet moth and belong to the same group of insects.

One of the other insects dependant upon the common rock rose is the Castle Eden Argus, a sub-species of the northern brown argus and a member of the widespread family of blue butterflies, including the common blue which also appears here. The Castle Eden Argus can be differentiated from the northern brown argus by markings on the fore wing (a black pupil to the white discal spot). The common brown argus also has different wing markings and is widespread.

The area is very much influenced by the maritine climate and the amount of erosion and land slippage, nevertheless there are vantage points on the cliffs and seashore from which to observe migrating seabirds.
32ha

BOWLEES VISITOR CENTRE (Durham WT) — *Spring through autumn*

This interpretive centre explains the land uses of Teesdale; there is also an area where unusual plants, rescued from a flooded valley, can be studied. A trail leads through

Cygnets   *Durham, Cleveland etc.*

woodlands to a spectacular waterfall where dippers and yellow wagtails breed.
1.4km – Map ref: NY 907283

CASTLE EDEN DENE (Peterlee Development Corporation) — *Spring, summer*

This is where the Castle Eden Argus butterfly was identified and it's probably the most unspoiled valley, or Dene, in the region. The ravine owes its shape to events of 10,000 years ago when a torrent of glacial melt waters cut down through the soft limestone creating a channel to the sea. Later deposits from melting glaciers overlaid the valley with clay which in turn was eroded back to the original bed of the stream by water cascading down the valley.

When the earth warmed after the last ice age there was a rapid growth of trees, and trees have clothed this valley for 50 centuries. Yew and ash are predominant where man has not been able to harvest the timber. However, in other parts of the ravine where ease of access and timber cultivation has become more viable oaks and sycamore have been planted and some conifers, which drastically alter the pattern of life. Bird cherry grows in the valley bottom along with alder providing food and shelter for birds.

The presence of rhododendron is a problem that will have to be dealt with for the dense ground cover afforded by these shrubs shades out and eventually kills tender plant species. Rhododendron has little effect upon the variety of mature native trees such as holly, elder, rowan, hawthorn, blackthorn and hazel, it is the seedlings that suffer from shading.

The ground cover plants are extremely varied and range from herb paris, with its green flowers, to a rather beautiful hybrid primula, a cross between cowslip and primrose; its flowers are like that of an oxlip. In spring a carpet of bluebells, wood anemones and a mass of green dog's mercury combines to create an altogether magical place.

The birdlife here is extensive with garden warblers, grasshopper warblers, blackcap, whitethroat and a host of native resident species including greater spotted woodpecker. The stream holds the occasional dipper and there is an extensive sett system occupied by badgers; roe deer and foxes also occur in the Dene.

The steep hillsides encourage soaring birds, and jackdaws and rooks often mob sparrowhawks or chase the buzzards as they ride the updraughts along the ridges over the valley. It is a place of great beauty and variety.
200ha – Map ref: NZ 410387

HAMSTERLEY FOREST (FC) — *Spring, summer*

This Forestry Commission woodland has a range of native broadleaved trees in small blocks. The Pennington beechwood, at 300 metres, being one of the highest beechwoods in the country. The size and variety of habitats throughout the forest means there's a good mix of mammals such as roe deer, badger, fox and red squirrel, with the smaller mammals represented by woodmice and short-tailed field voles.

The Bedburn Beck and its streams, which drain the forest, are always interesting for the birdlife that comes to drink and bathe, and redstarts, wood warblers, pied flycatchers and siskins make an interesting dawn chorus. Several areas of old pasture support orchids, and a number of other native limestone and grassland plants are to be found; yellow rattle, one of the indicator plants of unimproved grassland, is common and so too are cowslips.
4372ha – Map ref: NZ 093312

MARSDEN CLIFFS (South Tyneside MBC) — *All year*

These cliffs of magnesian limestone hold large colonies of breeding kittiwake, fulmar, herring gull and cormorant. The cliff-top and slopes are covered with typical limestone flora, common rock rose and bird's foot trefoil abound. Common blue butterflies also thrive here, and migrant species like painted lady and red admiral appear in large numbers in the summer. It's an excellent place to see seabirds on passage in spring and autumn and in winter you might see a snow bunting.
1km – Map ref: NZ 397650

MOORHOUSE WOOD (Durham WT/NT) — *Spring, summer*

Mixed coppice regime woodland with hornbeam standards constitutes this reserve, it's a developing habitat with good potential. The woodland floor has a marvellous showing of woodruff in late spring, and the shrubby areas encourage nesting songbirds, including some migrant warblers. Willow warbler and blackcap are common, as are titmice.
8ha – Map ref: NZ 310460

PENNINE WAY (CC) — *Spring, summer*

From Cow Green reservoir, past the spectacular falls at High Force, this section of the Way passes through some beautiful and fascinating scenery. High open moorland, golden plover, curlew, buzzard and the occasional raven vie with the river valley and dippers and wagtails.

It's a marvellous walk across Lunedale and out over the high ground of Balderhead reservoir, but it's not for the unprepared; always take proper equipment with you, adequate light protective clothing will repay your effort in having to carry it should the weather turn cold, wet or misty, as it can do so easily on all sections of this footpath.
45km – Map ref: NZ 815286 / 897067

ROSA SHAFTO (Durham WT) — *Spring, summer*

Over 90 species of birds have been recorded in this interesting woodland of mature beeches with oak, ash, birch and rowan; and the conifer areas actually add to the bird potential as nesting and roosting sites. The ground flora is varied and divided between wet woodland, meadow and open woodland, where there are wood anemones, sanicle, woodruff and thick scrambles of honeysuckle; wood cranesbill and wood avens grow by the pathways where there is good light. In the meadow there are damp areas where water avens and common spotted orchid grow. Altogether a fascinating and varied reserve.
30.8ha – Map ref: NZ 245350

SHIBDON POND (Durham WT/Gateshead MBC) — *All year*

Resulting from a depression in the ground caused by mining subsidence, this pond has filled with water and become an urban marsh and wetland. The habitats range from scrubby woodland, rich in bird species, to the pond itself which supports a considerable population of birds, fish and amphibians.

The reserve has a reputation for bats; on summer evenings, when the swallows, martins and swifts have finished feeding on the abundant insect life of the pond and surrounding marsh, noctule bats are seen flying high over the water taking their share of the bounty. The dragonfly population is worth of note, and the birdlife excellent — lesser whitethroats, willow, grasshopper and sedge warblers and water rail breed here. The winter bird population is very good with many species of wildfowl appearing when the weather is hard.
13.6ha – Map ref: NZ 195628

UPPER TEESDALE (NCC) — *Spring, summer*

This well known and beautiful area is amply provided with upland and river valley habitats. Birdlife ranges from buzzards and dippers on the high moorland to willow warblers, chaffinches and yellowhammers in the lower areas. Much of this area is of international importance to nature conservation, and there is an excellent interpretive centre at Bowlees.
3500ha – Map ref: NY 840280

WALDRIDGE FELL COUNTRY PARK (DCC) — *Spring, summer*

The upland fell and mixed woodland found here has much to interest the naturalist and walker. There's an area of heath and bog well known for its insect population, and bell heather and common heather grows with cross-leaved heath and bilberry. In the marsh, bogbean and a number of sedges thrive. However, it's not particularly good for birds.
130ha – Map ref: NZ 254494

WASHINGTON WATERFOWL PARK (WWT) — *All year*

In common with many of the smaller Wildfowl and Wetland Trust refuges and collections, care is taken to ensure that the public have a good view of the less common species, some of which are internationally endangered. The breeding of these birds is a priority, and the numbers of wildfowl that have been successfully reared may well have saved some species from extinction. There is also a wild area with a "scrape", a shallow man-made pond, where wild birds and waterfowl visit to rest and feed.
41.2ha – Map ref: NZ 330565

WHITBURN BIRD OBSERVATORY (Durham WT)** — *All year*

Access is restricted to this cliff top site which is renowned as a sea bird and small migrant recording station. Permits from Durham County Trust.

WINGATE QUARRY (DCC) — *Spring, summer*

A good exposure of magnesian limestone and lime-rich grassland can be seen clearly at this old disused limestone quarry. There are many rare and interesting plants in the quarry, and a small pond harbouring great crested newts and smooth newts. The mixture of habitats, and the richness of the limestone grassland, encourages butter-flies and moths, and the pond produces a good show of dragonflies in summer. Breeding birds include wrens and long-tailed tits.
22.5ha – Map ref: NZ 373376

ESSEX

Pre-Elizabethan Essex was a land of woodlands, stretching for thousands of acres and full of birdsong; the county's trees played an important part in England's history being used for the ships on numerous fleets, and for many of London's buildings. Life was hard but productive for the charcoal burners and foresters who made a living here, they coppiced and shaped the trees, some of which are still standing in Epping Forest. It was a landscape that the brilliant countryside observer, John Clare, would have known well. In his poem "London versus Epping Forest" he looks at the encroachment of London into this ancient hunting chase:-

"The brakes, like young stag's horns, come up in
        spring,
And hide the rabbit holes and fox's den;
They crowd about the forest everywhere;

The ling the holly-bush, and woods of beach,
With room enough to walk and search for flowers;
Then look away and see the Kentish heights.
Nature is lofty in her better mood,
She leaves the world and greatness all behind;
Thus London, like a shrub among the hills,
Lies hid and lower than the bushes here.
I could not bear to see the tearing plough
Root up and steal the Forest from the poor,
But leave to Freedom all she loves, untamed,
The Forest walk enjoyed and loved by all!

The geology is fairly straightforward with chalk and London clay overlaid in places with fertile sheets of boulder clay forming gentle slopes and wide flat lands. The conversion of much of the fertile lands on the boulder clay from forestry to arable farming is almost complete and the open prairies of wheat and barley have robbed the landscape of much of its diversity. Dutch elm disease, responsible for the death of millions of magnificent trees, such a feature of much of England, led to an open windswept aspect in parts of the county and it's a wonder that Essex has anything left of note from a natural history point of view. But there are a vast number of coastal reserves rich in waders, wildfowl and geese as well as the plants and animals that make up a viable natural coastal ecosystem. The eastern boundary is one long sea coast, indented with creeks and estuaries, bounded by sea-walls and defences where salt marsh has been enclosed for monoculture cereals and oilseeds. A great deal of this part of Essex is low lying and, left to its own devices, the sea would have encroached far inland, but successive drainage schemes have kept the tide back as Canute could not.

The two reservoirs of Abberton and Hanningfield are a must for wildfowl watchers, and a vital stopover for a host of birds, including the annual passage of osprey on their way to and from their Scottish Highland nest sites. If ever a southern site for osprey were to be considered this would be the place in which to establish breeding platforms for these majestic fish eating birds.

The proposal of Foulness Sands as the site for London's third airport some years ago caused a furore, and raised public awareness of this forbidding, but extremely rich wildlife area of island, sand and mud flats. The land is owned by the crown for the Ministry of Defence and access is very limited. However, this does mean that the sands provide a refuge in the truest sense for immense numbers of Brent geese and wildfowl, as well as excellent feeding grounds for migrant waders.

The Thames estuary, at the southern end of the county, is becoming more productive as attempts are made to permanently clean up London's river, and now there are more suitable places for wild creatures on the fringe of the city than there have been since Shakespeare's time. Nevertheless there's still a long way to go. Changes that have occurred during the past ten years in the economic geography of south east England have meant that many of the sleepy Essex villages have been invaded by prosperous home buyers, largely replacing the genuine Essex villager; and the intensive farming regimes of the past 20 years have stripped the land of trees, hedges and people. Nowadays many of the villages are no more than dormitories for London commuters. Modern roads have improved communications to the coastal villages, so that they too are within easy reach of London. Nevertheless you can still find those magical places where the sea-walls are so remote that you can wander along them, miles from another human being, in touch with nature in the raw. It's a landscape that would have been familiar to the eyes of John Ray, father of British natural history, when he lived in the county in the 17th century.

The Essex marshes and foreshore are featured in several of Dickens' books; the King's Head public house in Chigwell is the model for the Maypole Inn featured in "Barnaby Rudge". Dickens' justifiably gloomy view of London was tempered by the greeness of Essex, though it would be incorrect to say that he was a countryman, he appeared more at home in a built-up environment, and like many writers who usually set their works in towns and cities the countryside, when it does appear, is portrayed as a place of masked hostility. Even his view of East Anglian family life depicted in "David Copperfield" portrays hidden menace in the natural world, with the sea and the flat landscape more adversary than friend. Yet beneath it all Dickens' observation of the times in which he lived has given us an almost photographic record.

ABBERTON RESERVOIR (Essex Water Co) — *All year (especially winter)*

Abberton is one of the most important man-made reservoirs in the entire country, and provides drinking water for thirsty Londoners and southern Essex residents. The wigeon that gather here on winter days when the sun is watery and the east wind is like a knife's edge, wheel about the sky in scattered flocks or wing purposefully away to graze in the fields, it's a rare sight in south east England; teal, mallard, tufted duck, pochard, shoveller and golden-eye can number more than 25,000. Flocks of quarrelsome coot may be joined by birds that have come from as afar afield as Holland and Germany; and the waders that stop and rest on passage, as well as those that spend a good part of the winter at Abberton, run into thousands.

Why should this reservoir prove so attractive to the birds of marsh and estuary? The answer may lie in the loss of habitat in the region as a whole. The fertile Thames estuary once supported millions of birds, but the Essex marshes are now all but a memory, the river mouth is polluted and much of the estuary cultivated or industrialised. But, of course, the reservoir is on a flyway, a traditional route for migrant birds, witness the fact that the osprey that make their journey to and from nest sites in Scotland and wintering grounds on the west African coast twice yearly, appear so frequently at Abberton in early spring and mid autumn as to be counted regulars.

Other birds too use the reserve as a wintering ground because of the huge amount of food available. Birds of prey like peregrine, marsh and hen harriers and short-eared owls are frequently seen, and even an occasional merlin harries the flocks of finches feeding on the grass and weed seeds of nearby pasture.

The development of the coastline and further loss of wetlands, means that Abberton, which is large enough to remain open when other water nearby is frozen over, will continue to be a life saver for many species in very hard weather, providing a refuge for wild swans and some of the less common duck. The ringing station has proved most successful and some of the birds ringed here have been recovered thousands of miles away.

470ha – Map ref: TM 962185

CHALKNEY WOOD (Essex NT) — *Spring, summer*

A superb area of coppiced small-leaved lime, Chalkney Wood has been managed traditionally with a resulting superb display of bluebells in spring as well as a host of other woodland plants. The regime provides a series of excellent warbler nesting sites, and blackcap, garden warbler, willow warbler and chiffchaff breed here as do several pairs of nightingales that are a star feature. The insect population is good and the open areas provide

Tufted Duck   *Abberton Reservoir*

speckled wood butterflies with ample territories in summer; brown aeshna dragonflies can be seen in the open coppice areas.

25.2ha – Map ref: TL 873273

COLNE ESTUARY (NCC/Essex NT) — *All year*

The Colne estuary has seen some dramatic historic events during its long existence. The Romans fled from Colchester as Buddica's Celtic army went on the rampage, following a series of appalling errors of judgement by the ruling Roman administrators; and the mud must have claimed many artefacts of Romano British culture in the scramble to get away from the inflamed Celts and their red-haired Queen.

This estuarine habitat is tremendously varied, but like much of the coast of East Anglia, it is slowly sinking beneath the sea, but material brought downstream is building new banks and gulleys where the many worms and crustaceans, the foundation of the estuarine food chain, can live. The estuary is very productive and on the grazing marshes above the tide line a huge amount of seeds are shed which duck and finches, that throng the winter marshes, feed upon; in winter the mudflats are wreathed with waders at low tide — whimbrel, redshank, curlew, knot, sanderling and ringed plover, with some golden and grey plover, and alive with the sound of wildfowl.

Large flocks of dark-breasted Brent geese winter in the many creeks and saltings, these geese and their pale-breasted relative, which usually winters in the west of Ireland, were almost exterminated by wildfowlers, but legislation to protect them has resulted in a steady increase until now the population can be counted in thousands on the estuaries of Great Britain. They have a gentle growling contact call that rises to a crackling bark if they become alarmed; when frightened they burst upwards from the beds of zostera or eel grass that is their staple food.

Off shore, the estuary is the wintering ground for sea duck and divers, but the mass of these birds, including immense numbers of wigeon, teal and pintail feed and rest in shallow water, or on the salt-tainted grazing marsh which supports a wide variety of sea plants, including glasswort and sea lavender. Fewer people visit the reserve in spring and summer when the flowers are at their best, and the larks rise up into the sky and migrant butterflies from Europe, especially clouded yellow butterflies and humming bird hawk moths, delight the eye. Later in the summer, if the weather is hot, south easterly winds blow dragonflies and hordes of painted lady butterflies over the channel; it is also a landfall area for large numbers of migrating starlings after their North Sea autumn crossings.

608ha – Map ref: TM 075155

COPPERAS WOOD (Essex NT) ** — *Spring, summer*

Sweet chestnut, oak standard with coppice woodland and small-leaved lime constitute the main species of trees at Copperas Wood and there are a number of plants particular to ancient woodland, the most unusual being climbing corydalis, common cow wheat and sweet woodruff. The birds take advantage of the large range of breeding sites afforded by mixed age rotational coppice, and there are plenty of insects, including a large number of moths.

13.6ha

The following reserves are described below as one entity:-

The Backwarden (Essex NT)
Woods, heath and wetland — *12ha – Map ref: TL 782039*

Birch Wood and The Slype (Essex NT)
Part of a 54ha mixed woodland — *Map ref: TL 789068*

Blakes Wood (Essex NT)
Mixed woodland. *33.4ha – Map ref: TL 775064*

Danbury Common (NT)
Woodland and heathland — *63ha – Map ref: TL 782044*

Lingwood Common (NT)
22ha – Map ref: TL 783057

Pheasanthouse Wood (Essex NT)
Part of a 54ha mixed woodland — *Map ref: TL 787065*

Poors Piece (Essex NT)
Part of a 54ha mixed woodland — *Map ref: TL 788068*

Scrubs Wood (Essex NT)
Part of a 54ha mixed woodland — *Map ref: TL 787058*

Woodham Walter Common (Essex NT)
Part of a 54ha mixed woodland — *Map ref: TL 790065*

In the triangle formed by Chelmsford in the east, the river Chelmer in the north and the Crouch to the south, lies the Danbury Ridge, a complex geological mix of clay and chalk and gravel strata which produces an interesting variety of habitats making up the Danbury group of reserves which encapsulate, in a relatively small area, some of the traditional methods of forest and common woodland management practiced in lowland England for centuries. The origin of many of the woodland blocks appears to be rather ancient some, like Poors Common,

having been cropped as firewood, others like the orchid-rich Woodham Walter common have areas of stunted oaks relics of past regimes of woodland management. Whilst Blakes Wood is a microcosm of British woodlands, common land and open heath.

The opening up of the canopy has produced a very interesting woodland flora, and in Poors Wood, wild lily of the valley can be found, it also appears in Pheasanthouse Wood; Blakes Wood also has a particularly rich array of flowers with bluebells and early purple orchids and in Birch Wood wood anemones appear in large numbers.

The entire complex is perfect for birds, with a large population of breeding blackcaps, chiff chaffs and garden warblers in the scrubby areas, with nightingales occasionally being heard in the coppice woodland together with wood warbler. All three species of woodpeckers are found in Danbury woodlands with hawfinch and four species of titmice. The breeding success of these birds is assured by the ready supply of insect food and the ample nest sites. Insects in these woodlands include many moths species.

EPPING FOREST (Corp. of the City of London) — *All year*

When Henry I established a Royal Forest here in the 12th century, the woodlands were already very ancient, indeed parts might have dated back to the post glacial birch and lime woods of the Neolithic period. In the intervening centuries much of Essex's woodland has fallen before the axe and the plough. Indeed it's something of a miracle that any have survived at all, so close are they to London (by motorway the forest is within half an hour of the city centre) but perhaps it was the presence of the city, with its demands for milk, meat, firewood and building timber that enabled the forest to survive following the demise of the hunting regime that had previously protected it.

The most popular method of obtaining timber for firewood, poles for tools and hurdles on a continuous basis is coppicing, but this requires the exclusion of large grazing animals because coppicing produces easily accessible shoots, growing as they do from short stumps or stools. Pollarding on the other hand allows for grazing for the pollards are above the grazing line as the trees are topped while still relatively young and vigorous. The ground cover beneath is varied because topping the trees allows light to flood the woodland floor encouraging a flush of plants and grasses exploited by the graziers cattle and sheep.

Certain trees, usually oaks, were allowed to grow on for timber in parts of the wood where their crop of acorns or pannage would have an ecomonic value as animal feed. Grazing meant that natural regeneration of the forest by sapling growth was extremely low, and the virtual immortality of the pollarded trees was maintained by regular cropping of the new growth on a seven to ten year rotation; it also provided open deer "lawns" where scrub and gorse was nibbled out and only grass and low growing herbs remained. If the forest had continued to be managed as it had been for several hundred years there would have been a stable man-made series of habitats

Epping Forest   *Essex*

superb for certain wildlife. All that changed with the flowering of the industrial revolution and the carnage of the Great War.

The manpower to manage the forest properly was lost on Flanders' fields, some of the pollarded trees became overgrown and dangerously unstable and fell, and the drought of 1976 weakened many of the remaining trees. The canopy of standards has grown so dense it has shaded out much of the woodland floor so that few of the plants that charactise a pollarded woodland remain.

Grazing too has declined, and the deer that were the natural foresters have all but vanished. The deer lawns have become covered with scrub hawthorn and black-thorn and the heathy areas are overgrown or subject to intense human leisure pressures, for the forest is a lung for stressed London residents, and huge numbers of people with their attendant rubbish, have driven the decreasing wildlife into smaller and smaller areas. The soil types of sand, gravel and clay has led, over the centuries, to a large number of marshes and ponds, some of which are very rich in dragonflies and amphibians, but the reduction in trampling and grazing has also led to some ponds becoming overgrown, and their value for amphibians and waterbirds is greatly reduced.

But all this is on the debit side, and the huge acreage of the forest does ensure a number of habitats for breeding birds such as redstarts, wood warblers and all the common migrant leaf warblers which are found here. The pollards have many holes in their crowns and trunks which provide nest sites for titmice, however, the scrubby areas have robbed birds like nightjars of their breeding sites. The population of birds of prey is limited to the smaller species like kestrels, and increasingly sparrow-hawks, but larger birds of prey such as goshawk and buzzards are still subjected to pressure from game management on the surrounding farmland and country-side despite legal protection.

The insects are extremely varied, especially the beetle population, which ranks with the New Forest for numbers of species. Butterflies are mainly restricted to the common species, although moths are very varied.

Although the demise of pollarding has lowered the number and species of flowering plants, there is nowhere else so close to London with such an air of wilderness and natural peace — long may it continue.

2430ha – Map ref: TQ 412981

FINGRINGHOE WICK (Essex NT) — *All year*

This delightfully named reserve is headquarters and interpretive centre of the Essex Naturalist's Trust. Wet-land and marsh combines with an estuarine environment on the edge of the salt marsh, with a series of disused gravel extraction workings, all with a variety of associated habitats. The scrape hide gives a good view of the area looking over Geedon Marsh where immense numbers of brent geese, dunlin and curlew gather in winter.

The river Colne is tidal at this point and draws geese and a large number of wildfowl. There's something of interest all year round on this reserve with its scrubby woodland and ample nesting sites for warblers and nightingales, and resident birds exploit both natural and man-made habitats.

50ha – Map ref: TM 041195

HATFIELD FOREST COUNTRY PARK (NT) — *Spring, summer*

Not far from the airport at Stanstead and the border with Hertfordshire, Hatfield Forest was once part of the much larger Essex forest of which Epping is part though, unlike Epping, these woods were enclosed and managed as coppice with standards. Part of the woodland consists of hornbeam over coppice hazel which has resulted in a superb flora with such plants as primrose and sanicle. It is one of the most beautiful and fascinating woodlands in the whole county with a rich variety of wildlife all year; the birdlife is superb, and there is always the possibility of hearing a nightingale. Large mammals include fox and badger and the small predatory mammal population reflects the abundance of grassland and woodland rodents.

The parkland contains an area of marsh (Hatfield Forest Marsh — Essex NT** *3.6ha*) and a lake, which have proved excellent for wetland plants, birds and insects, and the lake holds a resident population of Canada geese.

420ha – Map ref: TL 546199

HITCHCOCK'S MEADOWS (Essex NT)** — *Spring, summer*

Hitchcock's Meadows consist of an area of lime-rich grassland, scrub and marsh, and are particularly noted for green-winged orchids and summer glow worms. In late summer and autumn Lady's tresses orchids can be seen.
3.8ha

LEIGH (NCC-Essex NT) — *All year*

Well known for its diverse flora this salt marsh on the Thames estuary supports five species of glasswort and common and lax flowered sea lavender, golden samphire, sea arrowgrass and sea wormwood all grow together with pale pink cushions of thrift. The mud is well covered with large amounts of eelgrass on which the thousands of geese, and other waterfowl that throng the reserve in winter, depend. The geese regularly flight between Foulness Sands and Leigh, and the rising tide drives flocks of small waders and larger redshank, grey plover and curlew up onto the saltings to roost where they are sometimes harried by wintering peregrine falcons and short-eared owls that quarter the marsh and the reclaimed areas seeking small rodents.

The plant population on the reclaimed land is a confused, but interesting, mixture, some arrived with the tippings used in the reclamation, and an abundant insect fauna thrives here, including the butterfly most associated with the county, the Essex skipper. The coastal influence brings many migrant butterflies and moths to the saltings and the flowery roughlands; in summer huge numbers of painted lady butterflies can appear when the weather and winds are suitable for them to cross the channel.
257ha – Map ref: TQ 835850

NORSEY WOOD (Basildon DC) — *Spring, summer*

Trees have been growing on the site of Norsey Wood for thousands of years; an area of sweet chestnut coppice is a relatively recent additon to the rotation, and the wood provides a unique series of habitats and nest sites for breeding birds. A variety of unusual plant species, including Midland hawthorn, make up the understory and butcher's broom and lily of the valley thrive on the woodland floor. There are several ponds in the wood containing a number of plants and dragonflies and damselflies are common.
67ha – Map ref: TQ 692957

OLD HALL MARSHES (RSPB) — *All year*
BLACKWATER ESTUARY (NCC)

These two estuarine reserves are of particular interest because of their remote nature on a promontory in the Blackwater estuary. They serve as a focus for many species of wildfowl and waders including the speciality of the east coast the dark-bellied Brent goose, a small and attractive creature only a little larger than a shelduck, which breeds in the high arctic and winters in huge numbers on the grazing marshes that comprise part of these reserves. Up to 4000 individuals collect here to feed together with thousands of wigeon, teal, shelduck and many thousands of waders. Grey plover, curlew, redshank and dunlin can be seen in winter and are frequently disturbed by passing hen harriers and short-eared owls, barn owls and merlin who regularly hunt over the reserve. Among the breeding birds here you will find water rail, bearded tit and common tern. Unusual waders are frequently observed including avocet.
Old Hall Marshes   1560 acres – Map ref: TL 950117
Blackwater Estuary   1171ha   – Map ref: TL 940070

SHADWELL WOOD (Essex NT)** — *Spring, summer*

This botanical treasure house exists because of a combination of natural and man-made events. The natural event is the presence of a drift of glacial lime-rich boulder clay perfect for the type of woodland management employed. Over 23 trees and shrub species occur here, and the coppicing of hazel, hornbeam and field maple under standards of oak and ash has produced a dapple of light and shade that changes slowly as the coppice poles grow from their stools shutting out the sunlight from the woodland floor.

When they are cropped after a period of seven to ten years the ground cover plants receive full sunlight again and the wood comes alive with cowslips, primroses, oxlips, early purple orchids, ramsons, goldilocks, celandine and a carpet of bluebells. The paths through the wood can be one mass of common spotted orchid, and greater butterfly orchid also grows here.

In winter colour is provided by holly and yew and as spring develops Midland hawthorn, guelder rose, blackthorn, wayfaring tree, spindle and wild privet form a complex series of habitats and nesting sites for warblers and native songbirds. Greater spotted woodpeckers drum on dead branches. It's a rich example of the type of woodland that might have been found in Essex during the Middle Ages.
6.4ha

STOW MARIES RAILWAY CUTTING (Essex NT)** — *Spring, summer*

Glow-worms and cypress spurge are two particularly precious inhabitants of this disused railway line; the

Short-eared Owl   *Old Hall Marshes*

butterfly population includes speckled wood.
1.2ha

THORNDON COUNTRY PARK (ECC) — *Spring, summer*

Hornbeams and oaks of considerable age grow in the original part of this ancient deer park, and lakes, streams and conifer plantings add variety to the rest of the reserve. There is a rich insect life, especially in the older part of the reserve where the oaks and hornbeams encourage a substantial fauna. Birds include green and greater spotted woodpecker.
144.4ha – Map ref: TQ 604915 / 635899

TIPTREE HEATH (Tiptree PC) — *Spring, summer*

Tiptree Heath presents an unusual habitat for Essex, cross-leaved heath and heath milkwort grow in the damper areas, and gorse, heather and tormentil thrive where drainage is better.
24ha – Map ref: TL 884149

WEELEYHALL WOOD (Essex NT)** — *Spring, summer*

An ancient wood best known for beautiful mature oaks and a superb showing of bluebells in spring. Some of the oaks are in excess of 300 years old and support a tremendous population of insects, many of them particular to oaks at a certain stage of maturity. The bird life is varied, all three species of woodpeckers are found here as are kestrels, sparrowhawks and barn owls. In spring there are a large number of warblers, and resident species including nuthatch, tree creeper and the common titmice.
31.2ha

WEST WOOD (Essex NT)** — *Spring, summer*

A highly developed wood of oak standards and some coppice with a large central area planted with Norway spruce, of value for nesting or roosting birds. Where the trees are broadleaved, the woodland floor is thick with oxlip, dog's mercury, bluebells, white flowered and garlic scented ramsons; bugle and ground ivy are common on the woodland edges while in the rides early purple orchids thrive, followed by masses of common spotted orchids.

Birdlife includes garden warblers, goldcrests and red-polls along the edge of the conifer plantings; and cole tit, great tit and long-tailed tits are common where they can find ample nest sites. The mammal population is considerable with muntjac deer and fox, the territorial bark of muntjac can often be confused with that of foxes. Sparrowhawks and tawny owls nest in the wood, and frogs and newts breed in a series of pools; these wet places also encourage marsh marigold, and later in the summer dragonflies quarter the rides feeding on insects, including unwary butterflies.
23.2ha

GLOUCESTERSHIRE

"Waking in the morning I saw squirrels in the yew trees nibbling at the moist red berries. Between the trees and the window hung a cloud of gold air composed of floating seeds and spiders. Farmers called to their cows on the other side of the valley and moorhens piped from the ponds. Brother Jack as always was the first to move, while I pulled my boots on in bed. We both stood at last on the bare wood floor, scratching and saying our prayers, too stiff and manly to say them out loud, we stood back to back and muttered them, and if an audible plea should slip out by chance, one just burst into song to cover it."

This lovely descriptive scene of the Gloucestershire morning is from Laurie Lee's "Cider With Rosie", and it speaks to me of my own childhood, of a soft autumnal morning with the sun slanting across my bedroom floor in my parent's cottage on the edge of Dartmoor. There's a distance of 60 miles or so, as the rook flies, from Laurie Lee's Gloucestershire village of Slad in the Cotswolds to the village of Bratton Clovelly in Devon where my mother, my brother and I spent the war; but I can't read this superb evocation of a country childhood and early adolescence without the strongest feeling of being in a time machine.

Lee's Cotswold countryside portrayed a ruminating pace of life and the endless enjoyment of a rural up-bringing that has nothing to do with material possessions, or even happiness. When you are feeling miserable, what better place to go and be miserable in than a quiet wood or a flower filled field.

Gloucestershire's landscape has many faces; the Forest

of Dean, the limestone outcrop at Symonds Yat with its peregrines, the broad Severn estuary where the tide rises and funnels into the narrowing throat of the river at Epney driving the waders high on to the mud banks. Man has made his home in this region for a very long time; the Celtic tribes of the Somerset Levels gave way to the Belgic warriors who built fortified villages on hilltops and buried their dead beneath round mounds. These fierce and artistic people shaped the county; where there was a hill to be cleared they cleared it with axe and fire.

The honeyed rock overlaid with soft soils encouraged pastoral farming, not the aggressive barley and wheat praries found further east where the rocks turn from cream to white under the influence of chalk. The land here produces the delicious double Gloucester cheese, crafted from the rich milk of water meadow-fed cows and the many springs, streams and rivers. The beautiful river Windrush rises in these generous hills and meanders, full of fish and fowl and insect life, across the northern arm of the county. This is also the birthplace of the Thames, it rises from a quiet hillside west of Lechlade; the springs that eventually become the mightiest and most English of rivers bubble, almost unobtrusively, from a crack in the bedrock.

Several regions take their character from the bedrock upon which they were founded and Gloucestershire is a particularly good example. Every village that stands untouched by modern developers is warm and gentle ornamented by gold and cream houses with woolly caps of thatch. Thousands of photographs of thatched Cotswold cottages litter the far flung corners of the globe, treasured as the comfortable image of the heartland of England.

As far as conservation is concerned the county has had some notable successes; the Wildfowl and Wetland Trust's Centre at Slimbridge being one of the most important. Here the premier Knight of conservation, Sir Peter Scott, held friendly court and painted wildfowl in his studio in the marshy goose-rich Severn valley. This fertile flood plain is now aggressively farmed, the geese and wildfowl out on the flats are no longer sheltered from the road by thick hedges and tall banks, there's an uncomfortable uniformity here now, but happily relieved by the Wildfowl and Wetland Trust refuge. People come from all over the world to see the collection of exotic birds and the arctic travellers that seek shelter in 'swan lake'.

The cowslips and orchids of Laurie Lee's Cotswold childhood may not be as common as once they were, indeed they are largely confined to nature reserves, but they are the seed corn of the county's natural recovery; waiting for the swish of the haymakers's scythe in the small meads of Slad, and the new move towards a green revolution of meadows and quiet woods will allow youngsters, fresh and green, to taste the cider of life for the first exhilarating time beneath a Gloucestershire haycart.

ASHLEWORTH HAM (Gloucester TfNC)** — *All year*

There's no access to this reserve which has to be viewed from hides adjacent to the public road. Nevertheless it's worth a look for the flat flood plain is very beautiful, due in part to the breadth of the skies and the colour of the hills beyond. It's a wildlife storehouse, the summer productivity of the meadows providing food for the wildfowl when they arrive from their far-off nesting sites; and in winter thousands of duck in mixed flocks take advantage of the bounty.
40.9ha

COTSWOLD COMMONS AND BEECHWOODS (NCC) — *Spring, summer*

Mainly beech woodlands of which Buckholt Wood forms a large part. Common rights still apply on these unenclosed common lands, though cattle are no longer grazed in the woods.

There is a wide variety of tree species including whitebeam, ash and wyche elm in the drier areas of the wood, and alder and willow in the damper parts; overall an abundance of hawthorn, holly, wayfaring tree, hazel, some wild cherry and yew. Needless to say the ground cover is also extremely varied and where the beech wood is thin enough to allow light to filter through to the woodland floor, bird's nest orchids and helleborines thrive and, where the soil is particularly alkaline, you may see clumps of green helleborine. Wild rose scrambles over bushes in the clearings and rides, and there's a superb show of primroses and bluebells in spring.

The bird population varies with the season. In spring the woods are loud with spring migrants and woodpeckers drumming and in winter, if the 'mast' has been good with beech nuts everywhere in the leaf litter, flocks of finches, including bramblings, jostle for food.
270ha – Map ref: SO 894131

COTSWOLD WATER PARK (GCC — Wilts CC) — *All year*

These immense gravel and sand workings appear on the map as a series of lakes spattered over the countryside from Somerford Keynes to Wick, where the course of the embryo Thames meanders through a landscape that hides beneath its turf even more huge deposits of sand and gravel; remnants of a tremendous waterway that once flowed along the valley.

Already more than 1500 hectares of land have been cleared and dug for their stony treasure and, as night follows day, the watertable has ensured the lakes would follow the digging. Gravel workings change the wildlife potential of an area; where there was farmed dry grassland, fields and woods, now there's a whole series of new habitats — deep water, marshes, reed beds, willow swamp and banks of sheared sand that provide nesting sites for martins and kingfishers. Open water encourages life all year round; migrating wildfowl are always attracted and even geese will stop to investigate the potential of a gravel pit if it's large enough.

Eventually more lakes and ponds in the Cotswold Water Park will be used for water sports, and the advent of the wet suit has meant that water-skiers and windsurfers can pursue their sports for as long as the water surface is free of ice. Such continuous activity will mean that birds feeding here in winter will have to go elsewhere,

Symonds Yat   *Gloucestershire*

which would be unfortunate for the water here is rich in lime and consequently very productive.

Ospreys and many other migrating birds such as terns and waders visit annually. However, migrants are only part of the picture, there is a healthy breeding population of waterbirds and the beginning of plant colonisation that will mean rapid change and a greater diversity of birds, insects and small mammals.

5666ha – Map ref: SU 026597

FOREST OF DEAN (FC) — *Spring, summer*

An immense spread of forest, and moorland, set in a wedge of land that lies between the rivers Severn and Wye. Unfortunately drastic alterations by Forestry Commission plantations of conifers and sheep grazing, has meant there's relatively little natural regeneration of broadleaved woodland. The region has a complex geology with coal seams still mined by a number of Forest of Dean resident miners, though this type of traditional drift mining is now relatively uncommon.

The forest is not one continuous area covered with trees as its name suggests; it is a mixture of woodland and open moorland with a varied rock structure showing signs of huge earth movements over millions of years. The river Wye has cut deeply into the limestone and sandstone creating rock faces like that at Symonds Yat, sheer and high and ideal for peregrine falcons to breed. There's an observation platform nearby where you can enjoy the astonishing sight of these wild birds feeding and teaching their young to fly and hunt; more than 100,000 people have seen them.

The rocky crags and hanging woods and the tall conifers provide nesting sites for two unusual birds, the raven and pied flycatcher, both at the eastern limit of their present range. Other birds in the forest include nightjar and tree pipit, crossbill and heron; and butterflies are abundant. Indeed most of our common woodland fritillaries breed regularly here with more than 30 species of butterfly and many hundreds of species of moths being recorded.

10,935ha

FRITH WOOD (Gloucester TfNC) — *Spring, summer*

Beech woodland on both sides of a narrow limestone ridge composed of very tall straight trees, gives Frith Wood an imposing aspect. The canopy is dense, but where adequate light reaches the woodland floor there's a good variety of flowers. The reserve boasts a number of long abandoned limestone quarries with their own habitat of ash, whitebeam and yew, dense layers of hart's tongue fern, traveller's joy, and wild roses grow where the sunlight is strongest. Dog's mercury, wild raspberry and several species of calcareous woodland orchids such as broadleaved helleborine also thrive here. The birdlife is

Weasel   *Frith Wood*

extremely rich, particularly in those areas where felling has taken place. Warblers are well represented with both garden and willow warbler; mammals include foxes, stoats, weasels and grey squirrels.
22ha – Map ref: SO 877086

FROCESTER HILL (Coaley Peak) (Gloucester TfNC) — Spring, summer

Scrub and limestone grassland predominates on this hillside which affords superb views across the Severn estuary to Wales. Linnets, yellowhammers and willow warblers nest in the scrub layer, and a quarry provides nesting sites for blackcaps and resident thrushes and blackbirds. There are butterflies aplenty with marbled whites and other species of browns such as ringlets.
5.6ha – Map ref: SO 794009

LANCAUT (Gloucester TfNC) — *Spring, summer*

The valley of the river Wye is spectacular, and very rich in plants and birds. The river is tidal at this point and its rise and fall is extreme. Successive quarrying operations have carved steps in the limestone and the salt marsh at the river's edge is narrow. These dry warm rock terraces support late spring flowers with valerian, ox-eye daisy and naturalised wallflowers making a particularly lovely display.

The steps give way to woodland clinging to the sides of the steep valley, and representatives of old woodland trees grow here; whitebeam, wild service and small-leaved lime are all found together with yew, oak and ash. In spring, before the canopy closes over and excludes much of the sunlight, there's a very good show of primroses. The mixture of habitats ensures a wide diversity of insect, mammal and bird species.
24ha – Map ref: ST 539967

MYTHE RAILWAY (Gloucester TfNC)** — *Spring, summer*

A mixture of wet and dry habitats encourages a diversity of plants and animals on this disused railway line site.

Wild liquorice and spindle berry grow together with comfrey; the large brown dragonfly (Aeshna grandis) is a regular visitor hawking for flying insects along the wetter parts of the reserve.
2.8ha

NAGSHEAD (RSPB) — *Spring, summer*

Nagshead reserve is part of the ancient Forest of Dean just west of Park End village. It consists of mature oak woodland with beech, birch, rowan and holly, and a stream with its own tree cover of alder with a few planted firs.

In spring, when the wood is beginning to come alive with birdsong, there's a beautiful carpet of bluebells, and the honeysuckle buds are opening ready to feed the white admiral butterfly caterpillars; the minute larva of this insect hibernates in the rolled up dead leaves of honeysuckle and, during winter, can withstand everything the elements may throw at it. When the leaves unfurl it emerges to feed in readiness for pupation and its eventual metamorphosis into a perfect butterfly in July. Other butterflies include speckled wood and silver-washed and pearl-bordered fritillaries.

Honeysuckle also forms an essential raw material for the nest of another hibernator, common dormice. They occur here in small numbers.

The birds on the reserve are many and varied; pied flycatcher and redstart nest in the boxes provided for them as do bluetits, great tits and nuthatches. Other breeding species include chiffchaffs, blackcaps, tree creepers, all three woodpecker species, tree pipits, crossbills and hawfinch; sparrowhawks take advantage of this productivity and are seen regularly.

There are hides beside the waymarked paths.
153ha – Map ref: SO 612078

POOR'S ALLOTMENT (Poor's Allotment Trustees) — *Spring, summer*

A fascinating juxtaposition of rock types produces a dramatically contrasting flora on this reserve. The acid sandstone is covered with all three species of common heather, bilberry and western gorse; while the limestone supports species adapted to alkaline soil such as rock rose and carline thistle.
28.3ha – Map ref: ST 559995

SAPPERTON VALLEY (Gloucester TfNC) — *Spring, summer*

This disused canal is gradually reverting to nature, and along the towpath the flowers reflect the original ground cover of the area with woodland species like yellow archangel. The canal margin is alive with dragonflies and birds and there's a beautiful stand of purple loosestrife and marsh marigold; on the water there are the leaves and flowers of yellow water lily.
3.7ha – Map ref: SO 939034

SLIMBRIDGE WILDFOWL SANCTUARY (WWT) — *All year*

This huge site began to take shape just after the Second

World War when the late Sir Peter Scott, saw the rarest of all our regular wintering geese, the elegant lesser white-front goose, on the saltings here. Through his drive and personal enthusiasm and the success of his appearances on television, the Wildfowl and Wetland Trust began and, despite tremendous problems, is now the leading wildfowl protection and preservation organisation in the world.

Many of the birds on display, a representation of most of the duck, geese, swans and flamingoes of the world, breed and the success of this policy is most apparent in the case of the Hawaiian goose or Ne-Ne. Less than 50 birds survived in the wild in 1950, and from three birds brought to the Trust at that time they have bred thousands. Barring a disaster, this particular species is no longer threatened and as a bonus many have been returned to the woods and lava fields of their Hawaiian homeland. This is but a part of the conservation and research success enjoyed by the Trust.

One of the most interesting aspects of this place is the range of habitats that have been created. Even tropical species are catered for in heated buildings, and humming-birds mingle with tropical duck in an accurate representation of a jungle wetland.

In winter hundreds of wild whooper and Bewick swans arrive here; they tend to shun actual contact with mankind, disregarding those who stare in wonder at them through the windows of the observation buildings although they tolerate members of staff because these recognised and trusted people distribute the daily food supplies. Geese from the high arctic winter on the Severn estuary salt marshes and join the feral flocks of full-winged geese dropping down to be fed with the others.

Winter also brings the wild geese and the bird-watchers, and there are many hides from the tall Acrow or the South Finger hides that enable you to watch the geese

White fronted Geese

in their thousands, a truly thrilling sight. Who knows, if you're lucky you might even see the bird that started it all, the beautiful rare lesser white- fronted goose.
800ha – Map ref: SO 723048

THIS ENGLAND WOOD (Woodland Trust) — *Spring, summer*

A small wood, fairly recently established, with over a thousand new trees which in time will develop into mature broadleaved forest with all the plants, insects, birds and mammals you would expect to find in natural woodland. It is already beginning to show some of its future promise.
2ha – Map ref: SO 875083

GREATER LONDON

A less promising area for wildlife would be hard to imagine than the massive sprawl of houses, shops, blocks of flats and industrial estates that comprises Greater London, but to make this assumption would be to commit a gross injustice to this city which, over the past ten years, has become more and more fascinating from a

wildlife point of view, and also to devalue the work of conservation and education bodies and many committed individuals.

I came to live in Chiswick in west London in the 1950s, quite a culture shock for me having been brought up in the wilds of Devon and Cornwall. The crowds of people, the

Staines Reservoir   *Greater London*

the bottom of the river through two to three feet of water, a sure sign that although conservation in the city has a long way to go there has been some definite progress.

But it is in the sky in spring and summer that we should look for the greatest success. The clean air acts of the 1950s and 60s stopped a million coal-burning chimneys belching out their filth, the trees that coped best with London's grime were the London plane trees, not only could they shed their smoke and soot-caked leaves, but also their dirt encrusted bark. Now the trees in London's parks and gardens sport healthy leaves and the city blooms; butterflies and insects fly in the clear summer air and swifts and house martins harvest the bounty.

Occasionally a kestrel colonises the high rise world of the "square mile"; a squatter nesting on ledges which by city real estate prices would cost a King's ransom; a mouse hunter whose means of catching prey has changed from hovering over mice in a grass field to diving, sparrowhawk fashion, at small unwary birds. Even the lordly peregrine is able to live in a town environment, and Regents Park has its heronry and its lakes, and Hyde Park the Serpentine where wildfowl from Siberia will accept bread from tourists.

From the air London appears relatively green in spite of all the buildings. Far more trees than you would imagine grace the streets, and in the suburbs the spread of gardens and the tens of thousands of bird tables provide a series of nest sites and a food resource allowing a far higher level of wildlife to the acre than you will find on the relatively sterile farmland of the counties surrounding the capital. The parks and municipal gardens form a series of wildlife havens linked by private gardens; and roads and railways leading in and out of the city and provide a complex of corridors along which foxes, badgers and a host of other wildlife can travel freely to recolonise other sites.

Predatory pressures are far higher in Greater London than in a less built-up environment, cats lay in wait, some as wild as foxes, others as tame as the snuffling hedgehogs whose round of the food-rich gardens begins and ends with dinner on the patio (a dish of dog food and fresh water) provided by environmentally aware humans. Many country people scoff at townies as though they were a species apart; but it is these townies who are the prime movers of the conservation movement, the majority who give their voices and their financial support to everything from saving hedgehogs to arresting destruction of the rain forests.

Most people think of conservation as something to do with the countryside, but the fact of the matter is that most of the conservation movement is centred in towns and cities. There is a tremendous interest in wildlife within the Greater London area, after all it's a matter of numbers, there are simply more people here (in one accessible group) than anywhere else in the country, and they are begining to question the quality of their lives and of the nature around them.

Nature reserves in London range from tiny backyard plots and canal banks where rosebay willow-herb,

tightly packed houses and worst of all the lack of nature was horrendous and for a time I hated everything. Gradually I opened my eyes and began to see the wildlife that shared the bricks and mortar, the small areas of parkland and the lakes, and before long I had discovered great crested newts in a lake in the grounds of Chiswick House.

On climbing over the wall and fencing surrounding Barn Elms reservoirs on the opposite side of the river I was enthralled to find a haven for birds that had travelled immense distances; and it was here that I met the people who were to set me upon the course that led to my present life as a natural history writer, broadcaster and artist.

What has London to offer on the brink of the 21st century. First, much cleaner air than Londoners have been able to enjoy for 100 years, secondly relatively pure water flowing along the course of the Thames.

Opposite the famous Kew Gardens there used to be a gas treatment plant, the river below its outfall was absolutely dead, nothing could live in the yellow, tar-smelling mix that gushed into the river like steaming chemical soup. But recently herons have been seen fishing just down-stream from where pollution once reigned and tufts of water weed are thriving in the gravel, you can see elephant hawk moths or a frog represent the height of conservation achievement, to the massive open lakeland areas of the reservoirs at Staines where duck and bird-watchers appear in their thousands in the mid winter cold. It's a growing centre for wildlife; as yet the reserves are only the more visible tip of a natural history iceberg.

London represents a great plundering of natural mineral wealth. Chalk from the ring of chalk hills surrounding the London basin is cooked into a dust of fine grey cement, gravels from the Thames basin are used for concrete, and brick pits dug into the clay have left a series of holes in the ground that have been flled either with rubbish or ground water. The rubbish has attracted a huge population of black-headed gulls, now they scream into the metropolis like commuters to feed, and when replete fly out again in long waving 'V' formations to roost on the gravel pits that have been allowed to return to nature and on the drinking water and canal balance reservoirs.

London has its own micro climate. Travelling along the road in winter towards the city, especially from the north, you can see the snow beginning to melt away, and feel the temperature increase. This special climate is a major factor in the success of London's wildlife, insulating it from the harsh reality of winter. The streaming clouds of starlings that travel into the centre of town for the evening, do so because they like the warm and cosy, if noisy, streets; and pied wagtails, birds that countrymen associate with rushing streams and waterfalls roost in their thousands beside the warm waste air vents of hotels and office buildings in Westminster.

Richard le Gallienne, a north countryman who migrated to London as so many do, to pursue his art as a writer and poet had a love affair with the city and his poem "Ballad of London" accurately reproduces the ambivalent attitude of like and dislike that many people feel towards the noisy exciting metropolis.

"A Ballad of London"
Ah London! London! our delight,
Great flower that opens but at night,
Great city of the midnight sun,
Whose day begins when day is done.

Like dragonflies, the hansoms hover,
With jewelled eyes, to catch the lover;
The streets are full of lights and loves,
Soft gowns, and flutter of soiled doves.

Upon thy petals butterflies,
But at thy root, some say, there lies,
A world of weeping trodden things,
Poor worms that have not eyes or wings.

BARN ELMS RESERVOIRS (TWA)** — *All year*

Barn Elms Reservoirs have great significance for me, for it was here that I met a Mr Brook. He introduced me to natural history as a study rather than a hobby; duck and wildfowl have been an abiding interest ever since. It was only after I went to work for the RSPB, at his insistence, that I discovered he was Viscount Alanbrooke, Churchill's wartime military advisor, a man who went to war with a pair of binoculars in his knapsack, not only to study the enemy.

These reservoirs have a reputation for smew, a most elegant saw-billed duck that winters in the London area. It is also where gadwall breed and where garganey stop off on their way back from Africa. In summer swifts and many other migrants such as sand martins appear, and kestrels scan the mown causeways for voles and meadow pipits. The heron population seems to be declining, but it may only be better fishing in the nearby Thames.
34ha

BRENT RESERVOIR (BWB) — *January through September*

The small road bridge at the lower end of the reservoir gives excellent views; there is substantial pressure from dinghy sailing, none the less a healthy population of duck winter here, especially the beautiful saw-billed smew. Dabbling duck are well represented, and heron too are seen fishing the shallows at the Silk Stream and Brent river entry. The reed beds are very productive as are the willow clad areas, and the playing fields overlooking the reservoir also serve as a roost for wintering lapwing.
47.2ha

CAMLEY STREET (London WT) — *May through July*

Camley Street is a classic urban nature reserve, a former coal depot on the side of the canal. The site has rosebay willow-herb in plenty, with reed sweet grass on the banks and the developing areas of willow and the grassland support butterflies, among them common blues. Sadly Camley Street is under threat from development.
1ha

DOWNE BANK (Kent TfNC)** — *All year*

Downe Bank was closely studied for 40 years by the eminent naturalist Charles Darwin, father of the theory of natural selection. The site is close to his home, Downe House, and is maintained as chalk grassland with hazel coppice. It's rich in plants like spurge laurel, and tooth wort grows as a parasite on roots of certain bushes. The gale in 1987 felled many of the trees and the view now would be familiar to the great man.
7ha

HAMPSTEAD HEATH — *All year*
NW1/NW3

That Hampstead Heath has survived at all is something of a miracle, but it has become a symbol, a lung, a place where people come summer and winter; and despite the pressure the common supports a large wildlife population. Ken Wood has a lovely show of bluebells and a small wetland provides for a wide range of plants and animals while South Meadows are managed as meadow grassland, harbouring birds like goldfinches in late summer. Generally speaking the bird population is considerable and tawny owls and kestrels are quite common.

Hampstead Heath is one of the best places in London to hear a fully developed dawn chorus in spring, in spite of the noise of jet aircraft the birds still make themselves heard.
324ha

HAREFIELD PLACE (Hillingdon Natural History Society) — *May through July*

Harefield Place Golf Course
Harefield Place began life as a woodland bird sanctuary, a role it still plays, for between the woodland, wet meadow and pond there's a good range of insects allowing for a valuable breeding bird population, this type of habitat also contains an abundane of small mammals.
3.9ha

LAVENDER POND (The Ecological Parks Trust Reserve) — *July through September*

Rotherhithe Street, SE16
Lavender Pond is totally man-made, water from the Thames supports the large number of fish in the pond, and there are dragonflies in some numbers while winter birdlife is augmented by visiting wildfowl and coot. There is also a pleasant mixture of alder and scrub and reed beds which have the potential to support a good insect fauna and nesting birds.
1ha

NUNHEAD CEMETERY (LB Southwark) — *May through July*

Linden Grove, Peckham SE15
Nunhead Cemetery contains an astonishing number of native plants, probably the original flora growing in the field before it was consecrated for burials in Victorian times. Dog's mercury and meadow cranesbill make an excellent showing in spring and summer and many common birds have established themselves. There are also plenty of mammals — urban foxes, short-tailed field voles and wood mice. Needless to say with such an abundant food supply kestrels and tawny owls hunt over the reserve.
11ha

PERIVALE WOOD (Selborne Society)** — *April through October*

Established in 1904 and one of the first nature reserves in the country. The woodland shows signs of being very ancient including wild service trees, particularly un-

Urban Fox   *Nunhead Cemetry*

common in the London area; red campion, wood sage and wood millet all indicate the woodland has been growing on this site for many thousands of years. In spring there's a lovely flush of green to the hazel coppice and a carpet of massed bluebells.
11ha

QUEEN MARY RESERVOIR (TWA)** — *All year*

Most of the major drinking water reservoirs in the London area are superb winter gathering places for wildfowl and Queen Mary's is no exception. Though some human disturbance has reduced its potential, black-necked grebe are frequent visitors, and large numbers of pochard roost here.
283ha

RUISLIP (Ruislip and District Natural History Society)** — *All year*

Ruislip Lido is quite famous; once it fed the Grand Union Canal, now the banks and surrounding countryside are totally naturalised. One of a select band of official London nature reserves the site has wetland, marsh, chalk grassland and some dry heathy areas; there are a large number of breeding birds with willow tits and long-tailed tits much in evidence in winter while the spring warbler population is excellent with blackcaps, chiffchaffs and garden warblers.

Ruislip woods have been here for thousands of years and the mixed aged trees encourage a tremendous range of birds, from common species like blackbirds and mistle-thrush to less frequently encountered birds like hawfinch, dumpy broad-billed seed eaters.

An ancient trackway runs through the oak and hornbeam wood, known as Mad Bess Wood, was used in the Middle Ages for "pannage", that is when pigs are allowed to root for acorns, a singularly effective form of woodland management.

4.5ha

SPRINGWELL QUARRY (London WT)** — *May through July*

An old chalk quarry overlooking the river Coln and one of the most interesting places on the outskirts of London. The vantage point from the top of the quarry is superb and there are many ledges in the chalk face where kestrels have been nesting for some time while lime-loving plants grow in the crevices where soil has collected; the flat land at the base of the quarry carries a typical flora of rich chalk pastureland. Stockers Lake and Maple Cross sewage farm are the autumn and winter refuge of wildfowl and waders, especially sandpipers.

This reserve has been well wardened and the Coln has long been a haven for redpoll and siskin, and it's one of their winter strongholds in the London area. They feed on the seed cones of the alders and when these have been stripped out the birds begin to forage in nearby gardens for peanuts.

0.5ha

STAINES RESERVOIRS (North and South) (TWA) — *All year*

There is something unnerving about standing on the central causeway between the reservoirs at Staines as jumbo jets lumber into the sky from nearby Heathrow Airport; although the noise of jets and the smell of aviation fuel doesn't seem to worry the duck that mass on the reservoirs in winter.

Over the past few years substantial repairs to these immense holding tanks have been carried out and it has been interesting to see just how deep they are. Such deep water and the steeply sloping concrete banks with relatively little plant growth deters dabbling duck from breeding. However, this makes very little difference to the thousands of duck that roost here during the day safe from most predators. Very occasionally there is a flurry when a wintering peregrine flies over and the flocks are thrown into confusion.

The numbers of some species are huge, 5000 pochard have been counted and 4000 tufted duck as well as many hundreds of teal and wigeon and less common species like smew, goosander and goldeneye, the latter diving to the concrete apron deep below the surface to reappear like corks after a minute or so. Sandpipers regularly appear on the sloping concrete sides picking tiny insects from the tide line as small waves, driven across the surface by wind, break on the concrete.

When any of the reservoirs are drained for maintenance huge numbers of lapwing and other waders congregate on the exposed food-rich mud on the bottom. The scale of such work often entails a long period when the reservoir is empty and the surface of the mud becomes covered with a film of green plants, the wildlife potential is at its highest level then for when the water stands 20 metres deep the fish are the beneficiaries of the vegetation.

172ha

SYDENHAM HILL WOOD (London WT) — *All year*

Part of the old south London forest, hazel coppice, hornbeam and oak form the mass of the woodland cover; bamboo and rhododendron have invaded the wood from an adjoining Victorian garden, but wood anemone, Solomon's seal and ramsons all flowers of ancient woodland are still found here, and there is a fine showing of wood mellick grass. The railway that once ran to Crystal Palace passes through the reserve, it is derelict now and a tunnel system has been barred to provide roosts for bats.

Birdlife is excellent, blackcaps, willow warblers and chiffchaffs breed as do greater spotted woodpeckers, and a pond has been created for amphibians where the birds come to bathe. Sparrowhawks and kestrels are both present, though neither breed here. The reserve is being developed as a working woodland thereby improving its overall potential.

11ha

THAMESIDE (Thameside Assocation) — *All year*

River Road, Creekmouth, Barking

A nature reserve on the least promising site of the now derelict Thameside power station complex being managed to produce an astonishing level of wildlife potential. Common spotted and southern marsh orchid hybrids occur on the fly ash reclamation pools, and the marshland attracts barn owls and short-eared owls to the considerable vole population. Unfortunately the area is under some threat from development of the nearby river frontage.

13.2ha

WALTHAMSTOW MARSH (Lea Valley Authority) — *All year*

Spring Hill, Clapton, E5

A site of special scientific interest which represents the last piece of unimproved grassland in the Lea Valley. The reserve supports a large number of plants including meadowsweet, and the sedge, marsh and reeds hold nesting sedge warblers. It occupies a perfect position as a resting and feeding site for farmland waders like snipe

who gather in considerable numbers in autumn and winter. Road development threatens.
35.2ha

WALTHAMSTOW RESERVOIRS (TWA)** — *All year*

Perhaps best known for its heronry which is going from strength to strength; other breeding species include Canada geese, pochard, tufted duck and the important, but declining, mute swans. They are also noted for waders while the numbers of terns on passage in autumn and spring may reach double figures. It is a most important nature reserve within the confines of the metropolis, and a particularly interesting place to go bird-watching.
133ha

WILLLIAM CURTIS ECOLOGICAL PARK (Ecological Parks Trust Res) — *All year*

16 Vine Lane, Tooley Street, SE1
An urban wildlife reserve created from unlikely conditions. Exposed house foundations provide cover and a pond provides wetland where frogs and newts breed; 300 plant species have been recorded and birds include herons and black redstarts, once common in post war London but now a rarity — in all more than 30 bird species have been recorded. An excellent use of urban dereliction to the benefit of wildlife and the many hundreds of children and adults who enjoy the natural history of the area.
2ha

WIMBLEDON COMMON — *All year*
(Parkside, Wimbledon SW19)

On the high ground there is a heathland flora with gorse and birch scrub extremely attractive to birds like yellowhammers, in the past linnets would have nested here. Lower down the oak and hornbeam woodland supports redstarts, willow warblers, blackcaps, garden warblers and nuthatches; tree creepers are frequent visitors and probably breed, and greater spotted and green wood-

Woodmouse   *Wimbledon Common*

pecker occur. Where the clay is thickest in the valley bottoms water has collected in the form of bogs and marshy areas where round-leaved sundew, bog bean and bog asphodel are found growing in the acid water. Over the mossy carpet that covers some of the wetter areas there's an excellent dragonfly and butterfly population. The amphibians include common frogs and toads, and while grass snake and common lizard are not common, they do occur.

The predatory bird population includes tawny owls, kestrels and sparrowhawks, and while urban foxes and badgers are found in quieter parts of the common there is not one single Womble, despite diligent searching by several generations of children. However, there are large numbers of grey squirrels, and woodmice in plenty and bank and short-tailed field voles, shrews and hedgehogs.
341ha

HAMPSHIRE
&
ISLE OF WIGHT

The first place of natural history interest to be mentioned when a discussion of Hampshire is in progress between naturalists and bird-watchers is the New Forest, immediately followed with equal enthusiasm by Langstone Harbour, for they typify the atmosphere of the county; beautiful English woodland, miles of heathland purple with heather enhanced by sythe-winged hobby falcons, edged by a coastline indented with natural harbours, mudflats and saltings, alive with waders and geese. Yet to say this was all would be to understate the county that can boast of Gilbert White's Selborne and the magic landscape of W.H. Hudson who lived in Bournemouth.

The high white points of the Needles lend a curious detachment to the Isle of Wight, a mere few miles offshore, but almost a separate county with its red squirrels and unique butterfly, the Glanville fritillary, found nowhere else. The island is a microcosm of a chalk downland habitat with all the flora and fauna found on unimproved chalk grassland. With a relatively small resident human population in winter it's a peaceful place. In summer however, the island's cash crop of tourists arrive by all means to take advantage of this peace, removing what they seek by their presence; the fate of all tourists seeking nature.

"At Farringford" — Tennyson

Should all our churchmen foam in spite
At you, so careful of the right,
   Yet one lay-hearth would give you welcome
(Take it and come) to the Isle of Wight;

Where, far from noise and smoke of town,
I watch the twilight falling brown
   All round a careless-ordered garden
Close to the ridge of a noble down.

You'll have no scandal while you dine,
But honest talk and wholesome wine,
   And only hear the magpie gossip
Garrulous under a roof of pine:

For groves of pine on either hand,
To break the blast of winter, stand;

and further on, the hoary Channel
Tumbles a billow on chalk and sand.

There's a central spine of high chalk hills mirrored in Hampshire where they form a rampart topped with Iron Age forts and breast-shaped burial mounds of ancient warriors and their horses, covered with a Persian carpet of wild flowers alive with butterflies.

Langstone Harbour   *Hants I.O.W.*

Ten per cent of the nation's ancient woodland lies within the county's boundaries, and though the hurricane winds in October 1987 felled many of the beeches on the hangers, and toppled ancient field oaks, the wildlife survived suprisingly well. Perhaps that terrible night made us think more about our landscape, changed overnight by a natural catastrophe. It also made us look more closely at human intervention — farming, forestry, and the lack of foresight on the part of road planners and builders.

Hampshire's population is growing rapidly which may threaten the county's secret places. Tourism is a bone of contention in the New Forest, but no more so than the Forestry Commission with their reliance upon alien conifers that has wreaked such havoc. Once there were butterflies in plenty, now they are far fewer in number and in species.

The heath fires in 1976 reduced the number and species of creatures living on the pockets of sandy heath found all over the county in a wide band up into Surrey. The Dartford warbler has been greatly reduced in numbers and range by fires, and by habitat destruction caused through industry and housing. The adder, *persona non grata* in an urban situation, and the smooth snake, a reptile tied to dry heathland, cannot survive the housing estates and factory complexes that have sprung up in the past decade; sand lizards and other creatures like the nightjar have given way before the road, the bulldozer and conifer.

However, there seems less impact here from modern farming methods than in many other counties in the soft underbelly of the country, perhaps away from the chalk hills with their corn, wheat and rape fields, the dry sandy soil is too acid, too fast draining to withstand the pressure of arable farming on a massive scale. Hampshire, like its neighbour Dorset, is not ashamed to be rural and willing to fight for the better aspects of the landscape. Heathland is one of our most endangered national environmental assets, Hampshire has an abundance and is justly proud of this natural heritage.

CARRISBROOKE WALK NATURE TRAIL (IOW Natural, History and Archeological Society) — *Spring, summer*

One of a series of Island walks taking you through deep cut lanes and open woodland where there's a badger sett. The trail is further enhanced by a small stream, and in spring it's a delight with migrant and resident songbirds.
6.4-8km – Map ref: SZ 484876

CATHERINGTON DOWN (HCC/Hants & IOW NT) —*Spring, summer*

This southern finger of downland is a living page of history, the banks of the ancient field systems are dense with chalk-loving plants, especially the uncommon round-headed rampion with its thistle-like blue flowers so attractive to butterflies and day flying moths such as burnet. Orchids include pyramidal and autumn lady's tresses.
12ha – Map ref: SU 689141

COMPTON DOWN (NT) — *Spring, summer*

At the end of the Pliestocene Ice Age the sea levels began to rise and melt water flooded the depleted oceanic basins, the sea cut through the downlands of southern England and northern France creating the Channel and separating the Isle of Wight from the mainland. As the river valleys and estuary system, now Southampton Water, were flooded, the soft chalk between the island and Dorset was swept away leaving chalk cliffs on either coast.

Compton Down forms the most southerly arm of this exposed chalk strata, and like all islands specialised plants thrived. However, like much of the Downs in southern England the Isle of Wight's chalk pastureland and sheep grazing were "improved" for agriculture, although this is one of the few places left where all the plants normally thought of as being associated with English chalk downland such as carline thistle, horseshoe vetch and a hundred others can be found.

Needless to say the butterflies are spectacular. Adonis and chalkhill blues, dark green fritillaries, gatekeepers, meadow browns and very occasionally marbled whites and, of course, the Island's speciality the Glanville fritillary whose larvae feed on plantains and hibernate in groups in the warm dampness of the undercliff. They are enclosed in webs like small spiders, preparing for spring and the serious work of eating. The butterfly is very attractive, but it is far rarer on the Island now than in former times being badly affected in the past by collecting.
40ha – Map ref: SZ 368854

CRAB WOOD (HCC/Hants & IOW NT) — *Spring, summer*

Growing on clay soil with flints and chalk Crab Wood is of considerable age. Predominantly oak over a varied understory, many mature trees have been heavily cropped

Glanville Fritillary   *Compton Down*

and others suffered in the hurricane of 1987. Among the other species are yew, ash, field maple and smaller shrubby plants like wayfaring tree and spindle bushes which grow on the richer soils. The less fertile damp soils have a covering of holly and willows, aspen and birch. Solomon's Seal, a plant of ancient woodland, occurs here with a variety of other beautiful flowers like primroses, violets, lily of the valley and honeysuckle, the food plant of the white admiral butterfly and beloved of the common dormouse which uses the thin papery strips of the bark to make its wren-like nests. The woods supports nightingales and nightjars; and there are many migrant songbirds in spring to compete with the resident thrushes, blackbirds and robins. Fallow and roe deer also thrive in this very attractive and productive wood.
36ha – Map ref: SU 436298

FRESHWATER MARSH (South Wight BC) — *Spring, summer*

This reed bed and marsh on the headwater of the western Yar is a superb mix of wetland plants, insects, birds and amphibians. The marsh is a blaze of colour when the purple loosestrife is in bloom and the flowers attract a large number of butterflies. The position of this reserve encourages landfalls of continental butterflies such as clouded yellows and the paler Berger's clouded yellow; painted lady, red admiral, peacock and small tortoiseshell butterflies are common. There is a very good breeding bird population with willow, sedge and reed warblers, and reed buntings in some numbers. The presence of cuckoos in spring is an interesting sight as they wait for the warblers to lay eggs so they can take over the nests.
16ha – Map ref: SZ 347862

KEYHAVEN-LYMINGTON MARSHES (HCC/Hants & IOW NT) — *All year*

A large area of particularly productive mudflats and salt marsh on the Solent facing the Isle of Wight. Its sheltered nature makes it very attractive to water birds and waders in winter, and the mixture of mud and marine deposits provides ample food for the molluscs and worms that inhabit the ooze. Thousands of dunlin winter here, feeding on the bonanza exposed by every low tide and flocks of Brent geese, sometimes 500 or more, feed on the eelgrass. There are also large numbers of wigeon, teal, long-tailed duck and many others; the most elegant of all the dabbling duck, the pintail, this long-necked bird comes to the Solent every winter in considerable numbers to join goldeneye and red-breasted merganser prior to the breeding season.

The waders also include godwit and huge numbers of lapwings, and herons fish in the low tide gullies for flounders and mullet. In very hard weather when the inland waterways are frozen kingfishers come down to the sea to find open water and fish for their small prey.
277.6ha – Map ref: SZ 300908 / 333945

LANGSTONE HARBOUR (RSPB)* — *Spring through winter*

Langstone Harbour has an ephemeral quality, perhaps because the mud and shingle vanishes beneath the tide; but it is this twice-daily flooding of salt water that makes the mudflats so productive for wildfowl and waders. Every winter up to 7000 Brent geese fly to this safe haven; they were almost extinguished in this country by uncontrolled wildfowling, but now have protection under the law and their numbers appear to be stabilising.

They feed on eelgrass and soft seaweeds that thrive in estuarine conditions and as this type of food is prolific here the birds are doing well. In places they are exceptionally tame allowing close inspection from the sea-wall and the several car parks around the harbour; pedestrians can get a good view from the causeway across to Hayling Island.

In the middle of the reserve several islands of mud and shingle support one of Britain's largest little tern colonies, there's also a sizeable common tern breeding area, but naturally there is no access to these sensitive sites where ringed plover and redshank also breed.

The waders draw bird-watchers from far afield. Grey plover are quite dramatic as they spin past on a brisk wind, and the wheeling dunlin flocks look like wreaths of smoke as they dash about in panic at the approach of a wintering peregrine falcon. The variety and numbers of duck are virtually unmatched in southern England and the complete protection of this site for nature is an international necessity.
554ha – Map ref: SU 697058

LOWER TEST MARSHES (Hants & IOW NT)** — *All year*

One of the best botanical sites in Hampshire, in summer the water meadows are a blaze of colour and life, thronged with dragonflies, damselflies, butterflies and day flying moths. The 450 species of plants include green-winged orchid, and the bird population is extensive with a superb selection of migrant breeding warblers including grasshopper warbler. In the late evening in spring the marshes are alive with the bleat of snipe "drumming". Sparrowhawks, kestrels and buzzards can be seen, and the occasional marsh harrier and merlin visits in winter; the considerable wildfowl include wigeon grazing the rich vegetation on the marsh.
110ha

LUDSHOTT COMMON NATURE WALKS (Ludshott Common Committee / NT) — *Spring, summer*

Situated in the eastern corner of the county this series of heathland walks are very productive. Adders and slow worms as well as common lizards are frequently seen. Adders tend to avoid any contact with humans or larger animals and though their bite is poisonous they are not naturally aggressive, sadly they have a poor public image and are often killed by foolish people thinking they are doing good, in fact the adder is a vital link in the economy of heathland.
Various lengths – Map ref: SU 850360

MARTIN DOWN (NCC) — *Spring, summer*

A truly wonderful area of chalk downland, used by Hudson as the setting for his book "A Shepherd's Life". The careful managment of downland involves sheep grazing to produce and maintain the short turf necessary to sustain the flowerly sward with its rare grassland plants such as field fleawort, bastard toadflax, the unusual dwarf sedge and myriad orchids such as bee, fly, fragrant, frog and burnt tip orchid all found here.

Bokerley Dyke and Grim's Ditch are sites of enormous archaeological interest containing Iron Age deposits and burial mounds clearly visible on the unploughed hillsides. This is a very special reserve and the wardens have been successful in maintaining the diversity by grazing and brush cutting areas that had previously lost much of their special character.

Butterflies include chalkhill, adonis blue, Duke of Burgundy fritillary and dark green fritillary, the food plant of the former being the downy undersides of cowslip leaves. Another important and declining butterfly is the silver-spotted skipper. Birdlife is immensely varied, especially where scrub has been allowed to invade; nightingales occur in spring. Stone curlew used to nest on the downs, but have ceased to breed here although they still feed on the short turf. Winter birds include short-eared owls, but barn owls are present for much of the year hovering over the mammal-rich turf searching for voles. Kestrels, sparrowhawks and buzzards also hunt here, the latter feeding on the rabbits so vital to the maintenance of the area. Reptiles are well represented with many adders who find the short grazed turf to their liking.

Hudson would still be able to find a flavour of his "Shepherd's" downland here, although elsewhere in the county and in adjoining Dorset and Wiltshire many thousands of hectares of chalk grassland have been ploughed. Martin Down shows us a tiny corner of the once vast tapestry. Nearby downland is under military control, but hopefully in the future it will come under the NCCs care and with proper environmental management will help to maintain the gene pool of this vital and beautiful natural habitat.

249ha – Map ref: SU 058192

Bee Orchid   *Martin Down (Hants)*

NEW FOREST (FC/others) — *All year*

Of all the pleasures few can compare to walking in the green shade of a quiet forest in spring when the air is alive with birdsong. The New Forest is the largest area of old woodland in north western Europe and owes its continuance to the infertility of the soil and basic stubbornness of the people who have owned the grazing rights for hundreds of years, but it is under a multitude of threats from housing, industrial development, roads, recreation and the Forestry Commission whose remit is to grow wood as quickly as possible. Sadly the sandy soil and wide heaths lend themselves to the planting of alien conifers and huge tracts that once held broadleaved forest have vanished in the gloom and infertility of pine needles.

The Forest was once the happy hunting ground of Kings and the deer still try to avoid man with good reason for together with the semi-wild ponies they are frequent road casualties. In the Victorian era entomology was one of the main pastimes of country parsons and the New Forest was a mecca for them where they could find huge numbers of different species. One of the Edwardian collector/ entomologist /artists, F.W. Frohawk, a superb observer of fine detail, was the first to notice the variation which sometimes occurs in the ground colour of the wings of the female silver-washed fritillary butterfly, a variety he named Valenzina. He also called his daughter, lady Valenzina Bolingbroke, after this butterfly.

The mammals of the forest are many, but generally it is the ponies that cause the most interest as they graze the close cropped turf of the natural forest lawns. In autumn and winter when most visitors have gone and the forest is left to the verderers who maintain its herds, the deer, for which the area was originally preserved in medieval times, come into their own. Fallow, red and roe deer all occur and recently muntjac deer have been sighted. The red deer are very rare as are the similarly-shaped and antlered sika deer from Asia which escaped from collections and a few bred in the forest.

Foxes and badgers are common as are stoats, weasels and feral cats, tame moggies that have taken to the country life. The sheer number of birds is astounding, a huge acreage of heathland, part of the general area of the forest, supports its own special birds, the nightjar is one and the stonechat another, and the hobby falcon with its long scythe-like wings and mastery of flight; they are most exciting to watch especially when the parents are teaching their young the art of hunting dragonflies. Fortunately the insect population is sufficient to stand the predation. Many other birds of prey, including the very rare Montague's harrier distinguishable by its bouyant flight occur over the heathlands and forest.

This is one of our national treasures, some of the trees were saplings in the time of William and Mary and there are other, even older trees, and although many are moribund they provide food for rare beetles and the woodpeckers that feed upon them in turn. The forest covers a very large area and it would be hard to explore it all, but it is worth the effort for it is a very special place constantly changing with the seasons.

37,560ha

OLD WINCHESTER HILL (NCC) — *Spring, summer*

There is a certain magic about this reserve with its ramparts of an old Iron Age multivallate fortified hilltop — Scrub is a vital habitat for a wide range of migrant warblers, there's plenty of it here with an abundance of lime-loving woody species such as spindleberry and in spring the birdsong is glorious. Yew woodland, typical of the forest cover on the Wiltshire downs and beech woodland with ash and coppiced hazel is much in evidence and the banks on top of the hill support an unusually large population of round-headed rampion, a relatively common plant before 90 per cent of the downland was altered by agriculture, now it's found only in a few favoured areas.

The turf is extremely rich in flowers including yellow wort, clustered bellflower, harebells and wild mignonette. The orchids too are superb with an unusually large population of frog orchids, one of the smaller species but fascinating for all that. In all 14 species have been recorded here. Birds are attracted to the many different habitats and yellowhammers sing from the juniper bushes, a particular plant of chalk downland.
60ha – Map ref: SU 647210

SELBORNE HILL (NT) — *Spring, summer*

The Reverend Gilbert White, justly acclaimed as the father of modern natural history, lived and worked here, noting the plants that grew on the common and the nearby Selborne hanger as he took his walks. The pollarded beeches are greatly overgrown as are the coppice stools, relics of an old method of woodland management that relied more on men and less on animals to keep the woodland floor open. The ground flora is varied and ranges from stitchwort, red campion and wood sorrel to dog's mercury, enchanter's nightshade, foxgloves, ferns and wild rose.

White noted with precision the day-to-day life of the plants, animals, birds and insects that shared his small Hampshire village world, and we are indebted to him for his observations.
97.4ha – Map ref: SU 735337

TENNYSON DOWN AND THE NEEDLES (NT) — *Spring, summer*

The massive eroded chalk point of Tennyson down appears unfinished, cut in sharply curving bays and eroded into white pinnacles of chalk rock known as the Needles, it is part of a larger block of downland that has been broken away by weather and the rising sea levels at the end of the last ice age. The Needles point to the chalk of Dorset and it is believed that a land bridge once existed between Tennyson's island and Thomas Hardy's county. The plants growing here today are dwarfed by salt winds, but like dwarf thistle, shortened clustered bellflower and harebell have adjusted well to the conditions.

Butterflies are one of the delights of the area which slopes down to the coloured rocks and sands of Alum Bay, continental species can be seen in large numbers and painted lady's are particularly evident. Marbled whites are among the special butterflies and the island's most famous insect the Glanville fritillary also occurs here, although nowhere is it common.
77.6ha – Map ref: SU 324855

UPPER HAMBLE COUNTRY PARK (HCC) — *Spring, summer*

There's little doubt that there has been a wood on this site for thousands of years for as well as oak there are small-leaved lime and wild service or chequer trees, and large clumps of wild honeysuckle climb to the light around some of the trees. In spring the woodland beside the river Hamble is a delight of bluebells together with another indicator of ancient woodland, butcher's broom with its spiky deep green leaves and brilliant red berries. White admiral butterflies are found here from late June to mid July flying as though on invisible wires in and out of sunny clearings.
163ha – Map ref: SU 490114

The following reserves are all part of The Wealden Edge Hangers:-

WEALDEN EDGE HANGERS (HCC) — *Spring, summer*
129.2ha

ASHFORD CHACE (HCC)
86.4ha – Map ref: SU 729266

RESTON ROUNDHILL & HAPPERSNAPPER HANGERS (HCC)
17.6ha – Map ref: SU 749271

THE WARREN (HCC)
24.8ha – Map ref: SU 728288

These beautiful and spectacular woodlands of beech and oak, seeming to hang onto the sides of steep chalk slopes, are a relic of the forest that once covered much of the Hampshire and Sussex chalklands. These have remained largely because they were the only crop that could be grown upon the steeply sloping ground, the natural cover of these hills would have been yew woodland; in the age of the long bow, yew was the raw material of the bowmakers of England, now it is mainly used for making small pieces of furniture while larger trees are used for veneer. veneer.

Below the yews there is little growth because the dense canopy shades out virtually every other living thing, but in other parts of the hangers where beech or ash are the main trees there is a greater diversity of woodland flora with helleborines, and in early spring dense beds of bluebells, flowers always associated with beech and ash woods. The bird population tends to vary with the tree and shrub cover, but in late autumn the sticky red berries of yew and their seeds, poisonous to men, horses and cattle are an important food source for thrushes from home and abroad. In spring the dense canopy provides excellent nesting sites for a host of birds, as long as there is open woodland nearby where the adults can find food for their young.

Regular cropping of the trees ensures their survival, when the trees are clear felled numerous opportunist chalkland plants such as mullein, musk thistle and rosebay willow-herb grow in profusion only to vanish as the canopy is closed again by newly grown trees; either through planting or natural regeneration this cycle can produce superb populations of common butterflies while the plants bloom.

WEST YAR NATURE TRAIL (IOW Natural, History & Archeological Society.) — *Spring, summer*

A riverside trail leading to fresh water marsh along the side of the river Yar. There is much to see, but autumn and winter are best for waders and wildfowl, while spring and summer brings a wide variety of salt marsh plants into flower including marsh mallow with its beautiful flowers and deeply cut felt-like leaves.
8km – Map ref: SZ 354897

YATELEY COMMON COUNTRY PARK (HCC) — *Spring through autumn*

Situated on the greensand of the North Downs beyond Farnborough, the open heathland and man-made lake at Wyndhams Pool supports a wide range of heathland species, heather, bell heather and cross-leaved heath occur depending upon the amount of moisture in the sandy soil. The uncommon heathland butterfly the silver studded blue is seen in some numbers in June and July and dragonflies are a feature of the type of habitat found here, there are many species including several damselfly varieties. The reserve is excellent for birds, and the presence of sparrowhawks and kestrels indicates the productivity of the area.
197ha – Map ref: SU 822597 / 838594

HEREFORD
&
WORCESTER

Lying in a well favoured triangle between Wales, the west country and the industrial Midlands, the Malvern Hills and Black Mountains wring just the right amount of moisture from the clouds before they blow over the low ground; in fact the two counties have a climate similar to Somerset or even further south.

The bedrock of Hereford and Worcester is mixed, but in the main very ancient, the soft rounded Malverns are some of the oldest rocks in the Midlands, laid down or extruded from the mantle, in the turbulent era known as Precambrian, the longest period in the history of the Earth and the most momentous. At the end of the Precambrian period, although life on Earth was at its most basic level, plants had begun to evolve and the previously sterile atmosphere of the planet began to receive oxygen into its gaseous envelope; the key that would lead to all higher forms of animals had been turned and the complex web of life begun in earnest.

In their lifetime the Malverns have seen mountains, continents and seas come and go, they have witnessed the rise of the coal swamps and their demise, and know the secret that brought the dinosaurs to their knees, for they were ancient when the Silurian rocks of the Woolhope Hills were a series of bright coral reefs alive with sponges and flickering with the jerky movements of cephalopods and the first primitive fish that swam over the pulverised coral sand between the reefs.

Old red sandstone and marls form the base of a variety of soils from the fertile river valleys of the Wye, the Roach and the Severn and the flowery uplands to the heavily cultivated Vale of Evesham, once a mass of apple trees laden with gorgeous Worcester apples. The people that grew these apples had a long warlike lineage, especially those who lived in the areas between the Wye and the Monnow, known as the Archenfield, which extends almost to Hereford where in Saxon times the Welsh made friends with the invader and for their support were rewarded by being allowed to keep their ancient customs and culture and to sit in council with the Saxon warlords. At Welshford, where the Roman road crossed the Wye, the river takes on its west country guise winding through steep limestone hillsides until it reaches the spectacular gorge at Symonds Yat.

Despite the M5 and M50 which slice through the area the effect of heavy traffic is felt less here than in other parts of the country. Summer time at Breedon is still unspoiled enough to make you sing, and it's easy to see why this hill formed such a vital link in "A Shropshire Lad" which Houseman wrote in 1896 and which later on was set to music.

"Oh see how thick the goldcup flowers
    Are lying in field and land,
With dandelions to tell the hours
    That never are told again.
Oh may I squire you round the meads
    And pick you posies gay?
- Twill do no harm to take my arm.
"You may young man, you may"

Here, as in virtually every other county in these crowded isles, the land has been exploited by man, often for thousands of years. There are brine springs, worked for salt since Roman times and the man-made demands upon the salt deposits, together with the natural action of water, have created underground cavities which have fallen in upon themselves producing slacks and subsidence ponds that teem with life and often harbour a salt marsh flora, despite their distance from the sea. It is marvellous to see how nature exploits every niche available to her.

If Breedon Hill in Worcestershire is best known as the well spring of A.E. Houseman's verse, then the village of Bredwardine in Herefordshire marks the end of the short life of the diarist the Reverend Francis Kilvert. It was here that he wrote the last chapter of his diary before his untimely death from peritonitis in 1879. His detailed reflections on the life, people and countryside of the late Georgian and early Victorian eras were set down with a gentle humour. Reading them you feel as if the whole of country life in those days were being discussed not just a small backwater. Kilvert's Diary is, of course, the reason why so many people make the pilgrimage to Hereford and nearby Clyro in Radnorshire to see his countryside for themselves. It still exists in small pockets, all are worth searching for, the same species of birds sing in spring, buzzards soar over the hills, the same type of butterflies feed on the same flowers and the rocks and trees are much as when he was alive.

BOYNES COPPICE AND MEADOW (Worcestershire NCT)** — *Spring, summer*

At the heart of this reserve is an ancient ridge and furrow field system, a type of agriculture dictated by simple ploughing methods dating back to a time when fields were managed communally on a strict system of crop rotation and pasture. Ridge and furrow, with its variable moisture content, produces conditions favourable to the growth of a great number of plants and insects that are now uncommon; plants such as the elegant dyer's green weed, a legume used by the cloth trade for 1000 or more years to make a yellow dye — (when mixed with woad it is transmuted into a beautiful green, hence it's name). Green-winged orchids also thrive here and the area is excellent for butterflies.
1.2ha

CHADDESLEY WOODS (NCC) — *Spring, summer*

A jubilee walk runs through this area of mixed conifer woodland growing on the site of an ancient wood; broadleaved trees include wild service and small-leaved lime which together with some of the ground flora indicates that the site has probably supported woodland for millennia. The many different broadleaved trees provide food for a large variety of birds while the conifers provide nest sites. Where the geology is variable there is a fine show of bluebells in spring.
100ha – Map ref: SO 914736

CLENT HILLS COUNTRY PARK (H and WCC) — *All year*

A large reserve with a wide range of habitats and a good number of mammals, including fallow deer. The woodland is particularly rich in tree pipits, redstarts and willow warblers, and plenty of predators including sparrowhawks and kestrels; both species breed in the park.
148ha – Map ref: SO 927798

COMMON HILL & MONUMENT (Hereford & Radnor NT)** — *Spring, summer*

Limestone grassland with a wide range of plants including pale cinquefoil and green-winged orchid. The snail population suffers predation from a colony of glow-worms.
2ha

DOWARD GROUP (Hereford & Radnor NT)** — *Spring, summer*

White rocks, Woodside and Leeping Stocks constitute an area where nature is returning to ancient woodland of oak and beech and a mixture of other species. Heathy areas and old meadowland enchance the variety of habitats.

The three reserves should be treated as one as each is closely related and their boundaries allow easy progression one to the other. Insects, birds and wild plants abound and in spring and early summer the area is a delight with woodland butterflies, green-winged and greater butterfly orchids, broadleaved and white helleborine and violets growing in profusion in the woodland margins, while the meadows provide a food source for the larvae of silver-washed and pearl-bordered fritillary

White Admiral - Wyre Forest   *Hereford & Worcs.*

butterflies. White admiral butterflies also occur and their numbers are increasing.
16.5ha

DUKE OF YORK MEADOW (Worcestershire NCT) — *Spring, summer*

An area of unimproved old meadowland famous for its show of wild daffodils and green-winged orchids; there is a good butterfly population including common blue and small copper.
2.3ha – Map ref: SO 782354

EADES MEADOW AND FOSTERS GREEN MEADOWS (Worcestershire NCT)** — *Summer*

These two meadows have very restricted access, but are a reminder of what hay meadows once looked like. The Maytime flowers are a delight and because the area has been managed for hay for centuries the plant cover is very varied with green-winged orchid, cowslip, adder's tongue and, where the soil is less well drained, ragged robin and cuckoo flower. The presence of the latter ensures a large number of orange tip butterflies while the bumble bee population is encouraged by the meadow's autumn plants. This is one of the best places in Britain to see the beautiful pink flowers of meadow saffron, a species of crocus.
12.2ha

HARTLEBURY COMMON (H and WCC) — *Spring, summer*

An important lowland heath with bogs and pools, a superb habitat for dragonflies — a delight in the late summer. The reserve supports a wide range of insects with butterflies and moths particularly abundant, and the rich insect life encourages swallows and martins, whinchats and stonechats.
91ha – Map ref: SO 820705

HUNTHOUSE WOOD (Worcestershire NCT)** — *Spring, summer*

A stream has cut down through the coal measures showing a profile of the varying types of rocks from limestone to sandstone and the coal seams themselves. The variation in the rocks imparts considerable diversity to the flora and there are some superb specimens of wild cherry growing on the hillsides; some are of great age and girth. The amount of dead timber left after the Dutch elm epidemic has added to the insect life and created nest sites and food for woodpeckers and other birds that take up squatters rights in old woodpecker holes. The number of woodland birds reflects the immense variety of insects and plants, and the abundance of nest sites ensure an excellent range of springtime nesting species.
24.4ha

THE KNAPP AND PAPERMILL (Worcestershire NCT) — *Spring, summer*

The woodland, wet meadow and streamside environment reflects a pattern of countryside management that has almost passed into history, but there are relics of its existence in the coppiced hazel and lime, alder, ash and pollarded crack willow indicating an old economy based on tree products. The understory of shrubs and plants encourages a wide range of birds and insects, and the woodland provides a safe haven for badgers and foxes with ample food for large and small predators. The meadowland is rich in wild flowers, including common spotted and marsh orchids while cowslips and primroses grow in close proximity and hybrids of the two species, resembling oxlips, occur frequently.
24ha – Map ref: SO 748522

LEA AND PAGET'S WOODS (Hereford & Radnor NT) — *Spring, summer*

These limestone woodlands have a superb show of plants on the woodland floor, including wild liquorice. The trees are typical of limestone woodland with wild cherry and ash and, together with the oaks found in Paget's Wood, are excellent providers of insect food for birds. Needless to say the range of spring warblers is superb with garden warblers, blackcaps, chiffchaffs and willow warblers.
9ha – Map ref: SO 597342 / 598344

MALVERN HILLS (Malvern Hills Conservators) — *Spring through autumn*

The Malvern Hills are formed from some of the oldest rocks in the country and are the remains of a range of hills worn to stubs by the passage of time. They have been exploited by man for road stone, and quarrying has cut into their rounded and rather infertile curves providing plants with a roothold and birds with nest sites. The wildness and ageless quality of the Malvern scenery attracts tens of thousands of visitors every year.

The plant cover is not spectacular, rather it is specialised and some plants like the stonecrop orpine have adapted to make the best of a difficult environment. The rounded beauty of the hilltops is enhanced by the deep valley woodlands and the birds and insects in these woods are extremely varied. If there is a typical bird of these hills it must be the buzzard, circling lazily in search of a meal on the thermals issuing upwards like natural springs of air from the sun-warmed ancient rocks.
600ha – Map ref: SO 768454

MARSH WARBLER SITES (Worcestershire NCT)** — *Summer*

A series of nine very aptly named areas of marshland and scrub providing nesting sites for up to one third of the country's marsh warbler population. Permits and information from the Trust.
9ha

MOCCAS PARK (NCC) — *Spring, summer*

An ancient deer park with associated beetle fauna. Three species of beetles occur here that are found nowhere else in Britain. The open parkland is excellent for birds, mammals and many other insects. It is a balanced habitat that has been modified by man and deer over the centuries.
140ha

NUNNERY WOOD COUNTRY PARK(H and WCC) — *Spring through autumn*

Nunnery Wood Country Park is ancient woodland managed by man for at least 900 years; the plant cover and trees reflect this great age in the variety of species. The wood has been managed by the traditional method of oak standards over coppice of hazel and hornbeam, aspen and ash and there is also hawthorn as a consequence of this management regime. Bird and insect life is extensive and in spring the normal range of migrant warblers may be swelled by a breeding pair of nightingales. The availability of food and dead and ageing timber encourages woodpeckers to nest and all three species are present. Sparrowhawks and tawny owls are among the predators of the abundant small birds and mammals; foxes are also present.
25ha – Map ref: SO 877543

RANDAN WOOD (Worcestershire NCT)** — *Spring, summer*

Randan Wood has been the site of a special study on fungi, over 300 species have been identified; the area would appear to have been part of an ancient forest with small-leaved lime and wild service tree, and the understory has a range of shrubs including alder buckhorn; tutsan grows here as does a strange parasitic plant ivy broomrape. Mammals are varied and include badgers.
4.8ha

UPTON WARREN (Worcestershire NCT)** — *All year*

This fascinating area was formed when the ground which had been undermined by salt extraction slumped and surface water flooded the depressions creating pools and lakes some of which were brackish. This produced a habitat similar to that found on salt marshes enabling certain plants to grow here such as sea-spurrey and spear-leaved orache.

The wetland is of great importance to visiting wildfowl and considerable numbers arrive in winter to take advantage of the food supply; it is also of great value as a place for migrants such as waders and terns to stop over; the elegant black tern oftern appears here on passage. The reserve is on a flight line that allows birds like godwits and whimbrel to rest and feed on their migrations, while the reed beds surrounding the largest of the subsidence pools are popular with breeding duck, warblers and grebes.

Swallows and house martins are common in summer and in winter small finches find a substantial food supply on this very important reserve.
24ha

WASELEY HILLS COUNTRY PARK (H and WCC) —*Spring, summer*

In spring this reserve, which includes the Sedgbourne Coppice Conservation Area, is a riot of bluebells, and later on the bird population is substantially swelled by the many breeding species that occupy the abundant nest sites in the scrubby woodland areas. Small mammals and foxes are common and kestrels and owls take advantage of a ready food supply.
54ha – Map ref: SO 979768

WYRE FOREST (NCC) — *Spring, summer*

A Plantagenet hunting forest, the Wyre has remained woodland mainly because man has used it as such. The regime of coppice with standards of oak, both pedunculate and sessile, has ensured that this superb environment with all its many insects, mammals, birds and plants should remain relatively intact.

The water that feeds the forest is Dowles Brook, a clear fast running stream with an immense head of life between its banks, such as salmon and trout, and that odd fishy hangover from a past age the lamprey. Within the confines of the forest some of the original tree cover has been replaced with alien species which provide only a fraction of the food resources. However, they do increase the number of nest sites available for certain birds, and long-eared owls sometimes breed here. The sheer diversity of the Wyre provides nest and feeding sites for a host of birds from the wrens and woodpeckers that live here all year round to the elegant hole-nesting pied flycatchers. Wood and grasshopper warblers are also found here as are most of the common warbler species and along the forest's margins, where there is scrub, blackcaps and willow warblers add to the dramatic dawn chorus.

Badgers and foxes are common and breed within the forest, and a wealth of small mammals are responsible for the presence of a healthy population of tawny owls and kestrels while small ground predators like weasels and stoats are common, though less noticeable. The insects and plants form the basis of the woodland economy and the immense productivity and diversity ensures a healthy overall population. One particularly odd creature is a caddis (Enoicyla pusilla) which lives its life not in water, but in wet leaf litter at the base of a tree; this strange insect larvae builds a tube into which it can retreat at the first sign of danger and from there it feeds on dead plant material.

Other insects are more showy and less retiring than the non aquatic caddis, and many species of moth are to be found in the forest canopy and foliage, including some that are nationally quite rare. Butterflies too are common in the woodlands and in the rides. The uncommon and beautiful high brown fritillary and its cousin the silver-washed fritillary vie for nectar on thistle flowers in high summer. This is one of the country's very special places, that it has remained relatively intact is something of a miracle, let us hope this state of affairs will continue.
300ha – Map ref: SO 759766

HERTFORDSHIRE

In times past Hertfordshire was a haunt of Royalty. Henry VII and Anne Bolyn had a secret meeting place near Hemel Hempstead and later their daughter, Elizabeth I, was a virtual prisoner in the beautiful confines of Hatfield House; in the 20th century the county was home to another equally famous and well loved Elizabeth, the Queen Mother, whose childhood home was St Paul's Waldenbury in the rural heart of the county.

These days Hertfordshire is interlaced with roads and awash with people flooding to the south east in search of prosperity. This massive influx has led to the degradation of many wild places, not helped by the agressive regime of farming encouraged by EEC agricultural policies such as the removal of many hundreds of miles of hedgerows, straw and stubble burning plus the loss of elms through Dutch elm disease. Nevertheless, the county still possesses much beauty, and the level of public awareness is such that any move to degrade the countryside further meets with stern objections.

Although I think of myself as a west countryman, I have lived for more than half my life in Hemel Hempstead the valley of the river Gade in Hertfordshire, a town like several other new communities in Hertfordshire that has quadrupled its population over the last thirty years, yet I can walk 150 yards from my front door to a rich ancient woodland full of birdsong and deep in bluebells in spring. Bluebells abound in Hertfordshire, as does that other indicator of ancient woodland, dog's mercury. These two plants thrive where the chalk and clay run side by side in overlapping strata. Much of the county is founded on chalk, from the Chiltern buttress around Berkhamsted and Tring to the wide, over-developed farmland of Royston where once, on Royston Heath, the chalkhill blue butterflies were so prolific they rose in blue clouds beneath the muzzles of the grazing sheep, so many were there that in the 1920s variations in the markings of their underwings inspired commercial collecting and study by several prominent amateur entomologists, foremost among them being P.M. Bright and H.A. Leeds, companions in the production of a monograph entitled The British Aberrations of the Chalkhill Blue Butterfly (Lysandra coridon).

Now all that remains of Royston Commons is a remnant of the field heath, the rest is gone to barley and rape. But to paint a gloomy picture of the wildlife potential would be to do it a disservice, and perhaps dissuade visitors. On the contrary there is much to be enjoyed. Superb woodlands with ancient pollarded beech trees, downland escarpments and disused watercress beds that bubble clear lime-rich water over shallow ponds where insects and fish form an abundant food source for migrant birds.

The Grand Union Canal runs through the county passing a microcosm of a landscape that has changed little since the well known political writer and keen observer of the countryside William Cobbett took his rural ride in the 1820s. He spoke of tall trees and meadows, some can still be seen today, and long may they remain. How a man-made watercourse can naturalise is seen in the rich flora and fauna along the canal banks, and the incredible diversity of birds, animals and plants that inhabit Tring reservoirs. Tring and its museum are associated with the Rothschild family; their collection has been left to the nation and now forms the country annexe to the British Museum of Natural History.

I have a personal connection with Tring reservoirs, having been an honorary NCC warden of the reservoir complex, and I'm in the process of creating a nature reserve within the grounds of another ex-Rothschild family estate, the world renowned health resort of 'Champneys at Tring'. Perhaps this is a pointer to the type of development taking place, where Hertfordshire's prosperity is used to improve and enhance its flora and fauna.

The Romans thought the valley of the river Ver a good place to set up their city of Verulamium, later to become St Albans. Despite being destroyed several times by the native population, on one occasion led by the Lady Budicca, the Romans considered that site to be so important they rebuilt it, each time more imposing than the last. After they left, the town fell into disrepair but rose again, like a phoenix from the ashes, in the form of building material, particularly tiles, which can still be seen in many of the county's ancient churches. Today the town is still a source of building materials, river terrace gravels are found in huge deposits, mined for the extensive industrial sites and roads that have erupted across the country, and the depressions left by the mining operations soon fill with ground water and naturalise into wetlands of considerable importance.

The Hertfordshire countryside provided inspiration for George Bernard Shaw who lived in the village of Ayot St Lawrence, a beautiful place with timber-framed cottages and a ruined church. The tradition of rural life seems strange in today's busy county yet there was a time when nightingales sang and glow-worms twinkled from hedges all over the county — in the 18th century the Berkhamsted poet Cowper was familiar with both these creatures.

"The Nightingale and the Glow-worm" — Cowper

A nightingale, that all day long
Had cheer'd the village with his song,
Nor yet at eve his note suspended,
Began to feel, as well he might,
The keen demands of appetite;
When, looking eagerly around,
He spied far off, upon the ground,
A something shining in the dark,
And knew the glow-worm by his spark:
So, stooping down from hawthorn top,
He thought to put him in his crop.
The worm, aware of his intent,
Harangu'd him thus, right eloquent —
Did you admire my lamp, quoth he,
As much as I your minstrelsy,
You would abhor to do me wrong,
As much as I to spoil your song;
For 'twas the self-same pow'r divine
Taught you to sing, and me to shine;
That you with music, I with light,
Might beautify and cheer the night.
The songster heard his short oration,
And, warbling out his approbation,
Releas'd him, as my story tells,
And found a supper somewhere else.

ASHRIDGE NATURE WALKS (Herts Natural History Society and Field Club/NT) — *Spring, summer*

Originally a Manor of thousands of acres, Ashridge was administered by a monastic order, then became the estate of the Earls of Bridgewater, better known for building canals. Now the land is owned by the National Trust and the historic house, with its hard 'clunch' stone chalk facing is a Management College.

The woods occupy only a tenth of their medieval size, nevertheless their diversity is almost unequalled in south east England, and they are superbly maintained by the Trust's foresters. Many of the trees are very old, some pollarded beech in Frithsden Copse have stood for nearly three centuries. Good management ensures a certain amount of dead timber remains on the forest floor to encourage insects and birds. The dawn chorus may have to compete with the occasional aircraft, but the content is rich and varied. The beech trees produce abundant seeds in 'mast' years, a major attraction for wintering flocks of bramblings and the occasional hawfinch that might breed in the quieter parts of the forest. Ashridge often produces a surprise, from the spring song of a visiting golden oriole, to the sudden appearance of a sparrowhawk taking chaffinches from the flocks that feed on crumbs dropped by picnickers. There are badgers and foxes and many small mammals; common dormice are present, although few in number.

When the bluebell plants that carpeted the woods in spring are full of seed and ready to burst open, the tall flower spikes of purple helleborine and their near relative the broad-leaved helleborine grow in the shade of the beechwoods together with bird's nest orchids.

1.2 and 2.4km - Map ref: SP 971131

BLAGROVE COMMON (Herts & Middx WT)** — *Summer*

When the glaciers that covered much of northern Hertfordshire during the Pleistocene period retreated, they left behind a strange mixture of soil types. Chalk and clay was scraped, or washed down, from the glacier's trailing edge and the resulting slurry compacted into chalky rubble and boulder clay, rich in nutrients and tending to impervious layers where spring water could be trapped beneath the topsoil. In time this produced perfect grazing conditions and hay meadows, but agricultural 'improvement' has left very few of the wet meadows.

Blagrove Common is one of the richest of its type. In spring and summer a wide variety of wild plants, especially orchids, thrive in the unimproved, grazed turf. It's an excellent site for the southern marsh orchid, and where the water is forced to the surface by an impervious layer of clay beneath, sedges and meadowsweet, marsh marigold and ragged robin are much in evidence. Grassland butterflies and insects are abundant and in late August the metallic wings of small copper butterflies shine in the sun as they spar with rivals and display while feeding on the soft blue flower heads of devil's bit scabious.

4.3ha

CASSIOBURY PARK (Herts & Middx WT)** — *Spring, summer*

The river Gade flows through this park, a quiet place trapped between motorway development and the busy expanding town of Watford. The river has to work for its living, rising from clear deep springs in the Gade valley above Hemel Hempstead, by the time it reaches the park it has flowed along the Grand Union Canal and carried freight and holiday traffic on its back, but it meanders through the park past alder trees and grassland rich in insects. There's still enough clarity and lime in the water to allow that interesting fresh water crustacean the crayfish to survive, along with minnows and the occasional trout.

The river runs through several areas where the water table is close to the surface allowing a marshy habitat to develop with willow and alder thickets, enhanced by disused watercress beds which have formed into pools and small lakes. This wetland provides superb feeding for nesting songbirds and in spring and early summer the whole of Cassiobury Woods rings with birdsong. In winter the alders attract siskins.

5.2ha

HERTFORD HEATH (Herts & Middx WT) — *All year*

Unlike the Dorset and Surrey Heaths, the soil at Hertford heath is based not on sand but on gravel, a relic of the Pleistocene Ice Age; this gravel and pebble bed rests on a base of stiff London clay which leads to a basically impoverished habitat that encourages plants like bracken interspersed with rowan trees and silver birch; heather, heath bedstraw and tormentil grow in thick mats. The woodland areas with their stands of oak, ash, beech and

Lemsford Springs   *Hertfordshire*

hornbeam together with a healthy growth of shrubs, impart a certain amount of fertility to an otherwise nutrient-starved habitat; birds and small mammals find ample feeding in the leaf litter and the fruits that fall from the trees and bushes. The woodland is also rich in fungi.

The London clay forms impervious depressions allowing water to collect creating pools and marshy areas where purple moor grass predominates; good for dragonflies and amphibians.

25ha – Map ref: TL 350106 / 354111

KINGS LANGLEY LAKE (Herts & Middx WT)** — *All year*

A loop of the Grand Union Canal forms the boundary to one side of this lake, the other being edged by industrial development; yet in the midst of this man-made habitat the variety of wildlife is considerable. In winter, wildfowl navigating through the valley drop down to rest (over 60 species of birds have been recorded here) and there are plenty of fish for fish-eating birds. It's an odd place to find common and arctic terns, or the occasional osprey, on route for Scotland in spring — and returning to Africa in autumn, hovering like a huge black and white kestrel as it searches the water for surface feeding fish.

5.2ha

LEMSFORD SPRINGS (Herts & Middx WT)** — *All year*

When the watercress beds ceased to be commercially productive they took on another more important role, that of a perfect wetland site for both migrant and resident waterlife; hides overlook the disused beds providing vantage points to observe green and purple sandpipers, water rails, and the reserve's speciality kingfishers.

Mallards breed here prolifically, and in spring the shallow water bobs with fluffy ducklings. There are also a very large number of unusual moluscs in the pure mineral-rich water and the reserve is noted for a colony of Roman snails. Star of Bethlehem is one of the more uncommon plants, and the insect fauna includes many dragonflies and damselflies, whilst the butterbur moth occurs at Lemsford Springs which is the only authenticated site for this creature in Hertfordshire.

Attempts to attract owls and kestrels by the provision of suitable nest boxes have been entirely successful.

3.7ha

NORTHAW GREAT WOOD COUNTRY PARK (Welwyn and Hatfield DC) — *Spring, summer*

Maintained by coppicing this wood has produced a fine range of habitats, superb for songbirds and breeding warblers and woodcock, though the latter is susceptible to disturbance. Generally speaking nightingales are uncommon in Hertfordshire but they have been heard frequently here. The ground flora numbers several species that indicate ancient woodland, and there's probably been a wood here for many thousands of years.

100ha – Map ref: TL 283038

PATMORE HEATH (Herts & Middx WT) — *Spring, summer*

One of the best examples of acid grassland on the Reading

beds of sand and pebbles. The heath was once heavily grazed by sheep which kept the scrub under control, now the management plan is to control the scrub manually to allow the rare and unusual plant life to thrive. Open heath plants such as marsh speedwell, heath grass and heath rush occur here and nowhere else in the county. The ponds are well known for a variety of dragonflies.
9.3ha – Map ref: TL 443257

PURWELL NINESPRINGS (Herts & Middx WT) — *All year*

As its name suggests this reserve is based on nine springs that issue from the Melbourn rock. Remnants of drainage channels, used in former times to control water levels, are now overgrown and the whole area encourages a wetland flora of considerable diversity with a bird population augmented by an influx of migrants in spring and autumn.
7ha

RYE HOUSE MARSH (RSPB) — *All year*

In the Lea Valley Park area, Rye House marsh consists of a range of habitats particularly good for birds. The pools and mud encourage sweet reed grass and willow and alder scrub, and on the wet meadowland ragged robin, pink water speedwell, fen bedstraw and common reed thrive. Sedge and grasshopper warblers breed here, and the loud explosive song of Cetti's warbler can be heard, while migrant waders such as spotted redshank and jack snipe are just some of the wide range of birds seen in autumn and winter. Siskin and beared tit are also occasional visitors.
7ha – Map ref: TL 387099

SAWBRIDGEWORTH MARSH (Herts & Middx WT/ ENT)** — *Spring, summer*

Lying in the valley of the river Stort this is the finest marsh of its type in the county, supporting a number of plants that are extremely rare in this region — marsh arrow-grass, marsh willow-herb and blunt-flowered rush. The reserve also shelters a rare mollusc, the slender amber snail, only found in one other site in East Anglia.

The marsh is managed by traditional methods of cutting and grazing and the willows are pollarded to maintain their integrity; the poles gathered from this operation are stacked to encourage invertebrates and small mammals to shelter and breed.
12ha

TRING RESERVOIRS (NCC and others) — *All year*

Built to supply water to the Tring Steps Lock Complex for the Grand Union Canal in the early 19th century by gangs of Irish workers known as Navigators or 'Navvys', this reserve has taken on the air of a series of natural lakes. Owned by the Rothschild estate and originally managed as a duck shoot, today it is under the control of the British Waterways Board and the NCC. The reservoirs assumed international importance as a wetland when the little-ringed plover and great-crested grebe began to breed here in the 1940s. (The breeding population of great-crested

Little Ringed Plover *Tring Reserviors*

grebe is higher here than at any other site in south eastern England.)

Scheduled as a reserve in 1955, the reservoirs have played host to many rare species. It would be tedious to list all the visitors, but there are regular sightings of osprey on passage, and in late summer hobbys bring their young to teach them to hunt.

Swallows, martins and swifts as well as dragonflies patrol the calm waters, particularly over the smallest of the lakes, Tringford; and in the largest, Wilstone, there's a huge population of fish and invertebrates and a species of very large catfish from the Danube, called wels. These were introduced in the early part of this century by the Rothschild family, one or two are caught by rod and line, as are extremely large pike; though none of the wels have grown to their full potential size, some fish of 50 or more pounds have been recorded. Wilstone is also one of the largest gull roosts in the country with 4000 to 5000 black-headed gulls recorded in winter.

The reservoirs have a particular claim to fame for the only British colony of reed nesting herons. They began to breed in the reed beds at Marsworth reservoir in the 1960s after the trees in which they habitually nested fell through disease. Since then their numbers have fluctuated, but to date four or more pairs continue to breed here.

Unusually for such an important wildlife refuge, public access is exceptionally good with hides overlooking all the important areas.
19ha – Map ref: SP 919141

WORMLEY WOOD (Woodland Trust) — *Spring, summer*

A piece of woodland a remnant of the huge forest that covered this part of the county, but still a marvellous example of oak standards with hornbeam coppice, a classic form of ancient woodland management. Wild service or chequer trees grow here, and there's a high population of springtime songbirds. The ground flora also indicates the ancient lineage of the wood with a beautiful carpet of bluebells in spring, and sweet woodruff growing in the thickest parts where the light is dim.

Some cultivation has taken place in the past, but this has now been abandoned and birch and scrub woodland with blackthorn and hawthorn have taken over, creating superb habitats for nesting warblers.
136ha – Map ref: TL 317062

KENT

Chaucer's Kent was very different from the busy county of today. The Canterbury pilgrims looked out over green lanes and a countryside clothed from hill to hill with a wealth of trees. In spring, when the pilgrim's journies began in earnest, the weald would have been dense with hawthorn and wild cherry blossom, and loud with birdsong, and the April showers would have done little to dampen their happy spirits on a pilgrimage that was not entirely holy in its approach.

England was rumbustious then, the common man enjoyed an extraordinary level of freedom before the disruption of the Black Death in 1346. The huge loss of man-power meant that those who survived found their strength and skill was held at a premium. The church too was in confusion for the plague spared neither saint nor sinner, and the iron grip of the monasteries temporarily relaxed through a lack of priests and monks. Conversely the sense of faith strengthened among the survivors, especially those who had adhered to religious principles during the worst of the epidemics.

Consequently pilgrimages became very popular, and the single most important site in the southern half of England was Canterbury with its cathedral and shrine dedicated to Thomas á Beckett, murdered there in 1170, and canonised as St Thomas of Canterbury. It was good for business too; the villages and towns that lay on the pilgrim's way across the county became wealthy and influential; leaving the rest a wilderness of deep woods and meres.

Geoffrey Chaucer's verses were realistic and earthy, he saw the countryside of Kent as it was at that time, woodlands, marshes, mills and farms, all part of a cohesive human settlement. The wildlife was, indeed still is, heavily influenced by the proximity of the southern coastline to the continent of Europe. European weather patterns overlap the county bringing with them migrant species as well as a hint of French summers, but winter can reflect the harsher side of the great land mass with powerful blasts of cold winds, isolating villages with snow drifts.

On the northern boundary, the Thames provides a rich habitat, nothing like the incredible productivity of waterfowl and waders here when the estuarine flats of the Medway provided much of the waterfowl eaten in the City of London. But by the time the young Charles Dickens left the confines of his native Chatham to visit the creeks and flats of the saltings that now constitute the RSPB reserve of High Halstow marsh, the rivers were hopelessly polluted with raw sewage, and the prison hulks that bobbed at anchor in the Medway unbelievably foul and verminous.

On a cold January day on the Medway marshes, with the sea mist rolling in, like a wet blanket over the scene, it's easy to imagine that you are Pip and have just discovered the half-starved shivering convict in the churchyard. What is missing in cinematic representations of this scene are the fluting wailing cries of waders, the sharp crank of heron, the whistle of thousands of wigeon and the harsh exciting calls of geese.

Spring brings a change in the content and volume of birdcalls to this region, which is gradually recovering from the excesses of two centuries of sewage disposal, so that now the herons, from the largest heronry in England in the oak trees of Northward Hill overlooking High Halstow marshes, can find ample supplies of flounders and eels to feed their reptilian broods; while snipe and redshank display, and gaudy shelduck parade their fluffy youngsters. The numbers and variety of breeding duck here is astonishing. Teal, mallard and shoveller share the territory, and its prolific summer food resources, with gadwall and garganey and a few pairs of elegant pintail.

Kent is much affected by the sea, and by its position as the gateway to Europe. Soon it will host an even greater throughflow of traffic when the Channel tunnel is completed; yet there are immense contrasts in the landscape, from intensive farming and high population levels on the weald to the chalk slopes of the North Downs with sheep towns bearing names like Denton Tappingham and Boughton Malherbe, where the chalk runs clear to the sea to form the ramparts of the white cliffs of Dover.

These downs were once covered by orchid-rich sheep pasture, now cereals and rape seed reigns. Happily some tiny areas remain, saved for posterity. Places like Wye and Crundale Downs and the green, waterless chalk valley of the Devil's Kneading Trough, a typical example of a chalk downland habitat now so rare.

However, it has to be said that too little remains of the once extensive woodland of the weald, although there are small pockets like the yew wood forming part of Westfield Wood north of Maidstone on the North Downs Way. In their own way the strange dark wilderness of the yew wood at Westfield and the shingle bank of Dungeness Point form a link with Kent's past. The yew woods survived because they were useful to man, and the shingle survived because a few domestic animals could find a living on what is effectively a desert environment.

One of the largest shingle banks in Europe, Dungeness supports a wealth of specialised creatures and plants including the marsh frog, an introduced European species that spread from the Romney marshes, and a rare moth elegantly named toadflax brocade.

Kent also has a coal mining tradition dating back before Roman times, and in places mining subsidence has affected the enivronment for the good of wildlife. One such place is an astonishing area on the Kentish Stour where the land surface has slumped down into old workings creating a wetland with one of the most beautiful reed swamps in the country. Bittern, harriers and the elegant, but vulnerable, bearded tit or bearded reedling breed here as a result of a succession of mild winters. In May their metallic contact and flight calls interrupt the chatter and churr of breeding sedge and reed warblers.

Spring is the best time to visit the Kentish woodlands. If it's birdsong you want to hear, you'll find more nightingales than anywhere else in the country, and rare orchids such as the lady orchid abound. It is a region rich in natural history surprises for the traveller, which is only fitting for a county that has always been associated with travel and pilgrimage.

"Sweet chance, that led my steps abroad,
Beyond the town, where wild flowers grow —
A rainbow and a cuckoo, Lord,
How rich and great the times are now!
Know, all ye sheep
And cows, that keep
On staring that I stand so long
In grass that's wet from heavy rain —
A rainbow and a cuckoo's song
May never come again:

CHURCH WOOD BLEAN (RSPB) — *Spring, summer*

Church Wood Blean is in two sections, one large block of 360 acres and one smaller block to the west of 80 acres, being part of a huge 7000 acre woodland sweeping in an arc north and west of Canterbury. These woods would have been in existence in Chaucer's day, to a much larger extent, and possibly different in species, since oak woods today have been reduced to mere pockets with blocks of conifers and sweet chestnut coppice; the latter having been planted to provide long straight poles for hop farming.

Woodland birdlife is varied, at least forty four species breed here, and in an attempt to increase the diversity of wildlife the species-poor chestnut coppice is being reduced and oak planted in its place. The fact that the soil is poor sandy clay has saved the woodland from the fate meted out elsewhere, where richer soils have been cleared in favour of farmland. Attempts are also being made to encourage nightjars to nest in open areas created within the woodland, and the redstart, a rare bird in Kent, has established a small breeding population. Three species of woodpecker, nuthatch and tree creeper nest on the reserve as does the shy hawfinch.

Despite the fame of its breeding nightingales, pride of place must go to the heath fritillary butterfly, found only here and in very few other sites in the west of England, its larval food plant, cow wheat, grows profusely along the oak wood margins. This beautiful insect has increased its numbers, with man's help, through careful habitat management, from 200 individuals in 1983 to more than 1500 in 1986. A pond dug by RSPB members in 1985 has also enhanced the insect and amphibian population; but sadly the woodland suffered badly in the hurricane of October, 1987.

440 acres – Map ref: TR 126593

DUNGENESS (RSPB) — *All year*

A grade 1 (SSSI), this area of nearly 2000 acres of shingle dunes and sandy, almost desert conditions, is a mecca for bird-watchers and entomologists, herpetologists, botanists, and twitchers; one of the first bird observatories in the UK was established here, and it's an ideal place to see many rare vagrants, especially from eastern Europe.

The Romney/Dimchurch light railway terminates near the lighthouse, and the southern shore of the promontory is dominated by the forbidding presence of the Dungeness nuclear power station and an MoD firing range. These contrasting land uses have, by their very presence, actually preserved many of the habitats on the Dungeness

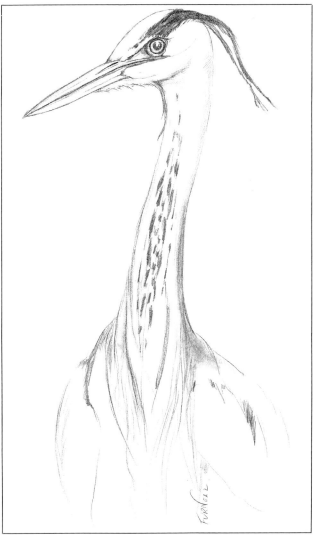

Heron　　　　　　　　　　　　　　　　　　*High Halstow*

Heath Fritillary on Foxglove
Church Wood Blean

ators like hen harrier, merlin, the occasional peregrine and short-eared owl hunt over the winter marsh; and avocet, curlew-sandpiper, spotted redshank and the unusual, but aptly named, Kentish plover have been recorded here. Spring and summer brings a change to the marsh and salt flats with sea-purslane, glasswort and yellow samphire.
1360ha – Map ref: TQ 926704

FARNINGHAM WOOD (Kent TfNC) — *Spring, summer*

An interesting joint project has been undertaken between Sevenoaks district council and the parish council of Farningham, resulting in a reserve of considerable size and great natural history interest. The diversity of soil types, from acid Thanet sands and Blackheath beds, to the upper chalk outcrops of the lower slopes, produce a fascinating variety of plants including lily of the valley on the acid soils and small-leaved lime on the lower slopes, and the rare and unusual Deptford pink grows on the southern boundary.

The woodland shows indicator plants such as butcher's broom, orpine and wood spurge, pointing to the fact that although the woods have been constantly used and exploited by man, they appear not to have been clear felled or cultivated. There's a range of breeding birds, including hawfinch.
176 acres – Map ref: TQ 536684

HIGH HALSTOW MARSHES (NCC) — *All year (especially winter)*

A remnant of a once extensive salt marsh in the Thames Medway estuary, part of the marshes that Dickens wrote about in 'Great Expectations'. In winter the whole marshland is alive with wintering wildfowl and waders, and the occasional gathering of greenland white-fronted geese. There is still a considerable amount of shooting on the Thames marshes, and High Halstow provides a refuge and stopover point for feeding birds.

Herons from the nearby heronry of Northward Hill fish for eels and flounders, and activity increases in spring as the young are hatched and the newly-fledged youngsters begin their fishing lessons.

The beautiful shelduck gather to feed and breed in spring, and are joined by gadwall and garganey, and a few pairs of pintail. Snipe drum in the early evening, and reed and sedge warblers can be seen and heard in the reed-filled draining ditches, and occasionally bearded reedling.
52ha – Map ref: TQ 799763

HOTHFIELD COMMON (Kent TfNC/Ashford BC) — *Spring, summer*

Once an ancient grazing common, Hothfield was declared a site of special scientific interest in 1986 on account of its series of raised acid bogs. The impervious layer of clay subsoil beneath the gently sloping sandy plateau of the common allows acid springs to well-up to the surface forming several mossy bogs. Over many thousands of years these have developed until some are several metres thick. Due to lack of management and grazing by cattle

foreland from exploitation, and in consequence there are large colonies of sandwich and common terns, black-headed gulls and a few pairs of Mediterranean gulls. Two species of grebe, the great-crested and the dabchick, also nest on the small pools and man-made flooded excavations which are exploited in winter by a large number of wildfowl. The same pools and pits become spring spawning sites for the marsh frog, an introduced species that has been singularly successful here. Viper's bugloss, a typical plant of shingle and dunes is abundant, and the site is known for rare continental migrant moths and dragonflies.
480ha – Map ref: TR 063196

ELMLEY MARSHES (RSPB) — *All year*

Habitat management has made the Spitend Peninsula on the Swale a major refuge for thousands of wigeon, teal, mallard, shelduck and white-fronted geese in winter. The coastal grazing marshes with their fresh water fleets and shallow floods are bordered by salt marsh on the north side of the Swale and are immensely attractive to waders, black-tailed godwit, curlew, dunlin and redshank. Pred-

Cetti's Warbler   *Stodmarsh*

and sheep, and more significantly rabbits, some of the bogs have become wooded with birch, willow, aspen and alder.

Since the area was designated a reserve, management has been stepped up and the scrub has been cleared from some of its old haunts. The site supports a number of wetland acid-loving plants such as bog asphodel, heath spotted orchid, and the insect eating sundew; the wet woodland provides a rich habitat for birds and mammals. Thirty-five species of birds have been recorded as breeding here.

56ha – Map ref: TQ 972457

NORTHWARD HILL (RSPB)* — *Spring, summer*

Justly famous as the largest heronry in England, these woods suffered badly during the Dutch elm disease epidemic of the late 1960s early 1970s. All the major elms in the reserve were lost, although many, with decaying trunks and branches, stand as stark monuments to the ravages of beetle-carried fungus.

The loss of these elms, and the increase of scrub woodland on the hillside, has provided a superb habitat for migrants such as garden and willow warblers, whitethroats, blackcaps and the reserve's speciality nightingales. The breeding population of nightingales at Northward Hill is extensive, and from early May onwards

they can be heard at all times of the day. The springtime dawn chorus here is incredible.

Early spring sees the return of over two hundred pairs of herons to the heronry, at which time paths through the woodland near the nesting sites are closed to the public. There are viewing points for visitors, but sadly the reserve suffers from vandalism.

54ha – Map ref: TQ 784761

STODMARSH (NCC) — *All year*

An accident of the industrial revolution led to the creation of this outstanding wetland reserve, when old coal workings subsided leading to extensive flooding and a series of shallow lakes, some of which have been colonised by vast stands of common reed. It's one of the finest reed swamps in southern England and home to hundreds of pairs of bearded reedling, reed, marsh, sedge warblers and occasional Cetti's warbler with its explosive startling call. The reed beds encourage rare and endangered species including Savi's warbler, marsh harriers and bittern. In spring and autumn osprey and black terns can be seen on passage, and in late summer hobbies hunt the dragonflies over the lakes and reed beds, while in winter the extensive flocks of wildfowl and passerines attract wintering peregrine and the occasional merlin.

160ha – Map ref: TR 222607

SOUTH SWALE (Kent TfNC) — *Autumn and winter*

Adjacent to the Oare Marshes reserve, South Swale comprises a complex of salt marsh and estuarine flats extremely attractive to wildfowl, especially Brent geese, shelduck, mallard, wigeon and pintail. Mixed flocks of waders also feed on the ample food in the mud flats; black-tailed godwits, grey and golden plover, curlew and large numbers of knot and dunlin.

The breeding species on the salt marsh include lapwing, reed bunting, redshank, yellow wagtail, sedge and reed warblers. The grazing regime is controlled to give the greatest diversity of plants, many of them typical of old saltings with sea lavender, sea purslane, golden samphire, and of course the eel grass on which the brent geese feed. Oare Meadow and Marshes (*Map ref: TR 007627/013647*) are part of the same complex and designated as part of the Swale SSSI after being recognised as a wetland of international importance by the 1973 Ramsar Convention.

165ha – Map ref: TR 068650 / TR 018640

LANCASHIRE & GREATER MANCHESTER

To the uninitiated Lancashire is a county of mills, clogs and smoke, and Manchester has a sad reputation for rain — both images are erroneous. The industry that drove the engine of the British Empire has become, like the Empire itself, a thing of the past. The coal industry is being run-down and the spoil tips landscaped and reclaimed for nature and for recreation; but the surge of new technology has shaken off the county's dirt and spring-cleaned the major cities of Manchester and Liverpool. The catharsis was painful for the population, and only now are the people of Lancashire coming to terms with a changed lifestyle no longer dependant upon wool, cotton, coal and shipping.

She's somewhere in the sunlight strong,
Her tears are in the falling rain,
She calls me in the wind's soft song,
And with the flowers she comes again.

Yon bird is but her messenger,
The moon is but her silver car;
Yea! sun and moon are sent by her,
And every wistful waiting star.
— song by Richard le Gallienne

Liverpool is the birthplace of one of my favourite poets, Richard le Gallienne, and the county also formed the inspirational key for poet and artist Edward Lear who came to Lancashire in the middle of the 19th century and stayed at Knowsley Hall, seat of the Earls of Derby. Lear was invited to paint the animals and birds in the private collection at Knowsley and while staying there he became a favourite with the Earls children, and in 1846 wrote much of his best known nonsense verse for them.

Lear was a rather complex person, a sad and solitary artist whose nonsense verse sublimated his desire to be accepted. He never married, probably because he suffered from epilepsy, which he kept a closely guarded secret even from his friends. He was considered a delightful companion by many who knew him, and perhaps it is unjust that he should be remembered mainly for his skill as a composer of humorous nonsense and the delights of the world of "Ongy Bongy Bo" rather than for his undoubted talent as a painter and illustrator of wildlife subjects.

The Lancashire that Lear knew is greatly changed, although the county can boast some of the most fascinating and varied scenery, from Silverdale to the limestone pavement of Gait Barrows, from the wide, fowl-rich mud and sand flats of Morecambe Bay to the salt marshes of the Wyre, few dune systems are equal in area or diversity of species than Ainsdale Dunes.

The climate is generally mild, due in good measure to the prevailing westerly winds off the warm Atlantic and the Irish Sea. This westerly airflow is responsible, in part, for Manchester's reputation as the best place for umbrella manufacturers to test their wares. The rising ground of the Forest of Bowland and the Penines receives the greater part of this rainfall which results in the creation of myriad small streams and becks that feed the larger rivers and provide a habitat for birds and mammals; the high ground is also a haven for upland birds. A number of the moors are employed for grouse shooting with restricted public access, but where there is sympathetic management for birds of prey and other predators, you will find a good population diversity.

The greatest threat to the Dee, Ribble and Morecambe Bay comes from pollution and development; a large amount of the most valuable land has been designated as reserves, or has statutory protection, but plans are on the drawing-board to build tidal barrages across Morecambe Bay with the intention of producing electricity from the impounded water and this would effectively destroy the wildlife potential of the whole area. Moreover it would irreversibly diminish one of Europe's outstanding winter refuges for wildfowl and waders.

The impact of man upon the landscape of Lancashire is substantial; much of the lowland is cultivated and many of the mosses and salt marshes that existed two centuries ago have been ploughed for crops; the silts and gravels left behind after the ice age creates superb farmland, and the less productive areas have been given over to development. Nevertheless it is a region of interesting contrasts — industry and urbanisation side by side with high deserted open moorland and wild seascapes. Little wonder the county has spawned such brilliant writers, artists and poets as well as creative engineers, themselves artists in metal and ceramics.

AINSDALE SAND DUNES (NCC) — *Spring, summer*

Fortunately the dune system at Ainsdale has received some measure of protection, for the presence of immense amounts of pulverised shell fragments within the overall mix of minerals in the sand dunes provides conditions favourable to orchids and other lime-loving plants. The dune helleborine flowers here in early summer and so does grass of parnassus with its beautiful white flowers shaped like rounded stars and smelling faintly of honey; the value of these dunes is clearly seen in the variety of plants and insects, birds and animals that inhabit them.

The dunes depend upon a consistent flow of sand from the sea bed and the tidal forces that deposit sand also encourage an abundant food supply for seabirds and off-shore fish eaters. But any dune system is vulnerable to blow outs, when wind erodes formerly stable dunes which have been stripped of covering vegetation by human feet trampling over them. These systems take many hundreds, even thousands of years to develop, but can be damaged in just a few years. Partly wooded with conifers, a small population of red squirrels enlivens a walk along the marked nature trails.
492.5ha – Map ref: SD 290105

BROCK VALLEY NATURE TRAIL — *Spring, summer*

Glacial sands and gravels, eroded by a torrential stream, form the basis of this nature trail. Dipper and pied wagtail, grey wagtail and common sandpiper can be seen along the streamside, and in May and June rare marsh stitchwort is a feature here, it is smaller than its common relative greater stitchwort with a grey-green tinge to the long pointed leaves.
2.4km – Map ref: SD 548431

CROXTETH COUNTRY PARK (Merseyside MBC) — *Spring, summer*

This substantial Country Park contains a wide range of habitats, from open pasture and broadleaved woodland, to wetland and open water and conifer plantings. It's an excellent site for birds, over 100 species have been recorded here, and the insect population is rich and varied too. There is also a wide variety of large and small mammals including foxes.
208ha – Map ref: SJ 399943

DAISY NOOK COUNTRY PARK (Oldham MBC/ Greater Manchester Council) — *Spring, summer*

A river valley where plants, birds and mammals can find refuge in the midst of an otherwise urban and formerly heavily industrialised landscape. The canal, part of the reserved area, is rich in fish and amphibia.
34.5ha – Map ref: SD 921004

EAVES WOOD (NT) — *Spring, summer*

High above the rich landscape of Silverdale, and looking seaward to Morecambe Bay, Eaves Wood hosts a mass of limestone plants and trees growing on the thin soils overlaying the limestone pavement. Red squirrels are resident here, and the birdlife is rich indeed with a large number of habitats providing nest sites and ample food for migrant warblers and resident species alike. There is also a good butterfly population.
3.2km – Map ref: SD 467762

ETHEROW COUNTRY PARK (Stockport MBC) — *Spring, summer*

Sandwiched between the bustle of the Manchester-Stockport conurbations and the open wildness of the Peak District, the wooded valley of the river Etherow creates a corridor for wildlife. The reserve of Compstall is included in this complex with marsh, river and canal comprising a good area of wetland which attracts a wide range of birds, mammals, plant and insects.
65ha – Map ref: SJ 965909

GAIT BARROWS (NCC)* — *Spring, summer*

One of the best areas in the whole of Lancashire for limestone pavement. The fact that the pavement and its immensely rich plant communities are to be found hidden away in the midst of woodland has saved it from desecration such as being quarried for ornamental stone for garden rockeries. The area is just like a natural rock garden with deep grikes, holes and terraces, evidence of a mighty glacier that planed the topsoil and rock away leaving the soluble limestone to the mercy of the elements. The naturally occurring carbonic acid in rain water has slowly dissolved the rock into fantastic shapes.

These pavements form a series of micro climates for ferns and rare plants, many of which are at the northern limit of their range. The rare dark red helleborine and fly orchid grow here and so too does the angular Soloman's seal, lily of the valley and deadly nightshade; an unusual mixture of plants. The soil on the pavement is too shallow to allow many trees to grow on its open surface, although small trees, including small-leaved lime, yew and juniper form a contrast to the carpets of biting stonecrop and cushions of bloody cranesbill.

Away from the open eroded limestone, where the glacier dropped drifts of pulverised rock, climax woodland has developed, and there is a further variety of habitats. The whole area is rich in insects, especially moths and butterflies, and the birds take advantage of the bounty. The springtime population of breeding birds is very high indeed.

The footpaths offer excellent vantage points and descend to the wetland area at Little Hawes Water through a variety of meadow and marshland habitats. Away from these paths the reserve is 'permit only' to protect the sensitive environment from disturbance.
70ha – Map ref: SD 480772

Ainsdale Sand Dunes   *Lancs. & Gt Manchester*

GLASSON DOCK & LUNE ESTUARY NATURE TRAIL (BWB/LCC/W & J. Pye Ltd) — *All year*

Excellent views to the estuary of the river Lune with a wide variety of habitats ranging from fresh water plants and aquatic life, to salt marsh and salt water marine creatures. The estuary is particularly interesting in spring, autumn and winter for passage and winter migrant birds.
3.2km – Map ref: SD 457562

HEALEY DELL (Rochdale BC) — *Spring, summer*

Created by the river Spodden, this deep cut valley is rich in ferns, mosses and liverworts. The woods are ancient in origin consisting mainly of oak and birch with introduced trees such as sycamore in some areas, which attract many breeding birds and winter visitors. The occurrence of lime-loving plants is due in large part to the presence of limestone rock ballast used to bed the sleepers on the old railway line, and this has resulted in a range of unexpected plants. The marshy areas support ragged robin and a series of hybrids of common spotted, southern and northern marsh orchids.
70ha – Map ref: SD 883159

LEIGHTON MOSS (RSPB)* — *All year*

Once this was an arm of Morecambe Bay, but in Victorian times a barrage and sea-wall was built and the land behind the wall drained and reclaimed. In the early part of this century the land fell into disuse, drainage ceased and the region flooded, beginning the process of open water to reed swamp and mire and ultimately woodland.

The open water, only a few feet deep, is already fringed by extremely productive reed swamp supporting birds and aquatic invertebrates, and is home to a northerly colony of bittern and bearded reedlings and the gargany, a duck which comes to breed in spring. Reed and sedge warblers are common, and so too are marsh harriers. In spring water rails can be heard, their strange calls issuing from the reed beds; and the density of these reeds makes them a perfect wagtail roost in winter and gathering place for martins and swallows in autumn. The sheer amount of insect food allows for a considerable population of hirundines and swifts to feed over the water.

Among the mammals on the moss is a pair of otters, they have bred in the seclusion of the reed swamp for a number of years. Red and roe deer are also here, and the abundant bird and small mammal population encourages birds of prey like kestrel, tawny owl and sparrowhawk. The regime of reed cutting results in a wide range of plants like purple loosestrife, hemp agrimony, bur marigold and greater water dock; the fen edge is constantly changing as plants come into flower throughout the spring and summer.
321 acres – Map ref: SD 478752

LYTHAM ST ANNES (Lytham BC) — *Spring, summer*

Sand dunes heaped up by the wind have formed a series of rolling hills, but they are subject to heavy pressure from summer holiday visitors to the beach on the seaward side. Tiny fragments of sea shells make up a high proportion of these alkaline sand dunes and in the damper areas, or slacks, a wide variety of flowering plants provide food for insects. Especially interesting are the day flying moths, the white satin, the cinnabar, whose caterpillars feed on ragwort and have bright black and yellow warning colouration in bands around their bodies, and the burnet moth. Butterflies like common blue and small copper are plentiful here, they both have more than one emergence during the year.
16ha – Map ref: SD 309307

MARTIN MERE (WWT) — *All year*

Over 10,000 pink-footed geese migrate to this wildfowl refuge every winter. Whooper and Bewick swans are regular visitors, and there is also a collection of pinioned water fowl from many parts of the world to interest the visitor.

The Mere is a vital stop-over for wildfowl on migration, the numbers of wintering duck increases as the weather becomes colder, and it's also an important site for waders with large concentrations of ruff in winter along with curlew and redshank and many other species. Green, purple, marsh, wood and common sandpipers all appear during the year, and hen harriers are regular visitors. Marsh harriers quarter the reeds, and in summer the hobbys cause alarm and consternation among the waterfowl and waders by hunting over the open water, whereas in winter it is the turn of the peregrines and merlins. In the meadows short-eared owls are a common sight as they search the grassland looking for voles.

There is a regular passage of terns, and the insect-rich water can attract the most elegant of birds the black tern.
36ha – Map ref: SD 428145

MORECAMBE BAY (RSPB) — *All year*

One of the natural history sights of the United Kingdom, especially in winter, the annual gathering of waders on the mudflats of this bay is dramatic; knot, sanderling, oystercatcher, redshank, curlew and about a tenth of Britain's wintering population of bar-tailed godwits flight and feed here, at times more than a million birds are feeding.

Reed Warbler   *Leighton Moss*

Wildfowl in their thousands form dramatic skeins across the sky and grey lag and pink-footed geese add to the wild bird symphony. Spring and summer are less productive for sheer numbers of birds, but there is a constant to and fro of species at all times of year feeding upon the bounty; nearly 165 species of birds have been recorded and the number is probably higher, but the immense area of sand and mudflats makes positive identification difficult even with powerful optical devices.
2485ha – Map ref: SD 468666

RIBBLE MARSHES (NCC)* — *All year*

The Ribble estuary salt marshes are exceedingly dangerous, but part of the area, Hesketh Marsh, is a sanctuary and study centre. The coast road across Crossens Marsh affords good views out over the estuary and the numbers of pink-footed geese constitutes one of the reserves specialities; being the largest concentrations of these geese in northern England. The estuary is also important for a number of estuarine breeding birds including shelduck and redshank, and it's full of interest in every season, although winter is best for the numbers and diversity of species.
3226ha – Map ref: SD 374208

SQUIRE ANDERTON'S WOOD NATURE TRAIL (Central Lancashire Development Corporation) — *Spring, summer*

Encompassing a variety of woodland habitats and a small stream Squire Anderton's trail is short, but interesting. Wood anemone, sweet woodruff and ramson indicate the age of the woodland, and tits and tree creepers are present all year with an increase in population in spring and summer when migrant warblers arrive.
0.8km – Map ref: SD 560337

WAYOH RESERVOIR (Lancs TfNC/NWWA) — *All year*

Wayoh reservoir and woodlands are blessed with an abundance of birds, plants and insects most of the year. In winter the interest is wildfowl on the open water, and in spring and summer it's flowering plants, insects and migrant songbirds. The scenery is dominated by a very attractive viaduct at one end of the valley.
50ha – Map ref: SD 732170

WYRE ESTUARY SALT MARSHES (Lancs TfNC) — *Spring, summer*

Of particular botanical interest, the Wyre estuary has a wide tidal range and the salt marsh, subject to periodic inundation from the sea, forms a carpet-like turf of common cord-grass acting as a trap for any water-borne nutrients. The flats provide excellent roosting for large numbers of redshank, oystercatchers and black-headed gulls while the sea-wall area is rich in plantlife that has adapted to the increase of salinity in the soil, although lime-loving plants like bird's foot trefoil and vetches thrive among the three species of sea lavender which occur here.
104ha – Map ref: SD 346486

LEICESTERSHIRE AND RUTLAND

Rutland is truly the heart of England, situated as it is in the geographic centre of the country. This tiny county, once the smallest in the land, and now supposedly assimilated into the larger county of Leicestershire and Rutland, retains a fierce sense of independence and pride of place.

Before the Romans came this was the land of the Celtic tribes of the Coritani who built their forts on Breedon Hill and at Burrough on the Hill, limestone outcrops from where they could survey the land below. The human condition changes little with time, and the same desire to live in an imposing palace on a hill led to the building of the turreted Castle of Belvoir, once described as the lordliest home in England (Windsor Castle excepted) overlooking the beautiful Vale of Belvoir.

The site was first chosen by a henchman of William the Conqueror, one Robert de Todeni, and the name of the original fortified house built in 1145 comes from the valley below originally called "Bella Viedere" (beautiful view). The unusual landscape, rugged grounds, and the lakes around Knipton make it a favourite place for visitors.

The county does not have a good reputation as a naturalist's paradise, yet remnants of the old forest of Charnwood can still be found growing on ancient rocks, where the ground did not yield easily to the plough. The forest remained almost unchanged into the beginning of Victoria's reign, and here you will see plants and tree communities not so very different from those that covered the land after the last Ice Age.

This forest was once a hunting chase, but has had to give way, in parts, to the march of agriculture and development. In Michael Drayton's poem "Charnwood Forest" (The River Soar Speaks of the Forest) he describes the changes that have taken place and the disappearance of the high palmed harts:-

Who will describe to life a forest, let him take
Thy surface to himself, nor shall he need to make
Another form at all, where oft in thee is found
Fine sharp but easy hills, which reverently are crowned
With aged antique rocks, to which the goats and sheep
(To him that stands remote) do softly seem to creep,

To gnaw the little shrubs, on their steep sides that grow;
Upon whose other part, on some descending brow,
Huge stones are hanging out, as though they down would
    drop,
Where under-growing oaks on their shoulders prop.

This poem tells a little of the fate of broadleaved woodlands all over the country. I wonder what the poet and cleric George Crabbe would think of it were he to return to the village of Muston where he lived and worked for 25 years, and where his wife is buried. Crabbe is better known for his poems about the Suffolk countryside and the fens rather than for his having lived in the top corner of this county where the Lincolnshire and Nottinghamshire flatlands pinch Leicestershire into a peak. Many of the quiet lanes and pastures that he would have known have gone, yet there are still a few places where the hand of man has fallen but lightly, where primroses and cowslips and green-winged orchids are able to push their heads up into the sunlight from the spring turf.

Though a small county, Leicestershire and Rutland is endowed with a fertile landscape of limestone and marlstone, and rocks of the coal measures. It is these carboniferous rocks that have helped to change the face of certain parts of the county quite dramatically. The coal that lies below the surface means wealth, and in the beautiful Vale of Belvoir coal reserves can be measured in quantities that will be exploitable until the middle of the next century. Whether the industry on which the original wealth of this county's economic power base was founded will be allowed to damage this priceless landscape will be a test of the ingenuity and skill of the planners and mining engineers.

Man's impact upon tiny Rutland has been dramatic with the creation of Rutland Water, the second largest man-made reservoir in England. This huge impounded lake is one of the best examples of conservation, education and recreation tied in with a water supply function. The boundary of the lake is under constant observation by ornithologists, and some astonishing rarities have been recorded.

Viewed from the ancient gathering place of Breedon on the Hill on a still summer's day, the landscape laid out below is quite breathtaking. The Celtic warriors who built the hill fort named it Bre, the old name for hill, and in the 7th century, a church was built here (a gift from the King of Mercia). It was considered a wonder of the age and some of the original runic carvings were taken and built into Peterborough Abbey. Later the old English name of "Dun" was added to the pre christian name of Bre by the monks. What they did not realise was that both words meant hill in different languages. Taken to its logical conclusion, the modern name of Breedon on the Hill actually translates as the hill on the hill. I'm sure this would have appealed to the rumbustious Celts, although I'm not so sure about the reaction of the ascetic 7th century monks.

AMBION WOOD & SHENTON CUTTING (Leics and Rutland TfNC)** — *Spring, summer*

A pleasant juxtaposition of habitats here — on the one hand a disused railway line and on the other an ancient wood with tall oaks and wyche elms and deep shade producing an impoverished but intensely interesting flora; where the midland hawthorn and coppiced hazel pre-dominates, the wood is more open, and early purple orchids bloom in the spring along with other plants of ancient woodland. Later in the year broadleaved helleborine opens its wasp attracting flowers.

There are a number of clearings in the wood some of which are wet and have an acid flora, whereas other areas are dry and support plants of the limestone edge such as goldilocks. The huge amount of insect productivity is excellent for migrant warblers; and in winter woodcock search the soft ground for worms. The area reflects a system of management that was popular in the past, one that produced a stunning variety of wildlife.
20ha

BOSWORTH PARK (LCC) — *Spring, summer*

Once a grand deer park, now a varied grassland with fine trees, several ponds and a lake, Bosworth is an excellent site for woodpeckers in spring where the old trees provide superb drumming places.
34.8ha – Map ref: SK 413033

BRADGATE PARK (Bradgate Park Trust) — *Spring, summer*

The high ground at Bradgate Park, covered with braken and grassland, looks down onto small remnant pockets of the Charnwood Forest. The reserve is based on ancient rock with a relatively low fertility and it is this fact, together with difficulty of access that has protected the area from development and agriculture. Part of the reserve also overlooks Swithland Woods and Cropstone Reservoir.
320ha – Map ref: SK 523116

BURROUGH HILL (LCC) — *Spring, summer*

Rising 600ft above sea level, this marlstone hill is one of the highest points in the county; it was a centre for the Celtic tribe of the Coritani. The weather stunts and twists

Garden Warbler   *Swithland Woods*

the few hawthorns that struggle to grow on the hillside, but lower down in the covert, bird and insect life is prolific, particularly the butterflies.
34ha – Map ref: SK 766115

CHARLEY (Leics and Rutland TfNC)** — *Spring, summer*

Once part of a far larger area, this small heath now constitutes the majority of the county's remaining example of this type of habitat with cross-leaved heath and heather, purple moorgrass, bilberry and crowberry. The rather odd and rare fern called moonwort also grows here. Birdlife is limited, but stonechats and yellowhammers and the occasional wheatear can be seen.
224ha

CROFT (Leics and Rutland TfNC)** — *Spring, summer*

The watermeadows of the river Soar hold a considerable variety of plants and birds. The river leaves the meadows through a water cut valley at Croft where the wetland species are enhanced by arrowhead, and the abundant insect fauna encourages insect-eating birds like swallows and house martins to feed in large numbers.
6ha

EYE BROOK RESERVOIR (AWA)** — *Winter*

Eye Brook reservoir has been popular with bird-watchers since its inauguration in the 1940s, and the view point from the minor road overlooking much of the best part of the reservoir has produced many rare bird sightings in the past. In winter, duck and swans use the water to roost, flying out at dusk to feed on the nearby farmland, or else they simply rest on the water during migration. Terns and

waders also use the reservoir as a stop over, but the latter are not easy to see from the roadside.
160ha

GRAND UNION CANAL (Leics and Rutland TfNC)** — *Spring, summer*

The whole canal is a linear nature reserve along which birds, animals, plants and insects can travel virtually unobstructed; this waterway, and flyway, has been part of the landscape for so long, it's now been accepted by both man and wildlife as natural. The winter traffic on the canal is now very limited which benefits a colony of Daubentons bats roosting on the roof and in crevices of one of the tunnels; and even the heavier summer traffic still allows the margin plants to develop.

The insect and aquatic life thrives in a series of fascinating habitats afforded by the variety of landscapes through which the canal passes, but the bird life depends on the time of year with spring in the more wooded parts being best because of the birdsong.
32km

GREAT MERRIBLE WOOD (Leics and Rutland TfNC)** — *Spring, summer*

A damp wood, remnant of a once larger block, Great Merrible Wood is now surrounded by farmland. Oak, ash and coppiced hazel with a shrub understory of guelder rose, hawthorn, dogwood, field maple and spindle berry flank the rides where meadowsweet encourages butterflies. Plants like herb paris and broadleaved and violet helleborine confirm the age of this wood which forms an oasis in a sea of agriculture and harbours a high bird population.
12ha

HERBERT'S MEADOW (Leics and Rutland TfNC)** —*Spring, summer*

Herbert's Meadow consists of unimproved heath grassland ideal for many plants, including fragrant orchid (flowering in one of the few sites in the region) and greenwinged and heath spotted orchid which occur in some numbers.
2ha

LAUNDE BIG WOOD (FC/Leics and Rutland TfNC)** — *Spring, summer*

Launde Big Wood is part of the old Leighfield Forest that has been cropped in recent times. The ground cover plants are varied, reflecting the different soil types and herb paris and early purple orchid, yellow archangel and giant bell flower all grow here; the beautiful and rare greater butterfly orchid can still be found in the wood which also boasts a considerable bird population, especially spring migrants.
40ha

RUTLAND WATER (Leics & Rutland TfNC/AWA) — *All year*

Created as a drinking water reservoir by flooding a valley, Anglian Water Authority produced the second largest man-made lake in England, and in the process provided a place where migrant waterbirds could stop and feed and roost. The wildlife potential of the reservoir has been further enhanced by careful management and the building of low banks which are flooded when the water levels rise in late winter, then remain wet when the levels fall; this continuity allows plants and invertebrates to enjoy a more stable environment and encourages birds and amphibians to colonise.

The siting of the reservoir along the flight lines and traditional migration routes through the Welland and Nene river valleys was an accidental bonus, and because of this Rutland Water carries a far higher bird population at migration times than would otherwise occur.

The potential for conflict between the requirements of recreational pursuits like windsurfing, sailing, water skiing and fishing on an area as great as Rutland Water could negate the security of the wildlife, fortunately the reservoir has been zoned so that these contrasting needs are catered for to the benefit of all concerned. The zoning is in three basic parts — the northern section, known as Burley Fishponds, has no public access being a protected reed swamp breeding site. The middle section of Egleton is open to local naturalist trust members and other permit holders, while the southern section, known as Lyndon is open to all. Those areas with public access are served by excellent hides and the birds have become used to the constant flow of visitors and are easy to see.

The number of birds appearing on the water, and on the 38km of shoreline, is astonishing, especially in the recognised migration seasons. Large exciting osprey regularly appear and, overall, more than 210 species have been recorded, including some very unusual ones like the manx shearwater, a bird more familiar with deep oceans, obviously blown off course.

Public interest in the area ensures that birds such as the long-billed dowicher, a rare vagrant wader from America, are properly identified; other transatlantic wanderers, the pectoral sandpiper to name but one, have also found temporary rest on the shores here, but it would be tedious to list all the rare and exotic birds, suffice to say that this is one of the finest inland sites for bird-watching, with immense numbers and many species; and the list grows longer with every season.

The breeding bird population is no less exciting, and some of them such as the oyster-catchers that utilise the gravel islands in the lake, would be considered more at home on a seaside shoreline rather than an inland water.

Nevertheless several pairs regularly rear their young here as do little-ringed plover, another wader that has increased in numbers with man's help.

The regime of agriculture around the reservoir takes into account the potential for pollution with toxic agrochemicals, and in consequence many of the meadows are managed as old unimproved pasture with a resulting superb display of spring and summer grassland flowering plants with large numbers of common spotted orchids.

The size of the lake and its position makes it a prime site for geese and swans; in very hard weather, when many other inland waters are frozen-over Rutland remains largely free of ice; and it is undoubtedly the lake which

draws bird-watchers to the shores every winter and at migration times; virtually the entire list of wildfowl and grebes that either visit or breed in the United Kingdom have been seen on Rutland's surface. The imposition of a reservoir as large as this could have been catastrophic but, on balance, the natural benefits — both now and in the future — from this lake would seem to be assured.
140ha – Map ref: SK 897049

SWITHLAND WOODS (Bradgate Park Trust) —
Spring, summer

One of the reasons why the Charnwood Forest was not felled and converted to farmland over the centuries is lack of fertility in the soil on which a large measure of the forest is founded. Where the soil is deeper and based upon younger limestone rocks, nature has vanished under the plough, and where sandy soil and heathland predominate commercial planting of conifers and hardwoods has been established; the ancient pre-Cambrian rocks and shales, relics of a long-ago eroded mountain range, produced harsh infertile soil on which only trees like small-leaved lime and oak were able to established themselves.

The slate found here was mined for roofing, but now the quarries are abandoned and flooded, and the acidic nature of the water does not encourage extensive plant growth, consequently the water is quite clear.

The ground flora also reflects the depth and acidity of the soil and varies from bracken and woodsage to stands of foxgloves, under the birch trees, and alders with their typical wet woodland plants.

The oaks and limes encourage a more open habitat where bluebells, great wood-rush, yellow pimpernel and common cow wheat grow. In the past the hazel under-story would have been used as raw material for wattles and hurdles, but left untended it forms small groves festooned with wild honeysuckle, which is such a feature of this type of Midland woods.

Wild honeysuckle is the food plant of the white admiral butterfly, a necessary adjunct to the lifestyle of the common dormouse, and forms a vital link in the flora of ancient coppiced woodland. Within the reserve there's a paddock, maintained by grazing, where a large variety of

Early Purple orchid   *Leics. & Rutland*

unimproved meadowland plants flourish, common spotted orchids are a feature in late spring, and summer flowering plants include betony, common saw-wort and the strange adder's tongue fern.

The large number of different habitats in this reserve encourages an abundance of insects and invertebrates, and a considerable population of large and small mammals. The birds too reflect the plentiful food with woodpeckers of all three species occurring together with nuthatches and a wide variety of native titmice, including marsh tits and long-tailed tits. Warblers are common with blackcap and garden warbler, chiffchaff and willow warbler; consequently birds of prey like sparrowhawk, kestrel, tawny and little owls are also present.
58.4ha – Map ref: SK 538129

LINCOLNSHIRE
&
SOUTH
HUMBERSIDE

Alfred Lord Tennyson lived at Somersby in Lincolnshire and wrote about the county in which he obviously found much inspiration.

"Lincolnshire Wolds and Lincolnshire Sea"
- Alfred Tennyson

Calm and deep peace on this high wold,
And on these dews that drench the furze,
And all the silvery gossamers
That twinkle into green and gold;
Calm and still light on yon great plain
That sweeps with all its autumn bowers,
And crowded farms and lessening towers,
To mingle with the bounding main.

The countryside of Lincolnshire and South Humberside is gently undulating where the wolds rise from the lowlands of the old flood plain of the wash north of Boston. Man created the landscape here fighting the elements with amazing feats of civil engineering, but he has cost the county's wildlife dear. The deep fens were drained first in Roman times and later in the 17th century by the Dutch, opening up many places that were once fit only for wildfowl and reeds; now fields of grain and sugarbeet, rape, celery and brassicas cover land reclaimed from fen and sea.

The limestone scarp banding the county from the Humber to the Wash was cleared long ago for grazing and only a few tiny pockets of ancient woodland survive to whet the appetite; once there were huge woods of small-leaved lime, ash and oak covering the uplands and bordering the immense lakes that flooded much of lowland Lincolnshire. These flooded areas were created as a result of glacial action which deposited a clay pan over a greater part of the southern county. This clay, and the flints and gravels that were deposited when the glaciers melted, dropping their burden of spoil at the end of the last ice age, produced a landscape of reed beds and meres, lakes and marshes alive with wildfowl. The reeds

and fens eventually turned into peat, exploited when the fens were drained and converted to superb fertile farmland, now few meres and little peat remains for the land is too valuable to be left to the wildlife. However, extraction of gravel and sand has created new wetlands within the county providing useful stop over places for wetland birds.

Along the coastline man has made less of an impact. Where the southern bank of the humber estuary bellies out into the North Sea past the once thriving fishing port of Grimsby, are a series of landscape features, dunes and coastal erosion, which suggests the North Sea is exacting tribute for the acreage that man has taken from it. From Saltfleet to Skegness salt marsh and dunes are embanked against the sea to prevent an incursion such as happened nearly 40 years ago when high winds and tides combined to break the defences and flood thousands of acres of low lying land in Lincolnshire and also Norfolk and Suffolk. This area is bound to be flooded again one day, especially if the rise in sea levels continues.

This is one of the few parts of Britain where the full force of the continental weather is felt, the easterly wind off the chill miles of North Sea blows dry and harsh, and the moist westerlies have usually lost much of their watery cargo to Wales and the Pennine chain. But the low lying nature of much of the region means that a drought would have to be unusually severe for the ground water level over the impervious clay to drop below the point where plant roots cannot reach it.

The region is not enormously rich in wildlife diversity. Those remnant areas where nature still holds sway are either on the coast or held in reserves. Many of the chalk downland flowers are a memory on the wolds, and woodlands are few and often impoverished by isolation or undermanaged for nature. Nevertheless there is much of interest here, especially the Wash, internationally important for wildfowl and waders.

The Wash is a huge estuary opening out onto the North Sea where immense numbers of birds over winter and where many others rest and feed during migration. On the sand bars and banks seals haul out to have their pups or to sunbathe in peace and quiet; and the fowlers who once made a living from the wildfowl in the fleets and marshes are redundant, their cannon-sized punt guns rusting museum pieces. The largest of these punt guns could fire a pound of lead shot of various sizes and kill or maim hundreds of wildfowl at one discharge. Many of the fowlers themselves met their end when the breech blew up in their faces, or they drowned as their frail craft were overwhelmed by the sea in an easterly wind.

The men of the fens were known as Fen Tigers and the author, Charles Kingsley, was inspired by them and the landscape to write his epic story "Hereward the Wake".

BARDNEY FOREST (FC)** — *Spring, summer*

Part of the old and far more extensive Bardney Forest, this piece of woodland is now kept by the Forestry Commission as an area of outstanding ecological importance. The coppice with standards is being continued in order to preserve the integrity of the lime and ash woodland, and the extremely rich bird and insect populations and the superb ground flora.
395ha

BASTON FEN (Lincs & S. Humber TfNC)** — *All year*

Baston Fen, based upon flood meadows and open water, is a mecca for bird-watchers in winter when large numbers of waterfowl arrive to take advantage of the ample food supply in the flooded meadows. Dabbling and grazing duck such as mallard and large numbers of wigeon gather here, and considerable numbers of waders rest on the shallow areas. In spring and summer, as the meadows begin to dry out, the flowers are particularly abundant with some specialists such as water violet and bladderwort appearing on the large list of over 200 flowering plants.
36.5ha

BLACKTOFT SANDS (RSPB) — *All year*

At Blacktoft Sands the large reed bed and lagoon are home to one of the largest populations of bearded tits in the country, nearly ten percent of the national breeding population are here. The reeds are particularly vigorous and form dense stands, taller than a man, and within the reed bed are grassy hummocks of higher ground where the soil is too dry for reeds to grow and which provide nesting for short-eared owls. The reeds are also excellent for a variety of reed living and nesting warblers and buntings, as well as water rail; while the salt marsh harbours nesting redshank and shelduck. The marsh harrier is a frequent visitor and in winter there's a huge population of duck, particularly teal, and a large flock of over 1000 pink-footed geese.
184ha – Map ref: SE 843232

BURTON GRAVEL PITS (Lincs & S. Humber TfNC)** — *All year*

Gravel has been extracted from glacial deposits dropped at the end of the last ice age and the resulting holes have filled with water to the benefit of the wildlife. The reserve has a number of lakes of various sizes and depths of water, encouraging a tremendous variety of waterbirds. Actual numbers depend upon the severity of the winter and prevailing winds, but it's an extremely important wildfowl and grebe refuge. The breeding population of birds in spring and summer is considerable, and insects include several species of dragonflies and butterflies.
36.8ha

CROWLE WASTE (Lincs & S. Humber TfNC)** — *Spring, summer*

The imagination can run riot on this worked out peat bog, once a great domed bog of enormous dimensions. Now the site is a maze of diggings and waterways where the workings have flooded, and there is a wide range of habitats from birch woodland to open heathy moor with cotton grass in the wet hollows; just the place for damselflies and dragonflies, and the most south easterly breeding site of the large heath butterfly whose larvae feed upon cotton grass. The flora is typical of bogs, with round-leaved sundew setting its sticky traps for insects that help to make up the nitrogen intake of this specialised plant. Adders and grass snakes are common, the latter in the wetter places where frogs feature on the menu. Adders tend to prefer drier places in the heather where lizards from the bulk of their prey. There are about 30 different bird species breeding on the reserve which adds to its fascination. This raised peat bog must have been outstanding before it was exploited by man.
116.8ha

DONNA NOOK & SALTFLEET (Lincs & S. Humber TfNC) — *All year*

This extensive coastal dune system, with its saltings and mudflats, forms a valuable winter reserve for birds ranging from harriers to shore larks; over 250 species have been recorded here. The breeding birds reflect the many habitats available and include whitethroat, little grebe, ringed plover, and the rare and elegant little tern which is extremely susceptible to public pressure on its shoreline nesting sites. The North Sea is one of the best places to see common and grey seals, and both species are found on this reserve.
900ha – Map ref: TF 421998 / 444958

FRAMPTON MARSH (Lincs & S. Humber TfNC) — *All year*

Tucked into the lower south west corner of the vast expanse of the Wash, Frampton Marsh is an echo of the past glories of this estuarine system. The marsh has been built up naturally by plants trapping the sediments — glasswort, common cord-grass and salt marsh grass — each of these three species is able to create dry land from the sea and silt. A host of marine and estuarine creatures, fish and crustaceans depend upon this system of creeks and saltings and in winter the place is alive with birds; waders flicker in huge smoke-like flocks wheeling and turning as they fly, and Brent geese beat in against the wind over the grey waters in thin wavering lines. The gatherings of goldeneye are a sight to behold as flocks of

The Wash *Lincs. & S. Humberside*

males in full breeding finery bob and posture to the females prior to the long flight north to breed.

The open skies and huge vistas either delight or intimidate, there seems no half measure, but whatever your feelings towards the dramatic grandeur, the undoubted value to wildlife cannot be ignored — from the tiny marine worms that inhabit the mud to the common seals that haul out to breed in large numbers. Despite the recent seal plague, the Wash is still one of the best places in the world to see large numbers of these engaging animals.

Spring and summer brings another face to the marshes with the flowering of salt marsh plants and the annual influx of migrant birds. The heavily industrialised farming of the fenlands and surrounding regions has lowered the breeding population of songbirds, but there's still a magic about the area that is hard to overlook.
271ha – Map ref: TF 364384

GIBRALTAR POINT (Lincs & S. Humber TfNC) — *All year*

The oddly named Gibraltar Point is a grade I natural history site where sea and land meet and mingle in a meld that is hard to define. The dunes are created by the sea, yet they repel the sea, building land with the aid of colonising plants like cord-grasses and marram whose root systems bind the sand and mud consolidating dunes and salt marsh. Inland the dunes are well established topped by dense stands of sea buckthorn, and alive in winter with redwings, fieldfares and parties of waxwings feasting on the berries and adding to the growth by establishing new stands of buckthorn, elder, hawthorn and wild privet, for where they roost their droopings, full of undigested seeds, fall on the sandy soil.

The point is relatively young, the most well established inner dune system being formed only in the middle of the 19th century, while the outer dunes beyond the salt marsh are still developing with the whole system appearing to march around the mouth of the river Steeping. Dune dynamics are constantly in motion, as the sand consolidates and becomes covered with vegetation new dunes build up in front, and between the banks of sand vegetation begins to flourish on the lime-rich soil composed of chalk and the pulverised fragments of a billion sea shells.

The presence of the river adds a further piece to the ecological jigsaw; fresh water from inland carries with it organic and inorganic nutrients to feed the organisms in the mud and also deposit more mud, this leads to a rich concentration of marine life that is preyed upon by fish and birds, also seals that wait offshore to run in on the tide to harvest the bounty.

In autumn and winter masses of wading birds congregate here, second only in numbers and species-richness to Morecambe Bay on the north west coast. Huge numbers of dark-bellied Brent geese and pink-footed geese may also appear as the dark days of winter leaden the skies, and the air is always full of the wings and whistling call of thousands of wigeon, teal, pintail and mallard.

In spring the skies lighten and massed flocks of returning migrants spin in to land, exhausted by their long journey, and take time to rest before spreading out into the surrounding counties. The breeding birds of Gibraltar Point are extremely diverse and range from small warblers and other passerines to the very important colony of little terns breeding on the shingle and afforded protection by careful wardening.

This is a very special place of ever changing moods, when the wind probes a weakness in the dunes a breach will appear and in a short time where there was once a bank, there is a valley. Moreover this changing face affords limitless opportunites for wildlife, be it plant, butterfly or bird.
428ha – Map ref: TF 556581

KIRKBY MOOR (Lincs & S. Humber TfNC)** — *Spring, summer*

An exceptionally rich and unusual area of moorland and heath in a county where this is not a common habitat. Reptiles at Kirkby Moor are varied with adders, slow worms and grass snakes all occurring. The woodlands are very productive with woodpeckers and birds of prey such as kestrels and sparrowhawks and the night shift includes tawny owl and little owl. There is an excellent breeding population of many dragonfly species and the butterflies include dark green fritillary. Mammals too are common with a large number of small mammals as well as foxes and badgers.
56ha

RUSH FURLONG (Lincs & S. Humber TfNC)** — *Spring, summer*

Strip farming is a relic of a long defunct system of agriculture, but it has somehow survived at Rush Furlong and the Trust is maintaining it for the diversity of its species. The reserve supports a large number of green-winged orchids and many other associated grassland plants indicative of ancient undisturbed grassland.
0.5ha

SALTFLEETBY-THEDDLETHORPE DUNES (NCC/ Lincs & S. Humber TfNC) — *All year*

The North Sea is continuously building and dismantling its shoreline, especially where Lincolnshire bulges out into the sea between the Humber and the Wash. Sand displaced from one site is deposited upon the beach further along the coast, given a steady wind off the sea and a turbulent tide, the construction of a dune system becomes a certainty. Whether or no it stabilises and becomes a permanent feature is in the lap of the Gods, but if the sand is colonised by sand fixing plants like marram, cord-grass and sea buckthorn then the land and not the sea will be the victor. These dunes systems are exceptionally rich in plants, insects, amphibians and reptiles, and the breeding and migratory birds that occupy this seemingly unpromising habitat enjoy the shelter afforded and ample food supplies in the way of insects, seeds, berries and small mammals.

There is a healthy colony of natterjack toads, a typical creature of the slacks, and common toads and frogs also breed here as do two species of newt. The orchid flora depends upon several circumstances of nutrients and moisture and the presence of shelly sand full of lime encourages them to grow abundantly. The marsh, such a feature of the reserve, has a very wide range of insects and a number of dragonfly and damselfly species. In winter the buckthorn is dressed overall with berries, and the migrant thrushes are to be seen in huge numbers feeding on the harvest.

478ha – Map ref: TF 465924 / 467917 / 478901 / 483893 /489882

SNIPE DALES (LCC/Lincs & S. Humber TfNC) — *Spring, summer*

Snipe Dales is in the process of being recolonised by oak, ash, alder and willow in the wetter areas. The reserve is developing beautifully which bodes well for a future filled with an abundance of birds and insects, especially butterflies and woodland warblers. In the wetter areas where marsh marigold and ragged robin grow the delightful descending cadences of the willow warblers can be heard. On the lower slopes a strong stand of gorse provides superb nesting areas for yellowhammers, linnets, and whitethroats which breed here. On an area of exposed soft sandstone a sand martin colony is established, but its success depends on events in far off Africa. It is to be hoped that time and rains in this desperate part of the world will allow for a greater survival of these attractive birds. Another national rarity, the barn owl, also appears here.

48ha – Map ref: RF 320863

TETNEY MARSHES (RSPB)* — *Spring, summer*

Tetney Marshes is one of the best sites in Britain for salt marsh dunes and foreshore. It is of particular importance for that national rarity, the little tern, which is very susceptible to disturbance by people on the beaches. Their breeding area is carefully wardened and restriction to non-sensitive parts of the reserve during the breeding season has ensured the increase of these attractive small terns. Many other birds visit or nest on the marshes during the year, including Brent geese, grey plover, bar-tailed godwit, knot, golden plover, whimbrel, curlew and sandpiper.

1300ha – Map ref: TA 360037

NORFOLK

It was Noel Coward who wrote disparagingly "Very flat Norfolk" and this is how many people see it, but there is more than one side to Norfolk! The exciting sea-shore for instance — picturesque at Blakeney, rich in wildlife at Cley next the Sea, and then there are the wild Brecklands. The wonderful colours and tones, the landscapes and the skies inspired the Norwich School of painters, leaving the world a legacy of beauty. Sadly the countryside that so enthralled Cotman, Crome, Cox and the like has been drastically changed by modern agriculture, but the wide open wastes of the wash, skirling with birds, are still a feature of the county, and the seascapes of the north Norfolk coast are still as beautiful.

George Crabbe, the poet, was enthralled by the north Norfolk landscape with its huge vistas, open gallops and particularly the wild places which inspired him to write this poem:-

"Peter Grimes at Aldeburg":-

Or sadly listen to the tuneless cry
Of fishing gull or clanging golden-eye;
What time the sea-birds to the marsh would come,

And the loud bittern, from the bull-rush home,
Gave from the salt-ditch side the bellowing boom.
He nursed the feelings these dull scenes produce,
And loved to stop beside the opening sluice;
Where the small stream, confined in narrow bound,
Ran will a dull, unvaried, sadd'ning sound.

Anna Sewell, the Norfolk born author of "Black Beauty" was also inspired by this landscape, she lies now in the quiet Quaker burial ground at Lamas amid the Irish yews while the young riders of a hundred pony clubs dream of owning such a horse.

The rides of Thetford Chase may thunder with the hooves of horses and ponies at weekends, but for the most part they are quiet, populated by fallow and roe deer and Norfolk's population of red squirrels. Both red and grey squirrels co-exist here, and although the red continues its downward population slide, other creatures will quicken the pulse of the naturalist. Birds of prey feature highly in these mature dense pine forests; the largest of the European round-winged predators, the goshawk, swoops along the length of the firebreaks its size, grey plumage and fierce yellow eye indicating its power and imparting a sense of menace. Despite being protected by law, they are subject to considerable pressure from gamekeepers, falconers and egg collectors, but it's possible they may spread out to other areas with sufficient cover and undisturbed hunting.

Once a very prosperous county, Norfolk's landscape was modified by man long before the industrial re-volution, for its wealth depended on sheep and huge numbers of these woolly goldmines quietly nibbled away at the grass of the central Brecklands. Sandy, remote and wild, the haunt of bustard and stone curlew and a fiercely independent race of shepherds, the Brecklands were created by man, as was much of the flat landscape of East Anglia. They are only a shadow of their former glory now, covered by conifer forests in an attempt to retain their profitability as the need for sheep declines. What is not already planted with conifers has become covered with scrub, after the myxomatosis outbreak when rabbits almost vanished, the process of scrub invasion accele-rated. The bustards that once lived in great flocks on the dry sandy heaths were shot out of existance by the beginning of the last century, and the stone curlew declined with the increased agricultural use.

After the last glaciation drifts of sand, pebbles and small boulders overlayed the chalk subsoil to a considerable depth. Where the chalk was closer to the surface or exposed by erosion, the land was suprisingly fertile and covered by dense forests of oak, ash, elm and lime. Over the centuries much of this forest has been felled, its place taken by agricultural monotony, but even here there's a plus for nature with the open ground and cereal fields providing nesting sites for rare Montague's harriers.

Norfolk's geological history has been turbulent, part-icularly because over the millennia sea levels fluctuated creating layers of silt and peat; in places this peat has built up to as much as 10 metres thick, and in medieval times was mined for fuel until a further rise in water levels flooded the peat diggings, when the Broadlands were formed. As they developed their own special character they were used by man for fishing, fowling, and reed cutting, used for thatch and bedding for animals. The Broads are now substantially disturbed and polluted by boating and farming interests, their former wildlife diversity has been suppressed, in some places virtually extinguished; yet those Broads where conservation interests have been able to control boating and access, and the quality of the water, are much as they were before the influx of tourism.

Another main feature of the county is the Wash, a huge shallow estuary where the rivers Ouse, Nene, Welham and Witham empty into the North Sea. This immense area of fertile sand and mud supports a huge amount of wildlife. From the invertebrates that form the basis of the food chain for birds and fish, to the common seals that haul out onto the sandbanks to have their young. Sadly seals are becoming less common since the outbreak of canine distemper in the summer of 1988 decimated populations all around the coast, not only in their traditional breeding grounds on the Wash sand banks, but in nearly every other seal colony. It is to be hoped that the efforts of a host of conservation organisations and wildlife rescue units will be able to find an answer to this very serious problem.

Perhaps the plight of the seals, the people of the seas as they are known by fishermen and sailors, may arouse the conscience of all the nations with North Sea coastlines and pursuade us to stop dumping our filthy rubbish into it, until then these lovely, soft-eyed, creatures will con-tinue to suffer from man's lack of care for his environment.

BARTON BROAD (Norfolk NT)** — *Spring, summer*
Barton actually consists of three broads, Barton, Turkey Broad and Irstead, the last two are best seen from the water. A navigation channel runs through them although access to the areas where swallowtail butterflies and bearded tits are to be found is restricted. There's a heronry here, and bittern also occur.
148ha

BLAKENEY POINT (NT) — *All year*
One of the earliest reserves to be instituted, the sand and shingle dunes at Blakeney Point are famous for rare and unusual migrant passerines. The point extends from the road at Cley next the Sea and juts out into a claw of shingle, enclosing the bay and sand flats behind in its grip. The wild weather that sometimes assaults the point and the bay makes this a perfect stopping off place for small birds exhausted by long sea crossings. In winter flocks of snow buntings fly the sands looking for food, and in summer these same beaches and sandy bays are host to nesting terns. Children from all over the country can visit the educational centre here and study a wild environment, sometimes in wild weather.
440ha – Map ref: TG 001464

BLICKLING HALL (NT) — *All year*
Beautiful parkland where ancient trees and buildings provide a host of nest sites for birds, especially the barn

owl which rears its young in specially prepared boxes in old farm buildings. Blickling and the Lothian barn constitute the headquarters of the Hawk Trust's Barn Owl Project and a display shows their work in owl conservation.

BREYDON WATER (Norfolk CC) — *All year*

The rivers Yare and Waveney empty into an estuary bounded by a huge area of tidal flats and salt marsh, well known for the excellent spring migration of whimbrel as they stop off to feed and rest on the long journey to their breeding grounds. The estuary also supports most species of waders, especially spotted redshank, black-tailed and bar-tailed godwits. Winter visitors include wigeon and the occasional scaup, while small groups of Brent geese gather prior to feeding on the marshes inland. The occasional short-eared owl can be seen quartering the marsh for food.
453ha – Map ref: TG 475051

BUCKENHAM BEAN GEESE HIDE (RSPB) — *December through February*

At the height of winter there are up to 200 bean geese on the grazing marsh, the only regularly wintering flock in the United Kingdom. Many other wildfowl favour the area, and can also be seen from the hide.
Map ref: TG 342067

CLEY AND SALTHOUSE MARSHES (Norfolk NT) — *All year*

Talk to bird-watchers about Norfolk and it won't be long before Cley next the Sea is mentioned, followed by a list of rare migrants as long as your arm. This sea-shore and area of salt marsh reeds is one of the best bivouac sites in the whole of east Anglia. When the rarities come, there are often more bird-watchers than birds, but the reserve is so large that it's always possible to be alone with your thoughts and the wildlife.

Spring and autumn is the time for waders and migrant passerines, and often the chance of seeing a peregrine or hen or marsh harrier hunting the reed beds. Indeed springtime on the marshes can be very productive when all the local nesting territories are disputed by any number of birds. Bearded reedlings are common as are sedge and reed warblers and be prepared for a passing osprey or a male ruff displaying (it is thought that this interesting bird may have bred here). One of the most attractive marsh birds is the golden plover in its full breeding finery, they gather here prior to flying north to their upland breeding sites.

Avocets returned to Norfolk to breed in 1977 and have been a great attraction ever since. Bitterns can be heard booming, and in spring the occasional pair of black-tailed godwits fly in to breed. Terns on passage regularly visit the sands, and sandwich terns once bred in some numbers, but no longer. The breeding success of little and common terns depends to some extent on the amount of disturbance they are subjected to, but they try to rear young each year.

The whole area between the marshes at Cley and the coastline up to Blakeney Point can yield surprises; in summer the arrival of hosts of migrant painted lady or clouded yellow butterflies completes a marvellous day.

A permit system applies for the marshland hides, but these are easy to obtain from the observation centre or from the Trust offices.
266ha – Map ref: TF 054451

EAST WRETHAM HEATH (Norfolk NT) — *Spring, summer*

A fine example of original Breckland over chalk subsoil. There was once a wartime airfield here, but a great deal of the Breckland habitat remains, including some meres (open areas of water) supporting large numbers of dragonflies. A particular characteristic of this area is the way that sand has created a moving scene of dunes with plants adapted to arid conditions. Where the wind has blown away sand from the underlying chalk, plants like wild thyme and mignonette have adapted and grow freely. It's particularly interesting to see wild mignonette growing close to viper's bugloss, a plant of acid sandy soil.

There are a number of conifer plantings, one of mature Scots pine, but others less compatible. Nevertheless the crossbills like the pines, and linnets the gorse bushes; and nightjar and wheatear are recorded as breeding here regularly. Hobby, merlin and long-eared owls are seen as well as the less exotic tawny owl. Adders, grass snakes and common lizards bask in the sunshine — all indications of the variations in the environment.
147ha – Map ref: TL 914886

HETHAL OLD THORN (Norfolk NT) — *All year*
One very ancient hawthorn tree thought to have been planted by King John in the 13th century.
0.05ha – Map ref: TG 172004

Avocet   *Tichwell*

HICKLING BROAD (Norfolk NT)** — *Spring, summer*

One of the finest man-made waterways in the whole of the country, and the largest body of open water in southern England formed from the flooded peat workings of a bygone age. The water is pure, and rich in plants, birds and insects; the British swallowtail butterfly is found here in some numbers feeding on the abundant milk parsley, although both the butterfly and its food plant are scarce nationally. Bearded reedling and bittern nest regularly, and you can hear the evocative booming of the bitterns in spring. Marsh harrier and the occasional Montague's harrier have nested in the reed beds.

The reserve is partly bounded by hay meadows where the ancient regime of cutting unfertilised grassland has continued unchanged to the present day, this has encouraged masses of wild flowers including the very rare and beautiful wild marsh pea. The wet marginal lands are grazed and in summer thick with southern marsh and common spotted orchids — the sheer unspoiled nature of this reserve makes it a haven for wildlife.
549ha

HOLKHAM (NCC) — *All year*

Holkham is part of the north Norfolk coast complex of reserves. Dunes, salt marsh, mud flats and agricultural land constitute an extremely bird rich area.
3953ha – Map ref: TF 892447

HOLME BIRD OBSERVATORY (NOA) — *All year*

The observatory is positioned on a bulge of land on the north Norfolk coast by Scolt Head which slows the westerly flow of incoming migrants. The belt of Corsican pines, behind the sand dunes, and the marram grass covering the dunes themselves, provide excellent shelter for small passerines; in consequence large numbers of birds including wrynecks and red-spotted bluethroats stop to rest before venturing on. Huge numbers of redwings and fieldfares take advantage of the berry crop on the sea buckthorn.

If weather conditions are right it's an excellent place from which to see plenty of sea duck and marine birds. The extraordinary is ordinary here; black terns and spoonbills may arrive unexpectedly, stay for a few days, then move on. All three species of harriers are a certainty in autumn, and the young osprey of the year are frequently seen heading south along the coast. In winter the reserve takes on another guise as huge numbers of Brent geese, often over 1000, visit the grazing marshes. They beat in low against the wind in thin waving lines growling their contact calls like a pack of terriers in full cry.
2.4ha – Map ref: TF 714449

OTTER TRUST (Otter Trust) — *Spring, summer*

Otters are one of our rarest breeding mammals, and you'll see both British and foreign species of these exquisite mustilids here. The Trust are trying to encourage the spread of these delightful creatures, especially in the light of the canine distemper virus which became prevalent in 1988 and which is almost bound to affect the seagoing Scottish otter population.
12ha – Map ref: TM 315884

SANDRINGHAM COUNTRY PARK (Sandringham Estate Parkland) — *Spring, summer*

Way-marked trails show the variety of this well known Royal estate. The woods consist of conifer and broad-leaved species, and there's also some heath. The result of this diversity is plenty of birds, plants and insects to delight both eyes and ears. Nightjars breed here, and hobbys and sparrowhawks are regular visitors.
240ha – Map ref: TF 689287

SCOLT HEAD ISLAND (NCC) — *All year*

Part of the north Norfolk complex of coastal reserves, the breeding tern colonies are the specialities of the island. The sand/shingle bar can be reached only by boat, but it's worth it for the superb range of birds and plants. Regular migrations of small passerines stop here, and quite a few rarities have been recorded. Excellent in autumn for shearwaters, sea duck and skuas.
738ha – Map ref: TF 805465

SNETTISHAM (RSPB) — *All year*

Snettisham is one of the very best places in the country for birds, the huge acreage of the Wash is of international importance as a feeding ground and roost for thousands of pink-footed geese and Brent geese. Also noted for immense numbers of shelduck, the reserve specialises in the numbers game; in winter more than 70,000 waders gather on the food-rich mud below the hides, and the Wash itself is particularly important as a site where wildfowl and geese and waders can find refuge from the wildfowling which still occurs on the foreshore. The flooded pits behind the foreshore are important for resting, feeding and nesting. To list all the duck and waders that gather here would be a difficult task, suffice to say that Snettisham is a jewel, fortunately not lost in the mud of the wash as were the crown jewels of King John.
3257 acres – Map ref: TF 648335

STRUMPSHAW FEN (RSPB) — *All year*

Situated on the lower reaches of the tidal river Yare Strumpshaw Fen comprises a complex set of habitats including large sedge beds bisected by the river, two broads with open water, a marsh with willow and alder woodlands and wet grazing marshes. Birds are of paramount interest here; marsh harrier, bearded tit and Cetti's warbler are some of the more unusual breeding species, and many duck, including gadwall, rear their young along with great crested grebe and water rail nesting in the reeds.

In winter the grazing marshes are renowned, for the largest flock of bean geese in the country gather together with immense numbers of wigeon and mallard, and on the adjacent fen at Buckenham there is a roost of hen harriers in winter.

Norfolk Field   *Norfolk*

In spring Chinese water deer can sometimes be seen feeding before the vegetation becomes too dense and they are hidden from view, and the insects here include occasional swallowtail butterflies and dragonflies.
447 acres – Map ref: TG 342067

TITCHWELL (RSPB) — *All year*

Part of the north Norfolk coast complex, Titchwell consists of tidal flats and salt marsh, reed beds, freshwater pools and a shingle beach and dune system. An increasing colony of avocets nest on the enclosed pools with gadwell, shoveller and little grebe and a small black-headed gull colony. In the reed beds bittern and marsh harrier breed, and common terns and little terns nest on the beach.

Spring and autumn bring their crop of passing rarities and black terns can sometimes be seen catching insects from the surface of the inshore pools; in winter the reserve is no less active with hen harriers roosting in the reed beds, scoters and eider duck floating off shore and regular visits from Brent and pink-footed geese.
206ha – Map ref: TF 750436

WALSEY HILLS (NOA) — *Spring, autumn*

One of the few high vantage points on this stretch of the north Norfolk coast. Understandably it is superb for observing the birds that travel along the coast, including the annual sea-bird migrations every spring and autumn.

The high ground also acts as a magnet for small songbirds, tired after their migration.
0.3ha – Map ref: TG 062441

WEETING HEATH (Norfolk NT/NCC)** — *Spring, summer*

A typical example of Breckland heath as it once was all over the area, the reserve is known for its butterflies and breeding birds. Early forget-me-not and rue-leaved saxifrage grow in profusion.
138ha

WINTERTON DUNES (NCC) — *Spring, summer*

Winterton Dunes are unusual because they have less sea shell fragments than commonly found in dune systems and this lack of lime has led to the sand being unusually acid, exactly the right conditions for heather and cross-leaved heath, both of which grow well here and on the grazing marshes behind the dunes. Marram grass stabilises the dunes against the wind with its deep mat-like root system so that other plants can take hold. The dune slacks attract natterjack toads, one of our rarest amphibians, they thrive in the warm sheltered environment; on the shore, in front of the dunes, little terns breed, but if subjected to disturbance their success is reduced.
105ha – Map ref: TG 498197

NORTHAMPTONSHIRE
&
THE SOKE OF
PETERBOROUGH

This is John Clare country. He was born at Helpston and was buried here in 1864 after a life spent in turmoil. Yet he captured the essence of his countryside in each exquisite line he wrote. How easy it is to imagine him on a summer evening penning the following verse — evening brings a host of wild creatures fearful of man, and his lines sum up so well this often unremarked conflict between man and nature:-

"Summer Evening"

The frog, half fearful, jumps across the path,
And little mouse that leaves its hole at eve
Nimbles with timid dread beneath the swathe;
My rustling steps awhile their joys deceive,
Till past — and then the cricket sings more strong,
And grasshoppers in merry moods still wear
The short nights weary with their fretting song.

The county we see today bears little resemblance to Clare's Northamptonshire. The woods he viewed have all but vanished, particularly the great Midlands woods that cover the portly girth of Britain's fertile midriff. In Norman times when deer, wild boar and wolves roamed the bird resounding woodlands and before shoemakers began to demand tannin from oak bark.

Rockingham, Salsey and Whittlebury forests retain a fragment of their former landholding, and numerous small copses and areas of shelter woodland kept for pheasant shooting, creates a deceptively wooded aspect; but most of the land is given over to farming, heavily exploited for cereals and oil seeds and other crops that require wide open fields. Nevertheless, even though the changes have been many and drastic, the county can boast some fascinating reserves, though the rolling hills may not be as dramastic as in some other parts of Britain, they nourish a large number of major river systems; the Nene, Welland, Tove and Great Ouse all rise from the deep limestone heart of Northamptonshire.

Economics have necessarily made great inroads; mining and mineral extraction and heavy industry once dominated this landscape, but over the past few decades technological changes have transformed the steel industry and towns like Corby are now a shadow of their former selves; the sheer amount of water needed to cool the giant steel works is no longer required and the sulphur and dust that was pumped out into the atmosphere no longer pollutes the air or the rivers. Fish that once lived very active lives in winter because of hot water outfalls into the rivers, have had to re-learn how to cope with normal temperatures.

The leather trade once depended upon water and tannin from oak bark and, together with the embryo steel industry, stripped the major trees from the landscape. However, the shoe trade needed a constant supply of tan bark such as a coppice woodland could provide, and coppice woodland is good for nature. As a conservation tool it has only really been appreciated since the end of the last war.

As the input of chemical pollutants from heavy industry declined and our rivers and streams, canals and brooks began to run clean again another aspect of pollution reared its ugly head, the uncontrolled expansion in the use of dangerous agrochemicals due to modern farming techniques and monoculture cereal and oil seed production. Many of the streams that fed major rivers became over-nutrified with the run-off from fields heavily top-dressed with soluble nitrogenous materials, or the even more destructive set of elements found in silage or intensive animal production.

In the north of the region the recently revitalised city of Peterborough with its new population may have a greater influence in maintaining the diversity of natural habitats than former more industrial regimes. The new housing and factory building will generate new gravel workings and eventually these will create more places for nature. I believe that Clare would not be entirely displeased with the way the countryside of his youth has developed; although some of the changes in the landscape have been shocking, at least he would be relieved by the rise in status and income of the mass of the population and the end of rural squalor and privation of many of his farming and industrial contemporaries.

BARNWELL COUNTRY PARK (Northants CC) — *Spring, summer*

Reconstituted from old gravel workings, the flooded areas in this park are now rich in reed and sedge species, with open water providing an ideal situation for duck, great crested grebe and water rail to breed successfully. More than 125 different bird species have been recorded here including the elegant black tern, large numbers of wintering duck and the occasional bewick swan in hard weather.

15ha – Map ref: TL 037874

BEDFORD PURLIEUS (Northants WT)** — *Spring, summer*

Within the boundaries of Bedford Purlieus, once part of the old forest of Rockingham, there are a number of differing soil types supporting plants like herb paris, sweet woodruff, greater and lesser butterfly orchid, common cow wheat, hard fern and great woodrush. Such a variety in a relatively small area encourages many butterflies, white letter and brown hairstreak are two of the more unusual species, and the white admiral butterfly finds ample honeysuckle bines on which to lay its eggs in July. Four species of fritillary butterfly, pearl bordered, the rare high brown, dark green, and the elegant, fast flying silver-washed fritillary all jostle on thistle flowers in the sunny rides.

Birds too find the variety of habitats and ample breeding sites provided through coppicing and woodland management to their liking, and the spring is as rich now as it would have been in John Clare's day.

22.8ha

CASTOR HANGLANDS (NCC) — *Spring, summer*

Castor Hanglands is a remnant of the ancient forest of Narborough, managed woodland of coppice with standards. Changes in the economy of the area lessened the need for tan bark and charcoal for industry and smelting and wood for building, and the forest was clear felled and left to revert to grazed common grassland. The wheel turned full circle, for as the land fell derelict and scrub began to invade the pasture, the trees reasserted their dominance.

Evidence of the woodland's age is found in the ground flora such as sweet woodruff, dog's mercury, wood sorrel and herb paris indicating that there may well have been woodland here since the end of the Pleistocene Ice Age. The reversion to woodland is not complete. There are areas of grassland, grazed by herds of fallow deer, where thriving plant and insect communities exist, and open water with its own flora and fauna and dragonflies and damselflies in some numbers in summer. The variety in the woodland, the woodland marginal vegetation and shrubs, provides excellent nesting for summer songbird migrants and native species. The reserve is well known as one of the best areas in the Midlands for the black hairstreak butterfly.

45ha – Map ref: TF 118023

KING'S WOOD (Northants WT/Corby DC) — *Spring, summer*

Part of the old Rockingham forest, King's Wood is mainly oak and ash over a hazel understory with some fine stands of large and very ancient oaks. The woodland plants and lichens indicates the age and quality of the wood, and the bluebells and woodland edge orchids attract botanists. The potential for nesting sites for birds means the spring birdsong is a delight.

45ha – Map ref: SP 864874

PEAKIRK WILDFOWL REFUGE (WWT) — *Spring, summer*

This wildfowl collection is set on the site of an old osier bed, and a duck decoy, which first appeared in records as far back as the middle of the 15th century, and is still in use for ringing migrant wildfowl. The bird population increases considerably in winter as wildfowl and waders fly in to join the captive collection. There is an excellent visitor centre.

6.8ha – Map ref: TF 168069

PITSFORD RESERVOIR (AWA/Northants WT)** — *All year*

Set in an area where there are few other large bodies of open water, Pitsford provides a safe refuge for a huge variety of birds. The reservoir has substantial marginal vegetation, muddy beaches and shallow margins where waders and migrant terns can feed and rest, both black terns and the rarer white-winged black terns occur on passage. Birds of prey thrive here and the twelve species recorded reflect the abundance of life on the reservoir as a whole. Autumn and winter are the best times when rare and unusual wildfowl and swans often fly in with the large mixed flocks of more common waterbirds; it's also a good site for goldeneye, and there is a substantial gull roost on the water that attracts unusual species.

172ha – (Overlooked from) Map Ref: SP 783701

Ne Ne Goose Peakirk Wildfowl (Northants)

SALCEY FOREST (Northants WT/BBONT/FC)** — *Spring, summer*

Part of the ancient woodland of Salcey, this remnant reflects some of the incredible diversity of this type of habitat. A huge range of birds includes nightingale, and the flowers are a mixture of ancient woodland species with primroses and bluebells being succeeded by carpets of goldilocks, wood sorrel, dog's mercury and early purple orchid; the speciality being the superb greater butterfly orchid.

Blackthorn, Midland and common hawthorn bushes provide cover and nesting sites for a host of songbirds, and butterflies abound in the rides on bright summer days. Mammals are well represented too with fallow and the small introduced muntjac deer, and there's a good fox population increasing as the rabbit population increases.
8.8ha

SHORT WOOD (Northants WT)** — *Spring, summer*

One of the richest, most beautiful woods in the Midlands, Short Wood is part of the old Rockingham forest, once a royal hunting preserve, but now known as perhaps the finest bluebell wood in the area. The flowers are typical of those found in ancient woodland, with particularly interesting species such as greater butterfly orchid, bird's nest orchid and broad-leaved and violet helleborine.

The wood has been managed by coppice with standards; but the method for coppicing the elms was unusual. The stools being 4ft to 5ft high instead of the more usual ground level coppice stool of hazel, oak or hornbeam, or pollarding where the new growth was encouraged above the grazing line of cattle or deer. Deer are relatively common here and the fallow bucks can be heard bellowing in the early autumn rut.
24.8ha

THORPE WOOD (Northants WT) — *Spring, summer*

A beautiful wood composed of oak and ash standards with hazel and field maple coppice. There's a good display

Goldilocks   *Salcey Forest (Northants)*

of bluebells in spring with nettle-leaved bellflower, and a large variety of birds including greater-spotted woodpeckers, nuthatch and many springtime migrants like blackcaps, willow warblers and garden warblers.
9.7ha – Map ref: TL 160986

THRAPSTON GRAVEL PITS AND TITCHMARSH HERONRY (Northants WT) — *All year*

The heronry consists of forty to fifty breeding pairs which makes it particularly interesting, while the reserve itself comprises a series of flooded sand and gravel pits gradually reclaimed by nature and affording nesting sites for wagails and little-ringed plover. The sheer banks of sand and gravel left after the workings were abandoned have become a thriving sand martin colony, a vital resource at a time when sand martins are declining because of drought in the African countries over which they migrate. There's also a section of disused railway cutting that is heavily overgrown with hawthorn producing a berry crop greatly appreciated by migrant thrushes. Thrapston lies on the Nene flyway, a migration route across the country, and the water attracts a considerable number of birds in winter when the feral population is swelled by wintering wildfowl, even bitterns can be seen in hard weather. This is a prime wetland site where any number of unusual birds may occur, and quite often do.
15ha – Map ref: TF 007796

WICKSTEED PARK (Wicksteed Village Trust) — *All year*

A nature trail provides access to this interesting park with a lake and pools which support a considerable resident waterfowl population enhanced by winter visitors; while the willows and alders attract mixed flocks of siskins and redpolls. Spring migrants arrive as the marsh marigolds begin to bloom and the shallow areas of the reserve come alive with sedge warblers and cuckoos. Periodically the lake is drained and the resulting muddy bottom encourages spring migrant waders and wagtails to stop and feed.
59.5ha – Map ref: SP 880773

Frog   *Northants/Soke of Peterborough*

NORTHUMBERLAND

The old granite of the Cheviots tells of a time long past when this entire area was a boiling mass of volcanic action, you can still find evidence of lava flows; the geology is as varied as the people and their domesticated animals, and the natural flora and fauna.

The Roman general Hadrian used the great curved ridge of the Whin Sill as a foundation for a rampart to prevent the wild tribes of Scotland, among them the Damnonii and the Selgovae, from spilling into the northern counties. However, it has to be said that the wall, constructed so carefully using local labour, stone and cut turf, was more of an architectural achievement than a defensive success for it seems the Scots ebbed and flowed into England whenever they felt like it, despite the efforts of the Roman legions.

The auxiliaries of the Roman army, under Roman officers, were drawn from many of the tribes of northern Europe, and there's little doubt that some of the soldiers who huddled in the rain on the watchtowers were southern British tribesmen. The reality of their life along the length of this rampart must have been somewhat different than contemporary report would have it, for excavations show that, far from sitting in splendid isolation on their lonely vigil, they enjoyed a healthy contact with the local inhabitants. They spent much of their time brewing beer, baking bread and teaching their children Alfa from Beta, and generally getting on with life as best they could in this the northern most outpost of the Empire.

It was a most incredible occupation lasting 400 years. Put into context with more recent history, it's the same length of time as between the reign of Elizabeth I and Elizabeth II.

The constant traffic ever since from north to south — south to north has resulted in some massive conflicts, but also some beautiful castles; sadly most are in ruins, monuments to man's aggression to his fellow man. The landscape somehow reflects this aggression in the harsh crags of the Whin Sill and the high isolation of the Cheviots. But it can be peaceful too on the open rolling moorland with the sound of golden plover and curlew floating on the wind, or down on the wide sandy bays where wind driven dunes pile up inshore to form a landscape the Romans would recognise despite the passing of 2000 years.

The wild men of the Marches shared the land with monks, and later the Vikings laid waste to the Monastery on Holy Island and the communities on the Farnes before roaring inland with increasing ferocity. Their power confirmed, they settled the sheep-grazed countryside and became part of the landscape, extending their influence into the next county and re-establishing the importance of Roman Eboracum which they called Yorvic.

The rivers Tweed and Till have their beginnings on the northern borders of this beautiful county; one fast and turbulent the other deep and quiet, they inspired this anonymous poem written in dialect.

Tweed and Till
Says Tweed to Till,
What gars ye rin sae still?
Says Till to Tweed,
Though ye rin wi' speed,
And I rin slaw,
For ae man that ye droun
I droun twa.
And there's no doubt that neither of these rivers are to be taken lightly.

Many of the streams and burns that run to the sea carry water from a host of mosses and bogs of deep water-logged peat built up since the end of the last ice age. The pressure of ice ground away the surface of many of the region's soft rocks exposing the deeper strata and the materials that were to change the economy of the county. It went from agriculture, especially the golden fleece from the backs of sheep, to the black gold of coal mines some of which run out under the cold North Sea where the roar of the waves can be heard underground in the cramped, frightening dark.

The coal seams that surface on the beaches of the Northumberland coast form steps of rock, like a flight of stairs worn by the same waves that separated the Farnes from the mainland 10,000 years ago. The fertile rim of farmland that forms a protective collar around the coast gives way inland to a harsh world of high wet moorland and peat bogs. Some of these are internationally important, but this has not stopped the March of alien conifers. Indeed the county carries an unfair burden of conifer plantations, leaving very little of the natural woodland.

The sea coast carries an echo of a long drowned plain that once extended far beyond the horizon and formed the bed of what is now the North Sea. Black jet and golden amber roll in on the tide and are polished on the beaches. The importance of this area lies partly in the fact that despite its dramatic beauty it is off the tourist map;

however, this is changing and more people are falling in love with Northumberland.

ARNOLD (Northumberland WT) — *Spring through autumn*

Arnold is one of the very few areas of semi natural woodland left in the county; sporting elm, sycamore, ash and scots pine with a healthy shrub layer and well known for its diverse breeding species. Its proximity to the coast makes it a prime spot for rare migrants and vagrant species such as the bluethroat, a small robin-like bird with a brilliant bib of blue feathers. In springtime the woodland is alive with birdsong and a gorgeous display of bluebells with foxglove and northern marsh orchid as the year progresses.
1.2ha – Map ref: NU 255197

BORDER FOREST PARK (FC) — *Spring, summer*

Based upon Keilder Water, a huge man-made reservoir, this area of Forestry Commission woodlands and moors provides a series of habitats from high moorland with curlew, wheatear, red and black grouse, and a few pairs of merlin to the mixed blocks of conifer woodland where you'll find siskin, short-eared owl, sparrowhawk and kestrel. The mammal fauna is diverse too and includes red squirrel, badger, fox, stoat and a substantial population of voles and woodmice. The reservoir also attracts both breeding and wintering duck.
45,325ha – Map ref: NY 633935

BORDER MIRES (Northumberland WT)** — *Spring, summer*

Of the nine sphagnum moss bogs here several are of international importance; they range from wet mires to drier sites and the vegetation is equally varied.
Various sizes

COCKLAWBURN DUNES (Northumberland WT) — *Spring, summer*

Typical coastal sand-dunes supporting clumps of thrift, buck's horn plantain and sea sandwort, while the limestone outcrops and spoil encourage bloody cranesbill, cowslip, autumn gentian and purple milk vetch. The seaward facing dunes shelter purple sandpipers, and turnstones feed on the tideline while off-shore flocks of common eider gather.
6ha – Map ref: NU 032482

FARNE ISLANDS (NT) — *Spring through winter*

Situated just off the Northumberland coast between the attractive village of Seahouses and magnificent Bamburgh Castle, these islands were separated from the land at the end of the last ice age by rising sea levels and the erosion of softer rocks by the immense pressure and abrasive weight of glacial action. The activity is evident in the layer of glacial drift on some of the larger islands. Mostly composed of very hard ancient rocks of the same group as the Whin Sill, there are some softer rocks and erosion has led to the formation of stacks so popular with seabirds.

In all there are twenty eight islands, though many are simply rocks that appear above the surface only at low tide, and have accounted for a lot of shipping over the centuries, before the advent of lighthouses. The rocks became famous during the Victorian era when the lighthouse keeper and his daughter risked life and limb to row out to the *Forfarshire* wrecked on the Farnes on 7th September 1838. The young girl's name was Grace Darling.

The North Sea is aggressive, and perhaps it is the turbulent conditions and smooth rocks churned by rushing water that has made this area such an excellent breeding site for the North Sea grey seal population. They are among the rarest seals in the world, and choose this place to have their pups. Sadly it has not saved them from the attentions of fishermen or government appointed culling teams who have killed them in their thousands. Now pollution and a variety of canine distemper is plaguing them and they are succumbing to respiratory infections. How many years will pass before the seals are able to develop a natural immunity is difficult to tell, but until that time their numbers will have to be monitored with some care.

Happily the gulls, auks and guillemots are in excellent shape and large numbers of puffins, called Tommy Noddies by the locals because of the way they nod their heads as they walk, breed on the main island (up to 15,000 pairs). As many as 6,000 pairs of guillemots nest on the stacks on any ledge they can find, but only a few pairs of their near relatives, the razorbills. St Cuthbert's duck, better known as the common eider, breeds in some numbers. Their eiderdown-lined nests built where anyone can see them for the female depends on her amazing camouflage of brown and cream to blend into the background. The eggs are taken by gulls, both black-backed and herring gulls, but they aren't molested by the fulmars who have colonised the islands since the early part of the century; several hundred pairs now breed wherever there is room for their scanty nests.

The guillemots and razorbills compete for nest ledgers with the gentle-looking kittiwake. Up to 4,000 pairs of kittiwakes seek nesting sites here in spring, many returning year after year to the same ledge. Shags and cormorants also nest here; the shag with its strange wild eye and fluffy top knot nests in some numbers on Staple Island. Inner Farne and Brownsman Island, and where the glacial till is exposed, waders such as oyster catchers and ringed plover nest on the stony ground. The stones and gravel also present a perfect nesting site for tern colonies and four species, including the very rare roseate tern as well as the more common sandwich and arctic terns, breed on Inner Farne, Brownsman and Staple Island.

Boats take visitors to and from those islands where landing is permitted; the National Trust make a small charge, but it's well worth it especially if the seals are bobbing about in the sea like so many large aquatic labrador dogs. They are so curious and always want to see what's going on.
32ha – Map ref: NU 230370

FLODDEN QUARRY (Northumberland WT)** — *Spring, summer*

In the very distant past the whole of this area was in the path of immense flows of molten lava from long extinct volcanoes, and in the section where quarrying has cut across the rock you can see the evidence of these ancient lava flows. Botanically the area is very interesting with a superb show of bluebells, many other wild flowers and ferns.
0.4ha

GOOSE'S NEST BLUEBELL BANK (Northumberland WT)** — *May*

This reserve with its lovely name has been set up to protect the finest display of bluebells in the county.
0.4ha – (Overlooked from) Map ref: NY 980852

GRINDON LOUGH (Northumberland WT) — *Winter*

Grindon Lough is a noted site for wildfowl; every year large numbers of shoveller duck, wigeon, teal and mallard gather to feed in the shallow water. Pink-footed and bean geese over-winter as do whooper swans, and goldeneye are also regular winter visitors.
88ha – Map ref: NY 806675

HARBOTTLE CRAGS (Northumberland WT) — *Spring, summer*

Once a wooded area the reserve is now maintained as heather moorland with sandstone crags with Harbottle Lough at the western end where wild swans and other wildfowl visit in winter. Birdlife on the high exposed moorland is typical with red and black grouse, wheatear, whinchat, ring ouzel, curlew, lapwing, redshank and snipe. Short-eared owls and the ubiquitous kestrel hunt the moorland fringes and merlins sometimes appear, though recently their numbers have been declining. Adders and common lizards sun themselves on the exposed rocks among the heather clumps, ready to vanish at the first sign of danger.
156ha – Map ref: NT 927048

LINDISFARNE (NCC) — *All year*

Lindisfarne is a wildfowl paradise — an immense area of muflats, sand-dunes, quicksand and open water. The productivity is astonishing with tens of thousands of birds gathering in winter; most notable are the light-breasted Brent geese, almost the entire population of this small relatively rare goose winters here arriving from their nesting grounds in Spitzbergen in early winter in long wavering skeins. Other wildfowl to find sanctuary here include great numbers of eider, long-tailed duck, shelduck, the dabbling teals, huge flocks of mallard and up to 25,000 wigeon.

Waders also make good use of this land of plenty, and it's thrilling to witness the arrival of thousands of dunlin, knot, godwits, grey and golden plover, redshank and curlew. Although the sheer numbers of birds does not always allow you the chance to see the rarities that often arrive mixed in with the flocks.

Watching the sea can be a most interesting pastime on Lindisfarne; grey seals haul out onto the sandflats or the mud, and terns and skuas can be seen on passage along the North Sea coast.

It is a very special place, and has been so for generations. On a clear day the monastery at the tip of the island stands out against the dunes. The dunes themselves, and the variety of habitats they enclose, shelter many plants, not least the northern marsh and common spotted orchid and marsh helleborine. The sands at Lindisfarne have been used for explosives practice and some areas carry a danger warning.
3278ha – Map ref: NU 096432

NORTHUMBERLAND NATIONAL PARK (Northumberland CC) — *Spring, summer*

The park is based upon the Cheviots, a range of hills that tell of a time when subterranean upheavals pushed up mountains and sent rivers of molten lava flowing across the twisted landscape of northern England and Scotland tens of millions of years ago. During the time that followed, up to the present day, rocks were deposited and eroded, rivers of water and of ice gouged their way over the surface leaving behind the features with which we are familiar today. Hard rocks like the great Whin Sill stand proud, a natural barrier across the landscape.

A National Park is a dynamic entity not a museum. Farming and forestry and the man-made lake at Kielder Water have altered and modified the countryside; even the mosses and bogs of the high ground have been affected by man's intervention, but where they remain they harbour special plants and insects, birds and mammals.

Most visitors to the park come to see remnants of Hadrian's wall, especially the stretch where the Roman engineers built along the top of the Whin Sill using the natural barrier of rock to keep civilisation on one side and barbarity on the other.

The height of the Cheviots induce a heavy rainfall and the streams that tumble from the hills are acid or alkaline depending on the chemical composition of the rocks over which they travel, which also dictates the life forms and plants of the shallow Northumbrian loughs. Dippers and ring ouzels are birds of the high country, and red and black grouse permanently inhabit the heather and the birch and rowan woods; the black grouse also take advantage of the extensive conifer plantations for cover. Birds of prey are a singular sight on the quiet open moorland where a few pairs of merlin, our smallest native falcon, still find peace enough to breed and the occasional peregrine hunts the wildfowl that haunt the winter loughs.

The landscape is one of contrasts, the rugged rocky faces and high ground of Newton Tors or Humbleton resembling parts of the Scottish Highlands with plants and insects adapted to a harsh environment and the evocative calls of nesting curlew and golden plover and redshank on the wind. Then there are the gentle wet valleys reminding you of Wales or the western moors, clad in oak and silver birch, full of the songs of redstart and pied flycatcher.

Access to the wildest places are for the hardy, well shod, well prepared walkers only; but even for the less mobile there is still much to see.
113,110ha

Northumberland Coast

PENNINE WAY (CC) — *Spring, summer*

A long distance footpath that follows Hadrian's Wall for part of its course; the countryside and its wild inhabitants echo the pattern of the National Park.
150km – Map ref: NT 853269 / NY 698479

RIVER TYNE GRAVELS (Northumberland WT)** — *Spring, summer*

The spate waters of the river Tyne bring a torrent of gravels and stones from its upper reaches and deposit them over the flood plain. This stony ground has provided a series of seemingly unrelated habitats; drifts of thrift more commonly associated with a maritime environment grow here in profusion, along with high ground and mountain plants such as alpine penny cress and mountain pansy. However, this hotchpotch of mixed species has a common factor, of harsh terrain and contamination by metallic elements. The water that feeds the gravel has flowed past the spoil tips of lead and zinc mines further up the water course absorbing heavy metals. Incredibly the plants have adapted to tolerate these conditions in much the same way that thrift on a cliff's edge can put up with heavy salt contamination blown on the sea winds.

At the edge of the gravel, close to the river's high water line where the spate rarely reaches, trees and scrub have established, holding the loose soil together and beginning the process of stabilisation. Away from the most intense areas of heavy metal contamination scots pine and grassland has become established.

The turf supports a wide range of flowering plants such as wood cranesbill, the beautiful sweet cecily and northern marsh orchid; and the gravel encourages waders to breed and stop over on migration. The fast fish-rich waters are inhabited by goosander and where drifts of sand and finer gravels have been cut back sand martins build their tunnels.
5ha

SILVER NUT WELL (Northumberland WT)** — *All year*

The Silver Nut Well is a natural phenomenon. A form of iron carbonate in the spring that feeds the well reacts with sulphur (a product of decay in the mud) and precipitates out on to the hazelnuts that have fallen into the well covering them with a metallic coating that both looks and tarnishes like silver when exposed to the air. The effect is made even more dramatic because the carpet of mud at the bottom of the well churns and boils with up-welling water, bringing the silvery nuts to the top of the mud and then swallowing them again.
0.05ha

NOTTINGHAMSHIRE

Nottinghamshire, heartland of England, birthplace of D.H. Lawrence at East Wood where his father was a collier — quite a contrast to the wealth and opulence of beautiful Newstead Priory where Byron spent his childhood and some of his happiest times in the wonderful setting of this ancient house and its superb grounds. But the county has changed much since then.

Nearly eighty per cent of the land is under agriculture and the forests for which the county was justly famous have been whittled away to mere pockets. Sherwood was once a royal hunting chase stretching across the country in a broad band following the dry sandstone and clothing the impoverished soils with a blanket of trees, but most of this medieval forest has disappeared under the plough or been felled for timber and charcoal. Some remnants were saved by enclosure when the royal chases were drawn into estates known as "The Dukeries" where the habitat and its wildlife have remained much as they have been for centuries.

Whether or not Robin Hood, undoubtedly the most famous of Sherwood's many residents, would recognise his old haunt is arguable; what is not in doubt is the fact that fragmentation of the forest has led to a diminution of the variety of birds, animals, insects and plants. In Mr Hood's day gos hawks would have been a familiar sight circling over the canopy and calling to one another as they set up their nesting territory. Nowadays sparrowhawks and tawny owls have inherited the forest, sharing it with an increasing number of human visitors.

Claylands produce fertile pasture, much of the finest land being in the beautiful Vale of Belvoir where cattle graze in an idyllic setting, but the seeds of destruction are sprouting even here. Deep beneath the beauty lie coal deposits, some of the largest in the country. Coal measures have already affected a large part of Nottinghamshire for the extractive industry always changes the face of the land, and with the presence of coal and other raw materials comes the development of towns and cities.

However, it has to be said that many of the spoil heaps from the older coal mines have begun to blend into the landscape although a geological anachronism, the deep deposits of ancient forest and mud banks buried almost a mile under ground for more than 300 million years have become the top dressing for a newly reconstituted landscape, exposed again to the rays of the same sun that once shone fiercely down onto a tropical swamp. Now those shales and fossiliferous sandstones are subject to frost and modern plants as they are recycled into a temperate climate.

Perhaps the greatest natural influence upon Nottinghamshire's countryside is the river Trent meandering through the claylands, imparting a sense of peace in spite of the enormous changes wrought by modern industry and agriculture.

The composition of the rocks that underlie the county are not such as to produce tremendously varied natural features, and modern agricultural machinery and chemicals have opened up the sandy soils, formerly covered by the great forest of Sherwood, to productive farming, drastically changing plant communities. The limestones and clays too have been exploited so that all that remains of their once varied floral cover are a few remnants found in nature reserves.

This area has been populated since the Neolithic age, and Castle Rock upon which the fortress of Nottingham Castle is built is perforated with caves that show evidence of long occupation up until the Middle Ages, the earthwork at Laxton also indicates the importance of the area.

The Trent floodplain with its cattle and hay meadows formed the basis for vast fortunes, spent acquiring great estates like Clumber and Thoresby where the last remaining areas of Sherwood Forest are enclosed. The line of wolds and hills that run from Lincolnshire to the west cut through the county though nowhere do they form steep bluffs as further south, the landscape here is gentle but where hills do occur, such as the rise at Hoe Hill, they provide vantage points over a large part of the county, especially lovely views of the Trent Valley stretching out below.

Small Copper Butterfly

It is perhaps taking imagination too far to suppose that Lord Byron dedicated his poem " She walks in beauty" not to some young society lady, but to the county where he spent such happy times.

She walks in beauty, like the night
Of cloudness climes and starry skies;
And all that's best of dark and bright
Meet in her aspect and her eyes:
Thus mellow'd to that tender light
Which heaven to gaudy day denies.

ATTENBOROUGH (Butterley Aggregates Ltd/Nottinghamshire WT) — *All year*

When the huge glaciers of the last ice age finally began to melt they produced rivers. At first a gentle trickle, but as the temperature rose and the rate of melting increased roaring torrents carried a cargo of shingle and fine gravels over the landscape. The river valleys created by these torrents sometimes formed beds for later rivers which is what happened in the case of Attenborough, with the Trent following the line of least resistance through the gravel deposits and over the clay basin.

This gravel has become a valuable commodity and the pits, which make up the reserve, are the result of decades of extraction and now a superb range of habitats are available, from mature lakes surrounded by thick vegetation and borderd by willow carr woodland to new pits with the scars of recent operations clearly visible on the banks. Such a variety provides a source of ever changing niches for birds, plants, insects and mammals such as the islands of gravel left in one or two of the pits which harbour safe nesting sites for common terns. The waterside vegetation allows for reed and sedge warblers to colonise and herons to fish, and a large number of waterfowl including garganey breed here in peace and security.

The area is well known for its dragonflies and sand martin colony — these latter birds love the steep banks of sand and spoil where they can tunnel their nest holes in safety, free from predation by rats. There is a wide range of predatory birds, and owls are particularly active because of the wealth of small mammals. Foxes too are common and feed upon mice and voles abundant in the healthy vegetation.
100ha – Map ref: SK 521343

CLUMBER PARK (NT) — *Spring, summer*

This huge estate is part of the original Sherwood Forest, the woodlands are rich in birds and insects and the lakeside reflects this variety. In spring and summer a great many birds and mammals come to the water to drink and to bathe while sparrowhawks hunt over the exposed lake margins.

Where the soil is sandy, and where the forest has been cleared and the ground heavily grazed by domestic animals or deer, heath is a natural successor with its own special wildlife. The woodlands are at their finest in spring when an influx of migrant birds adds to the power and variety of the birdsong and woodpeckers and nuthatch

Fungi   *Sherwood Forest (Notts)*

are common. The lake also provides a winter refuge for wildfowl and the numbers of birds increases dramatically in hard weather.
1273.5ha – Map ref: SK 645773

FAIRHAM BROOK (Nottinghamshire WT) — *Spring, summer*

The brook which gives its name to this reserve also gives it life; the fish, much in evidence, survive because of the considerable bounty of food living in the vegetation or washed down on the current. The area is very rich in insects and small mammals, the latter attracting predatory species including owls that hunt the reserve at night.

Spring brings a flush of flowering plants and the insects that feed upon them, and there is an excellent butterfly population with common blues and small coppers as well as many of the grass feeding species.
10.1ha – Map ref: SK 562338

HANNAH PARK WOOD (Woodland Trust) — *Spring, summer*

Hannah Park Wood is another small part of the Sherwood Forest mainly composed of high forest of oak and beech, but also a considerable area of yew woodland with a singular atmosphere of quiet. This reserve is excellent for birds, especially in winter when thrushes are able to take advantage of the heavy crop of yew berries.
5.6ha – Map ref: SK 590773

MARTIN'S POND (Nottingham City Council/Nottinghamshire WT) — *All year*

A marvellous area of urban conservation wetland, Martin's Pond was once destined to be built over, but now it forms part of the ecological benefits available to the citizens of the city of Nottingham.

The reed beds are best viewed from a walkway built over the water from where reed and sedge warblers can be seen in spring. The reserve is excellent for other birds too including willow warblers, chiffchaffs and reed buntings. In winter the marsh takes on a different face as birds such as water rail visit the reed beds — over sixty species of birds have been recorded here and many of them have bred as well. The site also harbours breeding frogs, toads and three species of newt while the fish population is

substantial and the while presence of fishermen during the coarse fishing season tends to reduce the numbers of shy birds, overall the reserve is very successful.
4ha – Map ref: SK 526402

MEDEN TRAIL (Nottinghamshire WT) — *Spring, summer*

Almost on the county borders where the magnesian limestone is the predominant geological feature, Meden trail runs along a disused railway line beside the river. There's a range of plant and insect species including common spotted orchids, guelder rose and ramsons which are common here as are nettle-leaved bellflower found in the edges of the ash woodland.
3.5km – Map ref: SK 506643 / 526646

OLDMOOR WOOD (Woodland Trust) — *Spring, summer*

On the outskirts of Nottingham, Oldmoor Wood is a vital link in the chain of wildlife sites in the city; the woodland is full of spring birdsong.
15.2ha – Map ref: SK 497428

RUFFORD COUNTRY PARK (Nottinghamshire CC) — *Spring, summer*

Part of the parkland known as The Dukeries which were once in turn part of the old Sherwood Forest. Bufford is particularly interesting for its trees and insects; the birdlife in spring is good with plenty of warblers nesting nearby.
73.5ha – Map ref: SK 642648

SHERWOOD FOREST COUNTRY PARK (Nottinghamshire CC) — *Spring, summer*

Sherwood is a remarkable ancient parkland forest with a parallel in Windsor Great Park where huge old oaks, some of the largest in Britain, have been growing for centuries; the resulting woodland over acid soils enjoys an open aspect and certain creatures, like some beetles, are found only in places where trees of great age exist.

The amount of food present in these oak and birch woods is tremendous and the birdlife is correspondingly large both in numbers and species, woodpeckers of all three species are present. The ground flora is never as diverse in acid woodland as that found on more alkaline soils, nevertheless immense stands of bracken cover the woodland floor and mammals range from deer to foxes, badgers and grey squirrels, while birds of prey include kestrels, sparrowhawks and even the occasional buzzard.
202.5ha – Map ref: SK 627677

TRESWELL WOOD (Nottinghamshire WT)** — *April through September*

Treswell Wood was mentioned in the Doomsday Book, and there is every reason to believe that woodland has thrived on this site for millennia. A regime of coppicing has produced a series of particularly rich habitats and the Trust has continued this practise with extremely beneficial results for the flora and fauna. One rather special insect, the speckled bush cricket, a flightless creature, is present in some numbers and thought to be part of the original insect population for being flightless it can only travel from wood to wood under certain conditions.

The wild service tree, another relic of woodlands from a past age, is also present here at the northerly limit of its distribution in this country. The wood is made up of many other species, and the coppice management ensures plenty of nesting sites for birds. The carpet of bluebells in spring is lovely and the presence of such reserves as Treswell gives us an idea of the natural diversity of medieval woodlands.
48ha

WILWELL FARM CUTTING (Nottinghamshire WT)** — *Spring, summer*

Another fine reserve utilising a disused railway cutting; there's a path running through a lovely display of lime-loving plants which in turn encourage insects, especially butterflies. In spring the site is alive with migrant warblers able to find ample song posts to practice their territorial displays. Whitethroats, greatly reduced in numbers because of drought in their wintering grounds in sub Saharan Africa, are beginning to make a come back and may yet regain their former numbers.
8ha

OXFORDSHIRE

So, some tempestuous morn in early June,
  When the year's primal burst of bloom is o'er,
  Before the roses and the longest day —
When garden-walks and all the grassy floor
  With blossoms red and white of fallen May
  And chestnut flowers are strewn —
So I have heard the cuckoo's parting cry,
  From the wet field, through the vext garden-trees,
  Come with the volleying rain and tossing breeze:
The bloom is gone, and with the bloom go I!

This extract from the poem "Tryrsis" by Matthen Arnold displays a love of the texture of landscape that once existed in the rolling Oxfordshire countryside. Now many of the hay meadows are memory to all but the oldest inhabitants of a farming community that still exists in a few quiet corners of the Thames valley, or tucked in alongside one of its many tributaries.

The fritillary meadows are a mere shadow of their former glory, and the watermeadows, once London's hay 'factories', are long redundant. Filled now with barley or oil seed rape, housing estates and 'The Business Park'. It appears that developers can't bear to see a piece of land that isn't covered in concrete and the most inappropriate buildings are erected on countryside that they consider to be going to 'waste', but which is in reality wild natural landscape and very much appreciated by anyone with even half an eye for beauty.

Fortunately there is still a great deal of the real Oxfordshire countryside remaining, particularly in the deep valleys and rolling hills of the Vale of the White Horse. The rocks beneath these hills are ancient, laid down when great lizards stalked the earth in the Jurassic and Cretaceous periods. The chalk and Oolitic limestone bedrock here exudes the flavour of the county, the limestone colours, sleepy Cotswold villages, the dreaming spires of Oxford's colleges, the gentle honey and cream tone that so delights the eye.

The eastern part of the county is covered with ancient beech forests, many planted for the furniture industry and now past their best, and where the chalk turf is open to the sky wild flowers play host to butterflies and moths in plenty. Here the hobby, that most beautiful of all the small falcons, finds safe nesting and happily they are beginning to increase in numbers as more cereal fields are returned to pasture and the ditches and ponds reinstated to the delight of dragonflies — and artists.

Oxford itself is a city so intertwined with the best of British culture that the honey stone reeks of past scholars,

Southern Marsh Orchid   *Parsonage Moor*

writers and poets demanding to be admired. It will never again be quite the same as Henry James described it:- "Oxford typifies to an American the union of science and sense, of aspiration and ease. A German university gives a greater impression of science, and an English country house or an Italian villa a greater impression of idle enjoyment; but in these cases on the one side knowledge is too rugged, and on the other, satisfaction is too trivial. Oxford lends sweetness to labour and dignity to leisure." How absolutely right he was!

Oxfordshire is an alkaline county. The acid tops of the clay-capped Chiltern Hills cannot disguise the fact that beneath the mantle of yellowish fine-grained clay embedded with flints, like Henry Moore figures, lies a pristine heart of purest chalk, and it is this which has determined the flora and the fauna and Oxfordshire's character.

ASTON ROWANT (NCC) — *Spring, summer*

Aston Rowant is one of the longest established chalk grassland reserves in southern England, it was desecrated by the Ministry of Transport when a huge wedge was carved out of the hillside to run a motorway through what was previously undisturbed countryside, isolating populations of grassland species one from the other, and exposing a face of white chalk that even today is showing little sign of the healing that time was supposed to encourage.

The hill tops are covered in woodland, mainly beech with some oak and thick undergrowth, and are rich in birds, in spring the variety is incredible. One of the residents, the hawfinch, a beautiful, almost exotic-looking bird with 'permanent waved' wing feathers and powerful beak, prefers the canopy and often you'll see them only when they're bathing or drinking from puddles in the pathways after heavy rain. The Trust has built a small artificial pond in lieu of a natural dewpond to provide drinking water for birds and mammals, though many of the dewponds that survive on the Chilterns are man-made.

Where the footpath enters the reserve proper 'Sarsens', massive slabs of sandstone, have been exposed leaving them propped at an angle like memorial tablets. Many millions of years ago the sandstone cap that covered this part of the Chilterns was complete, but time has worn away the stone until all that's left are these few remnants.

The grassland is the most exciting aspect of this extremely interesting area, many species of orchid grow in the thin sheep-grazed turf and butterflies are abundant. There is good regeneration of juniper on the hillsides which can be attributed to the management scheme; and a flock of sheep is used to control the encroachment of hawthorn scrub.

Kestrel and sparrowhawk hunt the slopes and hedges, but you'll need to look carefully as kestrels can often be mistaken for hobby falcons that sometimes hunt the large flying insects over the turf on summer evenings.
124ha – Map ref: SP 741967

BLENHEIM PARK (Duke of Marlborough) — *Spring, summer*

The Park boasts some very ancient oaks and, of course, the birds take advantage of their craggy structures. Tree creepers are common, as are woodpeckers, and it's not unusual to see jays taking acorns and hiding them in the grassland to last them through the winter. This is how many of the oaks were originally seeded, when the birds did not return for their cache.
897ha – Map ref: SP 442168

CHINNOR HILL (Berks, Bucks & Oxon NT) — *Spring, summer*

On Chinnor Hill whitebeam, wayfaring trees and yew, all typical of chalk soil, are complemented by a scrub layer that includes juniper. Chalk grassland plants depend upon the amount of sunlight reaching them, and autumn gentian and common spotted orchids are relatively common here.
26ha – Map ref: SP 766002

DRY SANDFORD PIT (Berks, Bucks & Oxon NT)** —*Spring, summer*

An old disused sand pit that contains a considerable range of lime-loving species including the rare marsh helleborine and fen pond weed.
8ha

FOXHOLES (Berks, Bucks & Oxon NT)** — *Spring, summer*

Situated in the midst of a private estate, Foxholes comprises woodland and grassland that has not been improved in recent times; in consequence the landscape is much as it would have been in the late Victorian era. Where the drainage ditches that served the rising ground and woodland above the river Evenlode have become blocked, the ground is marshy and fen-like with many wetland species such as marsh valerian and great burnet thriving in the damp conditions. The blocks of ash and oak over a dense understory of hawthorn and blackthorn and some hazel encourages breeding songbirds.

The wood continues up the hillside with open areas covered by a host of grassland plants and a considerable amount of meadowsweet where the ground is poorly drained. There are badgers and foxes in the wood and stoats seem to be increasing in numbers as the rabbit population rises; altogether a beautiful place showing the benefits of isolation.
72ha

HOOK NORTON RAILWAY CUTTING (Berks, Bucks & Oxon NT)** — *Spring, summer*

A disused railway cutting supporting lime-loving plants as well as those that thrive on rock faces. There is also an area of woodland in the process of development, but already capable of supporting many birds.
7.6ha

PARSONAGE MOOR (Berks, Bucks & Oxon NT)** — *Spring, summer*

An important lime-rich fen where a wide variety of wetland species exist in close proximity. Purple moor grass, common reed, meadowsweet, yellow tormentil and devil's bit scabious, the food plant of the marsh fritillary and one of the most beautifully patterned of the small fritillary butterflies.

The area adjoins Parsonage Fen, where the marshy ground and standing water encourage sphagnum moss and sedge, precursors to peat. The wet moss also provides a roothold for common butterwort, otherwise known as bog violet, and round-leaved sundew, which have adapted to the lack of nitrogenous material in the soil. The latter catches its prey in the shape of insects attracted to sticky blobs of a nectar-like substance on the leaves; the plant absorbs the tissue of the insect thus obtaining nitrogen.

At the edge of the marshy areas where the soil is more fertile you will see in mid summer the beautiful scarce marsh helleborine and southern marsh orchid. The insect fauna is extensive; scarlet tiger moths are resident in the wetter areas, the larvae living on the leaves and buds of comfrey; marsh valerian and hemp agrimony attract a wide range of butterfly species.

An interesting bird population thrives in the scrubby area with warblers taking advantage of the insects associated with the marshy ground. Sedge and reed warblers appear in spring when hawthorn and wild privet rings with willow warblers, chiffchaffs and blackcaps.
5.2ha

RIDGEWAY PATH (CC) — *Spring, summer*

A walker's path based upon an ancient trackway across the tops of the chalk hills from the Vale of the White Horse to the Bronze Age hill-fort of Ivinghoe Beacon in Buckinghamshire. On a fine day with the sun shining and a light breeze it's a very pleasant place to be with all the specialised chalk downland birds, butterflies and plants to be enjoyed. The path also presents some superb views across the county.

58km – Map ref: SU 259833 / SP 770013

SHOTOVER COUNTRY PARK (Oxford City Council) — *Spring, summer*

This country park, once part of an ancient royal hunting forest, is based on coppice woodland with standards and scrubby heath with heather, not at all common in Oxfordshire. Muntjac and fallow deer are frequently seen here, but it is the butterflies that make the trails very special; in mid summer purple emperors exploit the high oak canopy and white admiral butterflies glide, as if on wires, along the sunlit edges and rides. Musk mallow flowers come out in July making an absolutely superb show.

1. 2-4km – Map ref: SP 561063

WARBURG (Berks, Bucks & Oxon NT) — *Spring, summer*

Warburg is one of the largest of the BBONT reserves and is situated in the valley of Bix Bottom, an area rich in plant and animal life. The beechwoods, with their dense canopy, tend to suppress the understory, but the plants that do grow such as herb paris and Soloman's seal are very special.

Where grassland is established in the rides, old meadows and woodland clearings, typical chalk turf supports wild mignonette and cowslips and the rare meadow clary, giving an echo of Victorian chalk grassland; you will also see bee and fly orchids. The chalk soil not only provides a superb habitat for plants, but makes easy digging for badgers and foxes, both of which occur on the site; fallow and muntjac deer are frequently seen. Four species of reptiles including adder and slow-worm are also found here.

The birdlife is extremely varied with wood warblers and most of the common tit mice, including willow tit, and in spring and early summer the reserve is alive with bird-song. Recent management has greatly encouraged the insect fauna especially butterflies and many species of moths.

102ha – Map ref: SU 720880

WYCHWOOD FOREST (NCC)** — *Spring, summer*

Wychwood Forest once extended over a huge area of the Evenlode catchment and towns and villages such as Aston and Shipton-under-Wychwood reflect the extent of this ancient royal hunting forest. Now all that remains are a few small copses, plus this reserve representing a very rich piece of woodland habitat. There are a number of pools and wetlands which increase the wildlife potential; many species of insects, especially dragonflies, are evident in mid summer and the amphibian population is subtantial. The wood has been managed for coppice timber over a very considerable period, a regime which encourages an immense variety of woodland plants, insects, mammals and birds. One can only wonder at the dawn chorus in the original Wychwood forest.

647ha

SHROPSHIRE

This beautiful and peaceful land-locked county lies between Wales and the great Midland plain, and the landscape reflects the climate and the rocks both of which shape the character of the countryside and its wildlife. The mass of Wales and the heights of the Cambrian mountains drain the clouds of their rain so the region is relatively dry compared to its westerly neighbours, however the rain that falls on Wales drains to the sea through many counties, particularly Shropshire. The Severn begins in Shropshire and meanders across the county before bidding the Midlands farewell when its course deepens and its flow is empowered by a host of tributaries.

The county and its wildlife have been spared the worst excesses of the agricultural surplus, for the unsuitability of much of the land for arable farming has led to a regime of sheep and cattle, roots and grass, an excellent recipe for wildlife continuity. The industrial revolution laid waste many of the really large spreads of forest, now only a few remain at Edge Wood on Wenlock Edge and Hope Valley where a policy of broadleaved replacement is being followed. The curse of the conifer is the lot of many a quiet county with rugged uplands less suitable for arable cultivation, and Shropshire has suffered from the increased planting of trees for short term profit.

The sheer variety of rock types, from very young to very ancient makes this a geologically important area. The honey tones of the Jurassic limestone have encouraged quarrrying for building stone and for industry. Ironbridge and Broseley on the Severn is where iron crafting and the skills of the smelter were first refined; now most of the heavy industry and smelting have gone and the new town of Telford looks to the microchip rather than the girder for its future.

Along Wenlock Edge the limestone quarries lie abandoned or worked out, and nature has reclaimed ledges and crevices and drifts of quarry spoil for its own rock garden. There are other calcareous emergences to the north, carboniferous limestone reefs that in Wales would mark important coal seams, but here they have eroded to form lime-rich soils perfect for a host of plant species. Regional contrasts are even more apparent from Long Mynd where the high plateau, carved and shaped by ice, now provides a home for a wealth of moorland birds, though manage-ment for grouse shooting on much of the moorland has reduced the wildlife potential.

The glaciers that honed the roughness from Wenlock Edge deposited a drift of clays and marls, sands and gravels over the lowland plain, and in places where impervious clay settled, pools of water developed and meres and bogs built up; many have been overcome by time, but a few are still in evidence such as Colemere and Wem Moss.

A.E. Houseman wrote his famous poem "A Shropshire Lad" in Ludlow in recognition of the influence of this attractive county, etched deep into his writing. In his poem "Wenlock Edge" he celebrates the beauty and peace of the natural features of the Shropshire countryside.

'Tis time, I think, by Wenlock town
  The golden broom should blow;
The hawthorn sprinkled up and down
  Should charge the land with snow.

Spring will not wait the loiterer's time
  Who keeps so long away;
So others wear the broom and climb
  The hedgerows heaped with may.

Oh tarnish late on Wenlock Edge,
  Gold that I never see;
Lie long, high snowdrifts in the hedge
  That will not shower on me.

This same countryside was the birthplace and inspiration of Charles Darwin, father of the theory of evolution and natural selection who changed the way we look at the natural world and our own place in the scheme of things. And if ever a county had a claim to look into the future of the world it is Shropshire, or to be more exact Bridgenorth, for here in 1657 were heard the first cries of a baby christened Francis Moore who was to grow up to be a

Speckled Wood Butterfly   *Corbet Wood Trail*

famous astrologer and compiler of the "Vox Stellarum", better known as "Old Moores Almanac". First published in 1700 it was an instant success but thankfully his most dire predictions of the fate of the world are yet to come to fruition.

BROWN MOSS (SCC) — *Spring, summer*

Pools created by peat cuttings support a wide range of resident birds, and migrants are much in evidence in spring and autumn. Black terns appear on occasions taking advantage of the prolific insect fauna of the pools.

The water plants give the site particular importance with orange foxtail, floating water-plantain, floating club-rush and water-violet, and this prolific vegetation allows for a breeding bird population of at least thirty species. A creditable number for an acid site that has undergone considerable modification by man.
32ha – Map ref: SJ 564394

COLEMERE COUNTRY PARK (SCC) — *Spring, summer*

The immense glaciers that once crowned the nearby Welsh highlands, and the subsequent effect of huge quantities of melt water, following the end of the last ice age, left behind a legacy of water-filled depressions in the landscape of Shropshire roughly between the towns of Welshampton, Ellesmere and Newton. These depressions and the more than adequate supply of water encouraged the Victorians to build the Llangollen canal.

Many of these watery depressions were changed by time and the actions of both man and plants, gradually some of the shallower meres filled with vegetation which developed into peat as can be seen at Wem Moss. Others like Colemere and the smaller Blakemere are still open water though nature is continuing to recolonise and turn them into dry land. The open water is a magnet for wildfowl and migrant terns, especially black terns. Spring and summer is best when the reed beds are full of birdlife but in winter the wildfowl usually produce a few surprises, and large flocks of wigeon, teal and other dabbling and diving duck are common in hard weather.
50ha – Map ref: SJ 434328

CORBET WOOD TRAIL (Shropshire WT) — *Spring, summer*

This attractive woodland trail comprises a wide variety of trees, excellent ground cover and abundant insect fauna, including a fine selection of moths and butterflies, especially the speckled wood butterfly. The trees are mainly wild cherry with beech and oak, with a mixture of conifers, rowan and birch which provides food and nest sites for many species of small birds. The old quarry is geologically very interesting.
1.6km – Map ref: SJ 525238

EARL'S HILL (Shropshire WT) — *Spring, summer*

Earl's Hill is a great knob of Precambrian rock rising clear from the surrounding countryside to a height of nearly 1000ft above sea level and was formed when the world resembled an Hironomous Bosch painting of hell — a planet in ferment with boiling lakes of molten larva and red hot rocks pounded by a steaming sea, where clouds of carbon doixide and sulphur roared up in tempests of poisonous vapour; yet in all this inhospitable torment life was already beginning in the ooze on the sea bed. Bacteria and algae had begun the long march to conquer every fraction of the Earth's surface.

The hill has been a silent witness to momentous events encompassing life on Earth, but it has not always stood facing the elements. During its long existence it has been eroded by the forces of nature, not once but many times. Its present prominence is merely another chapter in its life story. In our times its flanks are dressed with trees and grasses and its summit and screes decorated gold with rare and interesting plants like rock stonecrop, a plant more at home on the cliffs of Devon or Wales. The slopes owe their lack of cover to sheep grazing in past years which produced a grassy sward over the thin soil, but as grazing pressure decreases so the diversity of plant cover increases.

In the woodlands that skirt the base of the hill a large number of birds and mammals find shelter and places to breed, and the stream that flows in the valley attracts dippers and pied wagtails. Migrants find the woods to their liking and pied flycatchers appear here while breeding birds such as wood warblers and redstarts are a welcome addition to the dawn chorus and, naturally, such a wealth of birds attracts sparrowhawks. The large vole population, thriving in the grassland is preyed upon by kestrels, and the updraughts and thermal activity encourages larger avian predators such as buzzards to quarter the hill; ravens are also regular visitors.

The varying habitats encourage a diversity of species from common dormice and badgers, that feed in the gloom of the woodlands, to the butterflies that enjoy the grasslands; more than half the total number of British butterfly species fly here in summer. The visitor centre is an old restored barn and houses an interesting display of what there is to see.
40ha – Map ref: SJ 409048

EDGE WOOD (Shropshire WT)** — *Spring, summer*

From Much Wenlock the Ape Dale runs south and west bounded on one side by the long low natural rock barrier of Wenlock Edge. A large amount of the original woodland has been replaced with conifers, but plenty of oak, ash and hazel coppice remains and there are also plantings of beech, although these tend to be dark in late spring and early summer reducing the diversity of the woodland flora. However, there are a huge number and variety of habitats within this linear forest reserve and spring is an excellent time to experience the superb display of flowering plants and woodland birdsong.
10ha

JONES' ROUGH (Shropshire WT) — *Spring, summer*

Growing on a lime-rich habitat Jones' Rough reserve consists of a number of yew trees and wild cherry with spurge laurel and stinking hellebore occurring on the

woodland floor. There is also an interesting area of vertical limestone rock faces and scree.
3.1ha – Map ref: SJ 247247

LONG MYND (NT) — *Spring, summer*

The fact that this area is managed for grouse naturally reduces its diversity; the open areas are mown to encourage heather for feeding the grouse, consequently the ground flora is diminished. However, it is a wonderful place to see a wide range of birds soaring on the updraughts; buzzards cruise effortlessly to and fro scanning the ground beneath.

In spring and summer you can hear meadow pipits and the stonechat's metallic chatter and see wheatears bobbing on the rocks before flying off flashing their white tail patches; the blackbird-like song of the ring ouzel is often the only sign of these unobtrusive birds. Long Mynd does not consist only of heather moorland, there are pockets of woodland where redstarts nest and tree pipits call and clear pure rushing streams where dippers feed and wagtails hunt for emergent insects.
1812ha – Map ref: SO 425945

THE MERE — ELLESMERE (SCC) — *Winter*

Although subject to considerable public pressure the Mere is an interesting place. The heronry provides an exciting spectacle as winter ends and the birds begin to set up territory, while wildfowl are still trying to make up their minds which season it is. The site is excellent for wintering wildfowl.
46.4ha – Map ref: SJ 403348

STIPERSTONES (NCC) — *All year*

Stipperstones is a wild place full of the remnants of man's excavations for lead and other metallic elements. It is said to be haunted, a place of enchantment, and the wild scenery and rugged rocks do impart a strange beauty; legend has it that a Saxon King lost a golden arrow somewhere in the Stipperstone Hills. But when you grow tired of searching for it you can watch the soaring buzzards and other fascinating high ground birds.
Map ref: SO 369976

TASKER QUARRY (Shropshire WT) — *All year*

The natural forces that shaped the Earth 500 million years ago can be seen in the rocks at Tasker Quarry. Dating

Common Dormice   *Shropshire*

from the Ordovician period the exposures show signs of volcanic activity and the presence of shales indicate intense seismic turbulence interspersed with quiet periods.
0.8ha – Map ref: SO 326957

WEM MOSS (Shropshire WT)** — *Spring, summer*

A depression in the ground left after the end of the last glaciation is the basis for this dome-shaped peat deposit formed over a period of 10,000 years from a shallow pool invaded by mosses and bog plants until the surface rose above the surrounding ground in the characteristic dome shape of a classic moss. The woodland surrounding part of the moss is rich in birdsong and insects, and the moss itself has a differing flora and fauna depending upon the amount of water in the peat and it closeness to the surface.

The whole of a natural moss is like a huge sponge and the plants and animals that live upon it depend upon the integrity of the water table within the dome; if the moss is interfered with or drained the peat degrades into acid moorland with none of the original diversity. Fortunately Wem Moss is a perfect example with many features intact. Reptiles and amphibians thrive here, and adders are extremely common. The insects of the moss include large heath butterflies and a marvellous selection of dragonflies.
20.8ha

STAFFORDSHIRE

Staffordhsire is one of those interesting middle England counties; to the south is industry and the sprawl of the Birmingham, Wallsall, Wolverhampton conurbation, yet just a few short miles from the whirl of "Spaghetti Junction" are the open moors and forests of the ancient hunting preserve of Cannock Chase where nightjars and long-eared owls enhance the summer nights. This is where Arnold Bennett set his saga of the five towns, it was the birthplace of Samual Johnson, the inspiration of Jerome K. Jerome and Isaac Walton, master fisherman and author of "The Compleat Angler"; how would he find the county and his beloved river Dove today?

Just north of Leek are the Roaches, high moorland where blue or variable hares and red grouse live. The high ground echoes in spring with a dawn chorus made up of curlew and dippers and the bright calls of meadow pipits and wheatears. Beside the northbound A523 lies a lake, a quiet place where duck and moorhen float and cluck; in the middle of Victoria's reign, a newly married couple stood and admired the sights and sounds. The lake is called Rudyard Lake and the couple Mr and Mrs Kipling!

Contrasting geology creates a diverse wildlife. The millstone grits found in this area resisted the power of ice age glaciers to erode them, not so the limestone, shales and sandstone which was ground away and carried onto the plains to form thick pebble beds and clay pans that encourage blanket bogs and mosses, some with the peculiar phenomenon known as a quaking bog where trees grow on the apparently solid surface of a blanket mire until their own weight forces them through the crust of peat and moss into the water that lies below. Walking on the surface of such a bog gives you the feeling that the ground is quivering beneath your feet, and it is a little unnerving to see the nearby trees shaking in unison with your footsteps. Needless to say some of the quaking bogs can be extremely dangerous.

Another strange feature of Staffordshire's landscape are the waterways that periodically vanish from their normal course down "swallet" holes in the bed of the river and return to the surface miles downstream through another natural phenomenon called a "boil" hole. This is caused by millions of years of watery erosion. Carbonic acid is a natural compound occurring in rain water, gradually it dissolves the limestone rocks and in time holes and channels appear through which more water percolates and the process is accelerated. Eventually a channel is cut underground that can accommodate most of the flow of a stream or river, and when rainfall is low in summer and the river's volume falls, the entire river disappears.

Swallet or swallow holes feature in rivers and streams that flow over limestone rocks, usually carboniferous in origin, indicating the presence of coal deep underground or nearby, and this is the case in Staffordshire. Here the remains of centuries of mining can be seen in spoil heaps and old workings where fossiliferous shales from deep beneath the ground are heaped up in huge cone-shaped hills. Many of these have been softened by time and planted and now serve the public as amenity areas since the mines that created them are closed.

Away from industry and its detritus Staffordshire is quite beautiful. On the eastern boundary with Derbyshire nestle the valleys of the rivers Trent and Dove. Doveable is especially lovely where the river has carved a channel down through the limestone to form an enchanting vale full of dippers and wagtails. Charles Cotton thought it lovely too and in retirement was able to enjoy the Dove, to taste its pleasures visually as well as pit his wits against the fish in the clear fertile waters, following in the footsteps of Isaac Walton.

"Retirement" — Charles Cotton

How calm and quiet a delight
    it is, alone
To read, and meditate, and write,
By none offended, and offending none;
To walk, ride, sit or sleep at ones own ease,
And pleasing a mans self, none other to displease!

Oh my beloved nymph! fair Dove,
Princess of rivers, how I love
    Upon thy flow'ry banks to lie,
    And view thy silver stream.
When gilded by a summer's beam!
And in it, all thy wanton fry
    Playing at liberty,
And with my angle upon them
    The all of treachery
I ever learn'd to practice and to try!

ALLIMORE GREEN COMMON (Staffordshire NCT)**
— *Spring, summer*

One of the rarest habitats in this country is genuine unimproved pasture, grasslands and hedges where nothing has been done to upset the natural chemical balance in the soil so that plants, insects, birds and mammals can exist in relative equilibrium one with the other. That is not to say the land and its inhabitants should remain static, the weather and population dynamics must play their proper role in the scheme of things. Such is the state of affairs prevailing at Allimore Green Common with hedges well established and maintained in order to provide dense semi-natural linear woodlands affording nest sites and shelter for a host of birds and insects. The beauty of this grassland lies in lack of drainage which has resulted in a rich wetland pasture with damp grassland plants like ragged robin, creating a series of habitats for both marsh and common spotted orchids. The butterfly fauna is extensive as is the population of moths.

The reserve gives you a tiny hint of the countryside that would have inspired the Staffordshire painter Peter de Wint. Now this type of landscape exists only in a very few sites.
2.5ha

BELVIDE RESERVOIR (West Midlands Bird Club)**
— All year

On the Shropshire Union Canal, not far from the Telford Aqueduct, lies the feeder reservoir that supplies the canal so that the locks will have ample water in times of heavy traffic. Nowadays the canal is busy only in summer as the raw material of industry travels by road and rail, but the traffic is essential for the good of the wildlife. The pleasure boats that ply the canal lower the water levels in the basin providing a much needed source of food for migrant species such as waders ranging from black-winged stilts to common sandpipers; also terns, especially black and common terns. The lower water level allows bankside vegetation and reeds to grow also providing nest sites for large numbers of water birds including ruddy duck, particularly common in the county. In winter pressure from holiday boaters eases, the water level rises and a greater area of water is available for wintering wildfowl and swans. The reservoir is a very productive site for unusual duck, and lying as it does on the course of the canal it is a perfect stop over for birds following open water south in hard weather.
122.4ha

BLITHFIELD RESERVOIR (South Staffs Waterworks Co)** *— Autumn, winter*

A drinking water reservoir of considerable size providing a magnetic attraction for migrant wildfowl and birds on autumn and spring passage. In winter a resident population of duck is augmented in hard weather by swans and small numbers of grebes, and the reserve acts as a winter roost for large numbers of gulls, both black-headed, common and herring as well as small numbers of black-backed gulls. In spring arctic and common terns and a few black terns pass through on their way to breed elsewhere.
760ha

BROCTON (SCC) — *Spring, summer*

At Brocton a public hide overlooks a deep gravel pit with considerable wildfowl potential; a number of species are resident including great crested grebe and tufted duck; lying as it does within Cannock Chase this open water attracts much wildlife. The surrounding scrubby woodland has plenty of nesting sites and an abundant source of food so the bird population tends to be high all year. However, in spring and summer there is a further large influx of migrants. Sparrowhawks are frequent visitors to drink and to bathe and in mid summer they hunt the small birds to feed their young. The barking calls of long-eared owls can also be heard on the reserve.
48ha – Map ref: SJ 967189

CANNOCK CHASE (SCC) — *Spring, summer*

Cannock Chase is a plateau of heather, conifer and Bunter pebble beds, an area of peace in a highly industrialised region. The highest point is an Iron Age hill-fort 800ft above sea level, a vantage point overlooking the Trent valley. The fort was most likely a central meeting point for tribes and chieftains rather than simply a fortified town built to prevent raiders from gaining access to the Cannock plateau.

There's a lot of history here, the land is divided between some of the country's most powerful families, and beneath it, especially at Rugeley (the Red Town) the coal seams were heavily exploited through the Victorian and Edwardian eras bringing great wealth to some of the landowners and providing the industrial foundation of many of the surrounding towns and cities. When Elizabeth I reigned the chase was a huge open oak woodland, with a natural proportion of other trees, supporting masses of wildlife. Charcoal burning was the beginning of the end and a succession of wars and rumours of wars wreaked havoc until now only sycamore coppice and the most famous of the Chase's woodlands at Brocton Coppice remain; much of the Chase has been given over to monotonous conifers planted in serried ranks. I believe I'm justified to coin the collective noun for these aborecultural mistakes as "A boredom of conifers".

At Brocton Coppice the trees are ancient, some being two or three centuries old and the wildlife, especially moth and beetle fauna indicates the fact that there has been forest on this site for a thousand years or more, yet it is the open moorland which is the greatest public attraction. Picnics and family gatherings are popular and people seem sensibly undeterred by the more than average population of adders, our only poisonous snake, realising that in truth adders are singularly unaggressive.

The bird population is enhanced by that master of camouflage, the nightjar. They can be heard calling in spring, a low continuous purring that is made by the male as he sits on a low perch, often a fallen silver birch, not fore and aft like normal bird, but along the line of the bole or branch. Its astonishingly good criptic colouration makes it almost invisible until it moves or opens its immense gape or flashes its liquid brown eyes. These birds feed nocturnally on large insects which they catch in flight; they particularly like huge moths as they flit over the bracken and gorse.

Other birds adept at camouflage fly over the Chase. In spring the most elegant of owls, the long-eared owl, will sit in a scots pine in broad daylight and be invisble as its plumage blends perfectly with the bark. This owl has benefited from coniferisation, and will thrive and breed, providing the trees are in blocks with extensive rides and firebreaks and where the owls food, in the form of voles and mice, is abundant. In the evening and at night the calls of these elegant owls echo through the forestry plantations like the staccato barking of a lost terrier.

Another beneficiary of conifer plantations is the deer; all three native species are present, and the introduced muntjac is to be heard as the males patrol regular boundaries. Fallow deer appear to be the most common species and large numbers are present.

The sheer size of the Chase is conducive to a wide range of plants and insects and the whole area is a delight for botanist and entomologist alike. Public pressure is a potential problem. Certain areas have been declared off limits for motor vehicles which protects both the deer and the habitat, and also lessens the amount of dumped domestic rubbish in the ubiquitous black plastic bags. It is to be hoped that in time the increase in the planting of native trees, more in keeping with the area and its wildlife, and the better protection of the more sensitive parts of the Chase will result in its continuance as a place of out-standing natural importance.
870ha – Map ref: SJ 971842

CANNOCK FOREST CENTRE (FC)

Information about the Chase is available from the Forest Centre and makes a good starting point for visitors to this area.
Map ref: SK 017171

COOMBES VALLEY (RSPB) — *Spring, summer*

A particularly important piece of old oak woodland previously deforested through a number of causes, not the least being grazing and charcoal burning which had

Dipper   *Staffs*

allowed bracken and introduced sycamore to dominate certain areas. After acquiring Coombes Valley the RSPB set up a plan to produce a regenerated mixed oak wood with clearings and hedges on the farmed areas.

The steep-sided valley was formed when a glacier gouged its way into the softer strata of rock, and the process was further helped by the presence of water in the shape of the stream that runs along the bottom. This stream is unpolluted and contains a sizable population of fish and insects on which birds as diverse as grey wagtails, dippers, kingfishers and herons depend. The woodland that has been replanted and managed so far supports a large population of migrant warblers, especially willow warblers, but in the older oak forest there are pied flycatchers encouraged by the provision of nest boxes; redstarts, tree pipits, wood warblers, nuthatch and all three species of woodpeckers. Several species of tits are common as are chaffinches, and tawny owls and sparrow-hawks predate the mammals and small birds.

There are active badgers setts in this particularly important wood which acts as a reservoir for the county's wildlife. Some species like the increasingly rare high brown fritillary butterfly do not otherwise occur within a considerable radius of Coombes Valley.
104ha – Map ref: SK 005530

DEEP HAYES COUNTRY PARK (SCC) — *Spring, summer*

A fascinating mixture of pools, marshes and woodland with some interesting meadows containing a wide variety of plants and animals and a considerable population of amphibians and reptiles. The variety of habitats is reflected in the spring birdsong and plants such as the greater butterfly orchid.
57.6ha – Map ref: SJ 962535

GREENWAY BANK COUNTRY PARK (SCC) — *Spring, summer*

The nearby canal, once an artery taking the life blood of the pottery industry from Stoke-on-Trent to the rest of the world, is fed from a reservoir situated within the confines of this Country Park. The works of nature have become more apparent than the works of industrial man with marsh marigold and water avens thriving in the wet areas. Breeding birds take advantage of the insect food living on the native trees planted in Queen Elizabeth II Silver Jubilee arboretum.
44ha – Map ref: SJ 888552

JACKSON'S COPPICE (Staffordshire NCT)** — *Spring, summer*

A small, but very fine acid oak wood over sandstone with a rich fern growth on the exposed sandstone rock faces and a mixed understory beneath the oaks, a prime site for breeding birds. Jackon's Coppice grows on the side of a steep valley with a stream feeding the valley bottom where a marsh has developed rich in ferns and flowering plants; the woodland and the marsh combine to produce habitats for more than sixty species of breeding birds and the

reserve is noted for grasshopper warblers, small birds with a call likened to the sound of a fishing reel ratchet as the line is drawn out. The pitch of the grasshopper warbler's song appears to rise and fall as it turns to and fro with wide open bill broadcasting its song to all points of its breeding territory. These birds are difficult to see and the sound level of the song is quite low. However, they will sing in the evening and at night when competition from other more powerful songs is less.
6.4ha

MANIFOLD VALLEY (NT/SCC) — *Spring, summer*

One of the most attractive walks in the Midlands where the swift flowing river Manifold plays hide and seek beneath the limestone rocks, descending through faults in its bed known locally as "swallet" holes and reappearing through "boil" holes. The limestone caves and strange rock formations high on the valley sides show the river's past activity as it cut its way down through the rock to its present channel.

The valley is home to dippers, smart black and white fast flying birds that walk on the river bed using their wings as a foil against the thrust of the current to hold themselves down while they search for insect larvae and caddis grubs. The rich creamy golden limestone provides a habitat for a wide range of plants, indeed some of the slopes support a flora more reminiscent of chalk downland modified by the shelter of ash trees. Common rock rose and common spotted orchid complete the illusion of downland, although the spectacular scenery avoids anything but floral confusion.

The spring birdsong varies wherever you may be along the seven kilometres of the valley path, from dippers and wrens in deep green secret places to migrant warblers and wagtails where the rocky course of the river allows intense sunlight to fall on the banksides. Water voles and shrews are abundant and the former can be seen munching on green stems paying little heed to the many humans who come to enjoy this beautiful river valley.
7km – Map ref: SK 100543

RUDYARD NATURE WALK (Staffordshire NCT) — *Spring, summer*

You'll find a variety of habitats along this man-made reserve based on a disused railway line and a stream. Where the old railway line was bedded the remaining chippings have a flora of their own while the more acid sandstone of the cutting and embankments themselves sport a series of plants such as gorse and heather tolerant of acid soil conditions; the stream creates a wetland area where snipe are frequently encountered. It is an excellent example of the productivity of such places.
5km – Map ref: SJ 955579

TILLINGTON-DOXEY MARSHES (Staffordshire NCT) — *All year*

These extensive marshes on the river Sow provide a suitable habitat for large numbers of waders and smaller waterfowl to stop and rest on their cross-country migrations in spring and autumn. Many reed and marsh warblers, martins and swallows find food over the open water in the form of abundant insects.
36.8ha – Map ref: SJ 915239

Fallow Deer   *Cannock Chase*

SUFFOLK

Suffolk has enjoyed agricultural prosperity for many centuries. From the time when Neolithic man began to clear the forests to the Elizabethan era when the remaining broad spreads of oak and ash were decimated to build houses, and also for the ribs and planking of ships of war and of commerce; what was left was felled for charcoal. These days very little remains of the ancient forest yet in parts of the county an echo of the past can be felt where coppice stools, nearly a thousand years old, still produce a crop of straight poles, and seem set to do so for another thousand years.

John Constable was instrumental in keeping Suffolk (at least his part of it) intact. The area around Flatford Mill is much the same as it was in his day. Not so the Suffolk Brecklands, the main home for the secretive and romantic bird of sandy heaths and quiet places, the stone curlew. To my knowledge Constable never painted these birds, he was content to capture the soft, lush, but man-made landscape of the valley of the Stour.

The image of the Brecklands is of a desert environment of harsh dry dunes and flying sand, yet they were veritable gold-mines, producing wool from the short herb-rich turf. Here and there the underlying chalk is exposed but where the soil has stabilised the plant growth is lush. In his poem "Suffolk Heathland" the East Anglian poet, George Crabbe, gives an indication of man's attitude to this harsh inhospitable landscape, so good for nature yet so hard on man that he has allowed much of it to vanish under conifer and cereals:-

Lo! where the heath, with withering brake grown o'er,
Lends the light turf that warms the neighbouring poor;
From thence a length of burning sand appears,
Where the thin harvest waves its wither'd ears;
Rank weeds, that ever art and care defy,
Reigh o'er the land, and rob the blighted rye:
There thistles stretch their prickley arm afar,
and to the ragged infants threaten war;
there poppies nodding, mock the hope of toil;
There the blue bugloss paints the sterile soil;
Hardy and high, above the slender sheaf,
the slimy mallow waves her silky leaf;
O'er the young shoot the charlock throws a shade,
And clasping tares cling round the sickly blade;
With mingled tints the rocky coasts abound,
And a sad splendour vainly shines around.

Modern agriculture has dealt a heavy blow to the integrity of the Brecks and indeed to much of the natural landscape.

The fertility of the boulder clay lands that once supported widespread forests, now produces cereals and oil seeds in huge quantities, the wide landscape and low undulations being ideal for the employment of harvesting machines and monotonous monoculture.

Yet at Flatford Mill and in the surrounding area of the Stour valley agriculture has combined with the thriving tourist industry to retain the sort of countryside that John Constable and Gainsborough held so dear. In their time, surprisingly, the trees and hedges would have been less lush and over blown, for in those days every aspect of the natural economy was used in day-to-day life; willows would have been heavily pollarded for withy canes, and hedgerow, woodland and riverside trees would have been cut to a height above the grazing line so that cattle and horses would not be able to chew the growing shoots which otherwise would grow on to produce poles. Other hedgerow and woodland trees were grown as standards, tall and straight, for timber to build farm gates and carts like the modified hay cart standing in the river in what is probably one of the best known paintings of all time: Constable's "Hay Wain". This jewel of the natural history scene is found not far from the North Sea coast where reserves like Minsmere and Havergate Island are names writ large in the history of successful conservation.

One of the problems facing Suffolk is its position. There are moves afoot to develop the unspoiled counties within striking distance of London; already a rash of new industrial sites has sprung up, draining the rural economy and work-force and mechanised farming has increased to compensate. The results are felt in a reduced wildlife potential and a lessening of the diversity of habitats.

Stone Curlew   *Cavenham Heath*

Where conifer woodlands are planted on uneconomic Breckland, stone curlew and red-backed shrike are the loosers, but so are we! Shelter belts of quick growing alien species opens up land for farming that has never been ploughed before. Changes in EEC regulations and "set-aside" plans may be the answer to the problem. Suffolk cannot be held in perpetuity as a living museum to Constable and Gainsborough, but the efforts that have been made in the Stour valley point the way to how careful landscape management can result in a beautiful rich habitat, and prosperity for agriculture.

BRADFIELD WOODS (Suffolk WT) — *Spring*

An extremely important woodland having had the benefit of a regime of coppice with standards continuous since the early 13th century, and probably even earlier. Bradfield Woods contains some of the oldest surviving coppice stools in the country grown for use as small pieces of timber for agricultural implements and larger planks and baulks for buildings and farm gates, fencing, carts and furniture. Man-made earth banks indicate a time when the woodlands and coppice shoots were protected against predation by deer and the peasant's wandering cattle.

Coppicing, the praise of felling a growing tree and encouraging the stump to send up new growth for harvest on a seven- to ten-year rotation, is a methods of forestry which makes a tree virtually "immortal". Only the root system and the short trunk remains, all the vigour is put into trying to produce a replacement trunk from latent buds in the bark. In turn these pole stumps bud new shoots, and so on ad infinitum.

The forest floor receives a burst of sunlight when the coppice is harvested which encourages a succession of species adapted to a wide range of light requirements. Bradfield has been recorded as having 350 species of flowering plants, some forty of which are woody shrubs; few other woodlands in the United Kingdom can boast such a rich flora.

The insect life that thrives on this abundant plant food is immense, an echo of the wildwood that once covered the boulder clay of East Anglia and because of the host of insects the birds too are innumerable. In spring the dawn chorus is tremendous with migrant warblers and night-ingales adding to the thrushes and blackbirds, dunnock and chaffinch that have come to accept the myriad niches afforded them by the special management whereby blocks of timber are felled in annual rotation so that nest sites are always available in just the right situation. Not only is this one of the oldest coppice woodlands in the country, it is also one of the most fascinating and beautiful.
64.4ha – Map ref: TL 935581

BULL'S WOOD (Suffolk WT)** — *Spring, summer*

At Bull's Wood hazel coppice with oak, ash and field maple standards create the right environment for typical ancient woodland flora, including herb paris and oxlip in spring with carpets of bluebells. Early purple orchids thrive here, and the wood is also very rich in birds.
11.6ha

CARLTON MARSHES (Suffolk WT)** — *Spring, summer*

Carlton Marshes reserve is made up of old flooded peat workings, dyked grazing marsh and old wet woodland providing a similar range of habitats to typical Broad-land, even though we're in Suffolk. Many of the flowers such as water soldier, marsh pea and milk parsley would be more at home on Norfolk soil. It is a productive habitat and attracts many different birds and insects.
46ha

CAVENHAM HEATH (NCC) — *Spring, summer*

One of the finest acid heaths in the Brecklands with a wide range of habitats of heather and a variety of other acid-loving plants, adapted to dry conditions, such as common centaury, stork's bill, thyme-leaved sandwort, sheep sorrel and lichens. Areas of birch woodland with gorse provides cover for a myriad of creatures, and by the river Lark where it's wetter the dry open heathy moorland changes to lush flowery riverside vegetation alive with insects and birds. Adders and slow-worms are found on the drier heaths and grass snakes find shelter and food on the riverside where the considerable roe deer population comes down to drink. The grassy areas support a number of small mammals, and kestrels hunt the open ground seeking bank voles. The bird-life is plentiful and reflects the variety of habitats in close proximity one with another. Nightjars are found on the heath in the shelter of the birch woodland and linnet and yellowhammer take advantage of safe nesting in the gorse bushes.
140ha – Map ref: TL 757727

DUNWICH COMMON (NT) — *Spring, summer*

Part of the Suffolk sheep downs known as The Sandlings, Dunwich Common was once extensively grazed. The consolidation and enrichment of the sandy soil has been the undoing of the sheep walks, it made them more suitable for agriculture and many are now under the plough.

Heather, of many sorts, and gorse bushes clothe the commons, and common broom creates a gorgeous splash of colour when it's in bloom. There is evidence of fire with ample stands of rosebay willow-herb, also known as fireweed for its propensity to appear, as if by magic, after heath fires. The heath is gently undulating, reflecting its relationship to the coastal region, and the cliffs of sand and shingle are constantly eroded by the sea and wind creating a perfect site for sand martins to build their burrows. The sand martin colony declined drastically during the early to mid 1980s, coincidentally with the droughts in central Saharan Africa, but it appears their numbers are now recovering.
85.6ha – Map ref: TM 476685

FOX FRITILLARY MEADOW (Suffolk WT)** — *Open one day a year, early May*

Considered to be the finest fritillary meadow in eastern England, some years there are more than half a million plants here; an absolutely superb display, and a reflection

Adder   *Suffolk*

of the fritillary meadows that were common until the outbreak of World War II.
2.4ha

GROTON WOOD (Suffolk WT)** — *Spring, summer*

Best known as the finest stand of small-leaved lime in the county, Groton Wood has been revitalised by a regime of coppicing that has only recently been reintroduced. The ground flora is extensive with many plants of ancient woodland including herb paris and bluebells, sweet woodruff and wood spurge; the unusual violet helleborine also grows here.
20ha

HAVERGATE ISLAND (RSPB)* — *April-August, November-February*

Take a boat from Orford Quay to reach this famous bird sanctuary. The first avocets to breed in this country, began their courtship ritual in the flooded salt marsh in the spring of 1947, now the colony has 120 pairs breeding, or attempting to breed, on the man-made land adjoining the lagoons. However, the island doesn't only support breeding avocets they also winter here in some numbers.

Sandwich and common terns also breed here, as do redshank, shelduck, ringed plover and oyster-catcher.

Havergate shows a different face in winter when short-eared owls and the occasional hen harrier quarter the marshland; pintail, shoveller and wigeon make up the bulk of the wintering wildfowl.
108ha – Map ref: TM 425496

LADY'S-MANTLE MEADOW (Suffolk WT)** — *Spring, summer*

Comprising three small meadows that have never been ploughed, this reserve has been scheduled an SSSI. It's the only site in Suffolk where lady's mantle grows and the wealth of orchid species includes green-winged and twayblade, early purple and common spotted orchid; cowslip in abundance, pepper saxifrage and rest harrow are also found here. A ditch running through the site is the source of the river Alde.
3.6ha

MICKFIELD MEADOW (Suffolk WT)** — *Spring, summer*

Mickfield Meadow is still developing after scrub clearance, but it presents a superb example of unimproved herb-rich wet meadow. The native plants include the exotic-looking snake's head fritillary and the introduced meadow saffron; there are cowslips, ragged robin and lady's smock; and where there's lady's smock you'll find the beautiful orange tip butterfly. Stands of meadow-sweet fill the meadows in late summer.
1.8ha

MINSMERE (RSPB) — *All year*

Minsmere is one of the most important reserves for bird conservation in the country ranking alongside Havergate Island. A relic of the Second World War when the area was flooded as part of the coastal defence system against invasion and accidental shelling, in time the farmland that once existed behind the sea-wall became reed bed and marsh. Through lack of disturbance during war time, birds like bittern, harriers and the beautiful avocet, established themselves and now there is a wide range of habitats.

There is a famous "scrape" a man-made shallow lagoon system where the avocets breed; the second largest avocet colony in the country is here, and in certain years the elegant black-winged stilt will set up territory and raise a family in the nearby saltings. On the beach the tern colonies, including little tern, are very productive, and wading birds and terns gather during the spring and autumn passage. Autumn is a good time to see the rare and the unusual, black-tailed godwits and spotted redshank are frequent visitors to the scrape. Winter-time is excellent for migrant species from high arctic with Bewick swans most years.

Bittern nest in the extensive reed beds and marsh harriers are often seen quartering the marshes for a possible meal. On the adjoining heath stonechats and nightjars breed, and the increasingly rare silver-studded blue butterfly particular to dry heath occurs here; adders too take advantage of the heath to bask in the sun, they are not aggressive and will vanish with hardly a trace at your approach.

Otters are seen on the marsh from time to time, though nationally they are becoming scarcer.
1470 acres – Map ref: TM 475680

NORTH WARREN (RSPB) — *Spring, summer*

Part of the Sandlings heathland of the Suffolk coast, North Warren is made up of grass heath with areas of gorse and birch on sandy soil; there's also a mature fen with reeds, meadowsweet and sallow. These differing habitats encourage many birds including skylark, nightingale and whitethroat and bearded reedlings which nest in the reed beds. Kingfishers are also regular visitors.
96ha – Map ref: TM 455587

ORFORDNESS (NCC) — *All year*

The largest colony of lesser black-backed gulls in the country rests on this sand and shingle spit. Naturally the NCC actively discourages visitors during the breeding season. However, there are large numbers of waders and waterfowl to be seen in winter.
205.6ha – Map ref: TM 430480

POTASH LANE HEDGE (Suffolk WT) — *Spring, summer*

Potash Lane Hedge dates back to the time of the Norman Conquest with eight to thirteen species of woody plants per thirty yards length, and a total of nineteen species of trees and shrubs overall.
275m – Map ref: TL 994404

REDGRAVE & LOPHAM FENS (Suffolk WT)** — *Spring, summer*

This large valley fen reserve is nationally important as the only site where the great raft spider can be found. Discovered in 1956 it is the largest spider in the country. There is a tremendous variety of fen and wetland habitats here, and an excellent warden's centre where the history of man's use of peat is illustrated, as well as the impact of the mineral-rich calcareous springs on the flora and fauna of the reserve.
134ha

THETFORD HEATH (NCC/Norfolk NT)** — *Spring, summer*

A fine example of the remnants of ice age glacial mixing of chalk rubble and pebbles and sand. The ground cover reflects the mixture of soil types, and where silver birch scrub and trees have developed into small copses the greatest concentration of bird species will be found.
100ha

WALBERSWICK (NCC) — *Spring, summer*

Many heathland birds use this sandy maritime haven, and the tideline is regularly occupied by waders with terns and gulls feeding off-shore. Inland the sandy heathland shoulder of the county is one of the places where once the red-backed shrike was regularly seen, but it's still particularly good country for slow-worms and adders, and the common lizards that form a food source for shrike both great grey and red-backed.
514ha – Map ref: TM 493742

WANGFORD GLEBE (Suffolk WT)** — *Spring, late summer*

The Glebe has an evocative air about it, suggesting a time long ago when the sandy Brecklands covered an area 100 times more than they do today. The sand is loose and blows on the wind forming a mobile surface to which the plants and animals need to adapt if they are to survive.
16ha

SURREY

Stand anywhere on the North Downs or the high greensand ridge that sweeps across the county, and the impression you will gain is not the accepted one of commuter-belt country, but a wooded rural aspect. Granted the growth of many of the old market towns has been substantial as improved roads have brought affluence into the quiet countryside and many tiny villages tucked away in chalk coombes off the downs, and it is something of a minor miracle that so much woodland should have survived intact for in the counties north of the Thames modern agriculture has had a devastating effect. But here the sandy soil is less fertile and the chalky turf doesn't provide enough of a bite for the ploughshare, there is much to be explored.

The region is drained by several rivers; the Thames, the Mole and the Wey, the latter being split into the canalised section of the Wey Navigation at Weybridge and Byfleet. The snarling traffic of the M25 interrupts the peace as does the constant noise from jet aircraft at Heathrow and Gatwick, but here and there, where the open water meadows are bounded by alders, these troubles seem a million miles away.

Many of the most interesting natural history sites are on the less productive downs or greensand ridges, some are subjected to heavy tourist pressures like the spectacular sandy amphitheatre of the Devil's Punch Bowl, a natural feature now overgrown with conifers. Most of the sandy heaths have been seconded to the military, one of the reasons why they are still undeveloped; the occasional tank roaring across the quiet heath is less of a drama to wildlife than cultivation or housing or the fate of so much of our sandy soils, the planting of alien conifers in dark dismal lines so that the previously glorious ground flora is shaded out and destroyed. Scots pine grows well upon these sandy heaths, but when growing naturally would never form such dense stands as planted by foresters, and never in straight regimented lines.

Some of the finest heathland is at Thursley, an immense stretch of open wilderness where nature is King. Much of this habitat was created by slash and burn agriculture thousands of years ago, and the landscape has never fully recovered its original cover of oak trees; now bell heather and heath carpet the ground and the butterflies flourish.

There has been a great deal of road building requiring the extraction of millions of cubic metres of the abundant sands and river gravels of the Thames basin, particularly around Staines, Weybridge and Byfleet — the ground is pock-marked with huge areas of open water that have naturalised as lakes and wetlands of immense value to waterfowl, grebes and herons. Many of these lakes are being converted to water sport parks which reduces the potential for wildlife, but given a little peace and time many of the pits currently being extracted will form valuable wetlands for the future. The demands of London and the south east for places to dump the detritus of modern living has meant that some of these pits have been infilled with refuse, a tragic waste of raw materials that should be recycled. Perhaps the presence of huge rafts of duck on urban and suburban wetlands will be the catalyst for change in the environment, for hundreds of bird-watchers gather on the banks of these productive wetland sites every winter weekend.

It was the late 18th and early 19th century travel writer and agriculturalist William Cobbet who said that he had never seen a prettier town and a more agreeable or happier place than Guildford, but perhaps he was biased for he was a Surrey man, born and bred in Farnham. His book "Rural Rides" was published just a few years before his death in 1835. In Cobbet's day Guildford was a small market town where sheep, wool and the produce from the nearby countryside were brought to be sold; it is also the last resting place of Lewis Caroll who died here in 1898 while visiting his sisters.

But it is perhaps Richard Jefferies who encapsulated the Surrey countryside best, indeed the very countryside of England. During years of painful illness when he was unable to walk through the fields his fertile mind furnished a landscape that has become synonymous with Victorian rural life.

"To-day through the window-pane I see a lark high up against the grey cloud, and hear his song. I cannot walk about and arrange with the buds and gorse-bloom; how does he know it is the time for him to sing? Without my book and pencil and observing eye, how does he understand that the hour has come? To sing high in the air, to chase his mate over the low stone wall of the ploughed field, to battle with his high crested rival, to balance himself on his trembling wings outspread a few yards above the earth, and utter that sweet little loving kiss, as it were, of song — oh, happy, happy days!"

BAGMOOR COMMON (Surrey WT) — *Spring, summer*

A particularly rich piece of acid commonland with birch and pine woodland and stands of oak. The reserve is superb for insect species, being noted for the diversity of its butterflies; purple Emperor appears here in late July among the tops of the oaks.
13.6ha – Map ref: SU 926423

BOOKHAM COMMONS NATURE WALKS (NT) — *Spring, summer*

The walks at Bookham Commons are interesting on account of their size and the diversity of habitats available. Mainly woodland and grassland with an invasion of scrub, the flora is exceptional, over 500 different plant species having been recorded; such a wealth of plant life indicates a large healthy population of insects and birds with both small and large mammals. Within the confines of the nature walks are a series of old fish ponds adding their own specialised life to the diversity; and there are many species of dragonflies and damselflies, and a good bat population.
Various lengths – Map ref: TQ 121567

BOX HILL COUNTRY PARK (NT) — *Spring, summer*

Box Hill is one of the most popular places on the North Downs and as such has to with-stand immense public pressure. In parts the soil is worn through to the chalk, yet despite this the area retains its very special flora and fauna such as the Roman snail that trundles slowly over the foliage rasping its way through vegetation in order to keep its large body healthy. It was thought to have been brought to this country by the Romans and farmed for food, it can only live in areas where there is a great deal of calcium in the soil which it needs to build its shell.

Other relics of the past are the trees from which the hill takes its name. Box is a small shrub-like tree with strong round evergreen foliage, its hard straight-grained timber was once much in demand for tool handles; the number of box trees over much of the chalk scrublands of southern England has declined to a pitiful few, but Box Hill supports quite a number as well as yew woodland, another typical chalk downland tree.

The hurricane-force winds that swept over the county one Thurday night early in October 1987 overturned mature trees and smashed branches, many of the larger trees were damaged, but the box and yew suffered less in comparison, their short stature and dense growth protecting them from the full power of the wind. With the demise of so many trees the ground flora has had a chance to see the light and new plants are growing where once there had been very few. On the hillsides, where the turf is short, orchids and other downland plants help to compose a varied chalk flora. The man orchid is one of the most unusual of the orchids, its yellowish green mannikin-shaped flower is a rarity in this country, as is the small and almost insignificant musk orchid. Bee and

pyramidal orchids also flower on the chalk turf along with carline thistle; and the birds you'll hear will include linnet and skylark, both are seen in some numbers despite the human intrusion.
253ha – Map ref: TQ 179513

THE DEVIL'S PUNCHBOWL & GIBBET HILL NATURE TRAILS (NT) — *Spring, summer*

On a clear day the view from this outstanding site is glorious, you can see several counties. The heathy trails are best in high summer when the heather and butterflies and birds are out in force. One of the most exciting places on the whole of the lower greensand ridge.
3 and 4km – Map ref: SU 890357

FRENSHAM COUNTRY PARK (Waverley DC) — *Spring, summer*

Together with Frensham Ponds, which hold particularly good bird and insect populations, the reserve shows the classic Surrey heath with adders and common lizards. Both these creatures are shy and will vanish at your approach, if you want to see one at close quarters pick an overcast day to go looking, for the reptiles try to raise their body temperature by lying on heather clumps. The nature trail near the ponds is excellent and you should be able to hear the extremely noisy reed warbler colony in the reed beds. In winter the ponds attract waterfowl of many species, including the beautiful and unusual mandarin duck.
311ha – Map ref: SU 849406

GODSTONE RESERVOIRS (Surrey WT)** — *All year*

The presence of a small colony of sand martins makes Godstone Reservoirs a very special site. Wintering wildfowl are generally few in number, but smew or goldeneye can sometimes be seen in hard weather. In spring and autumn the margins along the reservoirs attract waders, and terns will occasionally stop on their migrations.
18ha – (Overlooked from) TQ 362511

HEADLEY WARREN (Surrey WT)** — *Spring, summer*

An outstanding reserve. Headley Common is best where the chalk dowland turf is well developed, rich in herbs and mounded with ant hills. The south facing slopes are a mass of tiny flowers; cowslip, rock rose, horseshoe and kidney vetch, milkwort and chalk milkwort, the odd-looking yellow rattle, clustered bellflower, wild thyme, harebell and wild marjoram all making a glorious display and providing nectar for the bees and flickering butterflies, among which the chalkhills and common blues are very active in high summer. The rare and beautiful adonis blue is also seen here as is the Duke of Burgundy fritillary, a butterfly in decline as its habitat decreases. It is not actually a fritillary at all but a representative of the metalmark butterflies whose main stronghold is on the other side of the Atlantic in South America. The Duke of Burgundy is the only member of this family in Europe. This is a lovely place and the orchids (five species) and butterflies (thirty five species) draw naturalists from far and wide.
31.2ha

HORSELL COMMON NATURE WALKS (Horsell Common Preservation Society) — *Spring, summer*

A series of common land walks with a wide range of wet and dry heathland settings. Reptiles include grass snakes, adders and common lizards, while the bird population is enhanced by linnets, stonechats and yellowhammers. The area is also overflown by hobbys and sparrowhawks, and kestrels are relatively common.
2.4km – Map ref: TQ 989605 / SU 002605 / SU 007593 / SU 015611

NORTH DOWNS WAY (CC) — *Spring, summer*

The North Downs long distance footpath follows the line of chalk hills from Farnham to the north Kent coast and travels through some of the most beautiful scenery in southern England. The damage done to trees in the October 1987 gale shows up clearly from the path, but it is interesting to see how much regeneration has already taken place.
72km – Map ref: SU 844467 / TQ 429561

STAFFHURST WOOD (SCC) — *Spring, summer*

In this well wooded county it's good to see areas of ancient woodland being preserved and properly managed; the presence of wild service tree indicates that woodland has probably grown on this site since the ice retreated and the climate became damp and warm — about 7000 years ago. The Wealden oak forest was once very extensive, the invading Romans called it Silva Anderida, but in the Middle Ages demand for timber for building ships and churches and for charcoal as well as the requirement for more agricultural land meant that many of the finest trees were felled; now this remnant harbours an excellent population of songbirds and insects.
38ha – Map ref: TQ 412483

Goldcrest   *Staffhurst Wood*

Headley Heath

THURSLEY (NCC) — *Spring, summer*

Broadleaved woodland once covered this part of Surrey, but over the course of time cropping and grazing so impoverished the sandy soil that heathland became the dominant habitat. Thursley Heath is a marvellous place, it's no longer economic to graze the sheep which once kept the heathland open and free from birch and Scots pine, so certain areas have regained a sparse covering of trees, though not enough to shade out the glorious heather and cross-leaved heath.

Where it is wet, ponds and marshes have developed and dragonflies thrive in very large numbers, up to twenty six species are found here, and it is thought that up to 10,000 species of insects inhabit the heath. Some, like the silver-studded blue butterfly, are becoming rare nationally as their habitat decreases, but here they are common.

The plant life depends upon the presence of water in the sandy soil; where there are bogs you'll find asphodel and sphagnum mosses forming a deep blanket of peat; cotton grass, purple moor grass and cross-leaved heath marks the damp areas. The open heath resembles moorland, and the birds that inhabit this area range from winter rarities such as the large predatory great grey shrike to merlin, hen and Montague's harrier, peregrine and hobby as well as a breeding population of sparrowhawks and kestrels. It is an excellent area for raptors for there are many small birds, including a breeding population of redstarts and a few pairs of Dartford warblers as well as linnets, yellow-hammers and corn buntings.

Reptiles are a features of heathland and Thursley is no exception with the very rare sand lizard occurring along with grass snakes and plentiful adders; while amphibians include frogs and toads and several species of newts breeding in the ponds. In all a very special area of Surrey heathland.

250ha – Map ref: SU 900399

VANN LAKE (Surrey WT)** — *Spring, summer*

The old hammer pond at Vann is a relic of former times and extremely popular with birds and insects; the woodland surrounding the pond is thought to be on an ancient site with wild service tree and a huge range of woodland plants such as bluebells, common cow wheat, early purple and common spotted orchids. The reserve is noted for its fungi with over 550 species being recorded, and the birds too are extensive, over 100 species being listed. It is also thought that nightingales breed here.

11.2ha

WITLEY COMMON (NT) — *Spring, summer*

Close by Thursley Heath, Witley Common is typical heathland with a wide range of birds and insects usually found on this fascinating habitat. Hobbys are commonly seen in summer and the breeding population of small birds includes whinchats, stonechats and linnets. Sand lizards have been recorded, although they are rare. Adders are common.

150ha – Map ref: SU 936409

SUSSEX

"Though I have travelled the Sussex Downs upwards of thirty years, yet I still investigate that chain of majestic mountains with fresh admiration, year by year; and I think I see new beauties every time I traverse it." So said Gilbert White of this most attractive southern county heavily influenced by both the sea and the South Downs.

Sadly the hurricane of 1987 wrecked many of the finest old beechwoods, leaving trees scattered like straws, and although plans for restoration are underway this will take a generation or more; meanwhile the woodland floor in these damaged areas is receiving a blaze of sunlight after being sheltered for two centuries, the results for natural history will be dramatic, especially on flowering plants like bluebells.

The whale-backed downs above Arundel, Littlehampton and Worthing were once the province of huge flocks of Sussex Down sheep and the men who cared for them written about by many, particularly Berkley Wills, a Worthing shopkeeper whose descriptions of the life of the Sussex shepherds and the sheep fayres at Steyning are classic. The crook makers who supplied the shepherd's badge of office were master craftsmen capable of turning a working tool into a work of art.

Many years ago, I was lucky enough to meet a few of these hardy countrymen. When stationed at RAF Tangmere in the 1950s I was seconded to an air traffic control centre on Trundle Hill, the site of an Iron Age hill fort on the Sussex Downs above Chichester and, when off duty, spent many happy hours watching the last shepherds with their flocks working the downs. Once the modern agricultural revolution got rolling much of the downland was ploughed and there was no longer a place for the shepherd and his flock; the landscape they had created was interdependent — the sheep kept the grasses short enabling delicate specialised flowers to thrive in profusion, and the butterflies too benefited from the woolly lawnmowers. Adonis, chalkhill and small blues, and Duke of Burgundy fritillaries once rose in clouds before the grazing flocks.

Rudyard Kipling lived in Sussex and his love of the county and of the downs runs through many of his poems:-

"A Three-Part Song"

("Dymchurch Flit" — Puck of Pook's Hill)

I've given my soul to the Southdown grass,
And sheep-bells tinkled where you pass,
Oh, Firle an' Ditchling an' sails at sea,
I reckon you keep my soul for me!

Kipling had a taste for landscape, the great downland escarpment and the soft Wealden woodland, the open coastline with its broad goose-filled marshes inspired him to write some extraordinarily beautiful verse. I am a great admirer of his; granted some of his views would not meet with universal approval today, but we should remember that he lived in very different times; all I know is that when I read his poems of the downland or his evocations on the prehistory of the downland peoples I am there with the wind upon my face and the smell of the sea coming up to me on The Trundle.

Sussex can smile at the rest of us with supreme satisfaction for faced with the devastation of Dutch elm disease they did not simply wring their hands and do nothing, they got up off their derrières and organised the cutting of a "Cordon Sanitare" around their county, and so saved most of their beautiful majestic elms. I guarantee Kipling would have applauded their efforts.

Inland Sussex has excited much interest from naturalists and landscape managers, for the wreckage of the downs and the monuments of Neolithic man and his successors by uncontrolled agriculture is a crime that future generations will curse us for. Many sites of great archaeological importance are also of enormous natural history interest, but intensive subsidised chemical farming is responsible for much destruction. The coastline, however, managed to escape the worst excesses and the area around Chichester Harbour, though a yachting marina in summer, supports a healthy population of geese and waders in winter. The shoreline from Selsey Bill to Rye can be depended upon to produce waders and, in spring breeding terns in large numbers.

View from Sussex Downs

Despite the heavy pressures of tourism there are still quiet places and creeks where birds can find refuge, where plants can grow and where small mammals can live out their short lives undisturbed by man.

ARUNDEL WILDFOWL REFUGE (WWT) — *All year*

The Wildfowl and Wetland Trust has been in the forefront of nature conservation since its foundation by the late artist, broadcaster and premier knight of conservation, Sir Peter Scott; and this is one of a network of reserves strategically placed around the coast to attract wildfowl and provide somewhere for the public to see the less common species in close proximity. Duck and waders gather on the meadows and scrape and the lake where migrant wildfowl and other birds can find refuge; public hides enable you to observe the wild creatures as well as a collection of waterfowl from other countries.
24ha – Map ref: TQ 020081

ASHDOWN FOREST (Conservators of Ashdown Forest) — *Spring, summer*

Ashdown Forest is a huge heathery heath in the process of gradual change for as the site is grazed less and less the encroachment of scrub woodland tends to overshadow some areas; however, there is much of natural history interest here. The fallow deer are numerous and worth looking out for and other large mammals include badgers and foxes; the wealth of plants and insects and the many different habitats encourage small mammals and birds which in turn attract birds of prey; long-eared and tawny owls make the reserve particularly important. Hobby falcons are seen over the area in summer when they hawk for the dragonflies that thrive in the wet areas where round-leaved sundew and sphagnum mosses form mats of floating vegetation; there are many butterflies including small pearl-bordered fritillary and silver-studded blue, and the emperor moth is relatively common here.
2560ha – Map ref: TQ 432324

BEACHY HEAD NATURE TRAIL (Eastbourne BC) — *Spring, summer*

A favourite spot for tourists, the downland on Beachy Head above a sheer drop to the sea, is of particular interest in that the butterfly population, especially the blue butterflies is outstanding; the presence of chalk grassland is the determining factor for these insects. The site is also spectacularly good for sea-bird observation and of recent years peregrine falcons have tended to appear in winter.
2km – Map ref: TV 586956

BURTON POND (WSCC/Sussex WT) — *All year*

One of the largest inland reed beds in the county, the breeding species include water rail, reed and sedge warbler; and grasshopper warblers appear occasionally as do Cetti's warblers. Burton pond with its wooded banks topped with heathland is bright with yellow water lily in summer and is the haunt of grebe both great crested and little grebe. It is the only known site in Sussex where cow bane can be found.
31.2ha – Map ref: SU 979180

CASTLE HILL (NCC) — *Spring, summer*

High above Brighton, Castle Hill's excellent chalk grassland is typical of the kind of habitat once common in Sussex. There are many species of orchids and the interesting scabious-like flower known as round-headed rampion with its blue flowers and inward-curving petals. Such a habitat attracts many breeding butterflies especially white and chalkhill blue.
45ha – Map ref: TQ 367074

CHICHESTER HARBOUR/NUTBOURNE MARSHES (Chichester Harbour Conservancy) — *All year*

Together with nearby Langstone Harbour this reserve forms one of the most important wildfowl refuges in Britain, indeed it is of international importance. The dunlin flocks are sometimes in excess of 20,000 and other waders such as bar-tailed and black-tailed godwits, oyster-catchers, turnstone, knot, sanderling and curlew make a days bird-watching very exciting; there is always a chance of seeing a rarity, and avocets are frequent visitors to the food-rich mud. Thorney Island, where the RAF Coastal Command had an airfield is excellent for waders; when the tide is full and the waders are driven inland they gather in immense numbers on the higher ground and in winter the Brent geese arrive in vast flocks. Over 8000 crowd onto the estuarine complex where they feed on eelgrass and, with increasing frequency in recent years, other geese have begun to arrive, especially white-fronted geese. Hard weather brings duck as they flee from frozen inland waterways, and herons and kingfishers too are common in hard weather.

This place is a must for any committed bird-watcher. The wind can be cold and the weather uncertain, but you are always sure to see something exciting. Often a peregrine will be wintering on the marshes taking waders from the feeding flocks or a teal from the gutters as the tide runs in.
Chichester Harbour 1200ha – Map ref: SU 775005
Nutbourne Marshes 360ha – Map ref: SU 766051

CUCKMERE HAVEN (ESCC/Lewes DC) — *Spring, summer*

The river Cuckmere runs out to meet the sea in the shadow of beautiful towering chalk cliffs cut sheer as if with a cheese wire, and the Haven itself was created by a combination of sea and melt waters from inland glaciers. Deposits of flints and silt formed a base for the marsh in the river-cut valley, and rising sea levels in the 3000 to 4000 years following the end of the last glaciation eroded the soft chalk coastline so that the shallow sea bed is now composed of shingle banks and wave-cut chalk platforms perfect for marine organisms.

The reserve encompasses both land and sea, the river mouth is a favoured stopping place for waders and migrant songbirds and inland the high chalk downland

supports some particularly fine downland flowers including round-headed rampion and several unusual orchids, one of which is the burnt orchid. The usual plants of chalk turf are also found here squinancy wort, purple milk vetch, milkwort, wild thyme, wild carrot, yellow rattle, wild mignonette and carline thistle; also the horseshoe vetch, the food plant of the delightful chalkhill blue butterfly. Birds nest upon the Seven Sisters, fulmars especially favour these sheer cliffs with their strong updraughts, and kestrels too play in the upcurrents together with jackdaws that also nest here.
392ha – Map ref: TV 519995

DITCHLING BEACON (Sussex WT) — *Spring, summer*

One of the most dramatic aspects of the north facing slope of the downs, Ditchling Beacon rises steeply to a considerable height and the views are spectacular. The chalk downland turf is rich in herbs and common blue butterflies, these lovely creatures, totally dependant on this type of habitat, are commonly found at the end of July.
19.6ha – Map ref: TQ 329133

KINGLEY VALE (NCC) — *Spring, summer*

The naturally occurring yew woodland at Kingley Vale has been allowed to mature into a solid canopy of deep green shade. It is considered to have one of the finest views in England. On a clear day you can see out over the yew woodlands and the downs to the Isle of Wight.

In places the yews are interspersed with hornbeam, ash, oak and a few beeches, and the shade beneath is such that only a sickly bramble or two can grow. The branches are tangled and root where they drop in a jigsaw puzzle of tree and soil. The yews vary in age from less than a century to some gnarled giants that have seen more than three centuries and the reason for their presence is the chalk.

Above the woodland is the down where a host of plants grow in a perfect setting, flowers massed in hundreds to the square metre, small plants stunted by lack of nutrients in the soil, kept low by grazing and cut by wind and lack of moisture. Butterflies too are a feature, four species of blue butterflies including chalkhills and five fritillaries including dark green.

The plant life is the reason why Kingley Vale is so important. Bee, fly and frog orchids have been recorded with fragrant, pyramidal, common spotted and twayblade orchids in the marginal woodland. There is also a wealth of birds, though few venture into the dense yew forest. Warblers and small songbirds find adequate nest sites on the margins and predators such as sparrow-hawks and the occasional buzzard are seen. The former nests in the forest and kestrels are regular visitors as are hobby falcons in summer. Owls, especially tawny owls, are common and feed upon the extensive small mammal population of the margins and downs; barn owls also appear occasionally. Badgers, foxes and fallow deer are common and the shy roe deer is at home beneath the yew canopy. In all it is a magic place of immense interest to the naturalist.
114.4ha – Map ref: SU 824088

MALLYDAMS WOOD (RSPCA) — *Spring, summer*

Owned by the RSPCA Mallydams Wood is typical Wealden woodland marked by stream-cut sandstone ghylls, and the butterflies and plants found in this type of habitat such as white admirals and spotted orchids.
24ha – Map ref: TQ 857122

THE MENS (Sussex WT) — *Spring, summer*

Formerly common woodland where grazing rights precluded coppice management and pollarding. If this type of regime was carried on in the past it was abandoned before records were kept; in consequence the wood, especially those areas where mature beech trees have been allowed to reach their full potential, is in deep shade and little grows. However, parts of the wood are more varied and show signs that woodland has been growing here for millennia. Butcher's broom with its deep green spiny leaves and red berries is found here, and the birds are superb with all the usual woodland species including all three types of woodpecker. The lack of ground flora in the deep shaded areas precludes a good butterfly fauna but you can find the very special purple Emperor. The Mens is lovely in springtime when the woodland is at its most beautiful with new green shoots and the brilliant purple-blue flowers of bluebells forming a carpet beneath the trees.
155ha – Map ref: TQ 024236

PAGHAM HARBOUR (WSCC) — *All year*

Less commonly visited than nearby Chichester Harbour, yet Pagham holds a tremendous range of birdlife, especially in winter when the tide exposes vast acreages of mud, and waders such as grey plover and lapwing feed so intently that one can approach within fifty yards or less. Good quality powerful optical equipment is helpful here, something light in weight as the walk along the sea-wall is long, but it's well worth it for huge numbers of waders congregate to feed and Brent geese and the occasional flock of pink-feet will suddenly appear on the wind. (Over 200 species have been recorded.) The Ferry Pool is a well known spot for birds.
440ha – Map ref: SZ 857965

RYE HARBOUR (ESCC) — *All year*

A large bay formed through the drift of shingle and sand over millennia and changing sea levels which have provided a series of coastal and salt marsh environments almost unrivalled in the south east corner of the country. Gravel extraction has created several freshwater pits that have been eagerly colonised by plants, animals and birds. Winter is when most bird-watchers gather to see the immense numbers of duck and waders that arrive in hard weather. Spring and summer brings the breeding birds, especially little terns whose nests on the shingle are closely wardened in order to avoid disturbance by people using the beach.

In summer the butterflies and moths from the nearby European mainland adds to the entomological interest and clouded yellows, Berger's clouded yellow, Queen of Spain fritillaries and very active humming bird hawk moth all fly around the shingle margins where viper's

bugloss and sea pea find roothold. Other plants flourish in the well established shingle — lime-loving musk mallow with its lovely pink or white flowers. In spring the passage migrants are both varied and spectacular.
356ha – Map ref: TQ 942187

SOUTH DOWNS WAY (CC) — *Spring, summer*

The long distance way from Beachy Head to south of Petersfield in Hampshire runs through some of the most beautiful landscapes in southern England. The downs are important, with their superb chalk turf and many flowering plants and birds; undoubtedly the skylark reigns here, their song is in the air from the beginning of spring to late summer. However, walkers should note the damage to the archaeological remains caused by ploughing; it is estimated that nearly eighty per cent of these sensitive sites have been affected.
129km – Map ref: SU 762193 / TV 600972

WEST DEAN WOODS (Sussex WT)** — *Spring, summer*

Old oak woodland with hazel coppice, a relic of the woods that once covered much of this area. The ground flora includes wild daffodils, bluebells and early purple orchids growing in profusion where the light is strong enough on the woodland floor. During the October 1987 gale the wood suffered some damage and this will take many years to rectify, but in the meantime the more open aspect will enhance the wood's potential with more nest sites for songbirds springing up in the clearings where trees have fallen; these trees too will form a valuable food resource where they are allowed to rot back into the soil.
15.4ha

WOODS MILL (Sussex WT) — *Spring, summer*

The headquarters of the Sussex Naturalist Trust is at Woods Mill, and this relatively small area contains a wide variety of habitats. The mill itself is driven by water issuing from the chalk downs and the woodland grows on Wealden clay, the plant life reflects this with early dog violets, wood anemones, moschatel, lesser celandine, bluebells and primroses. There's a pool where children are encouraged to dip for invertebrates during local school visits, and a lake which produces a wide range of insects with dragonflies and damselflies in abundance. Heron and kingfishers visit the lake, and the alder trees in the wet areas attract redpolls and siskins. The main value of this reserve lies in its educational potential as well as providing a microcosm of habitats in a very pleasant setting.
6ha – Map ref: TQ 218137

WARWICKSHIRE
&
WEST MIDLANDS

Even if Shakespeare had not been born here the county of Warwickshire and the new region of the West Midlands would still have been well blessed with creative writers. George Eliot with her wonderful evocation of character drew on the differing aspects of the county's landscapes in her novel Silas Marner. A mine of literary talent flourished over the centuries within the rigorous institution of Rugby, the archetypal British public school, and used by Thomas Hughes in his classic novel "Tom Brown's Schooldays".

Rupert Brook, one of a generation of young poets who rose like comets and were snuffed out in the 1914/18 war before their potential could be fully explored, was also a pupil at Rugby and so too was the unique Lewis Carol whose creative imagination has delighted children and adults alike for generations, putting into words the private fantasy world inhabited by the unsophisticated mind of a child.

Is it the landscape that inspires such a creative drive? On the surface it seems unlikely that a region so heavily and uncaringly industrialised should nurture any creative thought, unless it be how to escape the urban sprawl, and the noise and the discomfort of Birmingham city centre. Although perhaps the complex motorway system could inspire thoughts akin to Alice's desire to run down a rabbit hole in search of some answers. But this is the county as we know it today.

When Shakespeare first became aware of the countryside around him, and the river that fed and watered the meadows where wild flowers grew in abundance, and where mute swans sailed elegantly through Stratford-upon-Avon there was little industry in the county. Writing about the Bard Ben Johnson referred to him as the Sweet Swan of Avon! This was not simply pure romantic imagery from one friend to another. For Shakespeare possessed a keen awareness of the countryside, and a love of birds, animals and plants that marks him out as a sharp observer and more than just passing knowledgeable. One of his most famous and oft quoted poems comes from:-

"A Midsummer Night's Dream"

I know a bank where the wild thyme blows,
Where oxlips and the nodding violet grows
Quite over-canopied with luscious
   Woodbine,
With sweet musk-roses and with eglantine.

In Shakespeare's time the countryside was still heavy with oak forests, and the valley in which Stratford lay was described as being well wooded with fine farmlands. Shakespeare's knowledge of birds was that of a true Elizabethan countryman; one who hunted hart, hind and hare, knew the merits of a fine falcon, appreciated the scent of woodbine in the forest and the sound of birdsong in spring. He was familiar with the shape and sound of kites and of eagles, for both were familiar sights over towns and cities.

He was obviously familiar with the practice of falconry, a sport that has given many words to the English language. To Shakespeare a mews would have been a place where trained falcons were kept, and he often referred to this ancient sport in his plays. In "Taming of the Shrew" he gives Tranio the following lines to describe Bianca:-

Master, your love must live a maid at home;
And therefore has he closely mew'd her up,
Because she will not be annoy'd with suitors.

Eagles were also common in the county, though it's likely that the eagle to which Shakespeare referred would have not been a golden eagle, but a white-tailed sea eagle, a bird not averse to carrion to supplement its diet of fish and whose bones have been found associated with other Elizabethan deposits; the eagle, supposedly of Kingly manner and courage, was not as regal as the Bard's pen painted it. Raven too were common in those less than sanitary days and Shakespeare uses them as birds of ill omen drawing on the deep-rooted folklore of the countryside. Celtic tales of the talking raven 'Bran' were never far from the fireside storytellers armoury.

The region has been a crossroads for centuries. Before the extensive road network there was the railway, and the prosperity that this means of transport brought to a previously uncomplicated landscape wrought immense changes, although in some parts of the west midlands ridge and furrow agricultural methods still show through, as corrugation in the fields. Ridge and furrow was an ancient, but efficient means of ploughing, using a simple implement; particularly economic in farming difficult wet or stony ground, and so ingrained in the land is it that it has remained, the fingerprint of a system which has resisted obliteration.

In the mid 1870s more than half the region's farmland was under pasture, the predominant species being birds and mammals of the open countryside and deep thick hedgerows; what a change to the current situation where agricultural 'improvement' has swept away many of these hedges.

Yet it has to be said that some interesting habitats have been created by industrial use. Lime, clay and brick pits, and Victorian ironstone workings have left a legacy of environments that have been recolonised by plants and insect species, and the populations are often larger now simply because of the workings. As in other parts of the country, where there has been exploitation of gravel and sand deposits, huge holes have been created. Often it is the fate of these holes to be filled in with houshold refuse and spoil, but sometimes a more enlightened attitude prevails and they are turned into nature reserves of considerable wildlife potential.

The changes that time has imposed upon this landscape have more to do with the economic health of the country than virtually any other region. The decline of heavy industry and the growth in hi-tech companies has led to a cleaning and greening of the formerly most polluted areas, and wildlife is returning to the suburbs of towns where urban foxes are a common sight as are kestrel's nests on high buildings. New agricultural polices such as the 'set-aside' proposals for farmland, may soon lead to a West Midlands region with a renewed potential for inspiration worthy of the birthplace of our greatest creative playwright.

BEDWORTH SLOUGHS (Nuneaton and Bedworth BC) — *All year*

A wetland site that came about by accident when the ground above the mine workings slumped, leaving a depression that was soon filled with water and swiftly

Mute Swan   *Warwickshire*

colonised by wetland plants and insects, small mammals and birds. The area is also known for the large numbers of bird visitors it attracts during the year and its considerable breeding bird population, more then seventy species have been recorded. The reeds and vegetation surrounding the open water constitutes one of the largest pre-migration roosts for swallows in autumn — it has been estimated that up to 25,000 birds use this reserve.
5ha – Map ref: SP 350871

BRANDON MARSH (Warwicks NCT)** — *All year*

The changes wrought by gravel extraction can have considerable wildlife benefits; the upheaval while the minerals are being taken creates a desert-like environment where nothing seems able to exist, but afterwards, if the craters are not infilled by waste and debris, the land will soon return to nature. This is what has happened at Brandon Marsh, the pits of varying depths and shapes support reeds and marsh, and open grassland and wet meadow can all be found within the confines of the reserve. Reed nesting species and sand martins are the jewels in the crown of this site; the latter build in the steep banks created by quarrying, and the water and marsh provides suitable food. Sadly these attractive birds declined in numbers due to the drought in Africa where they winter.

The reserve provides suitable habitats for many birds all through the year. In winter, geese, the occasional wild swan, and many hundreds of duck and grebes are present. Hard weather will bring waterfowl from a considerable distance to benefit from the deeper water which doesn't freeze over, and spring and summer brings the migrants, including marsh and reed warblers that breed along with cuckoos, who use the warbler's nests as foster homes for their single chick.

There are many species of plants including marsh orchids and the attractive gypsywort with its jagged bright green leaves. The dragonfly population, and the presence of swallows, martins and other small birds brings the hobby falcons to the marsh in summer as well as marsh harriers, osprey, short-eared owls, and the resident sparrowhawks and kestrels that breed nearby. The presence of rabbits and small mammals encourages predatory mammals, and weasels, stoats and foxes all help to provide a balance. The reserve has an enthusiastic band of supporters and an active ringing programme that helps to provide comprehensive records of the avian visitors to this fascinating series of man-made habitats.
53.6ha

CRACKLEY WOOD NATURE TRAIL (Warwick DC) —*Spring, summer*

An attractive trail through oak and birch woodland with bluebells and wood anemones. There are foxes and badgers here, as well as an abundance of small mammals, and the birds include yellowhammer, chaffinch and two species of thrush. In spring and summer there's an influx of migrant songbirds and it's an excellent area for willow warbler and blackcap.
1.2km – Map ref: SP 287737

DRAYCOTE MEADOWS (Warwicks NCT)** — *Spring, summer*

One of the few remaining unimproved hay meadows in the region. In spring and mid summer this site gives an indication of how Warwickshire and the West Midlands region must have looked in the early part of the century. The flowering plants include green-winged orchids in profusion with yellow rattle and many other indicator plants. The fertility of the meadow is maintained by vetches and bird's foot trefoil, leguminous plants that fix naturally occurring nitrogen in the soil by means of bacteria that inhabit nodules in their roots.

The variety of plants encourages a wide range of insects, and the butterfly and moth fauna is outstanding. Small mammals and shrews are common in the grass and are hunted by kestrels by day and tawny owls by night. The meadows are also the haunt of weasels and the occasional stoat will explore for mice and voles from the safety of one of the ancient hedges that bound the stream.
5.2ha

EDGE HILL NATURE TRAIL (Warwicks NCT) — *Spring, summer*

A northern extension of the Cotswold Hills, the views from this reserve are said to cover twelve counties on an exceptionally clear day. The trail has a wide variety of habitats from wetland to woods and open hilly grassland with a correspondingly rich bird and plant life.
3.2km – Map ref: SP 370470

KINGSBURY WATER PARK (WCC) — *All year*

Kingsbury Water Park is part of a larger complex of gravel extraction workings, some of which have been filled with a slurry of fly ash which has consolidated into mud forming a series of shallow wetland habitats complementing the deeper water. The whole complex is extensive, although a large part is used for forms of recreation other than nature study. Birds find the area very attractive and the list is long, more than five species of warblers and some waterfowl breed here. There are plenty of summer and winter visitors both avian and human and birds of prey are common, largely due to the availability of food in the form of small birds and mammals.

The insect fauna includes many species of dragonfly and damselfly and these in turn attract hobbys. In late summer when they are teaching their young to hunt over the water, they take swallows and martins as well as the dragonflies. Often unusual waders and terns can be seen from the hides overlooking the lagoons; black terns will visit in spring and waders stop on passage though some, like snipe, may be present all year.
213.8ha – Map ref: SP 204958

LAPWORTH CANAL NATURE TRAIL (NT) — *Spring summer*

A section of the Stratford-upon-Avon canal which has a run of fifteen locks. The wildlife interest depends on the time of year, but is most attractive in early spring or late summer.
3.2km – Map ref: SP 186708 / 188678

OXHOUSE FARM (Warwicks NCT)** — *Spring summer*

Oxhouse Farm reserve is dominated by limestone exposed where once a busy railway line cut through the site. The chippings that form the bed of the line, and the steep banks, provide an excellent site for a number of plants that cling to the rocky scree like so much jumble. Wild basil, dyer's greenweed, cowslip, the strange dead-looking carline thistle and the sharp-tasting salad burnet grow together with quaking grass. There are more than forty-five species of grasses here, including a few found only in one or two other locations in Warwickshire.

The limestone meadows through which the now re-dundant line runs, boasts a great variety of habitats, and the shrubby bushes of blackthorn, dogwood, elder and hawthorn encourage summer songbirds to nest and colonise. The insect fauna is outstanding, there are any number of butterflies here, including one synonymous with limestone and chalk grassland, the beautiful fast-flying dark green fritillary. Many butterflies have been recorded on the reserve, almost two thirds of the total species found in Great Britain can be seen, from the orange tip in early April to the late emerging comma and red admiral.

The abundant insect population does not stop at butterflies, large numbers of spiders and beetles and other flying insects are a magnet for birds and the site has a very extensive list with some unusual songbirds like the nightingale. Winter bird visitors include huge flocks of redwings and fieldfares, and the occasional great grey shrike.
7.2ha

SANDWELL VALLEY NATURE TRAILS (Sandwell MBC) — *Winter, summer*

Running through mixed species woodland this trail skirts a series of pools rich in dragonflies and damselflies. The bird population reflects the variety of trees and shrubs, with a good selection of summer migrants; in winter the pools are popular with wintering wildfowl.
1.2 and 2.4km – Map ref: SP 017914

SUTTON PARK (City of Birmingham DC) — *Spring, summer*

Best described as an urban lung on the outskirts of Birmingham, Sutton Park is subject to immense pressure from the city's inhabitants and consequently the chance of seeing a rarity is remote. Where the ground is boggy and the woodland dense, the public ventures less, but most of the heathy rolling land will feel tramping feet during the course of the year, with summer taking the greatest toll. The park staff also have an almost insoluble problem with litter.

Potentially, it is one of the most productive places in the Birmingham area, the trees are mixed coniferous and deciduous with dense stands of holly, and here and there woods composed almost entirely of birch. In parts, the heathland looks more like moorland with bogs and common cotton grass in swathes, and various wetland plants such as ragged robin grow in the damp valley

Shrew   *Draycote Meadows*

bottoms where the soil's fertility is higher than the surrounding acid land. In all, a precious area, and vital if wildlife in and around our towns and cities is to survive. All too often such heathland is given over to development and vanishes with virtually no record of their ever having existed.
859ha – Map ref: SP 103963

WAPPENBURY WOOD (Warwicks NCT)** — *Spring, summer*

Oak over old coppice woodland is one of the recipes for success in woodland management for producing the widest range of habitats and species within a given area. The ground flora at Wappenbury Wood is abundant with a large number of shrubby plants including buckthorn, hawthorn, aspen, willow and ash. The open rides are attractive to both large and small mammals, and deer are present in some numbers. The birdlife of this productive habitat is varied, and tree pipit and nightingale have been recorded as well as many breeding birds such as warblers and titmice and some of the more common finches. Over thirty species of butterflies have been recorded here.
103.2ha

WELCOMBE HILLS NATURE TRAIL (Stratford DC) — *Spring, summer*

A wide variety of habitats can be enjoyed along this trail with grassland, spinnys and woods and where the park-land trees remain, many have reached considerable proportions. Birdlife is dependant on time of year, being best in spring and summer, but interesting all year round.
2km – Map ref: SP 205564

WYKEN SLOUGH (Warwicks. NCT)** — *Spring, summer*

The small reed bed at Wyken Slough is an important urban roost for swallows and martins in late summer. The wetland birds are varied and include reed and sedge warblers and reed bunting, and the reserve has a well deserved reputation for its dragonflies and damselflies. The breeding amphibians make an interesting addition to the fauna, and small mammals are relatively common.
1.2ha

WILTSHIRE

The chalk downs of Wiltshire could almost be described as the birthplace of British culture, from the flint knappers of the Stone Age to the highly developed hill-fort culture of the Iron Age Celts with their earth mound graves and Henge monuments. Wiltshire's Salisbury Plain is dotted with the remnants of 5000 years of occupation, and up until the 1950s there were still huge tracts of sheep pasture where shepherds roamed with their flocks, the sheep cropping the turf to the consistency of a springy carpet.

The stones at Stonehenge have long caused men to wonder. Why were they put there? By whom? What was their power? We know the "Sarsens" came from deposits on the plain and the "Bluestones" that cap the uprights were floated across from Wales then dragged to the site. Prehistoric civil engineering meant a huge expenditure of muscle and sweat and was far less romantic than theories put forward of celestial navigators from another planet. Whoever did build this immense and impressive stone circle also raised the monument at Avebury and many other circles now merely negative impressions on the texture of the plain, some known and some hidden, their post holes obliterated by deep ploughing. Whatever their origin these stones exuded a sense of power, be it real or imagined.

Unfortunately over the past few years convoys of flowerpower hippies have clashed with authority over the use of the monument as a gathering place and access has been greatly curtailed to avoid damage — no curtailment has been placed on ploughing and planting cereals on the flower-rich sward. Salisbury Plain held a unique record of our Bronze and Iron Age past, and the Celtic warrior chiefs who ruled the open chalklands of Wiltshire and Wessex. The vandalism of so many priceless monuments, earth-works and Celtic field systems is one of the worst examples of uncontrolled agricultural exploitation in the whole country and will be bemoaned by many generations in the future.

Stonehenge is reputed to have quite an effect upon lovers, and Coventry Patmore's poem "Love at Stonehenge" tells its own story of the magnetism of the ancient circle upon the romantic soul:-

"In Love at Stonehenge" — Coventry Patmore

By the great stones we chose our ground
  For shade, and there, in converse sweet;
Took luncheon. On a little mound
  Sat the three ladies; at their feet

I sat; and smelt the heathy smell,
  Pluck'd harebells, turn'd the telescope
To the country round.

Grasses formed the basis of a landscape that was one of the richest in wild flowering plants of any to be found in Britain, and in the fullness of summer common blue, adonis and chalkhill blue butterflies were so thick among the grasses and flowers that when disturbed they rose like a beautiful blue cloud, and the larks too would spiral up from their nests.

I've long enjoyed a love affair with the plains and valleys and rolling chalk hills of Wiltshire, its burial mounds and stone circles. As a child I remember being driven along the main A30/A303 by my father on our many perambulations from our west country home to London during the latter part of World War II. In those days the military and the sheep held the grasslands of Salisbury Plain in thrall. Old shepherds, actually not all that ancient, but seeming so to a small child, could always be seen carrying a crook and followed by a dog. I always tried to persuade my parents to stop so that I could get out and listen to the larks singing and the crickets trilling on the summer air. I wonder if my love of the county stems from some race memory, for my ancestors originated in the small town of Tisbury in the valley of the river Nadder on the fringe of Wiltshire and Dorset.

Just outside Mere, the chalk folds were used by Celtic farmers to create majestic lynchett-terraced slopes topped by the ramparts of multivallate Iron Age hill-forts. These hillsides reflect the culture of Celtic warrior chieftains whose sheep and cattle opened up the plain, maintaining and creating huge tracts of upland pasture and who hunted the wild aurox and bison, deer and wild sheep. Here and there, where the soil was deeper on boulder clay, immense forests of tall beech and oaks thrived in the soft damp winds. Neolithic and Iron Age farmers and warriors of the tribes of the Belgae and the Atrebates laid them low for building and for grazing their cattle and sheep. Later farmers stripped the little that remained from the fertile river valleys leaving only remnants like The Great Ridge Wood and Savernake Forest.

Wiltshire still retains the largest area of unimproved chalk downland in the country; for hundreds of years the great country houses and estates that circle the Plain were ensured of wealth by millions of sheep from whose backs the finest wool was shorn, and plans are afoot to restore some of the land lost to the plough; we may yet be able to see butterflies in blue clouds rising in front of the grazing sheep once again. In the meantime land held within the reserves will provide a reservoir of wildlife ready to repopulate the open landscape. Stone curlew, the great bustard, lapwing and grey partridge once thrived in the county in immense numbers. Before the end of the century they may have returned in some numbers again.

BARBURY CASTLE COUNTRY PARK (WCC) — *Spring, summer*

An Iron Age encampment set high on a hill where the chalk downland is grazed by sheep. There are superb views, and kestrels and the occasional hobby can be seen playing in the updraughts or hunting insects over the edge of the escarpment.
52ha – Map ref: SU 157761

BLACKMOOR COPSE (Wiltshire TfNC)** — *Spring, summer*

One of the most famous butterfly sites in Wiltshire with many of the rarest and most beautiful of the woodland species, including purple Emperor and silver-washed fritillary — butterflies of ancient oak woodland. The presence of oak is significant for many insects, none more so than the exquisite little woodland butterfly the purple hairstreak whose larvae feed on the buds and leaves of oak. They fly high up in the canopy, and will come to shrubby vegetation attracted by honeydew exuded by aphids; the male has an iridescent patch of violet on the upper surface of the wing.

Blackmoor Copse is considered to be very old, in places the woodland has recolonised ancient field systems and in others, where the chalk is close to the surface, a rich calcareous shrub flora has developed, including plants such as wild privet. It's attractive to birds because of the ample nest sites and food; spring is best for birdsong and midsummer through to August is best for butterflies. Mammals range from woodmice and the less common dormouse to rabbits, foxes, badgers and roe deer.
31.2ha

COLERNE PARK AND MONK'S WOOD (Woodland Trust) — *Spring, summer*

A fine example of coppiced oak woodland with a very interesting flora indicative of ancient woodland on limestone. The plants include angular Soloman's seal and lily of the valley, and the sensitive management encourages an immense diversity of bird life.
44.4ha – Map ref: ST 835725

LAVINGTON HILL (Wiltshire TfNC)** — *Spring, summer*

Lavington Hill is a superb example of managed sheep-grazed chalk downland; the plants and insects reflect the interrelationship with ants and butterfly larvae co-existing in the short springy turf. Chalkhill and common blue butterflies are common in late summer, and the marsh fritillary butterfly, whose food plant is devil's bit scabious, is common in early summer. Anthills, often a feature of ancient chalkland turf, are frequently em-broidered with the pink flowers and dusty green foliage of wild thyme taking on the appearance of natural cushions.
9.2ha

NORTH MEADOW (NCC) — *May/mid June*

Eighty per cent of the total British population of the glorious, but slightly sinister looking, snakeshead fritillary grows in this ancient meadowland, a relic of a time when hay was a major economic crop. This type of habitat depends upon special treatment entailing mowing and hay production by traditional methods. Many other plants occur here including southern marsh orchids and cowslips in profusion.
39ha – Map ref: SU 099944

PEWSEY DOWNS (NCC) — *Spring, summer*

This wonderful spread of rolling hills, ridges, slopes and coombs is one of the best herb-rich downlands in the country. The insects and plants, birds and molluscs are totally dependant upon the continuation of grazing by sheep, or latterly by cattle though cattle tend to be too heavy on the steeper slopes and cut deep steps in the fragile shallow turf. The downs are part of a range of chalk hills that extend into Oxfordshire echoing the beauty that Salisbury Plain must have presented to Victorian travellers. Now many of the old sheep walks have been ploughed for cereals and rape and have no value at all for the chalk downland plants and wildlife.

The range of orchids on the unsprayed, unploughed turf is immense and includes the rare burnt orchid, and frog orchid, small plants with tiny greenish flowers. Round headed rampion, and devil's bit scabious, the foodplant of the marsh fritillary butterfly, occur as do chalk milkwort and horseshoe vetch, the latter being the foodplant of the chalkhill blue butterfly; there are large numbers of this increasingly uncommon insect here, also small blue and attractive brown argus butterflies, and many day flying moths in high summer. In chalk grassland the interdependence of the plant community is highly developed and several very rare species are found here; early gentian and turberous thistle are two. A generation ago many of the plants were quite common, such are the changes that man has inflicted upon the environment. But Pewsey remains a living monument to the productivity of nature.
166ha – Map ref: SU 115635

Wiltshire Downs

RIDGEWAY PATH (CC) — *Spring, summer*

The Ridgeway Path begins at the ancient monument and stone circles of Avebury and runs across the chalk hills to the oldest Bronze Age hill-fort in Britain — Ivingho Beacon in Buckinghamshire. This long distance way takes the walker through some of the most historically exciting land in the Kingdom, over downland and through scrub and woods with the opportunity of seeing a wide range of endangered wildlife and habitats.
30km – Map ref: SU 118681 / 259833

SAVERNAKE FOREST (FC) — *Spring, summer*

The saddest aspect of Savernake Forest is the conversion of so much of its acreage to conifer plantations. From Norman times until the 16th century it was the hunting preserve of the Kings and Queens of England and the richness of the wildlife of the original forest was immense, especially the butterfly and birdlife. Now it is largely impoverished, the greatest diversity being found in the rides and open areas, although there are large numbers of mammals including introduced muntjac deer. It is an unhappy example of how not to exploit our native woodland for commercial forestry.
1000ha – Map ref: SU 225667

TANNER'S WOOD (Woodland Trust) — *Spring, summer*

Once an elm wood largely destroyed by Dutch elm disease, the Trust are managing the area sensitively and nurturing a mixed species wood with careful plantings of native trees. It has become an excellent site for woodland birds, plants and insects.
1ha – Map ref: SU 033373

VERA JEANS (Wiltshire TfNC)** — *Spring, summer*

A small valley fen and reed swamp in the upper reaches of the Avon. Formerly on the site of some disused watercress beds, the reed swamp, wet grassland and marsh are extremely productive in a chalk habitat that tends to have relatively few running water courses. The meadow area is

Marsh Fritillary Butterfly   *Lavington Hill*

extremely varied and in spring and summer is a riot of colour with an abundance of insects, especially dragonflies and caddis; a fact reflected by the excellent birdlife. The reeds are well populated by warblers, reed buntings and pied, yellow and grey wagtails which all feed on the rich insect fauna. Kingfishers and herons fish the clear water flowing through the site, and there are a number of unusual and localised water plants such as marsh arrow-grass.
12ha

WYLYE DOWN (NCC) — *Spring, summer*

The short turf of Wylye Down contains dwarf sedge, a characteristic plant of the Wessex downland sward; orchids, bastard toadflax and dyer's greenweed all point to a long established sheep-grazed turf. There are a great many insects in the mid summer air feeding on the nectar from the abundant flowers.
34ha – Map ref: SU 002363

35

YORKSHIRE
&
NORTH
HUMBERSIDE

As in most of northern Britain the Yorkshire and North Humberside landscape has been shaped by glaciers. The end of the ice age saw a huge flat tundra-like grassland where the ice had retreated leaving a moraine of boulder clay and chalky limestone soils; and here and there great outcrops of millstone grit with deep peat bogs and poor grassland.

This is the largest county in Britain, boasting both the Pennines and Cleveland Hills where red grouse, merlin and curlew cry and fly on the winds that beat straight across the North Sea from the high arctic; yet the climate is not harsh, indeed some inland areas even feel the influence of the sea when the mists and fogs that roll off the Humber estuary bring moisture to a landscape that is far removed from the wet west. The Atlantic winds empty as they rise over the Pennines falling as rain or snow on the high moorland, and feed the rivers that tumble and rush to the Humber estuary across the flatlands of the Vale of York.

The rivers Wharf, Nidd, Ure and Swale empty towards the sea through a landscape of outstanding beauty and meet the Derwent where it joins the Ouse to drain into the Humber south of Goole. The source of the Derwent is found high on the Cleveland Hills, where the Severn, Dove, Rye and Hedge Beck rivers flow down as one over the plain of Holderness.

The Pennines are beautiful and desolate, given over to heather moorland where sheep and grouse find a living, and where the declining pairs of merlin chase meadow pipits and larks to feed their young in nests set deep in the mature heather. Where there are trees, they tend to be conifers, although the county has not suffered the blanket afforestation of its uplands like some other northern counties which may be due, in part, to the value of the moors as shooting preserves. They are within easy reach of the prosperous cities of Leeds and York, where technologically based industry, large retail consortia and tourism have breathed new life into a faltering economical system previously based largely on textiles, heavy engineering and coal.

It was in the industrial landscape of the West Riding in the 1860s that Charles Kingsley chose to set his story of child exploitation "The Water Babies". Those times are long past and the industrialised early Victorian Yorkshire that horrified Kingsley and drove him to expose it was only one aspect of Victorian Society. There was also a more creative side epitomised by the immense talent of one particular family, the Brontës, and although they spent most of their time in the vicarage on the hill at Haworth, their novels were set in various parts of the county. Emily writes about the moors in her classic novel "Wuthering Heights", both the darker and lighter aspects of the landscape; when Catherine's life is declared out of danger after the worst shock of what was denominated a brain fever, Emily returns her to normal life thus:- "The first time she left her chamber was at the commencement of the following March. Mr Linton had put on her pillow, in the morning, a handful of golden crocuses; her eye, long stranger to any gleam of pleasure, caught them in waking, and shone delighted as she gathered them eagerly together.

"These are the earliest flowers at the Heights", she exclaimed. "They remind me of soft thaw winds, and warm sunshine, and nearly melted snow. Edgar, is there not a south wind, and is not the snow almost gone?"

"The snow is quite gone down here, darling," replied her husband, "and I only see two white spots on the whole range of moors; the sky is blue, and the larks are singing, and the becks and brooks are all brim full."

To the south, the old black country towns of Sheffield, Rotherham, Barnsley and Huddersfield are cleaner, brighter places now where house martins come in summer, and where the landscape, for so long hidden by the smoke of heavy engineering and steel works, is clearly seen. There is much beauty in the rolling hills and valleys, and rivers like the Don and the Aire are beginning to run clean again.

The demise of heavy industry and mining has proved a boon for wildlife, with areas of cleared urban land resembling the habitats found on naturally occurring limestone pavement. Where coal mining has been pursued for centuries subsidence caused by the collapse of shafts and galleries deep underground, have created depressions at the surface some, like the now famous RSPB reserve at Fairburn Ings, are extensive representing valuable wetland; others if positively managed for nature, would soon provide a source of wildlife interest.

On the glacial deposits of the plains and the Vale of York, the farmland is very productive. However, changes in agricultural support policy may mean that in time much of this farmland will be allowed to revert to natural grassland and woodland, and the diversity of the countryside and its wildlife will be enhanced for the benefit of a growing tourist industry.

The coastline is as varied as the inland topography. The coastal path of the Cleveland Way runs between the high ground of the North Yorkshire National Park, through superb scenery both moorland and coastal to the south and the stunning chalk cliffs at Bempton, nearly 400 feet high with their tier upon tier of bird-filled ledges as famous as any on the east coast. From Flamborough Head to the curving finger of Spurn Head, best known for its migrant birds, the sea is forever trying to reshape the land, the coastal erosion and subsequent deposition of shingle, gravel and sand on the leading edge of Spurn Point provides an ever changing environment; sometimes hostile, yet providing nest sites and food reserves.

The beauty of Yorkshire and Humberside stems mainly from the contrast between the rushing torrents and high moorland of north and ·east Yorkshire and the soft productive farmlands of the Vales of Holderness and York. From the high heathery tops and peat bogs of the north York moors to the high white cliffs along the coast the region is most rewarding for the enquiring naturalist.

BEMPTON CLIFFS (RSPB) — *Spring, summer*

Bempton Cliffs is the most important site on the north coast of England for breeding seabirds. Bempton and Flamborough Head have the only major seabird colony on chalk cliffs; as if this were not enough the cliffs here hold the only gannetry on the British mainland. In 1869 an act of parliament was passed to protect the kittiwakes and other seabirds from exploitation, it was a foundation stone in the structure of the modern conservation movement.

The reserve is long and narrow and in places runs along the top of dramatic chalk cliffs nearly 450 feet high, its position on the coast, and the promontory of Flamborough Head make it a perfect landfall for migrants and a superb vantage point for seabird-watching during the spring and autumn passage. In spring and early summer, tens of thousands of seabirds lay eggs and rear young on the precarious slippery ledges. Kittiwakes and auks reign here, 80,000 of these gentle-looking gulls jostle for space over nerve-jarring cliff faces (the largest number being kittiwakes) and between 10,000 and 14,000 guillemots lay their specially shaped eggs on narrow ledges and in cracks in the chalk. Evolution has shaped the eggs like pears so as not to roll off the cliff ledges when the parents shift position.

The rest of the auk family is represented by razorbills and a large colony of puffins numbering up to 4000 individuals, and another bird increasing its numbers along these cliffs is the fulmar (they have reached over 4000 breeding pairs) and glide stiff-winged in the up-draughts and chatter and chuckle to one another as they sit on their eggs. But the bird that has made Bempton really famous is the gannet. They first began to nest here in the 1920s, since then their numbers have steadily increased and now stand at about 320 pairs. There's been a steady stream of rare and unusual birds recorded here, including alpine swift and bluethroat.

The land behind the cliffs is heavily cultivated and the chalk-loving plants are limited to the reserve, even so 220 species have been recorded and 15 species of butterfly also occur here.
4.8km – Map ref: TA 197738

CLEVELAND WAY (CC) — *Spring, summer*

Moorland and coastline form the basis of the impressive landscape through which the crooked horseshoe of this section of the long distance path progresses. Definitely not for the unprepared as parts of the path are very hard going with the land rising and falling over the Cleveland Hills. Mist and heavy rain in any season, and sudden snowfalls in early spring, can prove a hazard.

The North York Moors National Park, through which the Cleveland Way passes for a considerable part of its length, presents many contrasts. In winter, on the high ground, the prospect is bleak with the heathery sward over acid sandstone showing bronze against the hillsides and only a raven or a buzzard for company in the lowering sky. On the seaward facing section, between Whitby and Filey the wind off the cold North Sea can bring a chill mist to blanket the scene.

Yet in spring and summer it's full of birdsong; the magical nuptial calls of curlew, and the trembling bleat of snipe as they dive downwards towards the damp tussocky ground where the females sit, the stiff feathers on the outer edge of the male's tail vibrating in the air stream known as drumming. Elsewhere the path runs alongside flowery heath and meadows, past a coastline where the sun, shining on the North Sea, dazzles the eye, and your ears are filled with the laughter of the fulmars, the screams of terns and gulls, the subdued croaking of auk, and the high chak-chak yelps of jackdaws playing on the wind.
144km – Map ref: SE 607837 / TA 121808

FAIRBURN INGS (RSPB) — *All year*

On the face of it this area would appear to have little promise for wildlife, set as it is in the valley of the river

Yorkshire Dales

Aire and sandwiched between Fairburn and Castleford, with the busy A1 at one end of the reserve and the equally noisy A656 at the other.

Many decades of coal mining have resulted in slag heaps and a basic instability that has already led to the formation of several 'flashes' (shallow depressions caused when galleries deep underground collapse and the land surface slumps). If left undisturbed these depressions soon fill with water and are colonised by wildlife.

The western part of the reserve is being managed as a wash to relieve flooding further down the valley. This has produced a superb area of shallow flooded rough pasture which attracts large numbers of waterfowl, including a herd of whooper swans up to 100 strong, that regularly visit in winter. The wildfowl too are many and varied with pochard, goldeneye and goosander.

In spring and autumn the area takes on a different aspect with a flow of migrants to and from their breeding sites. Several species of terns, including black terns, appear when weather conditions are suitable, and the autumn swallow and wagtail roosts attract many human visitors.

Aesthetically it is not a pleasing site, but it is extremely important, proving that even in the most uncompromising industrial wasteland, valuable natural history refuges can be recreated. It also has immense future potential as the demands made by mining decline, and the inevitable land subsidence develops further wetlands.
680 acres – Map ref: SE 460278

FILEY NORTH CLIFF (Scarborough BC) — *All year*

Looking south towards the promontory of Flamborough Head this seaside and cliff reserve affords superb views of seabirds and passage migrants.
46ha – Map ref: TA 115813

GRASS WOOD (Yorkshire WT)** — *Spring, summer*

The beauty of Grass Wood lies in the way that nature has recolonised the water-stripped rock of post ice age Wharfdale. The ash woods have formed an open canopy where rare and beautiful plants have been able to find roothold in the fertile soil that has collected in the cracked and fissured limestone. On the steep sides of the valley plants like bloody cranesbill and herb Robert grow in profusion, while on the valley floor, away from the scouring action of the river, bluebells and lily of the valley are found.

In the clear waters of the river Wharf, dippers use the current to assist them in their bottom walking search for the plentiful caddis and stonefly larvae. The productivity of the limestone woodland and the plant cover of the rocky regions of the valley produces a huge insect population, including spring butterflies such as speckled wood and orange tip, and the birds reflect this wealth of food, especially pied wagtails, willow warblers and blackcaps.
79.3ha

HORNSEA MERE (RSPB) — *All year*

Two miles long by three quarter mile wide, this lake was formed by the action of glaciers though, unlike the Cumbrian glacial lakes which are very deep, Hornsea Mere is shallow-only 12ft or so at its deepest point. In many places it is less than 5ft in depth, and at the western end, where there is silting, the water is no more than 2ft. Its very shallowness, together with the high fertility of the water make it a particularly rich source of food for a variety of birds and insects, fish and other invertebrates.

In the past it was famous as a pike fishery, and huge pike are still to be found cruising the waters in search of fish and ducklings. Shoveller, mallard and a few pairs of gadwall breed on the reserve, though the pike and foxes keep the numbers reaching maturity to a somewhat lower percentage than would be expected considering the overall productivity of the lake.

The northern and western shores are wooded and access is not allowed due to the potential danger of silted up drainage ditches. Also at the western end the shallow water encourages a well developed, but rather dry, reed swamp which does not offer complete security to nesting birds, however the reed bed does support the most northerly breeding population of reed warblers on the eastern side of the country. Some sedge warblers and reed bunting also nest here.

In winter the Mere comes into its own, with huge numbers of wintering wildfowl and coot, in severe weather over 1000 have been recorded. Less than a mile from the sea the reserve is often visited by sea duck as well as the more usual fresh water birds. In spring there is a great gathering of goldeneye, and mute swans also come here in large numbers for their moult. 170 species of birds have been recorded on the lake, and in the reeds and woodland.

The plant cover is equally rich and depends upon water levels. Near the water amphibious bistort grows as does yellow flag. Further away from the water agrimony, lady's smock, ragged robin and enchanter's nightshade thrive. The insect fauna is extensive and includes many butterflies and moths; mosquitos are common by the Mere.
580 acres – Map ref: TA 198473

HUMBER WILDFOWL REFUGE (Humber Wildfowl Refuge Com.)** — *Autumn, winter*

This large area of saltings and mudflats, has huge numbers of pink-footed geese, duck and waders.
It's best in late autumn, early winter, and in hard weather.
1280 ha (overlooked from) SE 864242 - 936263.

Long-tailed Duck

Hornsea Mere

LEVISHAM MOOR (NYMNPC) — *Spring, summer*

Looking down onto the spectacular valley of the Hole of Horcum this huge area of heather moorland supports a wide variety of birdlife with red grouse, breeding curlew, snipe and golden plover. Peregrines are seen over these moors, and the national population of these birds is increasing as they begin to seek out eyries that have not been used for nearly a century.

There's a considerable amount of ancient woodland with a population of migrant warblers and native breeding birds, including green woodpecker; the small becks and streams that tumble from the high ground provide a perfect habitat for wagtails and dippers which are common here. It is a most important and varied piece of countryside.

840ha – Map ref: SE 853937

MALHAM TARN (FSC/NT) — *Spring, summer*

One of the best documented nature reserves in Great Britain and of particular educational interest due to the variety of habitats which include tarn, fen, bog and limestone grassland. This mixture of high and low ground, and the plants and insects that live in association with these environmental extremes, gives the area its particular interesting quality.

73.6ha – Map ref: SD 890672

NORTH YORK MOORS NATIONAL PARK (NYMNPC) — *Spring through autumn*

Truly a magnificient place where rivers run through courses cut 10,000 years ago at the end of the last ice age. Melt waters from the immense glacier that ground its way inexorably across the region, bringing with it remnants of its travels in the shape of boulders and rocks rushed towards the sea from as far afield as Scandinavia, the weight of the ice and the power of the rivers that flowed from its base as the thaw developed, left behind the legacy that we enjoy today as the North York Moors National Park.

Where the harder sandstones resisted the abrasive force of the ice they sit high and isolated above the softer rock, creating a superb variety of habitats from the high heather moorland, where golden plover plaintively whistle, to the flower-rich dales and woodlands where birds that winter in Africa come to rear a new generation. At the eastern edge of the park the land runs out into the sea through a series of coastal formations, like the fascinating wave-cut platforms at Robin Hood Bay where considerable natural history interest has been enhanced by landslips. There are more species here than can be found elsewhere along the British coast, except in Dorset where similar natural events created a parallel set of conditions.

Birdlife on the moors is extensive, and includes some of the country's rarest breeding birds; nearly 150 species have been recorded across the length and breadth of the Park, and the best time to see, or hear, them is in spring and early summer. Merlin frequent the high tops where they have been driven because the lower moorland is subject to increasing public pressure, nevertheless the wildlife, especially plants, is extremely varied. Orchid specialists will find many fascinating species, including the rather insignificant-looking, but very rare, small white orchid.

The management of the moorland for sporting interest can run counter to the benefit of conservation if predator control is not adequately supervised. An over zealous gamekeeper may undo the work of many years of conservation and push a rare creature to the brink of extinction as a breeding species. Fortunately peregrine falcons appear to be on the increase, despite grouse shooting; however, the same cannot be said for the merlin which is declining rapidly as a breeding bird. Other species are still holding their own such as the dunlin and golden plover which breed on the small areas of blanket bog.

Mammals include roe deer, the occasional red deer, fox, badger, red squirrel, stoat, weasel and common dormice. The latter are at the northern limit of their range and have never been common here. The sheer variety of habitats and their superb setting makes this area one of the finest in the country.

PENNINE WAY (CC) — *Spring, summer*

The contrasts between this long distance path and its sister, the Cleveland Way, on the other side of the county are remarkable. First, this path does not include coastal habitats, but it does have the distinction of being the first of what was to become a series of long distance walks. It follows the spine of hills and mountains of the Pennines and takes you through some spectacular scenery with an abundance of wildlife interest. Public pressure on the footpath increases every year and parts have suffered from erosion and the attentions of off-road motorcyclists; despite these few problems the Way rewards walkers and naturalists with many wonderful sights and memories.

160km – Map ref: SE 078047 / NZ 897067

SPURN PENINSULA (Yorkshire WT) — *Spring, autumn*

The shingle point of Spurn is constantly on the move at the behest of sea and tide, and is much affected by constant erosion on the Holderness coastline. When seen on a map its shape, where it juts out into the Humber estuary, is not at all logical, but the tides have driven the spit inland and threaten to overwhelm it during high spring or autumn equinoxials, especially when these coincide with south easterly gales.

Enclosed by the point the Trinity Sands, exposed on some tides, form rich feeding grounds for migrant and passage birds. The observatory is ideally placed to intercept migrants from Europe and Scandinavia which often appear in huge numbers. Redwings and fieldfares feed on the berries of sea buckthorn before moving on, but other birds simply rest. There is a regular passage of terns and skua, the latter harrying the former to make them disgorge their catch of sand eels, but lately both populations of these birds have been declining probably due to over-fishing in the North Sea and pollution from chemicals and plastic residues. The area of sandflats available to visiting waders and wildfowl makes Spurn a popular place with bird-watchers, but the breeding population of birds is not as high as it might be because of disturbance.

112ha – Map ref: TA 417151

WHELDRAKE-INGS (Yorkshire WT)** — *Spring, summer*

Regular inundation has been the salvation of this long established flood plain. Birds able to take advantage of the available food supply released by the flood water include many wildfowl. In spring and summer plants blossom as they receive a new supply of nutrients when the flood subsides, some, like the narrow-leaved water dropwort, are dependant upon the flood regime for their survival. The wetland areas provide nesting sites for a host of birds like shoveller duck, redshank, curlew and snipe. The mammals too depend upon the decline of the flood waters in spring for their food and homes, and the breeding success of predatory birds such as kestrels and short-eared owls is directly related to the abundance of voles.

160ha

YORKSHIRE DALES NATIONAL PARK (YDNPC) — *Spring, summer*

Spectacular scenery and variety is the hallmark of this, the third largest of the country's national parks. The prime landscape has been created by the effect of time and water upon the carboniferous limestone; in some places this is yellow and in others honey coloured, at Malham it is very pale.

On the high ground remnants of a once far more extensive millstone grit rock cover still caps some of the hills. The last ice age eroded much of this dome of rock, leaving the softer limestone open to the elements and the acidity of the rain. The slow dissolution of the limestone has led to a fantastic variety of caves and underground water systems, with fifty or more caves of national importance and several hundred miles of underground passages.

On the surface the limestone eroded creating limestone pavement, another relic of past glaciation when the moving mass of ice planed the soil and the rock away from the original landscape forming flat tables, hilltops and terraces of limestone devoid of topsoil. Almost fifty per cent of Britain's limestone pavement is in the Yorkshire Dales National Park. In time the acidic rain etched channels and furrows in the scoured surfaces where soil collected and plants and trees took root. Grazing pressures and deforestation has been carried out over the centuries, and now the only plant life able to survive is in the shelter and protection of the grikes or fissures in the limestone. Some of these have taken on the aspect of tiny valleys with their own micro-climate where rare and tender ferns and liverworts thrive in what otherwise would be extremely exposed positions.

In places careful management has allowed some of the once widespread woodland on the limestone pavement to regenerate, and many of the plant species that were once very common in the region are able to retain a toe-hold, and birds, mammals and insects proliferate.

The hills above Wensleydale drop sheer for 100ft before graduating into green sheep-grazed sward. On the valley bottom, the river runs beneath grey stone bridges with elegant spans above the scoured pebbly river bed where banks show the scars of past spates; spotted trout use every large stone to shelter from the force of the flow, and wait for the current to carry the caddis flies to them.

Heron stalk the shallows of this most beautiful area of small swift rivers, and although kingfishers are less common, they too watch the troutlets from vantage points ready to dive like a streak of rainbow for their meal. The dawn chorus is a delight, curlew are answered by their own echoes, golden plover pipe plaintively and snipe drum up the morning sun as lapwings tumble in the perfectly clear air. In the meadows drifts of sweet cecily, smelling like aniseed sweets, open to the first bumble bees. There are lambs and blackbirds and a sense of peace and tranquillity. A strong feeling that although man may believe himself to be the dominant factor here, a more powerful force has shaped the landscape.

176,113ha

WALES

CLWYD

My introduction to this part of Wales began on the other side of the Dee estuary when, as a young national serviceman I was posted to RAF West Kirby for 'square bashing', a process whereby callow youth is transformed into disciplined manhood with a great deal of seemingly pointless shouting. Having been blessed with the ability to run quickly it wasn't long before I found myself in the atheletic squad, my days were dedicated to running along the Dee estuary and over the Dunes, where I gazed longingly at the blue hills of the Clwydian range and the waves-lapped wader-rich mudflats.

Charles Kingsley captures the wild desolation of this mighty estuary:-

"The Sands of Dee"

O Mary, go and call the cattle home,
And call the cattle home,
And call the cattle home,
Across the sands of Dee:
The western wind was wild and dank with foam,
And all alone went she.

The western tide crept along the sand,
And o'er and o'er the sand,
And round and round the sand,
As far as eye could see.
The rolling mist came down and hid the land:
And never home came she.

In a way the flat plains of Clwyd are mirrored by the rich farmlands of the Cheshire and Shropshire plains; the glaciers that funnelled inland from the sea in the last ice age formed a substrate on which a great diversity of plants, animals, and agriculture, depends; and gravels deposited in the Dee valley are exploited for building materials leaving holes and water-filled pits that, in turn, are exploited by nature.

The land rises from the wildfowl-rich shores of the Dee, and the caravan and chalet-filled coastline of the Atlantic seaboard to a quiet countryside dotted with the remnants of coal and mineral workings. The extractive industries that explored the potential of these carboniferous deposits are almost a memory now, and the image of

Wales as a Principality based upon coal, choirs and chapel is long past and, it must be said, mourned by relatively few of those who had to endure the reality of the life of a miner. However, there is still a considerable industry extracting limestone from the thick deposits of shelly creatures that lived and died millions of years ago, and used now to make steel and clad our roads.

Did the sheer variety of landscape features fire a spark for adventure in the heart and mind of Stanley, the famous explorer, taking him from his quiet schoolroom in Brynford where he was an assistant master to seek Livingstone in the steaming heat of the Congo. This region was formerly known as Flintshire, and some of its famous sons do seem to have had a hard-edged quality about them. Gladstone lived at Hawarden for a large part of his life when he was not in parliament, and died there in the house he loved so much.

The contrasting habitats have naturally lead to a contrast in wildlife. However, it is probably the margins of the county that tend to attract most visitors seeking natural history delights. The Dee estuary with its huge wader and wildfowl flocks and the dune systems along the coast between Colwyn Bay and Point of Ayr are winter places. The summer influx of caravan and chalet dwellers see a different face, for the holiday-makers the dunes bloom with orchids and bloody cranesbill.

COED CILYGROESLWYD (North Wales WT)** — *Spring, summer*

A particularly interesting ancient wood with a wide variety of species; especially a good spread of mature yew trees where the dense canopy dictates the ground cover beneath. Elsewhere in the wood ash, oak and some holly with a healthy shrub layer provides an abundance of nest sites for small birds. The attractive pied flycatcher breeds here regularly, and woodland warblers also use the trees as song posts.

Where a reasonable amount of light falls on the woodland floor you'll find sweet woodruff, a plant with very particular habitat requirements, it's quite common here, as are a number of other unusual plants which grow in response to the underlying lime-rich nature of the soil. The green flowers of stinking hellebore, a plant of early

spring, use their heavy scent to attract the first pollinating insects to the pungent flowers; greater butterfly orchid and bird's nest orchid are relatively common, and the contrast in habitats is shown by the presence of giant bellflower, a northerly plant and nettle-leaved bellflower, more usually found in the south. Here they grow on the same site. Mammals are relatively abundant with wood mice, squirrels and increasing numbers of polecats.
4ha

CONNAH'S QUAY (CEGB/DNS)** — *Spring, through winter*

The land adjacent to the power station at Connah's Quay constitutes a major nature reserve within the Dee estuary complex. It provides a wide range of habitats deliberately managed for the benefit of the natural life that abounds in this rich area of mud flats, saltings, freshwater pools, scrub and grassland; about a third of the reserve is salt marsh with the usual glasswort and common scurvey grass plant cover.

The range of birds is extensive, and the autumn and winter flocks of waders and duck are only one of the many facets that bring bird-watchers from miles around; the resident populations of mallard and shelduck are augmented in winter by large numbers of wigeon, pintail and teal and these flocks are very mobile over the whole estuary. Waders are a feature of the salt marsh and the rising tide drives the black-tailed and bar-tailed godwits inshore. Such huge flocks of birds attract the attention of birds of prey and peregrines are frequent visitors spreading alarm among the resting and feeding flocks.

A brackish pool, which enjoys a varying salinity depending on the tide, has formed where a stream enters the reserve. Fish-eating birds like kingfisher, heron and two species of grebe are attracted to this habitat.

Part of the reserve is made up of reclaimed land on which rough meadows rich in butterfly food plants are found. These rough scrubby grazed areas have a suprisingly large and diverse bird population augmented in winter with migrant thrushes and the occasional hen harrier quartering the scrub or merlin chasing pipits across the open ground.
90ha

DEE ESTUARY (Various bodies) — *All year*

This immense estuary is a deep 'U'-shaped notch in the coastline, although the river Dee that feeds it seems hardly powerful enough to have created such a width and length of sand and flats. However, it had some help in the shape of a massive glacier that ground its way inland from the Irish Sea, pulverising solid rock as it moved slowly towards the Cheshire Plain at the end of the last ice age. The ice left huge deposits of sand and gravel on the plain much of which was re-deposited in the estuarine valley as the sea level rose. Over the following 10,000 years or more, the river continued the process and the result is what we see today, a sandy, muddy, shallow estuary where fish and worms and marine molluscs find a billion niches in which to breed.

Because of the prolific food supply the birdlife is staggering, nearly 150,000 waders feed on the invertebrates in the mud at every tide during the winter season; the supply of worms for their probing beaks is seemingly endless, indeed one species of worm has a density of half a million to the square metre. An estuary is a hostile environment for a marine invertebrate, twice daily changes in salinity, temperature and moisture content demands special adaptation, but the food supply available to those creatures that can adapt is astounding.

Sadly estuaries are looked upon as ideal for exploitation, and degradation often takes place with virtually no restriction. In the past many productive estuaries have been ruined for wildlife by uncontrolled dumping of sewage and industrial effluent and the demands of boating and shipping interests.

The Dee faces some of these threats, especially from the leisure industry, but its importance as a site where ten per cent of our total stock of waders overwinter is a powerful argument. Twenty-two of the twenty seven species of duck on the British list are regularly seen here, some in huge numbers. Pintail from the high tundra of Russia flock here in winter and shelduck, dabblers that depend on small marine snails, can number 5000 individuals. Other wild wings can be numbered in thousands too with wigeon, mallard and common teal. The visual treat of 40,000 waders in the air as a sparrowhawk or a peregrine disturbs the flocks is a sight to remember.

The estuary is protected from the full force of the waves by The West Hoyle Bank, a favourite place for grey seals to haul out. Their numbers have been reduced by pollution and canine distemper and may take some time to recover, but the sight of these charming creatures lying in the sun scratching and grooming their mottled shiny fur, looking for all the world like animated rolls of silvery linoleum, is one of the sights of the estuary. Seals have been persecuted for centuries by fishermen so they are not easy to approach on land.

In the old cooling ponds at Shotton, rafts have been provided for common terns to nest. Little terns also breed regularly on nearby beaches, but are extremely vulnerable to disturbance. The sheer abundance of life in the Dee estaury is one of the natural wonders of the country. It can only remain so with extreme vigilance, its sensitivity to change could so easily be overwhelmed by the demands of the industrial and population centres that surround it.
12,600ha

EWLOE CASTLE NATURE TRAIL (CCC) — Spring, summer

A perfect place to see primroses and bluebells in spring when the valley bottom is carpeted with them. The trail passes by ponds which support a good stand of yellow flag iris, and the dense vegetation encourages waterbirds to breed.
2.4km – Map ref: SJ 292670

LLANGOLLEN CANAL (CCC) — *All year*

The canal has become a linear nature reserve over the years with a fine show of monkey flower, a garden escapee that seems to have created its own niche along the bankside of many of our small rivers and canals. Mammals include the delightful water vole, an entirely vegetarian creature totally at home at the water's edge where there is little disturbance and where the level remains relatively constant. Young voles have to be wary at all times, especially as there is a healthy heron population here patrolling the banks.

Dragonflies are common as are damselflies, despite the number of fish of several species in the canal, and the towpath has become an informal nature trail. However, The Tan-Y-Cut section is the official trail with information boards.

17km – Map ref: SJ 198433 / 284378

LOGGERHEADS COUNTRY PARK (CCC) — *Spring, summer*

Famous for the limestone crags that tower 1800ft above the park providing a superb range of habitats, from the streams that tumble down the valley through deep woodland to open limestone grasslands and the almost rockery-like display of flowering plants clinging to the rocks.

The woodland has deep shade and open sunlit glades where dog's mercury and enchanter's nightshade grows in profusion. On the tree roots, particularly hazel, the insipid flower spikes of the parasitic toothwort burst from the ground, and in the canopy the spring birdsong is extremely varied and includes tree pipit and pied flycatcher.

On the hills above, the atmosphere changes with open limestone pasture exhibiting many of the characteristics of old downland. Where rain has leached nitrogen and essential trace elements from the soil, plants tend to become very specialised and in some areas the soil exhibits an acid Ph. Here and there birch, rowan, gorse and dogwood grow indicating the change of soil type, and on the alkaline soils colourful flowers like rock rose, bloody cranesbill, wild thyme, harebell, small scabious and common milkwort thrive in drifts.

On the river, which has a good head of small trout, dippers can be seen fishing for caddis larvae in the clear water and kingfishers are frequent visitors to the quieter pools; both pied and grey wagtail search the stones and vegetation or sport like flycatchers after the hatch of insects from the river bed.

27ha – Map ref: SJ 198626

OFFA'S DYKE PATH (CC) — *Spring, summer*

Offa's Dyke runs from Prestatyn to Llangollen, along the top of the Clwydian range through limestone country and heather moorland. This long-distance path marks the line of an ancient Saxon defensive position built to keep the warring Welsh out of England. The strategy is working in reverse now as walkers from England are attracted in their thousands to the beauty of Wales. The sight of red grouse, buzzard, rare merlin or the wild music of curlew makes this such a delightful place.

85km – Map ref: SJ 073822 / 267206

POINT OF AYR (Welsh Water Authority) — *Spring through winter*

The wild beauty and desolation attracts people and birds. The birds, especially waders, appear in their thousands in late autumn and winter, driven off the rich feeding grounds of the nearby estuary. Thousands of knot and dunlin twist and turn in the air like living smoke clouds, and the sound of mixed flocks of grey plover, godwit and redshank mingles with the sibilant whistles and scrapes of smaller waders like turnstones and the strident piping of oyster-catchers. The salt marsh at Point of Ayr is backed by sand-dunes with their own special flora where birds that winter in the estuary are able to find food and shelter. Snow bunting appear in some numbers in winter and the small mammal population and abundant small birds attract both flying and ground predators, especially short-eared owls and barn owls; these birds quarter the fringes of the salt marsh and the rough ground between the dunes. Predatory birds hunt the waders and abundant wildfowl, hen harriers, peregrines, kestrels, sparrow-hawks and the occasional merlin are attracted by the sheer numbers of prey.

542ha – Map ref: SH 125847

DYFED

The geology of this region provides a fascinating backward look into the family tree of life on Earth. The Precambrian rocks are in excess of 600 million years old, and the region's youngest sedimentary layers, found in the inland hills, are upper carboniferous limestone and more than three hundred million years old. These rocks have been eroded and ground away by weather and successive ice ages; the vast glaciers were often more than a kilometre thick and carried an abrasive cargo of boulders, pebbles and sands. Evidence of this can be seen in the Cambrian mountains where whole valley systems have been smoothed to a cup-shaped profile. Time has softened some of their outlines and clothed the steep slopes with dense sessile oak woods providing quiet places where rare and endangered species of birds like the red kite can find a safe haven to breed.

The twin evils of blanket afforestation and moorland improvement have wrecked many of the traditional sheep walks, and the small elegant moorland falcon, the merlin, is now found only on a very few favoured, undeveloped moors; it needs heather moorland and gorse and an ample supply of food to survive, but above all it needs peace and space and these are rare commodities. Legend has it that Merlin, magician to the legendary Dark Ages King Arthur, originated from Carmarthen, and town and bird have enjoyed a long and illustrious association.

One of the most important birds of the region, as far as Welsh mythology is concerned, is the raven, a robust lordly crow common in the last century. Now they find less carrion for their needs and their numbers are slowly declining. Where breeding occurs outside protected areas they are often considered pests and destroyed by poison and shooting. Few such large birds possess their mastery of the air; in late winter and early spring they tumble and spiral and perform feather-tearing loops as they make their spectacular nuptial flights.

Inland, heavy rainfall encourages a wide diversity of plant and insect communities, and where ancient glaciers found their last resting place, sand and gravel dropped from the shrinking ice sheets formed barriers blocking rivers and beginning a process of lake fen carr and marsh, and eventually creating raised bogs as at Cors Caron. Sheep too have helped form this landscape and keep open its wild places, the short flowery turf is sustained by their jaws. Agricultural efforts to "improve" the moorland pasture has meant that many thousands of hectares of the best sites have already been spoiled and many more are under threat. However, "set aside" subsidy schemes may make it worthwhile to leave unimproved pasture just as it is, unimproved!

Some upland valleys have been dammed to provide drinking water reservoirs for the Midlands, making use of the considerable rainfall. Moist winds blow from the Atlantic and as the clouds are forced upwards by the rising ground of the central Welsh hills they drop their cargo of water; this moist unpopulated environment leads to an excellent growth of ferns and lichens, and in spring a superb show of bluebells, often blooming late.

The sea and prevailing wet west wind has a great influence upon the natural history landscape and the reliable rainfall feeds many rivers. The Dyfi and Tefi, Tywi and Gwendraeth rush or meander to the ocean according to the influence of the rainfall over the high ground, and salmon and sewin (the Welsh name for sea trout) spawn in the fast-flowing streams where dippers and grey wagtails breed. Water and rivers have always been important to the Celtic culture of Welsh poets and bards, Welsh poetry found its zenith in the talent of Dylan Thomas. He lived in The Boat House at Laugharne and worked in a little blue shed looking out over the ever changing vista of the Afon Taf; though he died in America during a lecture tour he is buried in the chapel at Laugharne beneath a simple white wooden cross.

In his verse play for voices "Under Milk Wood" Laugharne is thought to be the model for his imagined town, which he calls Llaregyb:-

"First Voice"

Stand on this hill. This is Llaregyb Hill, old as the hills, high, cool, and green, and from this small circle of stones, made not by Druids but by Mrs Beynon's Billy, you can see all the town below you sleeping in the first of the dawn. You can hear the love-sick wood pigeons mooning in bed. A dog barks in his sleep, farmyards away. The town ripples like a lake in the waking haze. And if you stand at the water's edge on a quiet night when the curlew call as they beat in to roost on the sand flats over the coal black, fish-filled sea, it's easy to imagine blind Captain Cat listening to the sounds of the sea from his window "in the sea-shelled, ship-in-bottled, ship-shape best cabin of Schooner House."

The importance of this area for wildlife is seen in the nummber of rare birds and animals. The red kite and polecat once enjoyed widespread distribution in the broadleaved woodlands that covered much of medieval lowland Britain until Elizabethan times. Now the forests have vanished and the kites and the polecats have

Puffins   *Skokholm - Dyfed*

retreated into the remote woodlands of Dyfed, so too have the western population of red squirrels. Extensive coniferisation has provided habitats for some of creatures, but in the main the impact of conifers has been negative rather than positive.

Wales and the west country is where the ancient culture of the British Celts survived relatively intact until the beginning of the industrial revolution. South west Wales comprised a series of unique and culturally undisturbed Celtic pastoral and fishing communities. The latter, depending upon the abundant seabirds and marine mammals to a considerable degree, would have felt a bond of fellowship with the Anglo Saxon poets who echoed the wild Pembroke coastline and the bird islands of Skomer, Skoholm and the gannetry of Grassholm.

When standing on the cliff-top overlooking the tide-race that surges between Skomer and the headland of the Marloes Peninsula this feeling of being at one with the forces of sea and wind is almost tangible. Gannets and fulmars beat on the wind and shearwaters call, like the spirits of the old Gods, as they return to their nesting burrows in the island's thrifty turf. They have nested here for millennia, long before the Norsemen, who named these islands, braved the uncertain sea in their longboats to reap this abundant harvest of seabirds.

CORS CARON (NCC)* — *All year*

A superb example of a raised blanket bog formed when the valley of the river Tyfi was blocked by debris left by a melting glacier at the end of the last ice age. The resulting lake became silted up and over the millennia the reed swamp developed into a mossy bog until the centre rose above the level of the surrounding valley floor in twin domes of peat and humified plant remains. Access to the reserve is limited, but even on the raised walks where the public is admitted, you cannot mistake the magic of the place. Red kites can be seen frequently, and there are a few pairs of red grouse on the raised centre section; in spring the sounds of nesting curlew ring across the emptiness.

The habitat varies from acid bog comprising mosses to deer grass with sundews in the wetter areas. The margins are covered in purple moor grass, sedges and bog asphodel, and in the valley bottom where the river flows a wetland lakeside flora has developed with water lilies,

yellow flag iris and meadowsweet. Dragonflies and damselfly species are very rich, and the small rare red damselfly can be seen in the spring. There are also common lizards, and the occasional adder suns itself on the wooden walkways.
800ha – Map ref: SN 696632

GOODWICK MOOR (West Wales NT) — *All year*

Goodwick Moor owes its existance to chance. The reed beds and river system, remnants of a glacial moraine dam, are close to Fishguard and could so easily have been dredged or drained, and the valuable wetland lost. Instead the reserve provides summer haunts for many birds including sedge, reed and grasshopper warblers and the open water is a winter haven for duck and waders; otters are relatively frequent visitors, if rarely seen.
15.2ha – Map ref: SM 946377

GRASSHOLM (RSPB)** — *Summer*

On a clear day in late spring the island of Grassholm can be seen from Wooltack Point on the Marloes peninsula, resembling a white cone on the near horizon. It appears so because of the immense numbers of gannets that nest here and, even from ten miles away, the white plumage of the 25,000 adult pairs reflects the light. This is the second largest gannetry in Britain and access is restricted until the birds have finished incubating their eggs. Landings are permitted from 15th June onwards and the sevice runs from The Dale Boatyard — Bookings taken by The Warden, Dyfed TfNC, 7 Market Street, HaverfordWest, Dyfed (Tel: 5462).
30ha

GWENFFRWD/DINAS (RSPB)* — *Spring, summer*

These twin reserves are situated in the valley of the river Tywi in the central Welsh hills. Dinas has a beautiful scenic walk from the car park where a stream runs beside a raised wooden walkway. Dippers can often be seen here, as can mergansers flying down the valleys from the lake above Llyn Brianne dam. Walking through the wood that runs downs to the river can be a delight, in late May the understory is a carpet of bluebells, and pied flycatchers and redstarts are quite common.

From the river, the smooth-sided valleys, indicative of past glacial activity, rise to moorland with red grouse and the occasional merlin. Red Kites are the stars of the twin reserves, and they nest in the thick hanging oak woods that carpet the hillsides.

Access is restricted during the breeding season. Permits and information about the nature trails can be obtained from the car park kiosk at Dinas.
480ha – Map ref: SN 787470

PENGELLI FOREST (West Wales NT) — *Spring, summer*

Unusual single-age coppice oak woodland, forming part of the largest area of ancient oak woodland in Wales. There are a wide variety of plants and mammals, including polecat, foxes, badgers and a population of common dormice. The rich mammal and bird fauna encourages birds of prey, and tawny owls, sparrowhawks and buzzards are common.

The coppice oak wood forms a dense uniform canopy which encourages a multitude of insects and butterflies including oil beetle and dark and speckled bush crickets, and the white-letter hairstreak, a butterfly increasingly difficult to find in Great Britain since the onset of Dutch elm disease, as it lays its eggs on the buds of wyche elm. In high summer silver-washed fritillary butterflies can be seen in the clearings and along pathsides.

Migrant birds, such as the growing population of pied flycatchers, have begun to colonise the nest boxes provided for them and redstarts and wood warblers are frequently encountered in spring.

64.8ha – Map ref: SN 124395

SKOKHOLM (West Wales NT/Dyfed WT)** — *Spring, summer*

An island of international importance, Skokholm is a speck of old red sandstone roughly shaped like a diamond, three kilometres off the coast of the Marloes peninsula. It's a magical place that comes alive on moonlight nights in June with the weird cries of tens of thousands of manx shearwaters and storm petrels, like so many celebrants, as they return to feed their young secreted in nest burrows in the thrift and campion-covered turf. The breeding birds also include a healthy puffin colony, and a large number of auks and lesser black-backed gulls.

There are few records of continuous occupation by any other creature than the island's very special breed of wild rabbit, thought to have been introduced by the Normans as a food source, some of them do hark back to domesticated breeds with either long or dark-coloured fur. They are unique in being resistant to myxomatosis, mainly due to the fact that they are not host to the rabbit flea , the normal vector for this virus.

The West Wales NT and DWARF run several weekly courses:- bird-watching for beginners and photography and painting; the island is perfection for all these activities. Accommodation is basic, but adequate, and you'll find a host of like-minded enthusiasts and a wealth of wildlife to make you want to stay longer. (Information from the West Wales NT.) Occasional day visits are also available during the summer, usually on Mondays, and conditional on weather and wardening facilities. (Information from the extremely helpful Dale Boatyard.) The Dale Princess will take you to the island, and the short crossing through the tide race of Broad Sound is a delight of puffins, gannets, auks and sometimes shearwater flying to and from the fishing grounds and their nests.

96ha

SKOMER ISLAND (Dyfed WT) — *Spring through autumn*

Skomer has clear archaeological records dating from the late Bronze Age, indeed the island has been described as the most complete archaeological site in Britain with walls and buildings and a soil structure showing long term human habitation. Skomer also differs from Skokholm in its geology: Skokholm being made up of old red sandstone while Skomer is built of hard, light-coloured volcanic rock. This contrast is most obvious when the two islands are viewed from Wooltack Point, the softer hues of the red sandstone impart a warmer tone to Skokholm. The rocks and deep soil of Skomer are rich in a variety of wild plants, over two hundred species having been identified; one, the yellow-eyed grass, is American and thought to have arrived with one of the not infrequent transatlantic migrants that turn up, along with others from Europe and Asia during the spring and autumn migrations.

The Skomer vole, discovered by Cardiff chemist Robert Drane at the end of the 19th century, is unique. It was isolated at the end of the last ice age when powerful currents carved through Jack Sound leaving only a nib of rock known as Midland Island, or Middleholm, between Wooltack Point and Skomer. Visits can be made daily, warden controlled, and weather permitting in late spring and summer. Tickets from DWT offices or Dale Boatyard (as Skokholm).

415ha

WEST HOOK CLIFFS (West Wales NT) — *Spring, summer*

Visitors to Skomer and Skokholm cannot fail to notice the deeply indented cliffs when they steam away from the harbour at Martins Haven, they are composed of very ancient Ordovician rocks, a maritime habitat of extreme interest to botanists. The very rare prostrate broom, (subspecies Maritimus) is a classic sea-cliff-adapted plant, its prostrate form being capable of resisting the force of salt-laden sea winds, and there are at least five colonies on the headlands.

Sea campion, sea pink and spring squill carpet the cliff-top, and the interesting small wood reed grows where freshwater springs make the soil marshy. The Manx shearwaters from the nearby island colonies have made numerous attempts to establish themselves in the many rabbit burrows, but it seems the presence of ground predators such as foxes dramatically reduces their chance of success.

The insect fauna is fascinating, over ten species of butterfly are found, including two fritillaries, the pearl-bordered and the dark green.

8.8ha – Map ref: SM 762092

YNYSLAS DUNES (Cors Fochno Bog) (NCC)* — *All year*

The Interpretive Centre here helps the layman and expert alike to understand the mechanism of the dune system, and the natural history of this extremely interesting series of developing habitats. The bogs at Cors Fochno are not open to the public, but they form a vital part of the ecosystem.

The Dyfi estuary has its own peculiar climate dictated by the temperatures and air currents from the landward side of the Dyfi valley. The dunes almost enclose the mouth of the estuary, and the wide sand flats of the valley. On the foreshore is a drowned prehistoric forest, and a

wide variety of plants and insects, particular to dunes, and can be seen in spring and summer and especially orchids and helleborines in the shelly sand of the dune slacks and damp hollows. Waders and geese arrive in considerable numbers in winter.
1590ha – Map ref: SN 609942

YNYS-HIR (RSPB) — *All year*

One of the most varied nature reserves in Wales, running from the sand flats of the Tywi estuary, through oak woodland, to the heather and bracken covered slopes and high tops. The whole reserve can be seen from an excellent vantage point where the wooded section rises on a small knoll overlooking the river and the marsh.

Large numbers of waders gather in winter and the reserve's specialities are the Greenland and Russian sub-species of white-fronted geese who arrive in their separate flocks. Wintering peregrines and the occasional merlin are also seen, the red kite is a regular visitor all year, and buzzards too frequent the reserve. The woodland is alive in spring with the sound of migrant birds; pied flycatchers nest in the abundant boxes provided by the Society, and the newly constructed pool at the seaward end of the reserve is a mecca for migrants waders and waterfowl.

The hillsides provide a perfect vantage point for birds of prey, and yellowhammers who use the descending powerlines as songposts. Although this is an RSPB reserve with the accent upon birds, the entomology, botany and mammal fauna with polecats and badgers present for most of the year, provides a great deal of variety. There is a nature trail and a number of hides, including a heronry hide with limited access dependant on the breeding season. (Information Centre Aberystwyth: Tel: 0970 612125)
255ha – Map ref: SN 683963

GLAMORGAN
GOWER PENINSULA

It's quite a contrast from the sand-dunes of the Gower Coast to the valleys of the Rhondda, but this once ravaged area is becoming green again as economics and international changes in fuel policy have caused the closure of many old coal mines allowing nature to clothe the mining waste tips in a healing blanket of vegetation, giving an indication of the outstanding beauty of the principality before man's hand fell heavily upon it. Every where you look the landscape has been moulded and shaped by past events. The industrial landscapes created by coal fields and steel works blend into the folds and valleys. Perhaps it is familiarity that blinds us to their true ugliness whereas the more recent hi-tech complexes glare at us from the salt marshes and straddle estuaries of immense ecological importance.

Industrial Cardiff in the 1920s must have been a sterile seed bed for the creative mind, or so you would think; but the very hardship of those times seems to have struck a chord of creativity in many fine Welsh writers. Welsh language students will be drawn to the central library to read of stirring deeds in pre-Norman Celtic Wales as told in epic poems like "The Gododdin" by the 6th century Welsh poet Aneirin. His verses tell of a time when this part of Wales was covered in dense oak forests, when wolves and wild boar and wild cattle lived in the bird-loud clearings. Most of the forests have vanished now, and with them the large mammals.

The industrialisation of wetlands is a continuing problem throughout northern Europe, and a proposal to build a tidal barrage across the confluence of the Taff and Ely rivers is a case in point. It highlights the need for a more deeply thought-out long term policy on wetland management and environmental protection in sensitive areas. The coastline of the Gower Peninsula, almost a third of which is described as being of national significance for nature conservation, is so important that it was the first area in the United Kingdom to be designated (in 1956) of outstanding natural beauty. It is also a Heritage Coast under the umbrella of the Countryside Commission. The coastline supports a wealth of habitats, in particular the massive medieval dune systems of the Gower with their almost desert-like environment and the gull-whitened wind-blown speck of sloping rock that is Flat Holm Island in the Bristol Channel.

The geology of Glamorgan dictates the landscape rather more than in other parts of Wales. Because of man's impact deep beneath the earth's surface, carboniferous limestones and coal have been brought to the surface forming quarries and spoil tips and scarps that are slowly weathering and imparting their own particular flavour to the plant and animal cover beginning to clothe them. Elsewhere the contorted rock strata breaks the ground surface to reveal remnants of ancient bogs and forests turned to coal, and mud compacted into slate and gritstones and old red sandstone; geological memorials to deserts and dunes that baked beneath the sun 350 million years ago.

Despite the industrial scars and current efforts to attract new industry to the region, you have only to travel over the brow of a hill to enjoy the green valleys and wild places, perhaps not quite the same as when Richard Llwellyn wrote his classic "How Green was my Valley", but beautiful none the less.

ABERTHAW SHORE (Glam WT) — *Spring through autumn*

This reserve owes its existence to the winds and tides that crash in from the wide Atlantic bringing pebbles and sand and the detritus of a modern world which has piled up into a storm barrier. Behind this barrier is an area of extensive salt marsh and sand-dunes, the latter stabilised largely by vegetation. Ravens breed on the sea cliffs where purple gromwell and maidenhair fern grows.
36.3ha – Map ref: ST 043659

BISHOP'S WOOD (Swansea City Council) — *Spring, summer*

Within easy reach of Swansea, Bishop's Wood is popular with visitors both for its peacefulness and superb sea views from the cliff path. It's rich in birds, and small mammals; foxes and badgers also thrive here.
9.2ha – Map ref: SS 594878

BLAENRHONDDA WATERFALLS WALK (Mid Glamorgan CC/FC) — *Spring, summer*

At the head of the once heavily exploited Rhondda Valley this superb area and its falls is very popular with visitors in consequence the wildlife potential is affected by human disturbance; nevertheless the heathy moorland supports a wide range of birds. Buzzards and ravens are frequent visitors and dippers make the most of the clear rushing water to find food and safe nest sites beneath waterfalls and overhangs.
4km – Map ref: SN 922021

BUTE PARK NATURE TRAIL (Cardiff City Council) —*Spring, summer*

A wide variety of exotic trees as well as native broad-leaved species are found on this trail by the river Taff. The birds depend upon the wealth of tree cover and spring brings an influx of small migrants, as well as a plentiful growth of plants on the woodland floor such as dog's mercury indicating the age of the woodland.
3.5km – Map ref: ST 182767

CRAIG-Y-LLYN (Glam WT)** — *Spring, autumn*

Lake Llyn Fach lies in a typical ice-cut valley reminiscent of the Lake District. In the past a vast glacier ground its way through this area of sandstone leaving in its wake scree slopes and deep cold water around which plant communities became established. The presence of water lobelia at its most southerly location further enhances the illusion of a northern Lake while on the screes relict plants of high arctic and alpine habitats such as rose root, fir club moss and interesting ferns thrive. Birdlife is typical of high ground with ring ouzel and raven being encountered, buzzards are commonly seen over the reserve using the updraughts from the tall slopes and screes for soaring.
16.2ha

CRYMLYN BOG (Various bodies)** — *All year*

Crymlyn Bog is one of the most important wetland sites in Britain and the largest lowland fen in the principality; huge areas of sphagnum bog and sedge fen swamps are full of unique wildlife interest and birds and insects are legion. There is no public access, but the site can be viewed from the roadway.
234ha – (overlooked from) Map ref: SS 700963

CWM RISCA (Glam WT) — *Spring, summer*

The Glamorgan Trust for Nature Conservation has its centre here on this reserve which is based on oak, ash and small-leaved lime woodlands. An interesting pond, fringed by marsh, wet grassland and willows, is home to a variety of birds and insects, and attracts breeding moorhens.
1.6ha – Map ref: SS 881843

EGLWYS NUNYDD (Glam WT)**— *All year*

A prime site for wintering wildfowl, the proximity of this large reservoir to the Bristol Channel means that in hard weather many different duck are found inshore; diving duck and sea duck such as scaup, frequently appear as do eastern European fish-eating duck such as smew.
101ha

FLAT HOLM (South Glamorgan CC)** — *Spring, summer*

One of several islands in the Bristol Channel, Flat Holm is best known as a gull breeding sanctuary, with lesser-black backed and herring gulls predominating. In recent years the overall numbers of gulls have decreased, though there are still very large colonies of both birds. Plant cover is influenced by the nutrients available from the gull colonies, nettles take advantage of the ample nitrogen supplied by their droppings, and the rare wild leek is a feature here. There are frequent arrivals during migration times and it is conveniently situated for rare vagrants to make landfall.
28.8ha

Dyfi Estuary   Gower/Glamorgan

GELLI HIR WOOD (Glam WT)** — *Spring, summer*

Gelli Hir Wood is a relic of the Gower of medieval times. Before man began to clear the trees for grazing the area was dotted with a mix of tree species, ponds, heath and bogs. The plant and birdlife is particularly interesting and the reserve is known for its butterflies; a colony of silver-washed fritillaries established here has forsaken its normal foodplant of dog violet in favour of the more commonly available marsh violet. It's a lovely place in summer.
28.7ha

GLAMORGAN CANAL (Cardiff City Council) — *Spring, summer*

A variety of man-made habitats are being returned to nature as a railway and disused canal is being heavily colonised by wildlife; plants in the canal include yellow and purple loosestrife providing colour among the reeds and sedges that in places almost block the waterway. The reserve is rich in insects, amphibians and fish, and the trees that overhang and border both the railway cutting and the canal are full of birdsong; siskin and redpoll both birds of alders and wet woodland are found here, and brimstone butterflies are common in early spring.
23ha – Map ref: ST 143803

KENFIG POOL & DUNES (Mid Glamorgan CC) — *All year*

Kenfig is a huge dune system with all the variety we have come to associate with this very interesting type of coastal habitat. The dunes between Porthcawl and Port Talbot are formed by the prevailing westerly winds that drive the sand up from the tideline and onto the developing parts of the system. They have been established for some time, consolidated by marram grass, and are massed with flowering plants. Behind the barrier, formed by the dunes, a series of slack or dune pools have developed which are alive with swallows, martins and dragonflies in summer and provide a safe resting place for large numbers of duck in winter.
810ha – Map ref: SS 802815

MARGAM COUNTRY PARK (West Glamorgan CC)* — *All year*

Margam Country Park has the advantage of a heronry and a large herd of deer numbering 200 to 300 individuals.

The heronry is situated on the Furzemill Pond reserve and because of the possibility of disturbance to breeding birds visiting is restricted to permit only. However, the park itself is well served with waymarked trails that show a wide range of natural and man-made habitats. The watercourses and ponds are rich in insects, plants and birds and there is a good breeding population of wood-peckers.
240ha – Map ref: SS 813849

OXWICH NATIONAL NATURE RESERVE (NCC) — *All year*

During the 13th century massive gales lashed the Gower coast driving ashore huge amounts of shingle and sand, adding to the peninsula's already well developed sand-dunes. The sand bar system at Oxwich Bay, in existence since the early Iron Age 2500 years ago, was the recipient of a great deal of that sand blown inland to form a rolling dune system entrapping a small freshwater lake. At the seaward end the lake became salt marsh, and on the freshwater marsh the margins were colonised by reed.

At the end of the 18th century, Thomas Mansel Talbot, owner of the Penrice Estate, decided to enhance the appearance of his lands with an ornamental lake which he produced by excavating the marsh and building a sea-wall and a complex of drainage ditches and ponds. The original marshland was drained to provide pasture, but this fell into disuse during the Second World War, and as the ditches silted up and overflowed so a reed swamp and floating fen developed — now a vital constituent of the reserve. Together with damp woods, oak woodland and quarried cliff this forms a complex of habitats exceedingly rich in wildlife — 690 flowering plants have been recorded over the years, nearly a third of the total British species. Specialities are early marsh orchids and dune helleborines, flowering in the dune slacks and depressions; bloody cranesbill, a rare geranium, is relatively common here.

A wide variety of birds have colonised the diverse habitats; herons from the nearby Penrice Estate heronry fish in the lakes and ditches, bittern appear regularly as do bearded reedlings, Oxwich harbours their most westerly breeding colony. Buzzards are a common sight and breed in Nicholaston Wood as do sparrowhawks. The hides are open to the public with a pass obtained from the interpretative centre and guided walks are arranged at the height of the summer season.
260ha – Map ref: SS 501865

PANT-Y-SAIS (Neath BC) — *All year*

Seemingly trapped between the road and the canal Pant-Y-Sais is comprised of a stretch of very rich fen with common reed and a wide range of associated plants and insects, influenced by the canal and the materials used to consolidate the towpath. The variety of scrub, reed, open grassland and trees provides an abundance of habitats for birds and there is always plenty to see here all through the year, but especially in spring and summer when warblers, particularly willow warblers, appear. Sparrowhawks and kestrels are the two most common predatory birds, but the abundance of small mammals also encourages owls.
17.8ha – Map ref: SS 713939

SOUTH GOWER COASTAL PATH (Glam WT/NCC/NT) — All year
RHOSILLE NATURE TRAIL/WORMS HEAD

This whole section of the Gower Peninsula is composed of strongly tilted planes of carboniferous limestone, and as such is a treasure-house of lime-loving plants. Among them is goldilocks, which occurs in very few sites. One other is Berry Head in Devon, which could be an indication that the peninsula escaped the ice during the last series of ice ages.

The coastal pathway runs along spectacular grassy inclines where buzzards and the occasional chough play in the updraughts, along with the hang-gliders that skim the cliffs in the westerly flow. From Oxwich the path runs beside the sea through dunes, mixed ash and oak woodland, limestone heath and flower-rich maritime grasslands where bloody cranesbill forms cushions of purple-red flowers in spring, and where banks of wild majoram provide a nectar-source for a host of common blue butterflies and other related grassland species.

Time and water have eroded caves into the hard pale-coloured limestone where colonies of greater horseshoe bats roost; these cave systems show evidence of occupation into the last ice age. Where these rare bat colonies occur there is no public access.

The spectacular limestone buttresses on the landward side of Worms Head and Burry Holmes stand square against the force of the westerly gales that blow from the Atlantic and the Irish Sea across Carmarthen Bay, it was the power of the winds and tides that rush around this coast that eroded the promontories and created the two islands. Worms Head has the furthest westerly colony of breeding seabirds in south Wales with substantial numbers of auks and kittiwakes, and the seabird colonist of the 20th century, the fulmar petrel, which occupies nesting ledges on the limestone bluffs gliding stiff-winged in the up-currents above the untidy seaweed nests of the shags and cormorants.

On the landward side of Whiteford Point lies the dune system, salt marsh and estuarine flats of Whiteford National Nature Reserve (*800ha – Map ref: SS 438938*) and the marsh of Llanrhidiunel, they are less visited and subsequently less eroded, and the wide unaltered area of salt marsh is a magnet for wintering wildfowl and waders. The reserve's particular value lies in its work as an environmental and educational centre and the fact that this less exploited region of the Gower allows a fragile ecosystem to survive.
30km

TAF FECHAN (Merthyr BC/Merthyr Naturalists Society) — *Spring, summer*

Taf Fechan is greatly enhanced by the Ph of the millstone grit and limestone rocks. The tree cover is a mixture of ancient woodland with small-leaved lime, beech and bird cherry and introduced species like turkey oaks; the valley bottom where the influence of the limestone is less pronounced is spread with bracken. Over a long period the river has cut down through the valley and developed a large range of habitats for birds, insects, plants, ferns, liverworts, mosses and lichens.

Pied flycatchers and redstarts both live and breed in the wood as do green and greater spotted woodpeckers, wood and willow warblers — while dippers hunt in the river shallows and on the bed of the stream. Wagtails are common and breed every year, and in the sky above the steep-sided valley buzzards circle on broad wings contesting the airspace with ravens. It is a beautiful and fascinating reserve.
41ha – Map ref: SO 045097

GWENT

"Days That Have Been" — W.H. Davies

Can I forget the sweet days that have been,
   When poetry first began to warm my blood;
When from the hills of Gwent I saw the earth
   Burned into two by Severn's silver flood:

When I would go alone at night to see
   The moonlight, like a big white butterfly,
Dreaming on that old castle near Caerleon,
   While at its side the Usk went softly by:

Can I forget the banks of Malpas Brook,
   or Ebbw's voice in such a wild delight,
As on he dashed with pebbles in his throat,
Gurgling towards the sea with all his might?

Ah, when I see a leafy village now,
   I sigh and ask it for Llantarnam's green;
I ask each river where is Ebbw's voice —
   In memory of the sweet days that have been.

W.H. Davies was a thoroughly Welsh poet, motivated by a deep sense of belonging which shows in his work. This region, formerly known as Monmouth, attracted the cream of the literary talent of past centuries — Wordsworth and Tennyson both came here and the landscape was a spur to their creative spring. Wordsworth brought his sister with him and when researching for his epic poem "Idylls of the King" (the legend of King Arthur) stayed in Caerleon; the castle is clearly recognisable in his poem "Geraint and Enid".

Gwent's old red sandstone colours the soil a deep ocre. Beneath this is carboniferous limestone and the rich coal seams that have so altered the surface features of the land and the cultural identity of the people of central and south Wales. Many of the mines are worked out now or have been closed, and reclamation to heal the scars of the century of mining and industrial exploitation is slowly beginning to bear a bandage of green.

The spectacular millstone grit cap of The Sugar Loaf is evidence of the last glaciation with the soft rocks of the region being worn away to form valleys and depressions. Whereas the harder millstone grits withstood the grinding process for a longer period before they too were crushed into the gravels and silts that were left behind when the ice retreated. Along the Bristol Channel, where the land has been reclaimed by the building of sea-walls, there is evidence that fen existed on a broad coastal plain before the sea level rose and inundated the reed and sedge beds 6000 to 7000 years ago.

The main river is the Usk which, together with its tributaries and feeder streams, has the rare privilege of being relatively unpolluted, the headwaters are the spawning grounds for salmon and migratory sea trout otherwise known as Sewin in these parts. These rivers run fast and clear, rich in minerals leached from the rocks over which they flow; where the pools are deep and the beds unscoured by spate, dense blankets of deep green water plants hide a wealth of aquatic life. In the upper reaches dippers walk the bottom searching the stones for insect larvae. Many of these streams and small rivers have begun to live again after years of being used for coal washing when they ran black as ink for miles. Now they sparkle with clear water and provide a home for wagtails and kingfishers and small golden-sided brown trout.

CLEDDON BOG (GCC)** — *Spring, summer*

A remnant of the ice age, Cleddon Bog is a small basin mire containing a great deal of botanical interest; purple moor grass, heather and cross-leaved heath, and in the wetter areas bog asphodel, hare's tail and cotton grass. The bog is a living entity, and the area of willow carr and drier scrubby heath supports a good bird population with the pools having an excellent range of dragonfly species. *85ha*

FIVE LOCKS CANAL (Gwent WT) — *Spring, summer*

This reserve shows how quickly industrial scenes can restore themselves with nature's help. Once a busy waterway it is now a gentle slow moving backwater in a county of fast streams and rapid spate rivers; consequently it offers an unusual habitat. It is bordered by alders, trees and waterside and marshland, rich in insects and very attractive to birds. The watery environment encourages a wide range of plants, over 100 species have been recorded on the banks and in the water, and the slow moving flow is enjoyed by amphibians, toads, newts and frogs with tadpoles forming part of the diet of the fish and dragonfly larvae. An indication of the origins of the waters feeding the canal is the presence of dace, a fish more unusually found in well oxygenated fast moving waterways.

The birdlife is diverse with little grebe and moorhen, pied wagtails and the occasional kingfisher. High summer, when all the many varieties of waterside plants are in full bloom and the dragonflies and damselflies are on the wing, is an excellent time of year to visit; the slow waters attract more swallows, swifts and house martins than their fast flowing counterparts. In the evening, bats especially Daubentons and pipistrelles, take over as the daytime hunters go off duty.
1km – Map ref: ST 287968 / 292978

GOLDCLIFF-COLDHARBOUR PILL (Gwent WT) — *Spring, autumn*

This part of the foreshore on the Severn estuary has been declared a protected zone where no shooting is allowed. Huge numbers of duck and migrant waders can now enjoy a relatively low level of disturbance in an area of extreme importance to wildlife conservation.
6km – Map ref: ST 385825

LADY PARK WOOD (NCC)** — *Spring, summer*

Situated in the beautiful Wye valley, Lady Park Wood is a remnant of the sort of ancient woodland that once covered so much of the limestone soil of the west. Chiefly interesting in that it has had minimal management and been allowed to return, through the various stages of felled or partially felled ancient woodland, to the original wildwood state. The whole reserve is very rich in plants, insects, woodland birds and small mammals.
46ha

LOWER WYE VALLEY (Various bodies) — *Spring, summer*

The river Wye is unusual in that pollution, the scourge of so many rivers, seems to have been avoided, the water runs clear and pure from source to tidal reach and estuary through a series of quite astonishingly beautiful valleys. One particular creature that needs this purity for a most important part of its life cycle is the Allis Shad, a strange relic of the ice age that migrates from the sea to spawn in the upper reaches of the river. There is also a considerable head of salmon and sea trout, and their relative the non migratory brown trout.

The river is a living ecosystem and a history book of the geological events that have shaped this part of Wales and Gloucestershire. It has cut down through layers of limestone and red Devonian sandstone and in the process enjoyed many moods, from a wide river meandering across a flat plain to a rushing torrent carving its way through the soft rock in a series of spectacular rapids and falls. Now it runs slow and deep in its bed at the bottom of a long serpentine valley.

Where the valley bottom is wide and flat the river is flanked by water meadows and pastures, and where the sides of the gorges are too steep for pastureland trees grow to the water's edge giving the valley its particular beauty. These limestone woods are made up of most of the common, and uncommon, trees that would have been found in the primeval British forests, wyche elm, field maples, ash, large-leaved lime and common whitebeam; the less common trees include wild service tree, Cheddar whitebeam, and an exceedingly rare hybrid between wild service tree and common whitebeam. The distinctive foliage of yew trees adds a splash of green in the otherwise purple brown of the winter woodlands.

There has been relatively little interference in these woodlands over the millennia and coppicing, a feature of the woodland management, has enhanced rather than detracted from the diversity and survival of many species. The woodland floor is carpeted with sweet woodruff, dog's mercury, yellow archangel and bluebells, wild ransoms occur in deep pungent drifts. One plant, unique to this valley, is upright spurge — small with green flowers it grows only in the limestone woods here.

The richness of plants encourages an equal richness in the insect life. There's a wider range here, particularly butterflies, than anywhere else in Wales and the sheer numbers encourages breeding birds. The dawn chorus in mid May in the lower Wye valley and Lady Park Wood is a natural wonder. The valley is also home to large numbers of bats, both the woodland species, such as pipistrelle and long-eared bats that rest and hibernate in trees and also the cave dwelling bats, greater horseshoe, that find refuge in the water worn limestone caves in the gorge.

The winding course of the river is a natural flyway for birds, and there's every chance of seeing a peregrine or a goshawk; buzzard, sparrowhawk and kestrel also take advantage of the good hunting in the valley and the surrounding landscape.

35km

MAGOR (Gwent WT)** — *Spring, summer*

A remnant of the Monmouthshire fens, Magor is an embanked area of wetland created by man, and similar in some ways to the naturally occuring fenland of the Somerset levels. There is some evidence that the fens were originally part of a reclamation scheme by the Romans which developed into an area of great importance producing huge quantities of milk, meat and hay up until the present day.

The fields, no longer grazed and cut for hay, are a mass of wild flowers; wild angelica and purple loosestrife provide a paradise for bees, and great willow-herb, water mint and yellow iris are ideal for dragonflies to sit on and wait for passing prey. The dragonflies of Magor are recognised as being of immense scientific interest, and several species are very rare. The ditches, locally called "reens", provide a habitat for the dragonfly larvae and for many other aquatic invertebrates. The plant life in these reens is rare, with arrowhead and frogbit; and in the pools mare's tail and bullrushes grow.

A number of birds breed in many different habitats and the reed warblers form one of the largest colonies in Wales. Water rail and redshank, snipe and yellow wagtail are but a few of the breeding species and the variety of songbirds attracts sparrowhawks and kestrels.
24ha

OFFA'S DYKE PATH (CC) — *Spring, summer*

Part of the ancient defensive ditch and bank system designed to keep the Welsh out of England, running from Chepstow to the mouth of the Dee, a distance of 120 miles, an astonishing feat of engineering that gives some idea of the organisational ability of a ruler whose country had only recently begun the long recovery out of the Dark Ages after the effective collapse of Roman rule. The dyke and its long distance path runs through some of the most beautiful countryside; in places the wall was built on high ground, nearly 350 metres above sea level, and the wildlife to be seen along its length is both astonishing and fascinating.
70km – Map ref: SO 267323 / ST 553928

PETERSTONE WENTLOOGE (Gwent WT) — *All year*

On the edge of the Severn estuary, this is an area of embanked land and salt marsh reclaimed from the savage tides that scour the coast. The tidal flats beyond the sea defences are covered only at the highest tides, providing a differing set of habitats protected by the wall. The mudflats and marsh are a favoured haunt in winter of great numbers of wildfowl and waders. Avocet and ruff are not uncommon visitors and occasionally mixed flocks, thousands strong, of knot and dunlin appear at the tide line. As is usual in places where large numbers of small wading birds and duck gather, predatory birds are commonplace; merlins and peregrines, sparrowhawks and buzzards all predate the waders, and short-eared owls hunt for mice.

The summer population of birds, plants and insects is extremely varied with butterflies from as far afield as France being driven in on the late summer winds. Clouded yellows and painted lady butterflies frequently appear in the fields where thistle and hemp agrimony provide nectar. Drainage ditches and dykes offer a whole series of places where birds, insects and small mammals can find refuge and food. Water voles take advantage of the lush vegetation and breed extensively; swallows and martins find ample food stocks over the marshes and fields. In autumn there are great gatherings of hirundines prior to migration. The whole of this extensive reserve is a haven for migrant species, and in winter, while the area beyond the sea-wall is the province of migrant wildfowl and waders, the fields and hedges are alive with thrushes and finches from Scandinavia and northern Europe.
4km – Map ref: ST 278807

STRAWBERRY COTTAGE WOOD (Gwent WT)** — *Spring, summer*

Beautiful hanging oak woodland adorns this attractively named wood on a hillside of old red sandstone. The

openness of the wood and its many nesting sites encourages woodpeckers and other woodland birds.
6ha

WENTWOOD FOREST (FC) — *Spring, summer*

An old red sandstone ridge above the valley of the Usk supports this Forestry Commission woodland with a wide variety of habitats. Some of the lowland oak and beech woodland remains among the conifer blocks, and the high ground has a taste of heather moorland with its characteristic flora and fauna. Parts of the Forestry plantations cover the remnants of a once extensive bog system with ivy-leaved bellflower being one of the plants of this type of habitat while other blocks cover lime-rich soils where large quantities of sweet woodruff grow in the shade of ash trees.

Wentwood is well known for its bats, especially the larger noctule, though long-eared bats also occur in some numbers. Badgers are in residence as are fallow deer, common dormouse have also been recorded while the number and variety of birds to be seen depends on the maturity of the conifer blocks and adjoining woodland.

Where there are plenty of deciduous trees the birdlife is extremely rich in springtime.
1005ha – Map ref: ST 436936

YSGYRYD FAWR (NT) — *Spring through autumn*

A buttress of old red sandstone, a remnant of the rocky sandstone hills forming the black mountains, which juts out providing an upland habitat where gorse and bracken thrive. You can see to the cone-shaped rock of the Sugar Loaf, and the upland slope is favoured by soaring buzzards.

Parts of the forest cover that once clad this region many centuries ago can be seen lower down the slopes of rough scree and tumbled rock. Small flat steps have formed where a grassland habitat with small trees and a host of plants, more suited to a limestone meadow, have developed with wild thyme and harebell. Lower still, through a scrubby area where birds are commonplace, the slopes are covered with woodland which, though less rich in birdsong than the scrubby land, provides breeding sites for redstarts and other hole nesters.
83ha – Map ref: SO 330180

GWYNEDD

"Cader Idris at Sunset" — Charles Tennyson Turner

Last autumn, as we sat, ere fall of night,
Over against old Cader's rugged face,
We mark'd the sunset from its secret place
Salute him with a fair and sudden light.
Flame-hued he rose, and vast, without a speck
Of Life upon his flush'd and lonely side;
A double rainbow o'er him bent, to deck
What was so bright before, thrice glorified!

Charles Tennyson Turner drew a large measure of his inspiration from the landscape of this part of Wales where the Cambrian mountains lower on dull days as the west wind sweeps in the rain from the Irish Sea and the tops are covered with blankets of sodden cloud or wind-whipped tatters of snow. Yet, just as suddenly, the clouds will clear and the whole landscape smiles; reflected sunlight from the sheep-cropped grass glows on the lower slopes of the broad-hipped hills covering them in deep green velvet.

The mountains have given their name to a series of rocks laid down in the infancy of life on Earth, a period of considerable interest to geologists and naturalists alike, for the slates and rocks of the Cambrian period carry in their fine-grained surfaces and bedding planes, evidence of algae and the first vascular plants and primitive life forms and the strange crustacean-like animals called trilobites, one of the most successful life forms ever to have existed; they crawled and swam through the clear waters of six geological periods finally vanishing from the fossil record 280 million years ago during the Permian period.

The westerly aspect of this region enjoys a high rainfall, a naturally damp climate with warm maritime winds off the Irish Sea conducive to the progression of oakwoods, valley fens and lakes. As in so much of Wales, little of the original oak forest remains, it has been displaced by agriculture and forestry. However, there are a few remnants in the quiet ice-sculpted valleys and they are rich in plants and bryophytes, and loud with birdsong.

The highest of the mountains, Snowdon and Cader Idris, show evidence of erosion by time and wind and ice, and many of the steep slopes, where even sheep dare not traverse the loose cold-shattered scree slopes, still resist the encroachment of plant life. One of the unfortunate aspects of this beautiful rugged country is the attraction it holds for the military as a training ground for pilots in fast jets; but the shattering effect of the roar of a gas turbine engine at high speed and relatively close quarters is more upsetting to man and his domesticated animals than it is to wildlife; the ravens, buzzards and red kites that roam the Welsh uplands are not worried by the jets, they are attracted to the winds that burst upwards off the cup-shaped valley sides. On the high ground you can still find some of the highly adapted alpine-type flora, a relic of the time when this area laboured under an arctic climate.

The Gwynedd coastline is as much a place of wild winds and white seas as the north Cornish coast; there are fewer hard rock formations here than in Cornwall, and this relative softness of the rock strata permits dramatic erosion presenting a contrast of beaches, cliffs and stacks where birds and seals and plants can be seen in a most beautiful and dramatic setting. The islands off the coast are as varied as the rest of the region; the tiny island of Bardsey lying at the tip of the Lleyn peninsula has an excellent bird observatory and balancing the weight of the peninsula, so to speak, is Anglesea with its bogs and sand-dunes and its place in Celtic history. Anglesea was where the Celtic warlords and the Romans met face-to-face in the final battle that was to end the power of the Druids. Here were found torques and mighty slave chains, relics of a race of people who worshipped nature, especially water and springs.

Gwynedd is rich in water and all the aspects of nature that would have delighted the Celtic tribes; the passage of two thousand years has changed little, this region still provides ample scope to commune with nature and the elements, it is a place of inspiration like few others.

BARDSEY (Bardsey Island Trust)** — *Spring through autumn*

Bardsey is one of the best known of the island bird observatories. This tiny speck of land at the tip of the Lleyn peninsula is the first landfall for many rare migrants. The plant cover is kept close by rabbits, their ministrations and their burrows providing birds like manx shearwaters with easy nesting sites and well mown take-off platforms. There are also limited numbers of nest sites for auks and kittiwakes, and a few pairs of shags. Grey seals are often seen in the waters offshore, and they use the island to haul out in good weather.
175ha

BRYN PYDEW (North Wales NT)** — *Spring, summer*

An area of limestone pavement where the rock has been quarried; many rare and interesting lime-loving plants thrive here, including lily of the valley and dark red helleborine. The tree cover is typical of limestone hillsides with yew, white beam and juniper, and on the grasslands, on summer nights, the females of that rare and unusual beetle the glow-worm can be seen — the full-winged males

being attracted to the female's light. Glow-worm larvae feed upon the soft tissue of snails, and should be welcome in virtually every garden, sadly they are declining in nearly all of their former haunts for a variety of reasons, mostly man-made.
5ha

CADER IDRIS (NCC) — *Early summer*

The climb to the crags, scree slopes and lakes of Cader Idris is an exploration through a range of habitats from oak, ash and rowan woodland on the lower valley to the sheep-grazed short turf of the high ground and the spectacular ice-cut bowl and lake of Llyn Cau, an upland Cwm carved from solid rock by the weight and abrasive power of a slowly moving glacier. Evidence of the last ice age is seen in the plants that cling precariously to the shattered scree slopes. Arctic and alpine species are rarely found in Britain and moss campion is a specialist of the high arctic environment that must have prevailed over much of the region 10,000 years ago.

The variety of rock types is shown in the close proximity of acid bog and alkaline wetland plants and mosses; the reserve has several species of mosses that excite botanists, and two ferns, green spleenwort only found on lime-rich soils, and forked spleenwort which prefers acid soils. They are found relatively close together and such contrasts are found in many places on this huge reserve.

The wildlife is dictated by altitude and the seasons. In spring and summer wheatear and meadow pipit find food and nest sites in the lower sheep-grazed grasslands while higher up the landscape becomes the province of the raven and buzzard and the ring ouzel, the blackbird of the high crags and moors. The dramatic scenery attracts many visitors who impose undoubted pressure. However, this public involvement does have its plus side in maintaining the integrity of this most beautiful wild upland area.
392ha – Map ref: SH 730114

COED DINORWIG (GCC) — *Spring, summer*

Part of the Padarn Country Park, this wood provides a unique opportunity to study the flora and fauna of a Welsh oak woodland that has been protected from the depredations of sheep having been enclosed to prevent their access to the Dinorwig quarry.

The moisture in the wood encourages a prolific growth of plants and ferns, and erosion of the slate base rock has formed channels that are exploited by many mosses and higher plants. The woods support a substantial insect population that provides a ready food source for the many migrant birds that breed here, especially pied flycatchers and willow warblers. Predatory birds are much in evidence, buzzard and sparrowhawk being relatively common. Mammals include fox and the occasional polecat.
50ha – Map ref: SH 586603

COED LLECHWEDD (Woodland Trust) — *Spring, summer*

Active management in this woodland, in the form of

fencing, has allowed the ground flora to develop in a most exciting way, the exclusion of grazing animals has had a dramatic effect.
24.4ha – Map ref: SH 592318

COEDYDD MAENTWROG (NCC) — *Spring, summer*

This reserve contains a variety of habitats including Mary's Lake or Llyn Mair; the oak wood attracts a wide variety of spring migrants like wood warblers, redstarts and pied flycatchers which are relatively common. Other birds found here include hawfinch which are hard to see in the tree tops and green woodpeckers, just the opposite, they are hard to miss with their yaffly cry and loping flight. All three woodpeckers can be seen here, although the lesser-spotted woodpecker is not so easy to spot as they prefer the high canopy.

The meadow and marshland leading to Llyn Mair are rich in plants and butterflies in spring and summer; in winter waterfowl and swans use the lake to stop and rest; Whooper swans appear most years, and the duck population includes mallard, pochard and goldeneye. There is a nature trail through the woodlands.
68.5ha – Map ref: SH 652414 / 600410

CWM IDWAL (NCC) — *Spring, summer*

The beauty of this large reserve depends upon the majesty of the steep hillsides and Llyn Idwal, formed by the action of ice during the last glaciation. The hanging gardens of the Twll Du, or the devil's kitchen, give an indication of the wide variety of plants that exist in this relatively inhospitable region, but the effect of sheep upon the plant cover of the upland slopes has been drastic; only where sheep cannot climb is the real diversity of plants realised.
398ha – Map ref: SH 640590

GREAT ORME NATURE TRAIL (Aberconwy BC) — *Spring through autumn)*

The limestone of Gogarth carries on into the massive prominence of the Great Orme with its rugged cliffs and huge sea bird populations that take advantage of the many ledges and breeding places. Updraughts from the sea against the cliffs provide a playground for fulmars, kittiwakes and jackdaws and in late winter and early spring huge black ravens use the winds to display to their mates.

One of the more exciting birds found in this part of Wales is the chough. Now sadly a rarity, this crow is a master of the air and can be identified by its sharp, almost jackdaw-like cry which carriers on the wind. Over eighty five species of birds have been recorded on this reserve; buzzards and kestrels are more often seen over the open limestone grassland, peregrine are becoming increasingly common and in spring and autumn dottrel pause on their way to the high ground. The sea is also a productive source for as well as seabirds on passage there is often a good chance of watching duck and grebes.
2.8 - 5.1km – Map ref: SH 780832

NEWBOROUGH WARREN-YNYS LLANDDWYN (NCC) — *All year*

The jewel in the crown of Anglesea, this reserve constitutes one of the largest and least spoilt dune systems in the country. The sand is fine and rich, being made up of the powdered shells of a vast number of sea animals which gives it a very high calcium level making it extremely important for flowering plants. In early summer large numbers of orchid species, especially dune helleborines, can be seen growing in the dune slacks. Five hundred and sixty plant species have been recorded in this incredibly rich area which, on first examination, would appear to be a rather inhospitable habitat for plants, birds, mammals and insects, yet the reverse is true and on this productivity the rest of the dune economy depends.

The lack of cover is exactly to the liking of meadow pipits and skylarks and, consequently, they are the most common birds here. Lapwings also enjoy the open habitat, and curlew are often seen and heard between the well developed dunes. Kestrels thrive on the common lizards and small mammals found here, and in summer insect eating birds such as swallows and swifts find ample supplies of flying insects.

Inland, pools of standing water support an abundant plant and insect life but, due to handsome government sponsored inducements to landowners to plant trees on such sites in the period following the last war, a large area of Newborough Warren was blanketed with conifers such as Corsican pine. However, a number of broadleaved trees were also planted and the combination of woodlands, and the shelter afforded by the trees, has helped to consolidate the landward dunes, and thriving plant communities have sprung up.

The area known as Newborough Forest is bordered by the river Cefni and Malltraeth sands and a salt marsh which contains an area of sea rush considered to be one of the largest in the country. The sheltered nature of the estuary and its natural productivity attracts huge numbers of birds, especially duck and geese, mainly feral greylag and Canada geese. Malltraeth Pool is a superb spot for waders with bar-tailed and black-tailed godwit are regular visitors. The seaward side of the Warren is constantly on the move as the strong winter winds blow in from the Irish Sea bringing more sand and pulverised shells to advance the spread of the dunes; deep rooted marram grass buttresses the seaward dunes against the wind, and protects the entire system from erosion; too many human and animal feet could result in severe damage to the whole ecosystem.
633.5ha – Map ref: SH 406636

SNOWDONIA NATIONAL PARK (SNPC) — *Spring, summer*

The second largest National Park, the Lake District being the largest, Snowdonia has an impressive list of attractions for anyone seeking solitude and beauty and the very best aspects of the natural world. The whole area appears to be at peace with the elemental forces that created it, although this is a human concept, for the slow inexorable erosion that shaped it will continue.

The hard rocks of Snowdon, the highest mountain in England and Wales (standing 3559ft above sea level) resisted the grinding force of the immense slow moving rivers of ice which carried a cargo of abrasive rocky debris that shaped many of the region's serpentine valleys into the elegant cup-shaped outline so typical of glaciated landscapes. When the ice retreated it dumped glacial moraine at the end of these narrow valleys, forming natural dams and deep lakes of cold water which hold relic species of fish like the gwyniad, a creature that looks like a cross between a trout and a herring, silver coloured but without spots and with a small adipose fin forward of the tail. The gwyniad is a sub-species of the powan and as such found only in the depths of Lake Bala (It is dependant upon pure and very cold water for its survival). The area of this lake has been increased by a man-made dam, but this doesn't appear to worry the fish. Other sub-species exist in Scotland in Loch Lomond and Loch Eck and in Cumbria.

Another ice age fish is the arctic char, a salmonid related to trout. The Welsh char is a sub-species as a result of long isolation, Torgoch is its local name. In order for such creatures to survive an ample supply of water is necessary, and the position of the Snowdon range and the prevailing westerly winds takes care of this; as the wet winds cross the land they rise and the precipitation falls as rain or snow or damp fogs soaking the short sheep-grazed turf.

On north and east facing crags other relics of the last ice age remain, clinging to ledges; plants like the Snowdon lily grow only in this one area of Britain. This sensitive plant, and other highland flora like mountain avens, alpine bistort, alpine cinquefoil, arctic and alpine mouse-ear and alpine woodsia survive because the necessary conditions have remained constant, but below the craggy, hard to climb, scree slopes, where sheep have nipped the hillside diversity in the bud the potential for flowering plants is less.

On the high ground you'll find heather and bilberry, providing food for a number of bird species. Red grouse thrives on the short heather shoots and they nest here, in company with curlew and golden plover, the latter keeping to the wetter more boggy areas. Wheatear and meadow pipit take advantage of the piles of rock to build their nests and merlins, smallest and most endangered of our native falcons, prey upon the young of both species, although it is powerful enough in the air to catch an adult. They will chase skylarks, climbing above their prey as they strive to escape by gaining altitude.

Other birds of prey are seen frequently over the vast area of the Park, buzzards and red kites share the thermals and updraughts in summer, although the kites don't breed here, they have become regular visitors, especially at the end of the breeding season when the young birds have to move out of their parent's territory. Sparrowhawks and short-eared owls are relatively common where forestry work has created the correct habitat for them; and in the remaining hanging oakwoods you'll always hear a delight of birdsong in spring and

Wheatear   *Snowdonia National Park*

early summer. Many of the woods are home to pied flycatcher and redstart and hold a population of wood warblers and willow warblers.

The beauty of the Snowdonia National Park lies in its diversity from sea level to a thousand metres and more; the peace may be broken by the ear-splitting roar of military jet aircraft as they practice low level precision flying, however, this is but a tiny fraction of the modern world intruding into an ancient, almost timeless, natural beauty.
218,455ha

SOUTH STACK CLIFFS (RSPB) — *Spring, summer*
A wonderful place for seabirds with an abundance of cliffs, caves and offshore stacks backed by the maritime heathlands of Holyhead mountain; one of the most impressive and unspoiled areas of its type in Wales. Seabirds are the main attraction, though people come here to see the very rare chough, a smart red-billed, jackdaw-sized crow that has declined dramatically during this century until now it is found only in one or two places in Wales and Cornwall. Often the best place to glimpse the elegant chough is in the region of the car park near Ellin's Tower.

This reserve is perfectly situated for birds. The sea fuels the breeding success of thousands of pairs of auks, kittiwakes, shags and cormorants and a cacophony of jackdaws. However, the puffin colony is minute, they are holding on to this site by the skin of their beaks, but you can see them when they return from the sea in May. The exciting sound that reverberates around the breeding colonies can reach a crescendo when one of several pairs of peregrine falcons nesting on the cliffs, patrols the updraughts looking for a meal for their young. The cliffs are a perfect vantage point for watching birds, and every year there are sightings of manx shearwaters, gannets and skuas, and the rarer species like the pomerine skua.

Inland on the heaths, the gorse and heather are beautiful. In late spring and summer the silver studded blue butterfly takes advantage of the sunshine feasting on the heather nectar. The clifftops are a wonderful sight with cushions of thrift and carpets of spring squill.
316ha – Map ref: SH 205823

Polecat

POWYS

The border region of Wales and England is made up of hills and streams, and the ancient defences of Offa's Dyke run down the length of the principality following a line which, these days, dips in and out of Wales as if loath to leave it. The beautiful rivers of Powys are legendary and the Welsh poet, Thomas Vaughan, had a love affair with the river that is born from the old red sandstone hills of the Brecon Beacons. In his poem to the river Usk (Ysca in Welsh) **"So Have I Spent on the Banks of Ysca Many a Serious Hour"**, he pays homage to the river extolling its vitues:-

All this from thee, my Ysca? Yes, and more;
I am for many virtues on thy score.

Trust me thy waters yet: why — wilt not so?
Let me but drink again and I will go.
I see thy course anticipates my plea:
I'll haste to God, as thou dost to the sea;
And when my eyes in waters drown their beams,
The pious imitations of thy streams,
May ever holy, happy, hearty tear
Help me to run to Heaven, as thou dost there.

The religious feelings of the population of this part of Wales are closely linked to the landscape; even the tiny valley chapels, built from local red stone and capped with slate dug from the earth, speak of the foundation of the faith and life of the communities.

The changes wrought upon the Welsh ecosystem by mining, sheep farming and forestry can be seen in the uplands of the Brecon Beacons and the Cambrian and Black mountains, yet the hand of man seems puny when compared with the majesty of the natural scenery. The oldest sedimentary rocks, the slates of the Silurian period, and the fossilised iron-rich dunes of the old red sandstones, speak of mountains and hills ground down to powder during unimaginable spans of time and the forces that rendered the magma and basalts to mud and sand are still at work in our time. Although the farmlands of the Severn and Wye valleys and flood plains are immensely fertile they owe their productivity to the high ground of the Brecon Beacons and the erosion caused by millions of years of ice, weather and vegetation.

The rock types, combined with the altitude above sea level, help to control the natural life of Powys. The high ground does not encourage arable farming, sheep reign here. Summer brings tourism, and many of the tiny stone sheep worker's cottages become holiday homes, a place where people from the towns and cities can recombine with the countryside. For a few weeks the landscape is relatively redolent with life and the tiny lanes choked with holiday traffic, but out of season Powys returns to its wide peaceful vista where peregrine falcon and merlin, kite and buzzard quarter the open ground and search the oak-wooded hillsides for prey; where curlew and golden plover make wild music on the heather moors.

Perhaps because it lies so close to England, this part of the principality is peculiarly Welsh, both in its human population and in its landscape, perhaps this is a form of defence against incursion into a language and cultural indentity, under threat from beyond Offa's Dyke. The Dyke itself, built to keep the Welsh out of England, now acts as a national barrier, the other way around, to bolster the cultural identity of this least populated part of Wales.

But the solitude and lack of any real incursion from aggressive development, other than a few drinking water reservoirs, and a landscape partly blanketed under conifer plantations, has produced a series of unique habitats. Many of the oakwoods that remain are un-altered, other than demands for firewood, building timber and a little charcaol, and this has created woodlands rich in birds and mosses, plants and insects; a springtime theatre for a host of migrant songbirds.

Perhaps the number of sheep kept upon the hills is the only aspect that impoverishes the land. They are responsible for the lack of regeneration of the hardwood deciduous forests that are the natural cover in all but the highest part of the region. The limestone, lava, sandstone and slate are all capable of producing myriad woodland habitats, and if they were allowed to do so Powys would once again revert to the forests of Elizabethan times and become yet another facet to this jewel of a region.

BRECON BEACONS NATIONAL PARK (BBNPC) — *All year*

The Brecon Beacons are outstandingly beautiful as well as being one of the last truly under-populated areas in Britain. Indeed the topography makes this lovely place far

more suitable for sheep than for people with the uplands rising to nearly three thousand feet. Rank upon rank of old red sandstone hills have been shaped into steps by ice and water and time.

The Beacons are mother and father to many rivers and streams; the moist westerly flow of air across the wide Atlantic and the Irish Sea is thrust upwards by the combined barrier of the Beacons and the Cambrian mountains until, cooled by altitude, it gives up its moisture in the form of rain or saturating mists. These mists, and the predominantly acid nature of the rocks produce peat bogs of bright green sphagnum moss and cotton grass which act as sponges holding the rain and moisture and then releasing it as tiny streams that gather together until they become rushing torrents drawn by the force of gravity to the sea.

Not all the rocks that make up the Beacons are acid, here and there are outcrops of carboniferous limestone, relics of coral reefs that flourished in a tropical sea over three hundred million years ago. The abrasive action of huge ice rivers ten to fifteen thousand years ago exposed the upper surfaces of this reef and the action of rain, together with the run-off from the acid peat moorland, etched and furrowed the limestone. Gradually the cracks became chasms and the faults became huge water-worn cave systems such as Ogof Ffynon Ddu, Britain's first underground National Nature Reserve.

Intensive sheep grazing has removed many of the original plants, but where the going is too tough for these voracious creatures, highland type plants like globeflower flourish, and rowan bushes thrive by digging their roots into rock crevices and hanging on above dizzing drops where rivers and streams fall in a series of sparkling steps to the valley floor hundreds of feet below. Dunlin and curlew, redshank and golden plover nest upon the high ground in the tussocky grass, and a few pairs of merlin, the tiniest of the British falcons hunt small birds over the rocky landscape. The solitude and openness encourages birds of prey like peregrines, for although there are few sheer rock faces, there are enough traditional eyrie sites for these birds to set up territories and rear young, especially as they are closely wardened.

The oak woodlands in the deep ice-carved valleys encourage red kites to set up territory, and the wealth of summer migrants provides a happy hunting ground for sparrowhawks while an increase in rabbits (post myxomatosis) has allowed something of a population explosion of buzzards; the larger numbers of these birds has led to an outward expansion across Wales and into the Midlands where sadly, despite protection by law, they are shot and poisoned by some game managers and keepers.
134,421ha

CRAIG-Y-CILAU (NCC) — *Spring, summer*

A massive sweep of limestone capped by a gritstone plateau tells of great upheavals in the past that turned, tilted, scored and eroded the strata. The limestone hides a network of caves reminiscent of Gruyere cheese, among them the Agen Allwedd system which runs for twenty five kilometres lunging deep beneath the ground showing how the water that formed the caves etched and burrowed its way out and down to the sea. The cave systems harbour the protected roosts of lesser horseshoe bats.

On the plateau sheep grazing has reduced the moorland diversity with grasses replacing heathers, but where the sheep cannot climb on the high ledges many species of plants still thrive and in spring and summer the brilliant yellow flowers of globeflower, and the reds and pinks of mossy saxifrage delight the eye.

The area boasts many large mammals including badgers and foxes, the latter rather unpopular with farmers, although there is little actual evidence of predation of healthy lambs by foxes. The foxes find shelter in the lower woodlands where five species of rare whitebeam with beech, yew, wyche elm and oak make a varied habitat for many insects; on these insects feed a host of birds and small mammals.

The streams that flow down into the valley form a raised bog in a glacial depression; sundews and cotton grasses grow here, and a host of dragonflies and damselflies hawk over the peat grassland in spring and early summer.

The reserve is well known, not only for its cave systems, but for the marvellous variety of breeding birds; ring ouzels sing from high rocky outcrops and nest in rock crevices. In February ravens perform aerobatics over the snow-spotted high ground, while later in the year wheatears breed in disued rabbit burrows. Both buzzards and red kites soar over the valleys and the moorland.
63ha – Map ref: SO 188159

LAKE VYRNWY (RSPB) — *All year*

The heart of this beautiful moorland reserve is the lake, a flooded valley dammed during the last century by the Liverpool Corporation to provide drinking water to a large area of the Midlands; later the management passed to the Severn and Trent Water Authority. However, it is not only the lake that provides interest for naturalists, there is an area of open sheep-grazed moorland where a system of management has been employed that has helped to preserve red grouse and breeding waders. It is also an area of broadleaved woodland that supports a considerable bird population as well as a healthy number of small mammals on which the predatory birds and larger mammals depend.

Red squirrels inhabit the broadleaved woods, and in the mature conifer forestry plantations badgers are quite common as are foxes, and that speciality of Welsh woodland, the polecat, occurs, although it is not easy to see. Being an RSPB reserve you'd naturally think the accent would be on birds; not so, the management plan is such that all aspects of the highland and valley sites are maximised for their wildlife potential.

There are many species of rare and endangered plants, and a very large insect population with butterflies and moths including the increasingly rare high brown fritillary butterfly in mid summer.

Insects attract insect-eating birds, and these include the redstart and both species of common titmice, blue and great tit, and the minute and seemingly delicate goldcrest which finds a living all year round. Dippers and wagtails thrive along the banks of the valley streams that feed into the lake which is itself a fishing site for breeding goosander. There are also a few pairs of blackcock in the conifer plantations.

Lake Vyrnwy is noted for its birds of prey, peregrines, merlin and hen harrier are frequently seen, and buzzards, kestrels and sparrowhawks hunt the region by day while tawny owls make their presence felt at night; their breeding success is directly related to the number of voles present on the reserve.
17,520 acres – Map ref: SJ 020193

NANT SERE WOOD (Brecknock WT)** — *Spring, summer*

When the glacial ice vanished from the Brecon Beacons it left a legacy of smooth-sided valleys with a 'U'-shaped profile where the softer rocks had been ground away. In the bottom of these trough-like landscape features lay a cargo of fertile silts through which fast rivers flowed. The intervening millennia have produced a mosaic of mixed woodland on the hillsides that has been shaped by agriculture and sheep farming, and a series of riverside and marshy pockets that nature has wasted no time in exploiting.

The woodlands differ in species depending upon the amount of water in the soil. At the bottom of the valley, where the river gives way to walled fields the trees are few, mainly alders and downy birch, but higher up the hillside oak and coppiced ash predominates supporting a very high bird population with pied flycatchers, wood warblers and green woodpeckers. The ground flora reflects the amount of moisture in the soil, foxgloves, bluebells and herb robert are typical plants of the drier woodland, along with wood sorrel. Where the ground is more open and wet — meadowsweet and devils bit scabious grow with marsh bedstraw, watermint and bog asphodel.
17.5ha

OFFA'S DYKE PATH (CC) — *Spring, summer*

A continuation of the old post dark ages fortifications that were to have kept the Welsh out of England, or the English out of Wales, depending on your point of view. This part of the long distance path is as beautiful a landscape as you'll find anywhere in the country, and rich in wildlife too. The rapidly changing weather conditions, sometimes encountered, make it advisable to be properly prepared if your enjoyment is not to be spoiled.
115km – Map ref: SJ 267206 / SO 267323

OGOF FFYNON DDU (NCC) — *Spring, summer*

The limestone bedrock has been burrowed and fissured by water, creating one of the deepest and most extensive water-worn cave systems in the country. The limestone yielded to the pressure of the last ice age, and the effects of water and ice upon the bare rock have produced the natural phenomenon called "limestone pavement" where

the flat ice-planed rock is fissured with miniature valleys; within these protected micro habitats a range of wild plants has been able to flourish despite the harshness of the surrounding environment. In places the softer lime-stone abuts very resistant millstone grit, and the erosion levels create a marked contrast.
413ha – Map ref: SN 867155

PWLL-Y-WRACH (Brecknoch WT) — *Spring, summer*

A reserve that owes its diversity to a band of lime-rich cornstone and limestone interspersing the old red sand-stone. The contrasting ph of the soils produces an interesting woodland flora and a varied birdlife. The land surrounding the woods was heavily grazed by sheep, but fencing has improved the situation allowing tree regene-ration and an increase in wildlife diversity approaching that of the deeper oak and ash woods where sweet woodruff, bluebells, wood sorrell, dog's mercury, en-chanter's nightshade and dog violet thrive. The river provides a perfect habitat for dippers, and they can be seen feeding below the surface against the current. Grey and pied wagtails are also in evidence, and the spring birdsong is augmented by the many spring and summer breeding migrants that find food and nesting sites here.
8.3ha – Map ref: SO 163327

SCOTLAND

BORDERS

O Caledonia! stern and wild,
Meet nurse for a poetic child!
Land of brown heath and shaggy wood,
Land of the mountain and the flood,
Land of my sires! what mortal hand
Can e'er untie the filial band
That knits me to thy rugged strand.

Sir Walter Scott recognised the special character of the borders. Since Roman times it has been an area of conflict, its rich farming land, fortressed coastline and deep sheltered river valleys made it a desirable prize; the mighty Tweed with its mills and remnants of once immensely wealthy monasteries point to a time of pros-perity built on the golden fleece — wool.

There was life here long before man evolved. Fossil records show strange crustaceans and footprints spanning virtually the whole of the history of life on Earth. Ancient Silurian, and later Devonian rocks, show the passage of time where pressures in the Earth's crust have curved the strata into gentle domes and valleys, and geologically recent glaciations have eased away any sharp edges leaving the sheep-grazed rolling hills with a soft outline. The cold drift from the inland valleys helps to prolong winter, and over the millennia the sea fog, with its attendant rainfall, has led to the creation of deep peat bogs and mosses in the valley bottoms; these mosses are continuing to develop and provide safe refuge for a variety of flora and fauna.

The river Tweed is the jewel in the region's crown. It drains a higher than average rainfall from the sur-rounding uplands from the Cheviots, Lammamuir and the Moorfoot and Pentland hills. With its many tri-butaries it combines to form one of the best salmon spawning rivers in the British Isles. There was a time when Ettrick Water and the tributaries of the Teviot were home to otters, but persecution and pollution, and the intro-duction of alien mink (escapees from fur farms) has brought about the demise of these engaging animals.

Where the Tweed finally opens to the sea the sheltered estuary forms a haven for wintering swans and wildfowl; but it is the barrier of massive folded rocks along the sea cliffs that attract birds and bird-watchers alike. The cliffs at St Abbs Head constitute some of the highest in the land, and provide ample ledges and crannies for a host of sea birds. The North Sea has the well-earned reputation of being one of the most polluted bodies of water in the northern hemisphere, but in this region it is less polluted than elsewhere; the water, unusually clear and rich, has resulted in the creation of marine reserves at St Abbs Head and Eyemouth.

Generally speaking the Borders have escaped the notice of most holiday-makers, but the diversity and variety of wildlife habitats will certainly reward any who venture here.

BEMERSYDE MOSS (Scottish WT)** — *April through August*

The reserve is controlled to keep water levels higher in winter than at other times of year. Winter brings a special magic to this marsh of willow carr and sedges, for the open water attracts large numbers of wildfowl. The black-headed gull colony depends upon certain areas of moss drying out in spring and early summer; their numbers reach a peak in June when up to 2000 pairs are present. The marshland flora is typical and certain species such as the celery-leaved buttercup appreciate the wet conditions.
27ha

DUNHOG MOSS AND HARE MOSS (Scottish WT)** — *June through September*

Unique for its water beetles; some of the species on this reserve are relics of the last ice age. The beautiful grass of parnassus can be found in profusion in July and August and attracts the velvety Scotch argus butterflies that have a colony here.
4ha

DUNS CASTLE (Scottish WT) — *April, June*

In a region where wet mosses predominate, Duns Castle presents a contrast of species-rich limestone beech woodlands and man-made waterways like the Lochan of Hen Poo. The reserve is at its best in spring with bluebells and wild garlic and the sound of returning migrant birds. Pied flycatchers use the nest boxes in the woodlands to excellent effect, and the insect fauna is rich with a number of butterfly species. Mammals include roe deer and the increasingly rare red squirrel.
77ha – Map ref: NT 778550

ST ABBS HEAD (NTS/Scottish WT) — *May through July*

St Abbs Head is one of the best and certainly one of the most spectacular places to watch breeding seabirds, but not for any one suffering from vertigo. A titanic upheaval in the Earth's crust hundreds of millions of years ago has bequeathed a bewildering variety of cliffs and stacks, pinnacles and ledges, and on this geological jumble thousands of nesting auks and kittiwakes rear their young. The ten thousand guillemots that annually throng the cliffs are what most visitors want to see, and the thousands of kittiwakes and razorbills that occupy niches on the rocks in competition with fulmars give an indication of the rich feeding that is to be found in the clear waters nearby. The cliffs are truly majestic and form a vantage point for bird-watchers to enjoy the passage of seabirds up and down the coastline in spring and autumn.

The headlands are liberally sprinkled with rabbit burrows where wheatears breed adding variety to the thrifty turf; behind the cliff face the land slopes away in a series of hummocks and dips towards the Mire Loch. The composition of the underlying rock dictates the flora which is extremely varied and ranges from thyme and bird's foot trefoil and common rock rose to acid-seeking plants such as milkwort. The surrounding countryside has a reputation for good sites for migrant insects, and the resident species such as grayling take advantage of the open ground to sun themselves.
97ha – Map ref: NT 9168

CENTRAL

From the flat plain of the Firth of Forth with its refineries, coal waste tips and wader-rich mudflats the land rises and changes dramatically. To the north of Stirling the productive farmland slips into bracken covered uplands and sparse woodland with small fields where curlew nest, and where brown hares box in spring. Within a few miles, on the slopes of Earls Hill over 1400ft above sea level, the trees give way to a completely different terrain, almost arctic tundra covered with heather. On these high tops brown hares would be too vulnerable so nature has replaced them with the arctic or variable hare whose winter coat stays white until the snow melts.

The land rears towards the southern Grampian Hills showing the effects of age and weathering and the successive climatic changes over hundreds of millions of years that have moulded and scoured the glens. There are signs of long past, frighteningly powerful, geological events; the sheer cliffs of the Ochil Hills are evidence of a fault in the Earth's crust that once sheared in a gigantic show of natural power and Campsie Fells also reveal the region's violent past.

Towering over the Campsies is the Earl's Seat, and to the west the ancient volcanic cone of Dumgoyne looms silently. From the vantage point of Earls Hill the landscape rises and falls to the Fintry Hills. Despite the mass of Scottish urbanisation that swings in an arc from Glasgow to Stirling (with its imposing castle set on an outcrop of rock) to the Firth of Forth and Edinburgh, an air of peacefulness reigns and a great deal of wildlife thrives.

Gulls breed on the tiny upland lochs in the Fintry, Earls and Touch Hills. They will spend their first autumn on the shores of Loch Lomond before moving south ahead of winter; but before they go they make the most of the rich waters of this the largest body of fresh water in Britain. The shores of the Loch can boast their own microclimate, although when the winter wind is off the snow-covered Trossaschs it can be harsh indeed; nevertheless this does not deter the many species of wildfowl that roost on the waters or the fish that thrive within them; the powan, a relic of the ice age or even beyond is found here and in few other places. The hillsides around the Loch are dominated by woodlands, many of which are accessible only by boat, consequently the lack of disturbance allows for a large breeding population of warblers, pied flycatchers and redstarts.

On the Stirling Plain is the great peat bog of Flanders Moss and the wader-rich mud of Skinflats on the upper Firth. The contrast in climate can be extreme. While the heather and deer grass on the high ground are still under many feet of snow, it can be quite spring-like down on the plain and the first pied flycatchers will have returned to sing in Dollar Glen. Sir Walter Scott would still be able to remark upon "A scene of natural romance and beauty. . . High hills, rocks and banks waving with natural forests of birch and oak, as their leaves rustled to the wind and twinkled in the sun, gave to the depth of solitude a sort of life and vivacity."

BEN LUI (NCC) — *June, July*

An area of high ground well known for its superb examples of mountain flora. Limestone and mica schist ledges provide a roothold for a wide range of plants including rose root and yellow and purple saxifrage, globe flower and alpine saw wort, mountain bladder fern and mountain avens. Visitors should contact the NCC warden at Balloch.
798ha – Map ref: NN 2626

DOLLAR GLEN (NTS) — *April through June*

Steeply wooded with oak and a little ash and wyche elm, Dollar Glen is an excellent example of this type of

Loch Lomond   Central

Scottish deciduous woodland. In spring the predominant features are migrant birds, especially redstarts, pied flycatchers, willow and wood warblers. The ground flora indicates the age of the woodland with wood sorrel and dog's mercury forming dense carpets while the garlic scent of ramsons drifts on the breeze.
4ha – Map ref: NS 9699

FLANDERS MOSS (Scottish WT)** — *April through June*

Flanders Moss is a large area of a formerly extensive raised peat bog supporting typical mire fauna with sphagnum moss and cotton grass giving way to drier moorland plants on the margins. Snipe and curlew are particualrly abundant as is bog rosemary (also known as marsh Andromeda), a pretty and very local member of the heather family whose pink flowers open in late spring and early summer.
45ha

INVERSNAID (RSPB) — *All year*

The road to this secret and very productive reserve runs from Aberfoyle between Loch Arklet and Loch Katrin and leads to the northern end of Loch Lomond. The West Highland Way runs close by and there is a pedestrian ferry from Inveruglas.

The ground rises steeply from the lochside through woodlands to the crags above and the view from the top is superb. The burns that rush down through the reserve create their own habitat with abundant ferns and lichens. Badgers thrive here as well as feral goats and red and roe deer. The bird commmunties are tied very much to the habitat, from buzzards and ravens in the crags, grey and pied wagtails and common sandpipers along the sand at the lochside, and the woodlands are a wonder of migrants including pied flycatchers, wood warblers and tree pipits. Where the mountain burns run more slowly, forming small pools you will find dippers and in winter the loch provides bird-watchers with ample opportunities to see geese and migrant waders.
923 acres – Map ref: NN 337088

Feral Goats   *Inversnaid*

LOCH LOMOND (NCC) — *May-July* (Breeding birds and flowers) *October-December* (Wildfowl)

The beautiful freshwater Loch Lomond is one of the most popular tourist spots in all Scotland. The road runs beside the water for several miles and the views are superb, but in order to enjoy the true beauty and the abundant wildlife that exists here you will need to spend a little time. NCC wardens organise guided walks and it's well worth joining them. (NCC Reserve Manager, Balloch.)

The range of breeding birds is superb, from blackcock to redstarts, and there's always a chance of seeing an otter in the late evening fishing in one of the many burns that join the loch. The underwater scene is less easily studied, but a relic species of fish, the powan, is found here; it's a freshwater herring, a hang-over from the ice age.

The fish population is huge. Salmon and sea trout run up through the loch to their spawning grounds, and the native brown trout are distributed fairly evenly. Other freshwater fish, especially pike and perch, tend to live in the richer feeding areas at the southern end. This end is also favoured by the huge flocks of wintering wildfowl that visit every year, and whooper swans and Greenland white-fronted geese find food in the marshy areas. Loch Lomond is on a major flightline, and if the water levels are right, migrant waders stop to feed, especially on the exposed insect-rich mud where the river Endrick enters the loch.

The largest island of the cluster at the southern end is called Inchcailloch and geologically it is particularly interesting, sitting as it does, across the old highland boundary fault line with serpentine and old red and conglomerate sandstone among the different rock types and soils. The diversity of flora this creates is fascinating, with both acid and lime-loving plants occurring within a short distance of one another. These islands also provide a haven for migrants, and there are ample places for naturalists, or simply a seeker of beautiful scenery. *416ha – Map ref: NS 3598*

QUEEN ELIZABETH FOREST PARK — *April through October*

Queen Elizabeth Forest Park is huge, beginning at the eastern side of Loch Lomond and rising to the top of Ben Lomod, over 3000 ft above sea level. It's very popular because of the variety of scenery and habitats, and the lochside woods are full of bluebells and birdsong in spring and early summer. Further up the slopes, away from the loch the habitat changes, the trees grow fewer in number and where there were sessile oaks and alders on the lower levels, now Scots pine predominate. If you venture even higher the trees cease altogether replaced by heather and bilberry.

The higher ground is less explored, and here the tiny merlin, and occasionally buzzards, can be seen, and the red grouse and ring ouzel replace the familiar lowland birds. In the very highest places the trusting grouse, the ptarmigan, can sometimes be seen scurring away, but often looking back as if unsure of any real danger. Ravens and peregrine falcons are the predators of these high tops, and occasionally the broad wings of a golden eagle will cause ptarmigan and variable hare to freeze into immobility until the danger is past.

Around Loch Ard the woodland is more dense and the whinchat and wheatears are replaced by the wood warblers, tree pipits and redstarts. In fact the whole Park is a delight for botanists; to list all the species would take up too much space, but take a good plant book with you and I guarantee you will find plenty of interest.

SKINFLATS (RSPB)** — *September through March*

A site of special natural history interest in the midst of industrial development, yet one of the best places for wildfowl and waders in the south of Scotland. The large area of tidal mudflats attracts huge numbers of curlew, knot, dunlin and golden plover, and in mid winter the food-rich mud is probed by thousands of questing beaks — while the refinery in the background belches out the fumes and pollution of the modern age.
410ha – Map ref: NN 9385

WEST HIGHLAND WAY (Central) (Central, Highland & Strathclyde RC) — *All year*

This first, officially designated highland route, provides a wide range of landscapes from the gentle slopes of Loch Lomond to the rugged mountain territory of Ben More and beyond to the north. Weather conditions can change dramatically so it's important to be well prepared; but the sight of a hunting golden eagle or the call of a nesting golden plover is music to lighten your step.
152km – Map ref: NS 896744 / NN 113743

DUMFRIES AND GALLOWAY

When travelling to Scotland, devotees of the Scottish bard, Robert Burns, turn left at Carlisle towards his last resting place in St Michael's Churchyard in Dumfries. Worried about his health, and that of his children, Burns chose to spend his last days in this the mildest part of lowland Scotland. Here too J. M. Barrie, author of the perennial classic "Peter Pan" was educated, and may well have been inspired to a literary career by the legend of Burns, and his love of the Scottish countryside.

Winter comes early to the stark hills of the Rhinns of Kells, and the wet winds off the Atlantic rise upwards dropping their rain and creating a scene of bogs and marsh. There is evidence here of the final struggles of the Pleistocene Ice Age. Moraine deposits left behind where glaciers expired are particularly noticeable from Burrows Head inland to the town of Dumfries. The abrasive weight of the huge ice sheets carved and smoothed the landscape forming Lochs Doon and Trool in the glacial troughs. Galloway is subject to wet west winds, and S. R. Crockett captured the wild feeling of the place in these few lines:-

"Whenever I think of paradise, to this day my mind runs . .on a clear stream birgling among trees of birk and ash that cower in the hollow of the glen from the south west wind."

The ridge of hills from Moffat in the east to Newton Stewart provide some of the best westerly breeding sites for curlew and golden plover and springtime here can be magical with the wild cries of breeding waders. In winter it's one of the best places in the whole of Great Britain to see the rare hen harrier.

The farmland has suffered a change of use since the end of the Second World War. A decline in sheep farming on the hills has allowed the forestry industry to exploit cheap land prices and grants for coniferisation. Huge, previously unspoiled areas, have been lost to conifers, and there is now considerable concern over the acidification of some of the lochs which contain relic species of fish and invertebrates. Commercial exploitation of the lowland peat deposits have diminished a number of natural habitats, but there are many plusses and the region supports quite a number of plants at the northern and southern limit of their range.

The rivers that drain from the high ground find their way to the sea through ancient watercourses, and flow into broad and fertile estuaries forming saltings such as Eastpark and Caerlaverock on the Solway Firth. Huge numbers of geese, waders and wildfowl gather here in winter making the most of the largest unreclaimed salt marsh in Great Britain. The area also holds an enormous concentration of Spitzbergen barnacle geese, and vast numbers of golden plover and oystercatchers.

Here too is found the most northerly breeding site for natterjack toads in the shallow sunlit pools hard by the shore on the landward side of the merse; but it is winter wildfowl and waders that have attracted man to this region. First the wildfowlers, then the bird-watchers, now there is an uneasy truce between shooting and conservation interests.

CAERLAVEROCK (NCC) — *All year, (especially winter)*

Caerlaverock is one of the largest areas of unreclaimed salt marsh (or merse) in the country, and on a brilliant winter's day when the geese are flying and the wind is off the Solway it's a magical place. The entire Spitsbergen population of barnacle geese winter here, and protection has allowed their numbers to reach nearly 8,000. Also 5,000 or more pink-feet geese roost on the reserve together with thousands of wigeon and pintail (it's a major site for pintail with up to a thousand individuals being recorded). Once wildfowling took a heavy toll, but a permit system is in force now which gives the birds some respite from heavy shooting pressures in winter.

Huge concentrations of waders, especially oyster-catchers, use the marshes and mudflats in autumn and winter, but it's a dangerous place when the wind is behind the tide and the sea rushes up deep natural drains, any one venturing onto the saltings should do so only under guidance from the NCC's warden. Spring and summer bring a new set of sights and sounds. Natterjack toads have their most northerly breeding colony in the sunlit freshwater pools where the saltings meet the land and curlew and oystercatchers nest in the tundra-like

Natterjack Toad   *Caerlaverock*

vegetation of sea aster, red fescue and salt marsh rush. Peregrines hunt across the Solway Firth, and kestrels patrol the grassy margins, perching on the fence posts joined by wire which are festooned with dried seaweeds and grasses blown in on the wind.

There's a picnic area, sheltered on the landward side by small salt wind-stunted oaks and hawthorns, where long-tailed tits and summer nesting warblers can be seen.
5501ha – Map ref: NY 0365

EASTPARK (WWT/NCC)** — *Winter*

Adjoining the NCC reserve at Caerlaverock this Wildfowl and Wetland Trust area helps to ensure undisturbed roosting and feeding sites for the thousands of wildfowl and geese that winter here. Also a very large pond has been created, fronting the hide and an observation building, giving intimate views of many of the winter visitors including huge numbers of barnacle and pink-feet geese and a small population of greylag geese. The sizeable wintering flocks of whooper and Bewick swans are the subject of a study by the Trust with a decoy being employed to capture and mark the birds.

Duck to be seen here include wigeon, teal, gadwall, pintail, pochard, shoveller and tufted, and there's always a chance of seeing a rare species mixed in with the flocks. The huge numbers of waders and duck attract birds of prey and the merlin, a small falcon declining in numbers, finds the winter pickings easy; hen harriers too are frequent winter visitors, and the sparrowhawks that breed near the reserve make dashing sorties into the teeming flocks. Access is limited to warden assisted parties of up to fifty people; larger parties should book in advance.
524ha – Map ref: NY 052656

GALLOWAY FOREST PARK — *All year*

The land suffered from forestry work when the heather moors were planted to the detriment of the native flora and fauna; less than half the original area remains. Even so huge vistas of wild moorland and granite scarps delight the seeker of solitude and attempts to reintroduce the pine marten have met with some success, for abundant prey is available in the form of squirrels and rabbits and variable hares.

The range of the Awful Hand, five summits dominated by The Merrick, supports an alpine flora with arctic/alpine species such as dwarf willow and juniper; the oak and birch woods around Loch Trool still retain an atmos-phere of pre-forestry days. In spring there's a great variety of birdsong, and redstart and pied flycatcher breed in some numbers.

Throughout the highlands red deer present a problem for the saplings of Scots pine and broadleaved trees, they nibble the growing points preventing regeneration. There's a deer museum at Clatteringshaws and sizeable deer enclosures at Brockloch Hill as well as one at Murray's Monument which contains a herd of feral goats. These are attractive animals, but even more destructive to woodland than the deer. It's an excellent area for walking, the best way to see the region's unusual bird species. Hen harriers are frequently seen on the more remote open

bogs, and the occasional golden eagle, peregrine falcon and merlin will make any walk a memorable adventure.
6000ha

GREY MARE'S TAIL (NTS) — *April through August*

The Grey Mare's Tail can boast one of the highest and most beautiful water falls in Britain, tumbling from Loch Skeen, some 180ft above. The loch lies in a basin surrounded by limestone rocks. Feral goats eat the plants on the more accessible slopes, but in spite of their efforts the flora is unusually rich. A thriving common gull colony enlivens spring and summer on the shores of the loch, and ravens nest on the more inaccessible places on the cliff sides.
1016ha – Map ref: NT 182150

KEN-DEE MARSHES (RSPB) — *May, June* (Breeding birds) *October through March* (Wildfowl/waders)

The wintering ground of the largest flock of Greenland white-fronted geese in the country, almost two hundred individuals spend the winter here. The differing habitats and variations in water levels, because of pumping by the hydro-electric scheme, supports such diverse species, as Whooper swan, greylag, barnacle, bean and pink-feet geese, diving duck and waders; and breeding birds include sedge and grasshopper warblers.

The old hay meadows surrounding the reserve are very rich in plants, and the small oak woodland and scrubby marginal undergrowth contains a considerable breeding population of willow tits, wood warblers and pied flycatchers in their season.
158ha – Map ref: NX 6376 / 6869

WOOD OF CREE (RSPB) — *Spring, summer*

The great Wood of Cree is one of the largest broadleaved woods in southern Scotland; rich and diverse, this once heavily coppiced sessile oak woodland was managed for some years by the Forestry Commission and the NCC prior to its acquisition by the RSPB. It supports a wide range of species. Some like rowan, are adapted to the cold wet conditions of Scottish winters while plants such as angelica, sneezewort and bog asphodel speak of a warmer regime.

The powerful melody of spring birdsong in the canopy of the oakwoods is in stark contrast with the dark, almost silent, conifer plantations of the adjoining Galloway Forest. Birds found here, in their season, include red-starts, pied flycatchers, wood warblers, tree pipits, wood-cocks and greater spotted woodpeckers and on these a healthy population of breeding sparrowhawks depend.

The oaks provide nesting sites for buzzards; and dippers searching for stonefly larvae, submerge them-selves in the burns that tumble down though the wood. On the riverside marsh, common sandpipers and grey wagtails breed, while on the moorland above the wood, curlew and whinchat nest. Otters are seen here, but rarely, as are the shy roe deer; dark green fritillary and purple hairstreak butterflies are a delight in late summer.
200ha – Map ref: NX 385700

FIFE

Not for nothing was this rather isolated part of Scotland known by its proud inhabitants as the Kingdom of Fife. The Forth Road Bridge ended its isolation, but by that time the traditional industries of mining and farming were undergoing a dramatic change. Centuries of coal mining left huge ugly spoil tips, but many of these have been softened and contoured into the landscape, suitable for farming and recreation.

The main natural history interest is in winter when huge concentrations of geese and waders come to the Tay Eden estuary, and winter flocks of eider gather off the coast and around the mouth of the Firth of Tay, which can boast one of the very few sand-dune complexes in eastern Scotland.

The point of land known as Fife Ness is a seabird paradise, with ample cliff nesting ledges and easy access to the rich fishing grounds of the North Sea. Fife's position on the east coast has made it important as a bird migration route, a fact recognised as long ago as 1934 when a bird observatory was established on the Island of May. This dot of land is halfway between Fife Ness and the massive gannetry of the Bass rock and it presents a wonderful place for weary migrants to rest.

Inland the woodlands have been converted to conifers, but there are still places where Burns would have found the landscape to his liking:-

An' oh! the scene was passing fair,
For what in Scotland can compare
Wi' the Carse o' Gowrie?
The sun was setting on the Tay,
The blue hills melted into grey,
The mavis and the blackbird's lay
Were sweetly heard in Gowrie.

— Burns

BANKHEAD MOSS (Scottish WT)** — *May through September*

One of the few remaining raised peat bogs in Fife, Bankhead Moss is a dome of peat where an active growth of sphagnum moss is still developing within an area of farmed land. In the centre of the moss, where the acid soil is water-logged and infertile, the tree cover, mainly Scots pine and birch, is sparse, but around the edge where the drainage is better, natural regeneration of birch woodland occurs. There's a typical range of bog flora, and the birdlife is mainly curlew and snipe.
4ha

EDEN ESTUARY (NE Fife DC) — *April through June* (Breeding birds) *August through May* (Waders/duck)

The position of this sheltered estuary on the Fife peninsula has created a very desirable stopping off point for waders on migration, also for wintering wildfowl. Unlike the nearby large estuaries of the Tay and Firth of Forth, this small outfall to the sea is bounded by mud and sandy shores; the salt marshes are on a smaller scale too, but none-the-less interesting for the wading birds they attract. In autumn and winter large numbers of grey plover, bar-tailed and black-tailed godwit visit the sandflats.

The estuary plays host to a large breeding population of eider duck, they nest nearby and bring their ducklings to the estuary in summer. Other sea ducks, such as common scoters, gather in the estuary mouth and there's a shelduck roost of international importance, the numbers rising to a peak in March/early April just prior to the breeding season. The sheltered nature of the sandbars encourages common seals to sun themselves at low tide.
891ha – Map ref: NO 4819

FIRTH OF TAY (TAY-EDEN ESTUARY) *April through June* (Breeding birds) *August through May* (Waders/duck)

Mention the Firth of Tay and the conversation always comes around to the subject of wildfowl and the massive concentration of eider duck that gather here in winter, often the numbers rise to as many as sixteen thousand, a fifth of the British breeding stock. They are joined by huge flocks of returning geese, especially pink-feet, as many as 15,000 - 20,000 at any one time. These geese, and the greylags that also occupy the roosts, are the subject of wildfowling pressure and cause considerable seasonal conflict with farmers because of crop damage. However, the problem with the geese is of short duration and is mainly heaviest as migrating flocks move across the country.

The shape of the estuary is such that the sandflats and mud, on which the large population of waders depend, are far from the banks making them difficult to observe; however this does mean security for the common seals that can haul out in comparative safety. The size and productivity of the mudflats and sand bars encourage a wide variety of waders and duck to congregate between Newport and Monifieth — and goldeneye can be seen in winter.

There's no doubt that this estuary is a jewel; but dark clouds are gathering on the horizon as the pace of industrial development increases. Already oil spills have caused damage among the eider flocks just off the mouth of the estuary; they, and the flocks of common scoter and divers that use the coastal waters, are especially vulnerable from such incidents.

ISLE OF MAY (NCC) — *May through July* (Breeding birds) *April, May/August through October* (Migrants)

One of the country's first bird observatories was begun here in 1934 in order to record the passage of migrants to and from the continent of Europe and their travels across the hostile wastes of the North Sea. The island also reflects changes in the relative numbers of seabirds with a huge increase in puffins, although losses due to a crash in the numbers of sandeels will affect them in the medium term and may, if shortages of natural food continue, reverse the pattern of expansion of these charming birds.

May's tern colony is subject to considerable pressure from gulls, as both herring and black-backed species nest on the island. Along much of the British coastline there has been something of a decline in the number and variety of seabird species, but here the increase in the breeding pairs of shags is astonishing. From the first records kept, when it was rare to find a dozen nests, the figures now top

Pine Marten   *Culbin Forest*

a Other seabirds such as kittiwakes and auks have also enjoyed. an upward turn, possibly as a result of increased protection and control measures on the predatory gulls. Bird rarities are a relatively common experience on May, as its position makes it a special site for Scandinavian and low arctic birds blown off course.

57ha – Map ref: NT 6599

GRAMPIAN

The plain, with its fertile soils is attractive enough, but not the sort of terrain to turn the head of an artist. The Norfolk of the north it's been called by visitors, and its North Sea outlook, and climate of cold wet winds and big skies finds the parallel. But it's the mountains that draw the naturalist to this region; the dramatic Cairngorms and Grampians that have left their mark upon the imagination and creative spirit of a number of Scotland's many talented sons and daughters. None more so than the young Byron when, following his father's death and his mother's reduction in circumstances, he attended the grammar school in the old town of Aberdeen. He later said that it was the mountains that so impressed him.

. . ."ye mountains of the clime
Where grew my youthful years;
Where Loch na Garr in snows sublime
His giant summit rears."

— Byron

The rivers Dee and Don too have been a magnet for tourists since Victorian times, and the royal family's Scottish home at Balmoral shelters them, for a short while, from the eyes of the world's Press. The twin river systems produce a superb waterway for salmon and trout, and substantial stocks are still held despite heavy salmon fishing in the North Sea and the estuary.

The influence of the highlands on birdlife is felt in the breeding success of osprey on several of the lochs and crested tits and Scottish crossbills in some of the woodlands. The high ground of the eastern range of the Cairngorms is perhaps the most unspoiled wilderness to be found in Great Britain, and is a breeding place for birds such as the confiding dotterel and snow bunting and golden plover.

The harsh ancient rocks along the coastline have been seabird colonies for millennia, and long exploited by man; now most places that support large concentrations of birds are protected and numbers have increased dramatically. However, oil exploration in the North Sea, with its potential for spillage, is placing a question mark over the future of many seabird cliffs, as is extensive over-fishing and pollution. Already some seabird colonies on the islands off the east coast have suffered several disastrous breeding seasons when hardly any young have been reared to maturity. Hopefully their plight in this fragile environment will become better understood, and a solution to the problem may not be far off.

CULBIN FOREST (FC) — *Spring, summer*

Commercial forestry has stabilized the sand-dune system and, together with Scots pine, has created a new productive habitat. The mammal and bird numbers reflect this with an increasing population of crested tits, red squirrels and that highland speciality the capercaillie. There is a reasonable number of roe deer in the forest, and the presence of predatory mammals and birds highlights the productivity of the woodlands with wild cats and pine martens, sparrowhawks, buzzards, long-eared and short-eared owls regularly noted as breeding species.

The estuary of the river Findhorn, and Dorback Burn provide ample fishing for that rarity among predators, the otter; and there's also plenty of food for them in the Murray Firth. The Firth's benign influence upon the climate of the area provides a habitat for a large number of plants to survive at the very northern limit of their geographical distribution.
2400ha – Map ref: NH 9861

DINNET OAKWOOD (NCC) — *Late spring*

A small wood by Scottish standards, but its mixed species of pedunculate and sessile oaks allow for a far higher song-bird population than is usual in this part of Scotland, including the migrant species of warblers and spotted flycatchers.
13ha – Map ref: NO 464980

FOWLSHEUGH (RSPB) — *Late spring, summer*

The old red sandstone cliffs of Fowlsheugh are renowned for the wealth of breeding auks and kittiwakes. The bridled sub-species of guillemot occurs in some numbers as do razorbills, and fulmars in smaller numbers with a few herring gulls; but it is the kittiwakes and their constant clamour that impresses visitors, perhaps sixty thousand birds all calling frantically as they defend their territories on this seabird conurbation. Access from the cliff path is relatively straightforward, but the sheer height and rugged aspect of the cliffs makes them dangerous.
1 ½ miles of cliff – Map ref: NO 876805

GLENMUICK & LOCHNAGAR (Balmoral Estates/ Scottish W.T) *May through September* (Birds/flowers) *November* (Deer)

Well known because it forms part of the Balmoral Estate, this area, including the loch, has been immortalised by Prince Charles through its ancient fictional inhabitant "The Old Man of Lochnagar." Notwithstanding, there is a great deal of fascination for walkers and naturalists for this is red deer country where golden eagles, peregrines, ravens and hooded crows are lords of the skies. On the high tops dotterel and ptarmigan are to be found, and lower down the moorland is inhabited by red grouse, curlew, golden plover and that wild and beautiful falcon the merlin (rarely seen). The variable hares are preyed upon by eagles and foxes, but are not much concerned by man and will often stand on their hind legs to observe a passing human with interest.

This is harsh country where the birds and animals have their own special place in nature, where man is very much an interloper. It is a landscape to be treated with care, to venture out onto the high ground with poor footwear and unsuitable clothing is courting danger as the weather can change from sunshine to cold drizzle or even snow very quickly. Isolation and steep wet corries has allowed certain plant communities to thrive, and relict populations of plants left over from the early post-glacial regime are evident on high ledges — globe flower, red campion and woodrush grow ungrazed by deer and carpets of yellow and starry saxifrage, Norwegian cudweed, alpine speedwell and alpine willow-herb also grow here. There is a useful visitor information centre.
2572ha – Map ref: NO 2585

GLEN TANAR (Glen Tanar Estate/NCC) — *Late spring, summer*

The remaining amount of old Caledonian pine forest is pitfully small, but this reserve is said to hold one of the best examples; it is also drier and as such has its own special flavour. Here the wildcat is a predator as are foxes and otters, and introduced mink; red squirrels also occur. Fencing restricts the access of red deer and encourages natural regeneration of the pine forest. Roe deer have less of an impact and so are present, though rarely seen by casual visitors, but capercaillie, siskin and the Scottish crossbill can be seen.
4185ha – Map ref: NO 4891

LOCH OF STRATHBEG (RSPB)** — *October through March* (Wildfowl) *April through July* (Breeding birds)

One of the most exciting reserves in Scotland for wintering wildfowl, in the height of the season as many as twenty thousand birds cover the shallow water. The geese are mainly greylag and pink-footed geese, although barnacle geese do stop over on route to their Spitzbergen breeding grounds. The Society has arranged with the MoD for access across military land so prior arrangements must be made with the RSPB warden.
2065 acres

MORRONE BIRKWOOD (NCC)* — *Late spring, early summer*

This is a particularly interesting area in that it is almost entirely covered with downy birch woodland, a relict of a time when the climate of this part of Scotland was more akin to that of northern Scandinavia.
225ha – Map ref: NO 143911

SANDS OF FORVIE & YTHAN ESTUARY (NCC) —
April-July (Breeding birds) *August-December* (Waders/-wildfowl)

One of the least human-affected coastal dune systems in the whole country and as such of enormous natural history interest. The dunes are constantly on the move at the behest of wind and weather, but where marram grass is established the dunes have stabilised to allow eider duck to nest, it is the largest breeding group of these elegant ducks in Britain. Large numbers of shelduck breed here too as do four species of tern that nest on the Sands of Forvie reserve — sandwich and little tern among them; the former breeding in considerable numbers.

The estuary is home to pink-footed geese, up to ten thousand have been recorded here and many species of duck are regularly seen — scoters, long-tailed, mergansers and divers. Waders too use the sheltered estuary for food and to rest on long migrations, and there is quite a winter population of sanderling, turnstone and ringed plovers.
1018ha – Map ref: NK 0227

SPEYSIDE WAY (MORAY DC) — *All year*
A long and beautiful walk beside one of Scotland's most exciting rivers, frequently enlivened by the sight of an osprey fishing in the shallow water. The Way begins in Spey Bay and follows the line of the Strathspey railway.
48km – Map ref: NJ 349654 / 167367

HIGHLAND NORTH

The northern tip of Britain is perhaps the last wilderness left in the country, a place where the landscape is beautiful but unforgiving. The north Atlantic gales spend their power on the aptly named Cape Wrath, the sea boils with fury, and long Atlantic swells ride into inlets where otters fish undisturbed, and where grey seals haul out to sun themselves. The main breeding population of grey seals centred on the British Isles calves here in autumn and depends on peace and quiet and an ample supply of fish to survive, but the development of industrial salmon farming along the Atlantic coast has created environmental conflict. Sadly Scotland's history of exploitation of the environment and the highland peoples does not give reason to hope that all will be well.

And as he turns his gaze on either hand,
He sees the great, the terrible, the grand:-
The dreaded Pentland's rough and rapid flow,
The wide Atlantic; lit with evening's glow.
— David Grant

The last glaciation rested heavily on the north west, carving deep gullies in the softer rocks, the old red sandstone and limestone, it polished and shattered the harder igneous rocks, and even after 10,000 years some places have a little soil covering as when the glacier finally gave way to the milder climate of our present interglacial period. Winds from the west carry moisture which falls as heavy rain on the west facing hills while in the east, in the lea of these hills lies a milder, more fertile, region with farming and woodlands.

The wet west winds also promote raised peat bogs such as the Gairloch Conservation Unit, nearly 50,000ha allowing us a glimspe into the past with patches of the Caledonian forest still in evidence around Lochs Maree and Upper Torridon. This is red deer country; they are maintained as a commercial entity cropped on an annual basis by stalkers who pay for the privilege of killing them, and the deer and sheep and the estate managers together produce the new heather shoots to feed the unnaturally high number of grouse for the guns which in turn constitutes a controlling influence upon the regeneration of the old system of forest cover.

Not only sheep, grouse and deer dwell in these high places, eagles and greenshank breed here; the latter need peat bogs for their nesting sites and eagles the high crags and open spaces where they can build their eyries and find sufficient food in the form of mountain hares and carrion to see them through the year and raise their young, often only a single chick.

Move east, and you move into the milder Cromarty Firth. Huge autumn and winter gatherings of waders and geese cover the muddy sands of Nigg and Munlochy Bays. It is a region of the most astonishing beauty.

BEINN EIGHE (NCC) — *Summer*

This area has been designated an international Biosphere reserve under the UNESCO scheme and is invaluable for all the many fragments of formerly widespread Highland habitats including the remnant of old Caledonian pine forest that grows from the shores of Loch Maree up the hillsides to nearly twelve hundred feet above sea level. It is a landscape of alpine plants and moss-hung trees where wild cats and pine martens hunt in the quiet forest where foxes and stoats also live; as winter approaches stoats have the ability to change colour into a coat of pure white ermine.

Winter comes early to this region and stays late; nature rules with a rod of ice. Birdlife is specialised — cole tits and woodpeckers co-exist, and summer birds like redstarts also take advantage of the woodpecker's industry. Surprisingly willow warblers are regular songsters here arriving in April as the snow departs. Crossbills depend upon the continuance of mature Scots pine and are common in the woods above Loch Maree. High rainfall and pure air accounts for a wide range of bryophytes, lichens and liverworts. It is a place both forbidding and beautiful.

4800ha – Map ref: NG 9862

HANDA (RSPB) — *Summer*

The great stack of Handa is perhaps the best known seabird colony in the north of Scotland with its immensely tall cliffs and weathered columnar stacks full of ledges custom made for seabirds. Auks and kittiwakes take advantage of the many nest sites and the population is enormous. Guillemot stand shoulder to shoulder protecting their gravity defying eggs, and razorbills too nest in huge numbers.

The reserve does not consist only of coastline, inland several small lochs provide a place for freshwater birds to bathe and drink, and the island also has a small flock of barnacle geese to graze the short turf while areas of tussocky grass provide nest sites for a few pairs of arctic skua which make life hazardous for the eider.

766 acres – Map ref: NC 130480

INVERNAVER (NCC) — *Summer*

Invernaver boasts a series of habitats similar to the machair of the northern isles where sand driven inshore contributes to the fertility of the soil by carrying shelly fragments that neutralise the acid peat providing an excellent growing medium for many plants. Wind and a fairly harsh winter climate ensures that few trees of any size are able to grow, but a belt of birch woodland along the lower slopes of the Naver provides shelter for wild cats, foxes, badgers and otters. On the lochans and moorland bogs greenshank breed.

552ha – Map ref: NC 6961 / 681612

LOCH FLEET (Scottish WT) — *Summer* (Flowers/ breeding birds) *Winter* (Wildfowl)

This tidal basin is a magnet for birds all year round, but especially in winter when wildfowl come in considerable numbers — mallard, teal, red-breasted merganser, eider and long-tailed duck. In summer the reserve takes on another face, the breeding duck include eider and shelduck, and terns fish in the rich shallow waters. The sand bar across the mouth of the sea loch is a favoured place for common seals to haul out.

Inland the mainly planted forestry woodlands have a reasonable plant and bird population with breeding siskins and that showy grouse the capercaillie; crossbills take advantage of the seeds in the pine cones.

709ha – Map ref: NH 7796

MUNLOCHY BAY (Highland RC) — *Autumn, winter*

An extremely rich sheltered area of tidal mudflats on the northern shore of the Murray Firth chiefly noted for huge flocks of up to a thousand wigeon that winter and feed here; also a roost for greylag and pink-footed geese in late winter.

443ha – Map ref: NH 6753 / 657537

NIGG & UDALE BAYS (NCC) — *Late summer, winter*

A most productive area for birds and marine invertebrates; thousands of waders feed at low tide and flight out to roost on nearby farmland. There's a good eelgrass crop which attracts immense numbers of wigeon and to their chorus of whistles is added the throaty trumpeting of hundreds of whooper swans, but for sheer spectacle there is little to match the sight of ten thousand or so wintering greying geese. Other waterfowl include pink-footed geese and pintail in small parties. In all a very exciting place.

Map ref: NH 7873 and 7367

PRIEST ISLAND (RSPB) *Late spring, summer*

Priest Island should be renamed storm petrel island for on this piece of grass-topped inaccessible sandstone the largest colony of storm petrels, over ten thousand pairs, breed in burrows beneath the turf. A few pairs of greylag also breed beside the several freshwater lochs; otters too are here in small numbers.

121ha – Map ref: NC 9303

STRATHY BOG (NCC) — *Spring*

Dwarf birch and sundews are a common feature of this reserve reputed to be one of the best examples of a low lying blanket bog in Britain. It is a living example of a once common habitat now extremely rare through changes in climate and exploitation by man.

49ha – Map ref: NC 7955

TORRIDON (NTS) — *Late spring, summer*

Man has wrought great changes by felling the old pine forests, grazing sheep and encouraging deer; in centuries past wolves would have taken out the weak and unwary and kept the herds in check, now the wolf is a memory. Deer are capable of living in these threatening hilly areas even when the weather is inclement, where only golden plover, curlew and golden eagle would notice them. The deer control the regeneration of Scots pine woodland and the rainfall encourages a deep blanket of moss, often heavy with moisture. Pickings are thin and wildlife is specialised, but it is the beauty, the almost primeval atmosphere that makes it so fascinating.

Walkers should always be prepared for the saturating mists that frequently wreath the high ground; even on seemingly fine days the weather can change dramatically.

The action of glaciers has created particular landscape features, piles of glacial debris form regular hills and in Glen Torridon are so common it is known as the corrie of a hundred hills. The skyline is often enlivened with the slow regular wing beats or soaring flight of the most magnificent of our native birds of prey, the golden eagle. These and the swift flying peregrine are beginning to repopulate the highlands since their numbers crashed in the 1950s due to pesticide poisoning, mainly used in sheep dips and as seed dressings. These poisons are no longer used and the birds breeding success is higher in consequence, though there are problems looming with the increased leisure use of the Highlands.

6518ha – Map ref: NG 9059

HIGHLAND SOUTH

The region is enhanced by its majestic scenery. On a fine summer day, when the clouds cross the rugged Cairngorm mountains like galleons in full sail, and the curlew and golden plover commune with the wind, few places could be more beautiful, yet this landscape of forests and hills has seen more than its fair share of calumny. The highland clearances are a case in point bringing about the destruction of a centuries old way of life for crofters and clansman and the end of the widespread forests of Scots pine that once clothed these hills. A fragile one per cent of the old Caledonian pine forest remains but the gnarled trees, growing in an understory of bilberry and heather, look much the same as they did before the clearances.

"My Heart's in The Highlands" — Burns

My Heart's in the Highland's, my heart is not here;
My Heart's in the Highlands a chasing the deer;
Chasing the wild deer, and following the roe;
My Heart's in the Highlands, wherever I go.

Robert Louis Stevenson used these Glens and hillsides as the backdrop for his story "Kidnapped"; the drama of the surroundings fits the drama of the story. However, it seems unlikely that Stevenson himself ever enjoyed a night spent sleeping under the stars cradled in a bed of heather — the famous Scottish highland midges and mosquitos can make life unbearable.

The Romans feared the warlike tribes of Caledon who were toughened by the harsh climate, for cold air from the snow covered mountains can wash downwards unexpectedly in a bone chilling flood even in late spring; sensibly the Romans stayed south of the wall built on the orders of General Hadrian. Their laws and straight roads hardly impinged on the Celtic culture of the highlands. Even today, nearly two thousand years later, this rugged terrain has changed little and the thousands of visitors who make the long trek north in search of solitude and beauty can still find what they are looking for; peace and quiet reigns here enabling rare birds and animals to breed. Osprey and golden eagle, marten and Scottish wildcat prey upon the black and the red grouse and the huge numbers of waders that choose these isolated moors and woodlands to rear their young.

ABERNETHY FOREST (RSPB) — *Spring, summer*

The acquisition of this area of the Cairngorm slopes and old Caledonian pine forest, nearly ten miles across, is perhaps one of the most exciting conservation projects of the latter part of the 20th century. Lying in the heart of one of Scotland's most scenically diverse landscapes and cut by the river Nethy, it abuts the Loch Garten reserve. A two hundred year management plan is being worked out to enable natural regeneration of the Scots pine seedlings which entails excluding red deer that might damage the growing points. Some of the existing Scots pines are two centuries old and very large, but some are moribund, being saplings when wolves roamed the land. It's like a time warp, a glimpse of the past, when forests like this, with their turkey-sized capercaillie, unique Scottish crossbills and specialised crested tits, would have clothed the whole area and when swifts would have nested, not in the roof spaces of houses, but in old grren woodpecker holes in trees.

The woodland is full of mammals, the beautiful but destructive red deer, the shy roe deer, red squirrels, pine martens and Scottish wildcats all living interdependently much as they would have done before man colonised this area. The woods also support a wide variety of native plants, with specially adapted orchids such as coral root, creeping lady's tresses and lesser twayblade. The plants that form the understory range from heather and bilberry to juniper adapted to cope with twenty degrees of frost and the cold air that comes sweeping down from the high tops in mid January.

On the high ground you'll find dotterel and the increasingly rare greenshank which breeds here. The population of birds of prey is extremely varied, with golden eagles, peregrines, merlins, sparrowhawks and hen harriers; on the burns and lochans red-throated divers, teal and wigeon and the ever present dippers and grey wagtails can be seen.

21,000 acres

BALMACARA (NTS) — *Late spring, summer*

Looking across the sound, on a fine day, from the Kyle of Loch Alsh to Skye and the scatter of islands like eider ducklings around their mother, is to see the coast of Wester Ross at its very best. Here agriculture is in tune with the environment, crofts and tiny fishing communities dot the deep cut sea lochs and inland lochans and the variety of habitats from sea coast to sheltered woodlands creates a naturally productive area all year round.

2274ha – Map ref: NG 7930

CAIRNGORMS (NCC) — *Late spring, summer*

The mountains dominate the landscape providing an immense watershed draining into the river Spey which, in turn, controls the natural economy of the region. The increase in winter sports has put pressure on the wildlife that may, in the long term, prove damaging; the high top flora and fauna is alpine and birds like the ptarmigan find their resting and feeding grounds disturbed by skiers and ramblers. Even in summer the mountains may still hold small pockets of snow in sheltered corries which create a micro-climate in the valleys below as descending cold air chills the plants struggling to survive. Rarities such as least willow, mountain hawkweed, alpine lady fern and arctic mouse-ear survive in these hills only because of this late snow which ensures little competition for these specialists. Low growing arctic species are well able to survive among the heather and in open places rose root, mountain sorrel and mountain saxifrage flourish.

The alpine flora gives way to stretches of Scots pine woodland with a high proportion of native birdlife. The only bird exclusive to the British Isles is the Scottish crossbill, a colourful seed eater that opens pine cones with its specially adapted bill. Tiny crested tits and siskins breed here, particularly the pine forests of Rothiemurchus where there are considerable numbers of red squirrels and black grouse and the Scottish wildcat, a predator whose presence can be detected by its scent marks and scratching posts; even so it's rarely seen being largely nocturnal.

Abernethy Forest

Reindeer, once indigenous to these mountains, have been reintroduced by man, the reindeer moss which forms the bulk of their diet grows in sufficient quantities for their needs. Red deer are the most common large mammal but their impact upon the natural regeneration of many trees and shrubs has meant that they have to be culled by shooting if the woodlands are to stand any chance of growing past the sapling state.

The Cairngorms are home to several pairs of eagles and peregrin falcons, and merlins are often seen, although the latter's sensitivity to disturbance is only just beginning to be understood. But the osprey's breeding success in recent years has meant they are becoming increasingly common.

CRAIGELLACHIE (NCC) — *Summer*

Spring and summer visitors to Aviemore see a different land to the skiers; beautiful elegant silver birch woods clothe the lower slopes and provide a suitable habitat for a large number of spring migrants, while the dominating wall of rock is a favoured breeding site for peregrine falcons. Doubtless they are attracted by the smaller birds that come to feed in the woods well known for their abundant plant and insect life particularly a Scottish moth called the Rannoch Sprawler whose yellowish green larvae feeds on the newly sprouting birch leaves. The Aviemore species is larger and greyer than its Rannoch relative and the adult moths can be found in early spring feeding on the sap which oozes from injuries in the bark.

260ha – Map ref: NH 8812

CULBIN SANDS (RSPB) — *Winter* (Duck/waders)
Spring, summer (Flowers/breeding birds)

The southern shores of the Murray Firth is the favoured wintering place for sea duck, large concentrations of long-tailed duck, surf and velvet scoters and red-breasted mergansers. The area consists of salt marsh and foreshore with creeks and sandbars and large sandflats, a seaward extension of the inland dune system which, although forested, constitutes the largest sand-dune system in the British Isles.

Loch Garten

The creeks can be dangerous, but the flocks of waders are most impressive and varied with bar-tailed godwit and oyster-catchers, dunlin and curlew as regular visitors.
2,130 acres – Map ref: NH 901573

GLEN AFFRIC (FC) — *Spring, summer*

A tourist's delight, Glen Affric is scenically most attractive as well as supporting a wide natural history interest. Along the southern shores of Loch Affric and Loch Benevean the Forestry Commission manage a large area of native pine woods where deer have been controlled, and the level of natural regeneration has proved the value of this policy; there is also a plan to plant young trees grown from seeds gathered from the Scots pine trees already growing here. Such a regime favours native birds and animals, and a healthy population of Scottish crossbills, black grouse, capercaillie and red squirrels is growing steadily. Golden eagles hunt over the reserve and peregrines are frequent visitors in summer; and while the Lochs are favoured by goosander the burns and rivers that fill and empty from them are the haunt of dippers. In autumn the rowan and birch respond with a splash of colour, startlingly beautiful in contrast with the sombre Scots pinewoods.
1265ha – Map ref: NH 2424

INSH MARSHES (RSPB) — *Spring, summer*

Situated in the Upper Spey valley, where a drift of glacial moraine has raised the valley bottom, the river floods out on to the marshes below Loch Insh. There are excellent hides and an information centre on a bluff overlooking the lower part of the reserve where a black-headed gull nesting colony thrives in spring. The breeding bird population is rich and varied, including goldeneye, tufted duck, curlew, snipe, redshank, sedge and grass-hopper warblers.

In the woodlands redstarts, woodcock and tree pipits nest regularly and the occasional pied flycatcher breeds in the nest boxes. Osprey, hen harriers and buzzards hunt over this area as does the large predatory goshawk and its smaller relative, the sparrowhawk. In winter large numbers of whooper swans, pink-feet and greylag geese pass through on migration.

You may be lucky and see an otter or a roe deer from one of the hides. The marshes are a haven for many migrant's such as a pair of bluethroats who, in 1968, decided Insh was an excellent place to rear their young. Sadly the nest was predated before the eggs hatched and this remains the only authenticated record of these birds nesting in the British Isles.
1,922 acres – Map ref: NH 775998

LOCH GARTEN (RSPB) — *Spring, summer*

Famous in the annals of bird conservation; half a century after being extinguished as a breeding species in Britain, a pair of osprey, large fish-eating birds of prey, built their huge nest in the pines near this lovely Loch. Their first attempts to raise a family were frustrated by egg collectors and a lack of enthusiasm shown by local riparian owners who feared for their fishing. Pesticides present in the environment did not help and affected the hatching success of the eggs. However, the birds persevered and in the 1960s began to breed successfully; a carefully wardened hide and information centre was set up to allow the public to see the nest since when over one million people have seen the ospreys, now breeding in a number of sites in Scotland. It was an important success at a time when wildlife conservation was at an all time low.
2949 acres – Map ref: NH 978184

SPEY VALLEY (Strathfarrar NCC) — *All year*

The Spey is a natural artery running through this magnificent region, the spectacular valley can boast a past as geologically turbulent and unstable as the history of its more recent human inhabitants. The river meanders to the sea over a moraine-filled flood plain, and in summer the area is full of life, a far cry from the turbid winter scene or when the snows melt on the Cairngorms releasing floods of icy water turning the marshes into a huge shallow loch. This periodic flooding has created the largest flood plain marsh in Scotland, and the mud that comes down with the water helps to maintain the fertility of this important wetland area. The Spey is one of the best salmon rivers in Scotland, it's fished throughout its length and still supports otters in quite large numbers, but pressure from riparian interests, and the presence of escaped mink has led to the decline of this beautiful animal over the entire course of the river.

Man's impact on the Spey valley is dramatic. Tourism has altered the peaceful character of the region, bringing difficulties in reconciling prosperity and pollution, access and environmental degradation. The high, wild places, previously seen only by the occasional shepherd, crofter, deer stalker or lone walker in search of solitude, now have to bear the brunt of a constant flow of people; the losers are the birds and animals, plants and insects for which the high mountains and heathery slopes are their only home. The growth in tourism has led to theme parks, like that at the Rothiemurchus Estate, or the Highland Wildlife Park between Kingussie and Aviemore, and this may be the way forward, channelling thousands of feet away from the wild places, and allowing people a less damaging insight into the fragility and interdependence of this region.

LOTHIAN

It's interesting to conjecture what the face of this part of Scotland looked like before the onset of the ice age. The soft rocks have been all but worn away by the friction and pressure of countless millions of tonnes of ice, fracturing the limestone and sandstone into a paste of fertile rubble; the hard basalt plugs at the centre of long dead volcanoes withstood the onslaught, but the softer material of the cone was eroded. Not only would the countryside have been different, the animals and birds would have been subtropical, with hippos and forest elephants, and strange flamingo-type birds. All this was swept away with the ice, and with it the fertility of the uplands, to be replaced by the landscape we know today.

The rocks exposed by glacial scour were not all hard and unyielding. Some, like the carboniferous limestone on the Barns Ness shoreline indicate great wealth for deep beneath the surface lies coal and this mineral wealth and the development it brought had a secondary effect; it prevented the remainder of the Scottish forests vanishing into the charcoal fuelled blast furnaces of the iron and steel works. Coal mining is in decline now, and the spoil heaps and workings are blending into the overall scenery.

The Lothian woodlands are varied, some are relics of the ancient pine and oakwood that dominated this region up until three centuries ago, but they have been largely replaced with grouse moors and farmland, and the ever present scourge of Scotland's wild and beautiful places, regimented conifer plantations with their dearth of wild-life diversity. Nevertheless the coastline is beautiful with a wide variety of maritime habitats ranging from high craggy cliffs to the broad sand and mud flat found on the Tyne estuary with dune systems more reminiscent of the west than the east coast of Scotland.

The seabird colonies are immense. Bass Rock supports a gannet city of breeding pairs nearly ten thousand strong; the specific name of the gannet (Sula bassana) was chosen because of its association with this bird-rich volcanic plug. The seal colonies off Gullane Bay on the Hummel rocks suffered badly from the infection that so damaged the whole seal population in the North Sea but with careful management they may recover and rise to former numbers. We could not contemplate the Scottish coast without the silkies, the people of the sea.

But northward far, with purer blaze,
On Ochil mountains fell the rays,
And as each heathy top they kiss'd,
It gleam'd a purple amethyst.
Yonder the shores of Fife you saw;
Here Preston-Bay and Berwick-Law:
    And, broad between them roll'd,
The gallant Firth the eye might note,
Whose islands on its bosom float,
    Like emeralds chas'd in gold.

— Sir Walter Scott

ABERLADY BAY (East Lothian DC) — *Spring, summer* (Breeding birds/flowers) *Winter* (Wildfowl/waders)

This large bay, sand, mud-flats, dunes and grassland forms a vital link in the chain of quiet places where migrant birds can rest after long sea crossings and fuel up prior to resuming the journey to their northern breeding grounds. A large part of the flats is under water at high tide which presents a perfect opportunity to study the massed flocks of waders and wildfowl as they wait for the tide to turn. The shelduck and eider are particularly interesting, and in autumn seals haul out on the sandflats. They keep as far away as possible as they have been much persecuted and have every reason to fear man.

In winter sea duck gather in the outer Forth despite some pollution and while the number of scoters is declining long-tailed duck and eider are on the increase; at this time mud-flats are alive with dabbling duck. The region behind the mobile dune system harbours a fascinating plant life, grass of parnassus and autumn gentian grow where the influence of the calcareous shell debris enriches the sand and where water lays in dune slacks northern and early marsh orchids appear.
582ha – Map ref: NT 4681

BASS ROCK (Privately owned) — *Spring, summer*

A remnant of past volcanic upheavals that churned and split the rock formations of this region when Bass Rock was left standing proud and gaunt. For some time on dry land then as the sea level rose when the glaciers melted, it became an island, its safe nesting ledges a boon for the hordes of seabirds that throng these cold food-rich waters; its evolution as a colony is logical, cut off as it is from land-based predators.

Gannets are the rock's best known inhabitants for although there are many thousand pairs of kittiwakes and auks, the gannets steal the plaudits by sheer size and weight of numbers. Nearly ten thousand pairs nest here, the original gannetry on the cliff ledges expanding under population pressures to take in part of the cliff-top.
10ha – Map ref: NT 602873

Eider Duck   *Lothian*

EAST LOTHIAN COAST (East Lothian Countryside Ranger Service) — *All year*

The East Lothian Coastline presents a series of challenges. Contrasts in land use with which the birds, if not the human inhabitants, have come to terms and which the birds have used to their advantage. The fly ash beds of the Cockenzie Power Station are a case in point; built to dispose of fine ash from the coal-fired boilers, it is mixed with water and pumped into large shallow lagoons where it dries and compacts forming a surface not unlike mud-flats. Wading birds, displaced from other sites, soon realised that predators were not prepared to venture out onto this surface and now huge numbers of small waders roost on the ash beds. The flocks of knot in particular are numbered in thousands.

East of the mining spoil heaps of Preston Pans the winds howl over the exposed shingle of Gosford Bay and the wintering flocks of eider and diving birds; it's a prime site for wintering Scandinavian divers, and Slavonian grebes in flocks of a hundred or more, mixed in with red-necked grebe and great northern divers on the turbulent waters of the Firth.

Another haven for seabirds is off Gullane point. The summer flocks of common scoters number over a thousand, and in winter velvet scoters and long-tailed duck join in. The dunes at Gullane have been subjected to human pressure; erosion, a natural fact of dune systems, accelerated until they were in danger of being blown away altogether wrecking the entire habitat. Restoring the natural plant cover on the dunes, and a reduction in random access has reversed the trend.

Past Bass Rock, pressure on the coastline diminishes, and the Tyninghame estuary and old red sandstone cliffs support a thriving flora and fauna. The Castle of Dunbar overlooks the sea and provides an excellent vantage point; four species of skua pass this way, arctic and great skua often appearing in large numbers. The age of the rocks can be seen at low tide and the old red sandstone gives way to pale carboniferous limestone and sandstone, the former extremely rich in tropical marine fossils also found along the coast south of Barns Ness. The lime-rich base rock dictates the flora here, and there are many plants adapted to this particular habitat.

FORTH ISLANDS (RSPB) — *Spring, summer*

A group of small offshore islands Fidra, Eyebroughty and The Lamb which enjoy none of the spectacular scenery of Bass Rock. However, they are exceptionally well placed for breeding seabirds. The Lamb Island has large colonies of cormorant and auks and a smaller, but significant, nesting of kittiwakes while the other islands have puffins and auks and eider duck in considerable numbers. Lesser black-backed gulls and herring gulls restrict the success of colonial ground nesters such as terns, but common and arctic terns have bred here.

   Fidra – Map ref: NO 513867
   Eyebroughty – Map ref: NO 495863
   The Lamb – Map ref: NO 535866

GLADHOUSE (Lothian RC) — *All year*

An inland drinking water reservoir softened by a wooded shoreline. Small islands add a more natural look, and it has become a regular resting place for pink-footed geese; more than thirteen thousand have been recorded here. In winter over a thousand duck gather in mixed flocks, mostly mallard, but pintail and wigeon appear in some numbers as do diving duck, especially goldeneye and tufted. When the levels in the reservoir are lower than normal areas of mud along the margins attract migrant waders on passage.
162ha – Map ref: NT 3054

JOHN MUIR COUNTRY PARK (East Lothian DC) — *Spring* (Flowers/breeding birds) *Winter* (Waders/duck)

An extensive reserve taking in part of the fascinating Tyne estuary, dunes, beach and cliffs. Better known as Tyninghame, the estuary is sheltered by two sandpits — Sandy Hirst and Spike Island creating a resting place and feeding station for birds flying to and fro on migration. These two promontories hold back the flow of the fine organic silts that settle out to form the mud-flats and provide a home and food for a variety of organisms and invertebrates. This food supply is harvested by fish and fowl alike, and the wader population reflects the rich pickings to be found in the ooze. Over thirty species of waders have been recorded at Tyninghame, and these and the duck, geese and swans that winter here, make the vantage points on the estuary popular with bird-watchers.

The rocks are hard and of a great age, many are volcanic in origin and the flora reflects this with a wide variety of plants; some, like bloody cranesbill and bucks horn plantain are maritime in habit, unlike wild thyme which also appears, while on the steep cliffs of Dunbar the flora is more reminiscent of woodland with primrose, cowslips and oxlips growing in a majestic setting.
675ha – Map ref: NT 6480

RED MOSS OF BALERNO (Scottish WT) — *Late spring, summer*

Red Moss, known to be a fine example of its kind with great depths of peat (up to six metres) was once cut for fuel. It is typical with a drier central dome and wet edges where the sphagnum moss, of which there are six separate species, add mass to the developing bog.

In the surrounding wet area bog asphodel thrives with round-leaved sundew, a plant more normally found in a milder climate. In summer the marsh surrounding the central dome is bright with wetland flora such as ragged robin, marsh ragwort and cuckoo, and in spring and early summer the presence of so much shallow water is a magnet for amphibians, both frogs and toads breed here; needless to say the dragonfly population is substantial. Moths and beetles are the subject of a research project and the birdlife is typical of established wet woodland. On the open areas short-eared owls and the occasional hen harrier can be seen hunting.

23ha – Map ref: NT 165638

TAILEND MOSS (Scottish WT)** — *Spring, summer* (Flowers/insects) *Winter* (Wildfowl)

Tailend Moss is a particularly interesting reserve supporting a wide variety of insects, birds and plants all closely interlinked by a common denominator — acid peat marsh. The reserve is known for its wide ranging insect fauna, including most species of dragonfly that appear in this part of Scotland, some six have been recorded. On the wetter areas bog asphodel, sundew and craneberry occur, and on the dry upper domes of the moss heather predominates.

There is a substantial list of breeding birds here with curlew, snipe, mallard and redshank. In winter there is also a wide range of wildfowl on the open waters with whooper swans and both diving and dabbling duck such as wigeon and goldeneye.

29ha

THORNTON GLEN (Scottish WT)** — *Spring*

Another segment of the old Scottish broadleaved forest with a wide variety of trees, including field maple at the very northern limit of its range. Ash is the principle tree with elm, holly and hazel bushes.

Fittingly for a wood with its own deer hart's tongue fern grows here along with six other species of fern and the moist environment encourages many bryophytes. Breeding birds include a good number of migratory species; redstarts and pied flycatchers take advantage of holes created by the industry of the green woodpeckers.

6ha

ORKNEY

The Orkneys have a certain magic; so far north they sit closer to the arctic circle than to the parliament that governs them, and the climate is not what you'd expect either. The prevailing winds ought to freeze the land solid, but the warm waters of the gulf stream modify the temperatures, snow is short-lived and very hard frosts are rare. There is plenty of wind, but the lack of high ground keeps the wet westerlies at bay and the rainfall is no more than moderate.

The islands have been suffering from depopulation for more than a century which has spelt the end of crofting, especially on the smaller scraps of land on the North Sound. Nevertheless the people that stayed have made for themselves a fine life envied by many for its tranquillity and sense of satisfaction; although the reality of life on an island is hard with few modern facilities and a higher cost of living than on the mainland.

The wildlife here is very special, the lack of predators, other than domestic cats and dogs means that ground nesting birds have a better chance of success. The style of farming too, encouraged by conservation societies and grants from central government, has helped to maintain a way of life compatible with wildlife. The increasing interest in natural history in the rest of Britain means that the islands have become a marketable commodity and the tourist season now provides much needed work and finance to an otherwise subsistence economy. Providing tourism does not make unreasonable demands upon the native islanders, an influx of outsiders to admire their wildlife could be a valuable asset.

BIRSAY MOORS AND COTTARSGARTH (RSPB) — *Spring, summer*

Looking out over Eynhallow Sound and the Loch of Swannay, this undulating heather moorland has clothed the old red sandstone with a variety of swards from dry heather to blanket bog and a marshy area with streams. The bird of prey population is extensive which may have something to do with the large number of indigenous

Orkney voles; ground nesting kestrels take advantage of them too as do short-eared owls. A few pairs of merlin, a rare falcon on the mainland, seem to be holding their own finding adequate food in the shape of small birds. There is a high nesting population of hen harriers, colonies of arctic and great skuas or bonxies, and the larger gulls are also present. Other breeding birds include waders such as dunlin, oyster-catchers, golden plover and curlew while the smaller birds include stonechats and wheatear.
5781 acres – Map ref: HY 3719

COPINSAY (RSPB) — *Spring, summer*

Copinsay and Corn Holm support a vital seabird colony; the cliffs rise 18m from the sea and hold an immense variety of birds from the occasional corncrake or raven to vast colonies of thirty to thirty five thousand guillemots, ten thousand kittiwakes and hundreds of razorbills and fulmar petrels. There are puffins on the island but they are fewer in number than the more common auks and the attractive black guillemots jostle for positions on the rocks and ledges. There are also shag colonies, but their numbers are small. Colonies of herring, lesser black-backed and common gulls mean that an unguarded chick or egg falls prey to their powerful beaks.

On Corn Holm, a scrap of rock joined at low tide by a storm beach, arctic terns nest and on the Horse of Copinsay, the larger more robust cormorants build their seaweed Castles.
375 acres – Map ref: HY 610010

HOBBISTER (RSPB) — *Spring, summer*

Predominantly heather moorland with bogs and fen drained by the Swartaback burn; also low sea cliffs above Waulkmill Bay with a small area of salt marsh, and bogs with a flora that includes round-leaved sundew, butter-wort and bog asphodel. Birds are the principle interest with merlin and short-eared owl, hen harrier, red grouse, snipe, curlew, red throated diver, twite, lesser black-backed gulls and common gulls; while fulmars, ravens, eider duck, red breasted merganser and black guillemots nest on the coast.
1875 acres – Map ref: HY 381068 / 396070

NORTH HILL, PAPA WESTRAY (RSPB) — *Spring, summer*

A maritime heath composed of heather, sedge, crowberry and the arctic relict creeping willow, borders the low sandstone cliffs. Best known for its very large colony of arctic terns, which nest close to arctic skua, eider, ringed plover, oyster-catchers and dunlin while wheatears nest in holes in the ground. Some puffins and black guillemots breed here too, and large numbers of razor-bills, common guillemots, kittiwake and shag nest on the low cliffs with the rock doves. This was the last breeding site of the great auk in Britain before it became extinct. The plant life is surprisingly abundant with Scottish primrose, alpine meadow rue and mountain everlasting; frog orchid is also found growing here.
510 acres – Map ref: HY 496538

NORTH HOY (RSPB) — *Spring, summer*

North Hoy is best known for "The Old Man of Hoy", a pinnacle of rock eroded from the mainland by time and the sea, but there are even more spectacular features such as the immense cliffs at St John's Head which rise 1100ft. The reserve is composed of heather moor-land dissected by glacial valleys. Large populations of great and arctic skuas breed here as do red grouse, golden plover, dunlin, curlew, hen harrier, merlin, short-eared owls, twite and greater black-backed gulls. Guillemots, razorbills, shag and cormorant nest on the cliffs. A pair of peregrines predate the doves and seabirds. ravens too are resident and there is also a colony of manx shearwater in the turf along the clifftop. Mountain hares are also found here.
9700 acres – Map ref: HY 223034 / ND 203995

NOUP CLIFFS, WESTRAY (RSPB) — *Spring, summer*

One of the largest seabird colonies in Britain, Noup Cliffs harbours immense numbers of guillemots, razor-bills, kittiwakes, puffins, shag, cormorants, herring gulls and greater black-backed gulls. Ravens nest on the cliffs in early spring and grey seals and small cetaceans appear offshore. The site is dangerous and care is needed.
1 ½ miles of cliff – Map ref: HY 392500

Oystercatchers

OUTER HEBRIDES

Blue Islands are pullin' me away,
There laughter puts the leap upon the lame,
The blue Islands form the Skerries to the Lewes,
Wi' heather honey taste upon each name.
— Kenneth Macleod

The Hebrides share many of the problems and satisfactions of island communities, but the presence of thriving wildlife is proving a great help to the economy. Situated in the gulf stream wet westerly winds are a fact of daily life, but when the sun is shining and the corncrakes call few places can match these lovely islands. They have a long history, being a remnant of volcanic action, hard rocks have been softened by time and blanketed with peat and moraine as the glaciers retreated leaving behind a cargo of pulverised rock. In places the peat is very thick and where it meets the salt-laden winds from the Atlantic, sand and shelly fragments blown inland form a fertile and special grassland rich in plant life known as machair; this unusually fertile enclosed meadowland provides a prolific crop of hay, and is also home to the corncrakes. The islands have been inhabited for many thousands of years by the descendants of a Celtic race whose language still survives. Later the Vikings invaded and settled imparting Norse place-names to many areas. More recently depopulation has been dramatic, only fourteen of the islands are now permanently settled, the other one hundred and six named islands are deserted for much of the year. However, it has to be said that what is bad for people is sometimes good for wildlife and the peace and quiet are perfect for birds, seals and otters.

BALRANALD, NORTH UIST (RSPB) — *Spring, summer*

Still a crofting community North Uist exhibits prime examples of the machair community where sea-blown shelly fragments provided additional fertility to the peaty soil. There is a shallow acidic loch, an excellent spot for corncrake and the occasional pair of red-necked phalaropes, the female of which is the brighter of the two, she lays the eggs and leaves the male to incubate and care for the young. Lapwing, snipe, ringed plover and dunlin nest here in large numbers as do teal, shoveller, gadwall, wigeon and the mute swan which prefer the marshes. Other breeding birds include little and arctic tern, twite, eider and black guillemot. Bewick swans are regular visitors in winter as are greylag geese, and the island is also known for birds of prey and the many passage migrants seen in spring and autumn. Grey seals breed on a nearby island.
1625 acres – Map ref: NF 706707

LOCH DRUIDIBEG, SOUTH UIST (NCC) — *Summer*

This extensive reserve holds the most important greylag breeding colony in Britain. Other features include dwarf willows, trees stunted by wind. Much of the land has been denuded of tree cover by burning and grazing, but there are plenty of plants on the machair to produce a rich hay crop in June. The machair is attractive to corncrakes and this is an excellent place to hear them. Red-breasted merganser, mute swan, heron, buzzard and red grouse are all found here while waders such as snipe, redshank, dunlin, lapwing, twite and corn bunting are dependant upon food from the hay fields where they make easy pickings for any visiting merlins. Occasionally a golden eagle may be seen.
1677ha – Map ref: NF 7937

NORTH RONA & SULA SGEIR (NCC)** — *All year*

NCC Inverness must be informed of proposed visits. Renowned as one of the largest breeding grounds for grey seals. From September to December seal cows gather to give birth, and up to two thousand pups are born. The steep barren rock of Sula Sgeir is famous for its gannetry where each year a crop of squabs is legally taken by the Islanders of Lewis. North Rona is larger and was farmed even before recorded times; there is an important colony of Leach's petrel and storm petrel and large numbers of fulmars, puffins, guillemots, razorbills and kittiwakes nesting on the cliffs.
130ha – Map ref: HW 8132 / 6230

ST KILDA (NTS/NCC) — *May to July*

A dramatic site for seabirds, St Kilda is the repository of several natural history records. Hirta is the most remote inhabited island in Great Britain and has the highest cliffs at one thousand four hundred and ten feet, rising sheer from the sea at Conachair. The last great auk in Great Britain was killed on Stac an Armin in 1840; this and nearby Stac Lee are the two tallest stacks in Great Britain. St Kilda hosts the largest and oldest fulmar colony and the stacks at Boreray support a vast gannetry with over fifty thousand pairs, the largest gathering in the world; yet the smallest native is the most famous, the St Kilda wren, larger than its mainland counterpart and greyer in colour, it is still much in evidence. Other creatures have been brought to the islands, though the primitive soay sheep that make a living feeding on seaweed and poor pasture look much the same as sheep belonging to neolithic pastoralists.
846ha – Map ref: NA 1000

SHETLAND

FAIR ISLE (NTS) — *May through July* (breeding birds)
September, October (Migration)

Forty kilometres off the mainland of Britain Fair Isle is ideally situated for migrants from all over the northern hemisphere; the bird observatory is constantly capturing, ringing and releasing birds new to the British list. The islanders, mainly fishermen and crofters, long depended upon the birds that throng to their island in the breeding season. The seabird colonies that mass on the red sandstone cliffs and in the turf burrows along the coastline are extremely varied; thousands of puffins return to breed as do more than a hundred pairs of storm petrels. The cliff nesters breed in staggering numbers twenty five thousand pairs of fulmars, twelve thousand pairs of kittiwake, twenty thousand or more guillemots and several thousand pairs of razorbills pack the guano-whitened cliff ledges. Gannets also breed here, but in relatively small numbers — a new colony, established in the mid 1970s, has now risen to nearly 200 pairs.

The waters of the North Sea and Atlantic produce huge numbers of small fish which in turn provide the birds with food, though over-fishing by man has reduced the small species like sandeels once found in untold millions, and the breeding success of the auks and terns has suffered accordingly. Grey seals fish in the cold waters or haul out in the many sea worn caves in the soft red rocks. Inland the plant life is extremely varied and the presence of fertiliser from the droppings of large numbers of arctic and great skuas helps to maintain the fertility of relatively impoverished soils.
830ha – Map ref: HZ 2172

FETLAR (RSPB) — *Spring, summer* (Breeding birds)
September (Migrants)

In my days with the RSPB I remember vividly when the snowy owl, a frequent visitor to this group of islands, appeared on Fetlar and attempted to breed. They finally succeeded in 1967, and even today Fetlar is the only place in Great Britain proved to have successful breeding snowy owls. Moreover, the island can boast more than one species of bird; there is a wide breeding population of waders most exciting of which are the whimbrel and golden plover. Dunlin and curlew also breed here as do storm petrels and manx shearwaters and the burrows are hotly contested with the considerable puffin colony.

Otters are a feature, these engaging animals lead a far more marine type of existence here and perhaps because they have been less persecuted than on the mainland they are more active by day. Other mammals live around the island's shoreline; grey and common seals breed and their numbers are still quite strong despite the epidemic of distemper that affected the North Sea population of common seals. The very special wildlife here lives under the shadow of the oil terminal at Sullom Voe, tucked into a corner of Yell Sound; an oil spill occurring at breeding time would prove disastrous!
1700 acres – Map ref: HU 604916

FOULA — *Spring, summer*

There are literally tens of thousands of seabirds here of many species — puffins, guillemots, razorbills and kitti-wakes; fulmars in incredible numbers, in excess of thirty five thousand pairs breed on the cliffs where they first established themselves in the late 19th century. Foula is the repository of thirty per cent of the northern hemisphere's population of great skuas, while smaller numbers of arctic skuas also breed here. Tube noses are an island speciality with storm petrels and manx shearwaters, and the only definite breeding colony of Leach's petrel which have established themselves on this very precious island. Three thousand arctic terns are part of the magnificent mix of breeding birds.
1380ha – Map ref: HT 9639

HERMA NESS (NCC) — *Spring, summer*

The next stop north of Herma Ness is the arctic circle, the island is the furthest northerly point in Great Britain with very long arctic days and short nights in summer when the sun hardly sets. Winter is quite a different story and spring is always welcome, especially as it heralds the return of untold numbers of seabirds. The gannets have taken advantage of man's protection and their numbers have risen to a staggering five thousand pairs since they first appeared here in the late 1920s; they have been accompanied on their breeding stacks by a lone black-browed albatross since the early 1970s; the possibility of it being joined by a mate is remote because the conditions that would allow for it to cross the Doldrums from the southern hemisphere are very rare indeed; the fate of a single bird is always interesting. A few pairs of red-throated divers breed here, as do golden plover and whimbrel.

The seas that wash this island fuel the staggering numbers of seabirds with ample supplies of fish. Tens of thousands of puffins, guillemots, shearwaters and the islands speciality, the great skua (its numbers are approaching a thousand pairs) thrive on the bounty of the sea. The great skua is aggressive, their mastery of flight enables them to harry other birds into disgorgng the food they are carrying back to their young. Otters and seals

also take advantage of the prolific fish, and grey seals breed in the caves hollowed out by the sea. On land the plants are fascinating with moss campion and Shetland's speciality, an island sub-species of red campion.
964ha – Map ref: HP 6016

LUMBISTER (RSPB) — *Late spring, early summer*

Otters and red throated divers are the creatures to be seen at Lumbister, though there are many hundreds of breeding birds including waders like golden plover and dunlin. The twite, a small northern finch, breeds here and the merlin, a small declining falcon, is still seen with a reasonable degree of regularity in spring and summer. Otters are relatively common and less wary than their mainland counterparts, so there's a reasonable chance of

seeing one early in the morning or late evening.
4000 acres – Map ref: HU 509974

NOSS (NCC) — *Spring, summer*

One of the most important of the Shetland Isles for seabirds; erosion of the sandstone cliffs has created wonderful breeding ledges for auks and kittiwakes and some of the cliffs swarm with bird tenements six hundred feet from sea to grassy top, every ledge jammed full. In the breeding season sixty three thousand guillemots and twenty thousand kittiwakes make a fantastic sound on the headland; five thousand pairs of gannets breed here, but the fish-eaters do not have it all their own way for large colonies of skua and greater black-backed gulls exact a toll in fish and young birds taken from unguarded nests.
313ha – Map ref: HU 5540

SKYE
& THE
SMALL ISLES

What would the world me, once bereft
Of wet and wildness? Let them be left,
Oh let them be left, wildness and wet;
Long live the weeds and the wilderness yet.

EIGG (Scottish WT)** — *May through July*

Eigg reflects its turbulent geological past when volcanoes ripped through the baserock of ancient sands and limestones, creating a tangle of rock strata dominated by basaltic lava columns of pitchstone. These push the winds from the wide Atlantic upward wringing out the moisture from low clouds making the atmosphere wet and mild. The high rainfall encourages the ferns of which there are a number including Wilsons filmy fern.

The trees tend to be stunted and highly specialised and excellent examples can be seen in the hazel and rowan woodland that clings like a closely-cut hedge to the slopes facing the prevailing wind. These wind-trimmed woods support an interesting flora with carpets of bluebells in spring and a host of other plants like wood sorrel and wood anemone, wood sage and wild strawberry. Buzzards and ravens, and the occasional golden eagle soar along the buttresses seeking prey on the slopes

below. Any manx shearwater late leaving the burrow will have to run the gauntlet of the gulls and the watchers above. Where the land is cropped there are many orchid species and corncrakes breed in the summer.
608ha

RHUM (NCC) — *Late spring, summer*

A very important island in the northern hemisphere for birds, and recognised as such by UNESCO being designated a biosphere reserve which means a complete series of habitats protected for their unique ecological significance.

Rhum is best known for two ecological specialities; a nesting colony of manx shearwaters on the Hallival and Askival slopes and the reintroduced white-tailed sea eagle. The former are present in huge numbers, over a hundred and thirty thousand pairs burrow into the scree and turf and the sound of their return late at night is really exciting. The island has been carefully protected and studied by the NCC and the herd of red deer have been the subject of a research project for a number of years.

The return of the white-tailed sea eagles was the result of cooperation between commerce, conservation and the military for the first young birds were bought here by the Royal Air Force from Scandinavia funded by an insurance company Eagle Star. The project which began in 1975 reached fruition in the mid 1980s when the first birds began to pair. Since then they have nested and some young were fledged, and though it is early days and there have been losses among the parent birds and their young, on the whole the project is a success; other birds of prey include peregrine falcon who are very successful here. Many birds have been induced to stay and nest by tree planting which has ensured sites for them, now blackbirds are to be heard singing in the wildness of this fascinating island.

Other island specialities are butterflies which have intense colour variation from those on the mainland; dark green and small pearl-bordered fritillaries and common blues are abundant, making an extra special contribution to the island's wildlife.

10,684ha – Map ref: NM 3798

TOKAVAIG WOOD (Coille Thocabhaig) — *Late Spring*

Situated on the lower lobe of the main island of Skye this area of relict woodland is in the full flow of the westerly airstream from the Atlantic, in consequence it's damp; limestone and sandstone outcrops add to the potential and the range of plants and insects reflects this richness. The limestone carries ash, bird cherry and hazel and the more acid sandstone has a covering of oak woodland, while the moist conditions are conducive to the prolific growth of ferns and lichens.

81ha – Map ref: NG 6112

STRATHCLYDE NORTH

I will away to the Kyles
And the rain-shadowed isles,
Mosses of the sea,
And on far elfin strands,
On wide, unwandered sands,
I shall be free.

— Lewis Spence

From sea level to the purple hills of Rannoch Moor with the deer and merlins and the high cold call of curlew, there's a strange isolation which belies the close proximity to the bustle and clamour of the modern world. But it's all illusion for this part of Scotland has felt the hand of man since Celtic warlords cocked a snook at the invading Roman armies; communities have long farmed, mined and exploited the land. In many ways the forests of Strathclyde were more easily exploited than most, for a great deal of the original woodland was broadleaved rather than Scots pine; the remaining broadleaved woods have a superb show of trees and attendant wild communities and owe their continued existence to coppicing or pollarding, the former being more popular as it provides a more easily managed crop of poles and small timber; but the rapacious mouths of sheep and cattle and laterly deer, have suppressed the natural regeneration of coppice woodland, other than in fenced-off nature reserves.

Elsewhere conifers march rank upon rank across the landscape like a dark green tide suppressing the heather and gorse; the merlin and short-eared owl have gone, so too have black grouse and red grouse from the high peaty moorland, and curlew and ring ouzel are unable to nest among the tall regimented stands. The deep ploughing necessary to plant conifers drains the land, the peat soon dries out and begins to erode; in times of drought and forest fire the peat, product of ten thousand years, is burned away along with unique plant and animal communities.

For a short while, before the trees grow tall and shut out the light, there's an upsurge of life and short-eared owls can take advantage of the prolific short-tailed field vole population, but later on as the canopy closes over, the ground becomes sterile fit only to shelter the shyest of our native cervids, the roe deer; they venture out when evening falls to feed on the grass margins. Fortunately conifers cover only a part of this landscape and perhaps the region is best known for the islands — Mull, Jura, Islay, Tiree and Coll and the promontory of Kintyre all conjure up a series of natural history delights, and inspired Mendelsson; his Hebridean Overture and the evocative "Fingall's Cave" so accurately describes the pulse and flow of the sea.

Volcanism created the basalt octagonal supports of Fingal's cave and the intense geological variety found in this relatively small area. Later natural events and the restless sea blew dunes of fine shell-rich sand far inland forming fascinating environments that man tamed and cultivated; in Gallic this grassland interspersed with wild flowers and orchids is called "Machair", it's a special type of hay meadow flora with its own particular bird, the corncrake, which finds the method of agriculture in these remote islands to its liking, even so they are not common and their ratchet-like call is a delight to any naturalist.

ARDMORE (Scottish WT)** — *April through July* (Flowers/ Breeding birds) *September through March* (Wildfowl waders)

Ardmóre is particularly interesting for the range of habitats within its boundaries. The promontory, part of the Clyde estuary, consists of mud-flats, tidal salt marsh and foreshore where a host of birds and plants find shelter and food all year round; in summer the salt marsh areas are rich in flowering plants. The reserve shows the influence of past geological events and the raising and lowering of the sea level that is part of the nature of the Earth; there are some excellent examples of raised beaches and relict sea cliffs that have eroded into slopes. The foreshore provides a number of habitats and in winter there are large flocks of duck and waders feeding in the pools and probing the mud for worms and molluscs. *194ha*

ARGYLL FOREST PARK (FC and others) — *All year*

Designated in 1935 this is the oldest forest park in Scotland. Over the intervening fifty five years a great many facilities have been developed for walkers, naturalists, camping enthusiasts and even subaqua divers who explore the submerged caves in Loch Long. The park offers a tremendous range of landscapes from sea-shore to the ridge of hills known as the Arrochar Alps. You'll find relic species of plants and animals that grew after the end of the last Ice Age.

Bounded by water on three sides — two sea lochs and Loch Lomond to the east — there's a decidedly watery feel to the area which affects the temperature; twenty miles inland the hills are in excess of 1000m and the winter climate would normally be very hostile with little able to exist in the harsh conditions. However, the sea exerts its influence; even on the highest point of the park arctic alpine plants are able to flourish, and ptarmigan and mountain or variable hares breed, even hen harriers breed.

This is the territory of ravens, golden eagles, peregrines and very occasionally merlin, though the latter appear unable to withstand the increase in human activity often associated with commercial forestry and leisure pursuits. Buzzards, larger and infinitely more adaptable, are a common sight and make the most of the prey afforded by the forested areas as do the bird hunting sparrowhawks that patrol the forest rides on the look-out for siskins, tits, goldcrests and crossbills.

Both red and grey squirrels are seen and capercaillie can be heard and seen in spring performing their courting display. On the outskirts of the woodland black grouse have their Lek's or jousting grounds where the cock birds display to attract the grey camouflaged hens. The park is so large that animals as shy as otters can find peace and quiet and the rivers and sea lochs afford excellent fishing for this endearing mustilid.
240sq.km –

Ardgartan – Map ref: NN 272034
Glenbranter – Map ref: NS 112977
Kilmun – Map ref: NS 160825

BURG/MULL (NTS) — *All year*

Principally botanical in interest, nevertheless there is a wide range of birds here with terns frequenting the summer shoreline. There's also a very ancient landmark, a tree thought to be at least fifty million years old fossilised in the columnar basalt of a volcanic eruption that churned up this part of the Earth's crust shortly after the dinosaurs became extinct.
617ha – Map ref: NM 426266

CARRADALE (Scottish WT) — *Spring*

Overlooking Kilbrannan Sound, Carradale is famous as a sea-watching venue, the wealth of smaller sea mammals is remarkable and you can often see killer whales "Orca" and smaller dolphins and from the low grassy clifftops. Seabirds too are frequent visitors as are terns sea duck and skuas, and another speciality are otters who feed on the abundant marine life close to shore.
70ha – Map ref: NR 8137

INVERLIEVER (FC) — *All year*

An immense forestry holding composed of many habitats from damp deciduous mixed species woods and conifer plantation to high moorland. Bird and mammal populations are varied and comprise sika and red deer with roe deer in the wooded areas; other large mammals include a healthy badger population. On the moorland hen harriers nest and golden eagles can be seen, and red grouse are present all year. In spring the high ground is perfect for wheatears fresh from their migrations; the woodland birds depend upon the type of tree cover, redstarts nesting in pockets of deciduous woodland while the tiny and populous goldcrest prefers conifers.
13,383ha – Map ref: NM 9410

LOCH GRUINART/ISLAY (RSPB)** — *All year*

Situated at the head of Loch Gruinart, this reserve is invaluable for the huge flocks of Greenland Barnacle geese that winter here. The geese have aroused some bad feeling in the past with the agriculturalists on the island, but it is hoped the islanders will be able to gain economic benefit from the thousands of tourists who will come to see the wildlife whether it be barnacle geese or the hundreds of waders and duck and considerable flocks of white-fronted geese and swans that also winter here, or perhaps the sight of an otter fishing for butterfish. Chough can be seen from time to time, these elegant red-billed crows are nowhere near common and they are a delight to watch, particularly for their mastery of flight.
4087 acres

TAYNISH (NCC)* — *April- July*

Taynish looks out to the quiet waters of Loch Sween and the many islets; the coastal waters are unusually warm and shallow, perfect otter country and these charming mammals are frequently encountered in quiet bays, a number breed on the islets. The reserve comprises deciduous woodland, bog and heathland. The woodland is said to be the largest surviving remnant of ancient deciduous woodland in Scotland; much of it is oak with a mixture of ash, holly, rowan and hazel. Consequently, birdlife is extremely varied with redstarts, wood warblers and woodpeckers. In winter the interest switches to the coast where large numbers of duck, especially wigeon, and fish-eating birds such as mergansers and herons arrive to feed in the shallow water.

320ha – Map ref: NR 7384

STRATHCLYDE
SOUTH

Despite the fact that Glasgow, the most important commerical and industrial centre in Scotland, lies within the boundaries of the region, there is much of natural history interest here. In fact the very presence of Glasgow's population and its demand for food led to a regime of agriculture that has been less destructive of the woodlands and pastures than in other parts of lowland Scotland. Though the estuary of the Clyde is heavily industrialised, there are pockets of wildife significance, particularly the islands and the Knoll of Ailsa Craig far out in mid channel and, of course, the beautiful Isle of Arran.

Yon wild mossy mountains sae lofty and wide,
That nurse in their bosom the youth o' the Clyde,
Where the grouse lead their coveys thro' the heather to feed,
And the shepherd tends his flocks as he pipes on his reed.

The geology consists of ancient rocks of the Silurian and Ordovician period, the ice which blanketed the region in the last ice age mixed and matched the soils and left behind a range of uplands, ice worn valleys and drifts of moraine that have formed the basis of fertile farmland or upland bog dependant upon the elevation of the land. The gulf stream runs offshore and insulates the coastline from the harshness of a northern winter, though this kindness is tempered with abundant rain carried inland on the wet westerlies. The west winds blow dunes along the Strath-clyde coast in abundance forming a desert-like habitat where plants and animals struggle in the harsh dry soil, nevertheless many species have adapted well.

BARONS HAUGH (RSPB) — *All year*

Flooded land, marsh and woodlands make up this series of rich habitats on the edge of the Clyde, almost in the centre of Motherwell. In winter the reserve is full of wildfowl, especially whooper swans numbering as many as fifty in hard weather; other wildfowl include wigeon, teal, mallard, pochard and the elegant tufted duck. Many birds come here to nest and roost, and as spring approaches redshank, grasshopper, sedge and garden warblers, tree pipits and kingfishers breed in the woods and parkland.

240 acres – Map ref: NS 755552

BALLANTRAE (Scottish WT) — *Spring, summer*

One of the most endangered breeding terns, the elegant little tern, nests on the shingle spits — these birds, though few in numbers are the stars of the area; and on the lagoons that intersperse the shingle spits mergansers and shelduck feed and roost. The shingle itself harbours many plants that have adapted well to a life constantly under threat from salt — sea campion and sea sandwort are common.

22ha – Map ref: NX 0882

CLYDE ISLANDS / ARRAN — *All year*

An island made even more fascinating by the accident of geology for the great fault line that bisects Scotland runs through the middle creating a greater diversity of rocks for its size than in any other part of Great Britain. The geology is reflected in the structure of the hills and plains; at 2868ft. Goatfell (NTS) is dramatic, a rock climbers delight with sharp sides and rugged granite peaks, part of the lower slopes have been forested, but quite a few areas remain where the hand of man has fallen but lightly. Here golden plover breed and are observed by golden eagles overflying glens which in turn provide refuge for peregrine falcons, and where ravens soar on the updraughts.

On the plain a great deal of forestry has taken place and crossbills are able to breed; siskins too find shelter and ample breeding sites in the conifers, but hen harriers and the red-throated divers that nest on small areas of freshwater need open peaceful scenery in order to thrive. However, red squirrels are found in some numbers and red deer are also present.

Holy Island is an offlier to the main island mass but shares the adder, a reptile that does not appear on any other of the Clyde islands. For its size Holy Island has a far higher population of seabirds due in part to the steep rugged topography, but even this pales into insignificance when measured against the incredible productivity of Ailsa Craig, up to 20,000 pairs of gannets breed on this stump of land green-topped and white-flanked with birds. Many other seabird species especially auks and kittiwakes breed here too, and the overall population can rise to a staggering 30 - 35,000 pairs of breeding seabirds. The gannetry has long featured in the local economy, gannets having been taken for food for centuries. Now they are in little danger directly from man other than the threat of oil spill or chemical pollution of the fish on which they feed.

ENTERKINE WOOD (Scottish WT)** — *Spring through autumn*

One of the best features of this mixed woodland is a pair of tree hides bult to overlook an active badger sett so that the public can watch these shy attractive animals. This is such a good idea for it greatly enhances public awareness of the value of conservation.
5ha

FALLS OF CLYDE (Scottish WT) — *Spring, summer*

One of the most beautiful of Scotland's numerous beauty spots where the river tumbles step by step down a series of spectacular waterfalls with deep dark runs of clear relatively unpolluted water where trout swim and king-

fishers hunt the shallows. Here and there, where abundant insects are to be found, grey wagtails are common and along part of the watercourse woodlands and pasture provide a variety of habitats for many different birds and mammals; willow tits tend to be very local in distribution, but other scrub and woodland nesting birds include spring migrants like garden warblers and chiffchaffs and later on spotted flycatchers. Mammals are abundant in the woodland and badgers, foxes and two species of common bats, natterer's and pipistrelle, are frequently observed in early evening. Roe deer and red squirrel are also common.
55ha – Map ref: NS 8841

FEOCH MEADOWS (Scottish WT)** — *Mid June, July*

The lime-rich base rock produces a tremendous range of ancient meadowland plants. Particularly interesting are the frog and small white orchids with tiny flowers easily overlooked; not so the more showy and beautiful greater and lesser butterfly orchids. Such an abundance of flowers is a magnet for bees and other insects, especially butterflies.
10ha

LOCHWINNOCH (RSPB) — *Spring* (Breeding birds) *Winter* (Wildfowl)

Relatively little known outside Scotland, Lochwinnoch is of great interest for its many different habitats from open water to secluded pools and rough scrub woodland ideal for breeding waterbirds. The Society have created a series of breeding rafts within the compass of the hides and there is also a tower hide providing particularly good views winter and summer. It is a very productive area, over sixty five species are known to have nested and more than a hundred and fifty species have been recorded, including greylag geese. It's a particularly good place to see snipe.
388 acres – Map ref: NS 359581

TAYSIDE

Tayside is one of the most exciting areas in Scotland for naturalists, from the high ground and inland lochs to superb reed beds and coastal reserves on the eastern seaboard; the region ranges from heavily farmed fertile lowlands to the high ground of the Grampian mountains where eagles and dotterel are found. The highland fault runs through the region and the effects of past geological dramas associated with this have shaped the countryside and its wildlife.

There is a great deal of lime-rich land, including some limestone pavement, and many glens and lochs bear witness to the weight of ice that lay across the region during the last glaciation. As the ice melted debris ground the landscape into a series of smooth hills and valleys rounding away the rough edges and depositing sands and gravels in the valley bottoms and in many river beds. There are salmon and trout rivers aplenty and though some have been tamed by hydro electric power they are still dramatic when in spate with the salmon running up their ancient migration routes leaping the spectacular falls.

The lowlands have little of the ancient broadleaved forests that once clothed their fertile soils, but on the high ground there are still remnants of the old Caledonian pine forests; though most of their exciting diversity has long disappeared, felled or converted to alien conifer plantations. Some areas like the Black Wood of Rannoch give a flavour of the past, a time when wolves called in the glens. Capercaillie are relatively common in these pine forests, this is their natural habitat, but the birds you see today owe their existence to reintroduction from Scandinavia, the native birds having been shot out in Victorian times. Not so the osprey its reintroduction was less direct, the birds that nest here now arrive with the spring, and like those at Loch Garten, they excite great public interest. The more pairs that breed, the more will survive the long and difficult migration to and from Africa.

Where the river Tay meets the sea in the productive estuary of the Firth of Tay huge reed beds provide a winter haven for duck and geese. The cliffs have a role to play too in the nesting season and though not as dramatic as other Scottish sea cliffs, nevertheless the red sandstone heights north of Arbroath are a vital link in the chain of seabird colonies. Along the coast the winds that drive in off the cold North Sea carry with them sand and pulverised shell fragments forming sand-dunes and producing a particular set of environmental conditions for specialised wildlife.

Tayside, however, is about geese, immense flocks of grey geese of international importance. Reserves like Vane Farm protect these birds, they no longer run the gauntlet of indiscriminate shooting as in the past. The Montrose Basin is a particularly fine site for wildfowl and waders in autumn and winter though subject to considerable public pressure from recreational use. The pressure on Scotland by the recreation industry is substantial and Tayside has felt the strain in many ways from walkers, winter sports enthusiasts and coastal golf and leisure parks along the sand-dune systems.

ATHOLL — *All year*

From Dunkeld to Blair Atholl the landscape is intensely varied, especially around the junction of the two ancient plates constitute the highland boundary fault line. This demarcation zone between the lowlands and the more rugged high ground is approached through an ice-worn 'U'-shaped valley of great beauty. The pass at Killicrankie is in wilder country, lowland Scotland having been swept away in a landscape of rugged hills home to only the hardiest of birds and animals such as the variable hare, red deer or grouse. In the 18th century much of this land would have been wooded with oaks on the low ground and Scots pine and dwarf willow on the high tops.

The variety of rocks is remarkable, some rich in lime others proved in the heat of past seismic upheavals that once rocked the areas when the highland fault was active; all are capable of producing ground flora of extreme variation. However, that speciality of the Scottish scene,

commercial conifer plantings, have made their impact upon the countryside and the wildlife, often to their detriment.

Between Dunkeld and the Loch of Lowes is the Wood of Craig, a beautiful oakwood with a substantial understory that includes rhododendron; the wood shows signs of being coppiced in the distant past for charcoal and tanbark, but its existence means the area is extremely rich in birds especially during the annual spring and autumn migrations. Birds of prey are common and not unnaturally include a healthy sparrowhawk population as well as buzzards.

The whole area is riven by rivers from the Tummel and Garry, both impounded for hydro-electric power generation, to the meandering course of the Tay. These rivers are home to trout and salmon and though the hydro-electric dams have greatly reduced their productivity there are still good runs of fish in the Tay. Building dams in these spate rivers is a two-edged sword, they provide adequate open water for waterfowl in winter, but they do restrict the flow of the watercourses and change their character. Fortunately the Tay has been spared some of this management and the river still finds its way through a maze of shingle islands that constantly change position as they are eroded and rebuilt by the flow.

BALGAVIES LOCH (Scottish WT) — *Spring, summer* (Flowers/breeding birds) *Winter* (Wildfowl)

A sheltered loch with rich fen and willow carr woodland extremely popular with wildfowl in autumn and winter, it provides a refuge in an area where conditions can be harsh, and the large flocks of greylag geese that flight in during winter evenings are a superb natural spectacle as are the flocks of mixed duck with wigeon, teal, goosander and shoveller. In summer the loch takes on a different hue with a great deal of marginal vegetation; roe deer are present and otters have been recorded with reasonable frequency.

40.5ha – Map ref: NO 528508

BALNAGUARD GLEN (Scottish WT)** — *Spring, summer*

This reserve is at its best in summer when the common blue and Scotch argus butterflies are abundant. The soil is loose glacial drift that erodes without adequate tree cover which in the past was provided by birch and rowan, both being dwarfed by the harsh conditions. The gorge that runs through the reserve is in total contrast to the moorland above; its sides are thickly wooded and dense stands of blackthorn provide superb nesting sites for small songbirds especially chaffinch. Other woodland breeding birds include redstarts and pied flycatchers while plants such as alpine bistort, fragrant orchids, cowslips and rock rose show the presence of lime-rich rocks. Mammals include both brown and variable hare, and red and roe deer, the former more a visitor in hard weather or when the does have very young fawns. Foxes and stoats are reasonably common and predatory birds include short-eared owls and sparrowhawks.

67ha

BEN LAWERS (NTS/NCC) — *Summer*

A relic population of lime loving arctic alpine plants is evident here, the rocks, mainly lime-rich schists, fracture and crumble making a loose almost scree-like terrain where specialised plants can gain roothold and where they are not grazed out by sheep or other herbivores — plants such as rose root, red campion, angelica, wood cranesbill and alpines like saw wort, alpine forget-me-not and alpine cinquefoil.

There are a few good areas for birds on this harsh uneven terrain, red grouse and wheatears can sometimes be seen, but this site is primarily for plants, and the small mountain ringlet, whose food plant matgrass (Nardus stricta), grows in exactly the right conditions. Warden-guided walks afford the best views of plants and insects for the layman.

3104ha – Map ref: NN 6138

BLACK WOOD OF RANNOCH (FC) — *Spring, summer*

An extremely important woodland as it represents part of the ancient Caledonian pine forest and birchwood once widespread over a great deal of Scotland until the end of the 18th century. The Forestry Commission are to be applauded for their efforts to restore the integrity of this site by removing exotic species and allowing natural regeneration of native Scots pine; there are some fine mature pines among them a few that are more than 250 years old, they provide a good source of food and ample nest sites for a great many birds who depend upon mature Scots pine woodland.

Capercaillie are common as are black grouse and Scottish crossbills, and siskins also breed here. In summer redstarts and spotted flycatchers breed, and the mammal population consists of roe and red deer, and red squirrels. Scottish wildcats have been increasing over the past decade. Long-eared owls and sparrowhawks are normally encountered in the woodland and the abundant small mammals are preyed upon by stoats.

2350ha – Map ref: NN 589561 / 536540 / 617573

KILLIECRANKIE (RSPB)** — *Spring, summer*

An SSSI, part of this reserve is a Grade 1 site. The sessile oakwoods rise to moorland through the gorge of the river Garry, wyche elm and alder grows on these steep hillsides too. Above the gorge is an area of pastureland, and above this the ground rises through birchwood to the crags and a ridge of heather moorland. Red squirrels and roe deer are plentiful, and there are a number of plant species dependant upon altitude and exposure ranging from mountain saxifrage higher up, to orchids on the lower more sheltered pastureland.

However, it is the range of birds that makes this such an important site. Wood warblers, redstarts, tree pipits, garden warblers and the occasional crossbill nest in the woodland; such a wealth of small birds attracts sparrowhawks, who also breed here, and buzzards are relatively common which indicates the numbers of small mammals and rabbits. The increasing population of green woodpeckers in this part of Scotland are able to find ample food and nest sites as do the smaller and less vocal greater spotted woodpeckers. High up on the crags are ravens, and the sight of a golden eagle or a peregrine falcon is not uncommon.

950 acres

LOCH OF THE LOWES (Scottish WT) — *Spring* (Breeding birds) *July* (Young ospreys - if present) *Winter* (Geese)

Of all the birds that have appeared at this fascinating lochside site, the ospreys probably arouse the greatest interest; these majestic birds have been on the Loch for more than twenty years and have reared a number of young to swell the Scottish osprey population. There are many other birds mainly associated with water and the Slavonian grebe, usually thought of as a winter visitor, built a nest and reared young, a very rare occurance south of the Grampian hills. Wildfowl, including hundreds of greylag geese, enliven the reserve in winter.

98ha – Map ref: NO 0544

MONTROSE BASIN (Scottish WT/Angus DC) — *All year, (especially winter)*

When seen on a map this huge area of productive mud-flats gives the impression of being neatly clipped out of the coastline with one of those hole punchers used by ticket collectors. The estuary of the south Esk river is a mecca for waders, the numbers of redshank and curlew is staggering in spring and summer, and dunlin, knot and oyster-catcher enliven winter skies as they race the rising tide over the mud. Thousands of whistling wigeon are among special sounds, and greylag and pink-footed geese roost here in considerable numbers, the presence of pink-feet is particulaly important. One of the problems of being so close to a major town is the conflict of interest with leisure and field sports enthusiasts, but when these are reconciled the site will resume its former importance as a natural history area.

1125ha – Map ref: NO 6957

VANE FARM (RSPB) — *All year*

Vane Farm is a protected area where visitors can be relatively close to many of the birds that feed and roost on Loch Leven. They drop in to Vane Farm to glean the farmland for potatoes, a crop specially planted for them, and there's often a chance to see snowgeese or the white-fronted geese among the immense numbers of greylag and pink-footed geese.

There's a visitor centre and observation hides at Vane Farm and the RSPB have created a scrape to attract the birds which has been an outstanding success. Such huge numbers of birds are bound to attract birds of prey and peregrines frequently hunt over the vast area of the Loch.

298 acres - Map ref: NT 160991

NORTHERN IRELAND

COUNTY ANTRIM

The blue hills of Antrim I see in my dreams,
The high hills of Antrim, the glens and the streams;
In sunlight and shadow, in weal and in woe,
The sweet vision haunts me wherever I go.
— Seosamh MacCathmhaoil

From the high north west of the county, with the stupendous giant's causeway of basalt columns, to the soft marine shores of Belfast Lough, water is dominant. The wet west winds that dictate Ireland's climate drop their cargo of rain and create a brilliant landscape of shaded green interlaced like a Celtic runic jewel with silver streams.

The whole of Northern Ireland owes its topography to the action of ice and the power of water. When the Irish Sea ice sheet melted at the end of the last Ice Age the land

Cruising in Ireland at Knockninny

surface reappeared, smoothed and reassembled, from beneath the grinding weight of billions of tons of crushing glaciers, only the hard igneous rocks to the north west survived the linishing leaving behind a legacy of drifts of gravel known as "drumlins" and fields of glacial moraine. The long warming of the post glacial period, together with intense rainfall, brought about streams and bogs, pools and loughs where troughs, gouged out by ice, filled with water and with life.

The soil is thin, supporting only grazing for cattle and sheep, but the people are used to the rigors of climate and rainfall. Nevertheless Antrim, with its abundant wild life and natural beauty, especially when the sun shines, is redolent still of the words of Seosamh MacCathmhaoil.

BREEN OAKWOOD (D.O.E. for NI) — *Spring, summer*

Mature relict oak woodland where sessile oak, birch and rowan predominates is rare on Dalradian soils, but Breen comprises a fragment of the woodlands that once covered much of the region. The moist nature of the habitat is reflected in the abundance of ferns, lichens and mosses and the woodland floor is thickly carpeted with woodrush. In spring and summer it's alive with birdsong, and the large insect population that thrives in the oak trees makes the wood a popular nesting site for warblers. *21ha – Map ref: D 124337*

EDENDERRY (Ulster WT)** — *All year*

A small area of marsh and woodland lying close to the headquarters of the Ulster Wildlife Trust and the River Lagan. The woodland, once part of the old estate of "The House at Edenderry", has a beautiful ancient and very large sweet chestnut surrounded by a number of naturally sown oak saplings, probably the work of jays of which there are many in the area. Edenderry is well known for its butterflies, especially small copper and small tortoiseshell, and the winter berry crop on the Irish yew and hollies attracts wintering thrushes.

190

The marsh is bounded by pasture, but it can be treacherous away from the marked riverside footpath.
2.76 acres

GARRY BOG (Forest Service Dept. of Agr) — *All year*

Part of a much larger raised bog system, the surface of Garry Bog is typically very wet, acid and impoverished with a dense plant cover including sphagnum moss, sundews and bog asphodel. Cranberry is a particular feature and although generally speaking bird life is limited, curlew and other inland wading birds find the site to their liking.
6.5ha – Map ref: C 938298

GAINT'S CAUSEWAY (National Trust) — *All year*

This wonderful natural monument is the result of the action of ancient volcanoes, Basaltic lava flows cooled into regular-sided columns and were exposed to the elements during the passage of tens of millions of years. The fertile Celtic imagination embued the rocks with a special magic and associated them with the giants and heroes of Ireland's mythology; and when you see this incredible place it's not at all surprising that they did so!
71ha – Map ref: C 954453

GLENARIFF GLEN (D.O.E. for NI) — *Spring, summer*

Situated within the most famous of the beautiful Nine Glens of Antrim, the reserve lies in a gorge and boasts a spectacular series of waterfalls; and the spray and moisture of this water system encourages a rich growth of ferns mosses and liverworts.
10ha – Map ref: D 210205

GLENARIFF LAKES (Forest Sevice Dept. of Agr) — *All year*

A series of three mountain lakes four miles south west of Waterfoot. Sedges are the principle ground cover here with large expanses of cranberry. The rare sedge (Carex pauciflora) has been recorded on this site, which is also a well known breeding refuge for redshank; wildfowl, including tufted duck, use the reserve in winter.
12ha – Map ref: D 195188

GLENARM (Ulster WT) — *Spring, summer*

This steep, wooded glen is the most secluded of the Nine Glens of Antrim. A footpath runs beside the course of the river Glenarm and where the path enters the reserve the river is wide and pebbly and favoured by herons as a fishing place. Further into the Glen the river's course is confined into steep rapids, falls and deep pools, a superb habitat for mosses and liverworts, ferns and plants of damp places. The bird life around the rapids is restricted, but the wooded banks of the glen are rich in species.
336ha – Map ref: D 301132

ISLE OF MUCK (Ulster WT)** — *March, September*

Access to this quaintly named famous seabird island refuge is strictly controlled as the landing area is somewhat dangerous; however there are many viewing points from the nearby coastline where the seabird colonies can be observed through binoculars and telescopes. Two thirds of the island's perimeter is bounded by rocky cliffs where black guillemots, kittiwakes, razorbills, fulmar petrels and a small colony of puffins nest.
13.78 acres

RATHIN ISLAND CLIFFS (RSPB) — *Spring, summer*

Access to this SSSI island reserve is by ferry from Ballycastle. Comprised of heathland and wetland with extensive grassland and basalt cliffs the main interest here is the variety of cliff sites for breeding birds and the large colonies of guillemots, black guillemots, puffins, razorbills, fulmars, shag and kittiwakes. Black-backed gulls nest on the top of the island and there are some manx shearwaters in burrows in the turf above the northern cliffs. As well as all this glorious multitude there are peregrines, buzzards, ravens and choughs; and the island forms a high vantage point over the sea where the passage of many different seabirds can be observed. (The reserve of Kebble can also be found on Rathin Island — 125 hectares managed by the DOE for N.I.)
Rathin Island Cliffs — 2½ miles — Map ref: (seabird colony can be viewed from D 093516)

REA'S WOOD — LOUGH NEAGH (D.O.E.for NI) — *Spring, summer*

One of the woodlands within the Loch Neagh complex of nature reserves. Rea's Wood boasts a rich fen woodland and a wide variety of insect fauna while the adjoining lake is well known for wintering wildfowl.
26.5ha – Map ref: J 143855

SHANES CASTLE (RSPB) — *All year*

This reserve is on an estate, part of which is open to the public, and adjoins the shores of Loch Neagh. It supports a variety of wetland habitats including alders and willow scrub where small breeding birds from the nearby parkland find ample food supplies in the breeding season; in the woodland you can see red squirrels and fallow deer.

There are several day and night flying birds of prey such as sparrowhawk, buzzard and long-eared owl and the abundant migrant songbird population includes blackcaps. In winter the shores of the Loch form a vantage point to see large flocks of wildfowl, and Bewick swans and greylag geese appear most years.
88 acres – Map ref: J 136874

SLIEVEANORRA (D.O.E. for NI) — *Spring, summer*

A footpath leads to Slieveanorra from the road and you will find four plots of land that illustrate the development of a peat bog with various stages clearly visible. This unplanted peat moorland is dedicated to the preservation of the red grouse, a bird generally in decline in Ireland, and for this reason no dogs are allowed here. It is also particularly important as the moorland has been surrounded by recently planted coniferous woodland.
49ha – Map ref: D 132865/D 135265/ D 147274/ D 155280

Slieveanorra Moor (Forest Service Dept. of Agr)
225ha – Map ref: D 140265

STRAIDKILLY (D.O.E. for NI)* — *Spring, summer*

Located between Carnlough and Glenarm, Straidkilly is an area of dry hazel wood on a steep east facing slope. It's an excellent place for small songbirds who find the low canopy to their liking.
8ha – Map ref: D 158305

SWAN ISLAND (D.O.E for NI)* — *Spring, early summer*

Managed by the R.S.P.B. as a tern breeding colony, access during the breeding season is prohibited.
0.1ha – Map ref: J 422993

COUNTY ARMAGH

Tucked in between the Newry Axis to the south west and the Caledonian Hills to the north west is the rift valley, a remnant of the landscape before the sea change wrought by the last great glaciation and the upheavals of the earth's crustal plates severed the land bridge between Scotland and Ireland.

The rift valley is seen to greater effect in Scotland where it carves through rugged terrain composed mainly of hard rock and where the great weight and power of the glaciers were unable to completely soften the outlines, but in Ireland, the destructive and abrasive force of an ice sheet a mile thick planed away the softer sedimentary rocks leaving a gentle rounded landscape with only remnants of the original limestone and the Tertiary granites that rise to form the Mourne Mountains 2000 feet above sea level.

The granite uplands were the last to be uncovered from permanent ice fields, and the land below, on the carved plain, was to be changed again in a welter of melt water, rocks and gravels deposited in heaps known as drumlins or lines marking channels such as the ones seen today where the outflow from Lough Neath runs to the sea emerging through the fiord-like Carlingford Lough.

The predominant westerlies create a fertile rolling lowland landscape of green with many streams, small farms and a variety of crops, changing to sheep grazing pasture as the land rises to the abrupt outcropping of hard rocks. The song "The Mountains of Mourne", beloved of exiles from this region tells poignantly of the mountains' soft sweep to the sea — the last sight of land from the deck of the ferry to England.

BRACKAGH MOSS (D.O.E. of NI)* — *Spring, summer*

Brackagh Moss is a large area of peatland that has been cut with a number of exposures showing the development of this fascinating natural resource as well as the fragility of this type of environment. An abundance of plants and insects are found here as recolonisation begins.
110ha – Map ref: J 019507

CARNAGH (Forest Service Dept. of Agr) — *All year*

A series of small lakes and mixed woodlands is all that is left of an old estate, nevertheless the woodlands are rich in spring birdsong and at the end of the summer an abundance of different sorts of fungi are to be found within the reserve's confines. The lakes come into their own in winter when many species of wildfowl can be seen; the presence of otters makes this a very interesting place.
12ha – Map ref: H 828295

HAWTHORN HILL (Forest Service Dept. of Agr) — *All year*

The diversity of tree species at Hawthorn Hill indicates the age and natural history value of the wood; red squirrels are found here, and a flock of wild goats.
29ha – Map ref: J 038193

Mountains of Mourne   *Co. Armargh*

LOUGH NEAGH ISLANDS — LOUGH NEAGH (D.O.E of NI)* — *All year*

These islands, which dot the surface of the Lough, provide important nesting sites for duck, terns and gulls, therefore access is restricted on many of them during the breeding season.
66ha – Map ref: J 053616

MILFORD CUTTING (Ulster WT) — *April through September*

Two miles south west of Armagh City, this reserve comprises two acres of disused railway cutting with a north/south orientation which makes it ideal for butterflies and wild flowers. The east bank is higher and has a wide range of flowering plants while the west bank is more shrubby and the floor of the cutting, once the bed of the railway tracks, is now marshy. It's an excellent reserve for migrant songbirds in spring and early summer.
2 acres – Map ref: H 859428

MULLENAKILL AND ANNAGARRIFF (D.O.E. of NI) — *Summer*

These adjacent reserves are part of the Peatlands Park; rich indeed in rare plants they are also of outstanding entomological interest.
99ha – Map ref: H 893610/H 905611

OXFORD ISLANDS LOUGH NEAGH (Craigavon Borough Council) — *All year*

This promontory of land on the shores of Lough Neagh supports a series of well established reed swamp communities, while on the higher land the grass and scrub provides perfect nesting and wintering sites for small birds. There's a visitor centre here and hides to enable you to get a better view — and also adequate footpaths.
66ha – Map ref: J 053616

LONDONDERRY

To my mind the shoreline is of greater beauty than the inland region, but beauty is in the eye of the beholder. The sand hills that stretch for miles along the seaboard towards Port Stuart and where the Bann finds the sea at Magilligan Strand are places of sheer loveliness, and both here and in the deep inlet of Lough Foyle wildlife teems. From Strabane the Foyle is a mecca for wintering and migrant wildfowl and waders, from Longfield to the Roe estuary there are abundant feeding and roosting stations for birds in winter and great flocks of whooper swans and lesser numbers of Bewicks arrive to rest and feed on the Lough and farmland.

The coastline north east of the Lough shows the power of the wide Atlantic for the westerlies deposit sand on the shoreline which is blown inland to form great dunes, some of the least spoilt in the British Isles. A whole ecosystem has been created with desert-like conditions of harsh shifting dry sand liable to 'blow out' in gales unless the deep roots of marram grasses can secure the dunes for other creatures and plants to colonise and stabilise.

Dune systems are perhaps the least valued of our natural habitats, often their rolling contours lie in strips between the land and the sea, ripe for exploitation as a tourist amenity, but dunelands are not capable of sustaining heavy public pressure without severe damage and the location and utilisation of the Ballymaclary dunes ensures a degree of control that will help to maintain them.

Inland where the Foyle gives way to the Finn and the Strule you'll find the hard ancient rocks of the Sperrin mountains, old metamorphic schists which have been softened by the action of ice and the passage of tens of millions of years of erosion by the elements.

BALLYMACLARY (D.O.E.of NI)** — *Spring, summer*

At the base of Magilligan point, and forming part of the firing range, the reserve at Ballymaclary must be visited only in the company of the warden; nevertheless this large area of relatively unspoiled dunes and damp dune slacks with their rare plant and animal communities should not be missed.
227ha – Map ref: C 697364

BANAGHER GLEN (D.O.E.of NI)** — *All year*

This reserve consists of three deep glens cut in the Dalradian rocks and which have produced a habitat of damp mixed woodland with a rich bryophyte community.
30ha – Map ref: C 672045

CRAIG-NA-SHOKE (Forest Service Dept. of Agr) — *Summer*

The erosion of peat has produced deep gulleys causing mushroom-like formations; these are seen particularly around the area known as Mullaghmoor where high rainfall on the moorland has produced Dendritic erosion and channels in the peat resemble the branches of a tree. Two club mosses are present including the rare (Lycopodium alpinum and Lycopodium selago). Land-slips caused by the peat surface slumping under the influence of water and erosion have given rise to terraces and lower down, the drier slopes support a varied montane grassland flora.
90 ha – Map ref: C 746005

LOUGH FOYLE (RSPB) — *Winter*

The reserve at Lough Foyle embraces the south east foreshore almost to the Roe estuary from Longfield Point and consists of wide mudflats with a fringe of salt-marsh shingle and shell ridges. The Lough itself is an outstanding refuge for wintering waders and wildfowl, the thousands of duck of many species that gather here (including flocks of wigeon, mallard and teal) are especially impressive.

Large flocks of pale-bellied brent geese also depend upon the Lough and white-fronted geese frequent the reserve, grazing on adjoining farmland with large gatherings of Bewick and whooper swans. The Foyle is well known for wintering flocks of snow buntings and the passage waders include spotted redshank. Wintering waders such as bar-tailed godwit and grey plover add to the excitement of the scene, and as at many of the R.S.P.B.'s sites visibility of the birds to visitors is excellent and facilities for the disabled are available.
3300 acres

MAGILLIGAN POINT (D.O.E.for NI)** — *All year*

Part of the complex of sand dunes and slacks lying within the M.O.D. range. The effect of wind and tide is particularly apparent along the coastal fringe. Warden accompanied trips only.
57ha – Map ref: C 665387

ROE ESTUARY (D.O.E.of NI) — *All year*

A tidal estuary which, with its extensive mudflats, forms an important wintering and passage site for wildfowl and waders. The sandbanks and salt marshes provide excellent refuge for waders at high tide.
474ha – Map ref: C 640295

THE UMBRA (Ulster WT) — *All year*

The showpiece of the Ulster Trust for Nature Conservation, The Umbra is a marvellous area of dunes and dune slacks with beaches and foreshore backed by woodland at the base of Eagle Hill. Considered to be the most unspoilt duneland in the whole of Northern Ireland and the newer dunes, though lacking some of the rarer insect and plant species of the main dunes, are none the less remarkable for their flora and fauna. It is a site that depends upon the destructive and constructive force of wind blown sand for its very life.
30ha – Map ref: C 724355

COUNTY DOWN

In the North of the county the city of Belfast is divided by the River Lagan and Belfast Lough; the city itself, with all its bustle and strife, is in stark contrast to the peaceful country at the southern tip of Down where the Mourne mountains rise above Dundrum Bay and the Irish sea.

The carboniferous limestone rocks of Strangford Lough show signs of scratching and polishing for the pink base rock is worn and furrowed, often overlaid with a thick blanket of boulder clay deposited over the ice-linished landscape by melting glaciers. Strangford Lough is of great international importance for wildfowl conservation for nearly three quarters of the European stock of light bellied brent geese winter here, and the mudflats at the northern end of the Lough are among the most productive and least altered examples of this type of habitat in the whole of Northern Island.

The peace and beauty of the county lies in its small fields and high mountains. Fertile, yet demanding, this is the land of the legendary hero Cuchulain, a champion of the Celtic chiefs. But too much of the history of the six counties is written in blood and obscures the true wonder of an area that boasts a sheltered coastline around Rostrevor and Warren Point, where native plants and insects enjoy an almost sub-tropical environment.

The calming influence of the high ground of the Mournes is felt in the mirrored surface of "Lough Cuan" the Irish name for Strangford Lough (the name translates into English as Calm Harbour). The Norse warriors of the 11th century gave the lough its name of Strangford because twice every day, in thrall to the tide, the lough fills and empties through the narrows between Strangford and Portaferry in a powerful tidal race. This tidal flow encourages a wealth of life in the mud and sandflats and one can imagine the roar of tens of thousands of wintering wildfowl as the tall dragon prows of the Norsemen's longships breasted the calm waters of the Lough.

BALLYQUINTIN POINT (D.O.E. of NI)* — *All year*

An exposed area with all the signs of the wind and sea in the flora and fauna and in the habitat that supports them. The reserve consists of a series of raised beaches on a rocky shoreline, the bushes that fringe the beaches are dwarfed by the topiary of wind and salt spray. It is an excellent place for winter migrants.
16ha – Map ref: J 624456

BELVOIR PARK (Forest Service Dept. of Agr.) — *Spring*

Although this reserve now comes within the urban area of the City of Belfast it was once part of an old estate (Belvoir Forest). These days it is heavily used by the public and the level of wildlife is naturally reduced, but depsite this pressure there's an abundance of migrant and resident songbirds. The regional office of the R.S.P.B. is situated in the park as is the Lagan Valley Regional Park warden and The Forest Service Educational Centre — the latter organise walks in the area.
15.4ha – Map ref: J 342698

BOHILL (D.O.E. of NI) — *Spring, summer*

This woodland reserve survived clear felling in the past and has been regenerated with a great deal of holly which, in turn, has produced an excellent habitat for a butterfly rare in Northern Ireland, the holly blue. They breed here in some numbers, especially in years when the weather is hot and dry. The open woodland and clearings are excellent for breeding migrant songbirds and for wintering thrushes, especially redwings.
2.8ha – Map ref: J 396459

CAIRN WOOD (Forest Service Dept. of Agr) — *All year*

Cairn Wood is a feature of County Down's landscape rising as it does over 900ft. Once an outlier of the Clandeboye Estate now its greatest value lies in its beauty and importance as a mixed woodland of considerable diversity. Beech trees predominate but oak and alder also occur providing for a varied wildlife, especially insects and birds. The open clearings in the wood are composed of grass with rushes and on the elevated section you'll find clear heathy areas with gorse.
40ha – Map ref: J 455774

CASTLE ESPIE (Castle Espie Conservation Centre-/Wildfowl and Wetlands Trust) — *All year*

This important joint venture was one of the last wildfowl refuges to be sanctioned by the late Sir Peter Scott before his death in 1989. Situated on the shores of Strangford Lough it has been run as a wildfowl refuge since the late 1970's by Paddy and Julie Mackie and has a fascinating history of development and decay, industry and conservation. Visitors are afforded ample opportunities to study birds, both captive and free flying, for there's a network of lakes and hides to observe the wildfowl that throng the area in winter. It's estimated that 70% of the European population of light bellied brent geese winter on Strangford Lough and can be seen from Castle Espie. Captive breeding of endangered species of wildfowl is a major part of the Trust's work and the red-breasted goose is a monitored species here; but it is the host of wild swans, geese and duck that choose to winter under Castle Espie's protection that provides a fitting tribute to a considerable conservation effort.
60 acres.

CLOGHY ROCKS (D.O.E. of NI) — *All year*

The tidal shoreline here supports an interesting fauna with seabirds and migrant species. Offshore the rocks are ideal for common seals to haul out; visitors are asked not to disturb seals during this time.
27ha – Map ref: J 594478

DORN (D.O.E.of NI) ** — *All year*

Formed by a naturally occurring rocky barrier across an inlet in Strangford Lough, this reserve is ideally situated for common seals to breed, while the muddy rocky foreshore provides an excellent feeding station for large numbers of wintering waders and wildfowl.
790ha – Map ref: J 593568

Strangford Lough   *County Down*

Castle Espie

GREEN ISLAND & GREENCASTLE POINT (RSPB) *
— *Spring through autumn.*

A promontory in the north east of Carlingford Lough, five miles south west of Kilkeel, this reserve comprises rocky shore and islets and is an important breeding area for colonies of roseate, common and arctic terns with a few oyster-catchers and ringed plover. The breeding terns may be viewed from the coast road at Greencastle which avoids disturbance, and access to the islets and the tern colonies is strictly prohibited for obvious reasons. At nearby Cranfield Point lighthouse there's a breeding colony of black Guillemots.
2 acres – Map ref: J 241118

HOLLYMOUNT (D.O.E.of NI) * — *All year*

In 1745 a tidal barrage was built across the Quoile estuary which has long since suffered the upstream silting common to such projects; now nature is taking a hand and the marshes and fen are developing into carr woodland, especially since major drainage works, instituted in the late 1950's, have lowered the water table. It is an excellent site for songbirds and small mammals with attendant predators.
12.5ha – Map ref: J 466399

INISHARGY BOG (Ulster WT)** — *Spring, summer*

Inishargy is an isolated bog lying in a drumlin hollow, a mosaic of habitats with typical fen vegetation such as sphagnum bog and on the higher ground colluna cover. Isolated clumps of willow and alder encourages small birds, and the royal fern, otherwise uncommon in the region, occurs here.
17.30 acres

KILLARD (D.O.E of NI) — *All year*

An interesting combination of a rocky foreshore and lime-rich dunes over glacial clays is found here, a combination conducive to an extremely wide range of plants and insects. The reserve is particularly noted for its plants, especially orchid species.
68ha – Map ref: J 610433

MURLOUGH (National Trust)* — *All year*

The reserve at Murlough is a very large area of stable sand dunes built up over a shingle basal layer. Dry conditions with some slacks present difficulties for plant life and it's interesting to see how nature has adapted to totally colonise this habitat; birds and small mammals are much in evidence, especially in autumn and winter.
283ha – Map ref: J 410350

NORTH STRANGFORD LOUGH (National Trust)* —
Autumn, winter, early spring

North Strangford Lough supports one of the least altered and most enviromentally interesting areas of mud flats in Northern Ireland. The reserve, which is extensive,

protects a wide range of birds in autumn and winter, and the area is particularly noted for wildfowl and waders.
1015ha – Map ref: J 508706

QUOILE PONDAGE BASIN (D.O.E. of NI)* — *Winter*

Formerly the tidal estuary of the river Quoile, Quoile Pondage Basin is now a very fertile lake rich in plant life and providing a valuable wintering area for wildfowl. The countryside centre offers an excellent interpretation of this special site.
195ha – Map ref: J 500478

ROSTREVOR OAKWOOD (D.O.E. of NI) — *Spring, summer*

The oakwood here, growing on ancient Silurian boulder soils is considered to be native woodland, part of the post glacial oak woods that once covered much of the area before man intervened. The flora and fauna is typical of this type of habitat with a very rich bird population particularly in spring and summer.
20ha – Map ref: J 186175

COUNTY TYRONE

The Strule river runs through a landscape created at the end of the last Ice Age when the gigantic ice sheet which covered so much of the western seaboard of Scotland and Northern Ireland began its inexorable retreat setting free from its icy grip an immense amount of gravel, clay, boulders and sand. It was this material that provided the destructive force of the glaciers and the combination of vast weight and abrasive power smoothed hills and levelled mountains leaving only basaltic plugs of long extinct seismic events as reminders of the past topography.

Torrents flowed from the base of ice cliffs creating features such as the Gortin Gap with its channels and drumlin swarms. The flow of damp air from the wide Atlantic ocean streaming into Donegal Bay produced a steady downpour that over the millennia helped to form the massive peat deposits and filled the great basin of Lough Erne crafting a jigsaw puzzle of islands and water.

The rainfall gave birth to streams and rivers in profusion with evocative names like Fairy Water. Indeed water dominates this land-locked county. From Mullan point in the east to the curve of Washing Bay Tyrone borders the wildfowl-rich waters of Lough Neagh, and from high bogs, rich in sundews, to foreshore rich in waders and wildfowl you will find a microcosm of typically Irish habitats.

ALTADAVAN (Forest Service Dept. of Agr) — *All year*

This small wood is the only representative of its type of old semi-natural woodland in the locality. Situated on a rocky knoll it's populated by oak and hazel with birch and some rowan, holly and blackthorn.
1.9ha – Map ref: H 596495

ALTAMULLAN (Forest Service Dept. of Agr) — *All year*

At the heart of this reserve is an old farm and sawmill, long since abandoned and returning to nature. The mill race has collapsed and is on the way to becoming a marsh and the mill leat has developed into an interesting wetland habitat. Trees range from ancient and decaying Scots pine and larch, to naturally regenerated scrub woodland; in all a superb place for songbirds and insects.
8ha – Map ref: H 160820

BLACK BOG (Forest Service Dept. of Agr) — *All year*

Green hairstreak butterflies lay their eggs on the leguminous species of plants found on this bog and hummock reserve with its interesting marsh flora, while the larvae of the marsh fritillary butterfly live on devil's bit scabious.
48ha – Map ref: H 642812

BOORIN (D.O.E of NI) — *Spring, summer*

A heathy area has developed on the well-drained soils here which derive from the drift of glacial deposits. A wood composed of oak and birch grows on the steep north facing slope.
58ha – Map ref: H 497846

COTTAGE FARM (Ulster WT)** — *April through October*

Situated on the banks of the river Strule, Cottage Farm reserve is, as you might suppose, based upon a working farm and was instituted to illustrate how a viable commercial enterprise can still possess much of natural history value. There are a variety of habitats including a cut-over blanket bog, mature woodland, an old flooded quarry and the banks of the river Strule — a wide range of sites for a wide range of birds, animals and plants.

Access is strictly by prior arrangement — please contact Mr M Archdale, Cottage Farm, 97 Carrigans Road, Omagh, Co Tyrone Tel: Omagh 52573.
105 acres – Map ref: H 436795

DRUMLISH (Forest Service Dept. of Agr) — *Autumn*

Drumlish consists of strips of broadleaved trees between coniferous woodland and is best known for fungi — sixty different species have been recorded here.
1ha – Map ref: H 352665

KILLETER FOREST GOOSE LAWNS (Forest Service Dept. of Agr) — *Winter*

As the name suggests this is where you'll find the Greenland white-fronted goose in winter. These geese, generally a declining species in Ireland, find this area of bog and rough ground between conifer plantations to their liking. Both this reserve and the nearby reserve of Killeter Bog are rich in plant species, especially sundews and sedges such as white-beaked sedge on which the geese graze in winter.
15.8ha – Map ref: H 093798/ H 078826

KNOCKAGINNEY (Forest Service Dept. of Agr) — *All year*

A small area of semi-natural woodland with a good range of shrub species, this reserve provides a suitable habitat for a herd of fallow deer; October is the time to see the bucks at the rut. In spring the area is alive with the territorial calls of native songbirds and summer migrants.
6.2ha – Map ref: H 714453

KNOCKMANY (Forest Service Dept. of Agr)* — *Spring, early summer*

Planted in the early 1920's, part of the reserve's woodland had developed into a "Heritage" stand of Sitka spruce and Douglas fir with a sizable population of red squirrels. Together with the wetlands of Ardunshin Lough and the associated reed-beds and wet carr woodland, the entire area is very rich in wildlife. No access from October to January.
31ha – Map ref: H 541550

MEENADOAN (D.O.E. of NI)** — *Spring, summer*

One of the very interesting bog areas found in the six counties. There is a clear succession of bog flora going back over the past twelve thousand years. Access - please contact Warden.
20ha – Map ref: H 244718

COUNTY FERMANAGH

The tail end of the Caledonian rift valley is still weakly defined in this region where the beautiful Lough Erne lies over its faulted bed. The bedrock is deeply scoured by the action of ice and the remains of long dead glaciers can be seen in the drumlins and drifts of glacial moraine. Here and there softened scarps of limestone have been honed to gentle curves by ice action and the effects of thousands of years of erosion by the elements; and the overall impression of the region is one of great beauty and fertility.

In the county town of Eniskillen lies the famous Portora Royal school which produced many notable scholars and artists, in particular the brillant Oscar Wilde and the creative aesthetic Reverend Francis Lyte, whose ministry work took him far from Ireland to the Devon fishing town of Brixham where he was the vicar of All Saints Church. As well as ministering to his congregation he wrote hymns; his talent was prodigious and he is best remembered for Praise My Soul the King of Heaven, played at our wedding, for my wife is from one of the old Brixham families and, of course, the deeply moving "Abide With Me". Ulster men have played their part in helping to form the culture of half the world, as Ireland's sons and daughters have left their homeland for countries far and wide.

The beauty of the Lough Erne lowland with its undulating drumlin swarms was very attractive to the early Celtic inhabitants; full of fish and fowl the many rivers and loughs and forests and fertile farmlands made rich pickings and evidence of the region's turbulent past can be seen in fortified settlements such as the round stone tower on Devenish Island more than eighty feet high and still showing parts of the wooden floors that housed its inhabitants, safe against marauders.

On the river at Belleek are banks of stone where the craft of eel fishing was carried on. The clear, fertile waters of Fermanagh have long been famous for their fisheries for both man and wildlife and the quiet backwaters of the county can frequently surprise a casual walker startled by the harsh "crank" of a heron disturbed at its meditative fishing, or delight by the sight of a kingfisher dashing low over the still surface of a gentle stream or stopping to fish from a lakeside branch.

The legend of The Swans of Lir tells of children doomed to wander forever after being changed into birds by their stepmother, and saved only from their feathered fate by St. Patrick. Such tales are easy to believe when you're standing by the side of the lough on a windless summer day and the tranquillity of the blue, glass-still, surface is broken only by the stately passage of mute swans.

AGHAGREFIN (Forest Service Dept. of Agr) — *Spring, summer*

Once heavily cut, this low lying bog has now been abandoned because of drainage problems and the rocky outcrops that form ridges through the area roughly east to west. The variety of habitats created by the abandoned turf cutting have been colonised by a wide range of moisture-loving plants while on the drier ridges tree cover has begun to invade showing promising signs for the future. Insects and birds, particularly wintering snipe and woodcock, find this complex area very much to their liking.
40ha – Map ref: H 210657

AGHATIROURKE (Forest Service Dept. of Agr) — *Spring, summer*

A multi-faceted site, Aghatirourke takes in bog, limestone pavement, scrub woodland and high heather covered hills. Complementing all this is evidence of past human habitation at Myalla with stone circles and a double chambered stone cairn, the earliest feature dating from 1800 BC. The base rock is upper mountain limestone of the lower carboniferous period formed in a shallow tropical sea probably as coral reefs.

The high rainfall and solubility of the rock has led to features such as "swallow" holes and fissured limestone pavement, and where the water has dissolved the rock on the high ground a blanket bog has developed with gulleys where varied woodland with rowan, ash, hazel and some oak has grown up. This moist habitat encourages profuse growth of ferns. Bird life varies according to the time of year and in spring the woodlands are alive with migrant songbirds while the high ground is the haunt of curlew and snipe.
695ha – Map ref: H 161315

BLESSINGBOURNE (Ulster WT)** —

Lough Fadda forms the hub of this nature reserve, part old estate woodlands and part wetland, and the margins along the lough are rich in plants and amphibians. The woodland suffers a little from rhododendron encroachment nevertheless, where this foreign invader has not shaded out the seedlings, the trees and shrubs and flowers are doing very well. It's an excellent site for birds with water and woodland-loving species in close proximity.
30 acres

CARRICKNAGOWER (Forest Service Dept. of Agr) — *All year*

A most interesting area of scarp and dip scenery with a wide variety of plants and insects. On the wet moorland you'll find butterwort. The north facing sandstone and boulder cliff faces provide a habitat for the rare filmy fern while on other cliff faces wintergreen thrives.

The wetlands are comprised of two lakes, the larger, Carricknagower, has a very good marshland flora including sundews while the smaller Lough Naman provides for a good winter wildfowl population.
86ha – Map ref: H 012544

CASTLE ARCHDALE ISLANDS (Forest Dept. of Agr)* — *Spring, summer*

Access to these three islands in the lower Lough Erne complex is by boat which means that the mixed deciduous woodland on soil derived from glacial drift has remained relatively undisturbed.
52.6ha – Map ref: H 148607/H 155603/H 158588

CASTLECALDWELL FOREST (RSPB) — *All year*

This reserve, predominantly a conifer forest on the shores of Lough Erne, includes a group of low drift islands, marginal reed and marshy woodland. It is particularly noted for its breeding population of common scoters which nest on the low-lying vegetated island. They share this habitat with heron, red-breasted merganser, tufted and mallard duck. On the pebbly sandy surface of the less vegetated islands small colonies of sandwich and common terns breed as do black-headed gulls. Great crested and little grebe are to be seen in the bays, and the forest supports a considerable range of breeding birds including siskin, the predatory sparrowhawk and long-eared owl. Corncrakes are a particular feature of the open areas.

In winter the wildfowl find the site to their liking and large numbers of various species flight in to the lake. There are frequent appearances of whooper swans in winter.
37 acres (plus 554 acres managed in conjuction with the Northern Ireland Forest Service) –Map ref: H 009603

COOLNASILLAGH (Forest Service Dept. of Agr) — *Spring, summer*

The farmland here, with its pattern of fields and hedges, is gradually returning to nature as the hedgerow trees seed

the pasture. There's a wide variety of bird and butterfly species and the site is famed for its spring display of flowering plants.
4.2ha – Map ref: H 433331

CORNAGAGUE WOOD AND LOUGH (Forest Service Dept. of Agr) — *Spring, summer*

Consisting of a small area of marshy woodland this reserve is dominated by willow and alder with a little holly on the drier ground. The lake is excellent for aquatic insects, particularly dragonflies. The area has developed to its present stage of colonisation following the cessation of peat cutting.
3.1ha – Map ref: H 474303

DOHATTY GLEBE (Forest Service Dept. off Agr) — *All year*

Base-rich soils and limestone cliffs have produced a wide range of plants, insects and birds. The reserve rises almost to the summit of Benaughlin, nearly 1200 feet, and two cairns, one on high ground and the other on the lower slopes provide an interest for archaeologists. The area, especially the scree slopes, is also noted for whinchats, a rare bird in this locality.
28.6ha – Map ref: H 180310

GLEN WOOD (Forest Service Dept. of Agr.) — *Spring, summer*

Oak woodland on heavy clay soils that has the appearance and some of the ground flora of ancient oak woodland despite the fact that it is not a naturally occurring forest, but was planted some time ago. Nevertheless it is rich in songbirds and butterflies.
4.8ha – Map ref: H 172330

Lough Erne *County Fermanagh (Nr. Kesh)*

HANGING ROCK AMD ROSSAA WOOD (D.O.E. of NI) — *Spring, summer*

Spectacularly attractive carboniferous cliff with ash woodland at its base. An excellent site for insects and birds.
15ha – Map ref: H 110365

KILLESHER (Forest Service Dept. of Agr) — *Spring, summer*

Woodland growing on base-rich soils with a predominantly ash, birch, hazel and rowan tree cover. The area is noted for its display of spring flowers, especially bluebells, dog's mercury and enchanter's nightshade.
3.7ha – Map ref: H 121358

MAGHO (Forest Service Dept. of Agr) — *All year*

Extending over a large area of limestone cliff and scree and onto the natural woodland margins of Lough Erne, the sheltered gulleys and rockfalls provide habitats for ferns and mosses with a host of birds on the lower slopes close to the Lough, including the common scoter which breeds here.
74.2ha – Map ref: H 080578

MARBLE ARCH (D.O.E. of NI)* — *Spring, summer*

A beautiful wooded limestone gorge, mainly ash but with some coppiced hazel understorey and a few areas of oak and beech. At its best in late spring.
24ha – Map ref: H 123350

NAAN ISLAND (Forest Service Dept. of Agr) — *All year*

Although accessible only by boat this reserve is a fine example of extensive reed swamp and marginal woodland where water birds, including heron, can find an undisturbed haven.
4.6ha – Map ref: H 296318

REILLY AND GOLE WOODS (D.O.E. of NI) — *Spring, summer*

An interesting and rich area of developing oakwood and scrub woodland, the latter found in Gole wood is the result of woodland clearance during the second world war. Now the reserve is very well suited to the needs of spring migrants and small mammals and squirrels. The ground flora is at its best in springtime which is also the best time for birdsong.
67ha – Map ref: H 340255/ H 336247

MONEYGAL BOG (Forest Service Dept, of Agr) — *All year*

This fine domed raised bog is one of the best examples in the country. It has been relatively unexploited, apart from some minor turf cutting on the periphery, and it's home to a wide range of specialist plants as well as the many wintering and breeding waders that abound here, including golden plover, snipe, redshank and jack snipe.
47ha – Map ref: H 241880

MULLYFAMORE (Forest Service Dept. of Agr) — *All year*

A raised bog where a small population of Greenland white-fronted geese feed upon the prolific growth of white-beaked sedge.
13.2ha – Map ref: H 105797

THE MURRINS (D.O.E. of NI) — *Spring, summer*

When the great glacier that covered this part of Ireland finally died at the end of the last Ice Age, the waters that flowed from the base of the melting ice sheet carried with them immense amounts of powdered rock in the form of sand and gravel; this was the basis of the Murrins. Twelve thousand years later there is a large stretch of heath with all the fascinating associated flora and fauna.
54ha – Map ref: H 565780

POMEROY (Forest Service Dept. of Agr) — *Spring, summer*

An educational forest site noted for its stand of Scots pine, some of which are several centuries old. Other parts of the estate support a variety of tree and shrub species that encourage a range of birds and insects, plants and fungi and there is also a wetland area where turf was removed in the past, but where mosses and wetland plants are recolonising successfully.
21.5ha – Map ref: H 712723

TEAL LOUGH (Forest Service Dept. of Agr) — *All year*

An area of bog and lough well known as a breeding site for teal, there is also a considerable colony of black-headed gulls in spring and early summer. The complex is made up of hummock and pool bog with a large variety of plant species, especially sundews and cranberry which abound in the short ground flora, while the pool contains a wide variety of sphagnum moss species.
40ha – Map ref: H 731880

TERMON GLEN (Ulster WT)** — *April through November*

A delightful area of estate woodland, about a century old, containing a mixture of hard and softwood trees and so providing a wide range of habitats for birds and insects; the woodland flora is representative of this type of habitat in Northern Ireland. A stream runs through the woods and feeds a small lake with two islands. It has been an area of interest to man for thousands of years and evidence of this is found in two Neolithic dolmen tombs.
25 acres – Map ref: H 625715

BIBLIOGRAPHY

A Choice of Thomas Hardy's Poems by Geoffrey Grigson Published by Macmillan

A Complete Guide to British Butterflies by Margaret Brooks & Charles Knight
Published by Jonathan Cape Ltd. Thirty Bedford Square, London.

A Field Guide to the Dragonflies of Britain, Europe and North Africa by J. d'Aguilar, J-L Dommanget,
R. Prechac
Published by Collins, 8 Grafton Street, London

A Field Guide to the Birds of Britain and Europe by Roger Peterson, Guy Mountfort, P. A. D. Hollom
Published by Collins, 8 Grafton Street, London W1

A Field Guide to the Insects of Britain and Northern Europe by Michael Chinery
Published by Collins, St James's Place, London

A foot in England by W.H. Hudson
Published by Oxford University Press, Walton Street, Oxford OX2 6DP.

A Guide to the Hill-Forts of Britain by A.H.A. Hogg
Published by Paladin Books, Granada Publishing Ltd, 8 Grafton Street, London W1X 3LA

A Literary Atlas & Gazetteer of the British Isles by Michael Hardwick
Published by David & Charles (Holdings) Limited, South Devon House, Newton Abbot, Devon

A Shepherd's Life by W. H. Husdon with a Foreword by Phil Drabble
Published by Macdonald Futura Publishers Ltd

A Shropshire Lad by A. E. Housman
Published by The Richards Press Ltd.

A Writer's Britain by Margaret Drabble
Published by Thames and Hudson Ltd

Bird Migration by Chris Mead
Published by Country Life Books, an imprint of Newnes Books, 84/88, The Centre, Feltham, Middx

Birds and Broadleaves Handbook by Nicholas Smart and John Andrews
Published by Royal Society for the Protection of Birds, Conservation Planning Department, The Lodge, Sandy, Bedfordshire SG19 2DL

Britons and Saxons The Chiltern Region 400-700 by K. Rutherford Davis
Published by Phillimore, Shopwyke Hall, Chichester, Sussex

Butterflies by Paul Whalley
Published by Mitchell Beazley Ltd,
87-89 Shafterbury Avenue, London W1V 7AD

Butterflies of the British Isles by J. A. Thomas
Published by Country Life Books, Hamlyn Publishing Group Limited, Bridge House, 69 London Road, Twickenham, Middx.

Cider with Rosie by Laurie Lee.
Published by Hogarth Press.

Collected Poems and Verses For Children by Leonard Clark
Published by Dennis Dobson

Collins Field Guide to Freshwater Life by Richard Fitter and Richard Manuel
Published by Collins, Grafton Street, London

Cowper Poetical Works edited by H. S. Milford
Published by Oxford University Press, Ely House, London W.1.

Discovering Walks in the Chilterns by Ron Pigram
Published by Shire Publications Ltd.,
Cromwell House, Church Street, Princes Risborough, Aylesbury, Bucks HP17 9AJ

Dylan Thomas Selected Works
Published by J.M. Dent & Son

Eleven British Poets An Anthology edited by Michael Schmidt
Published by Methuen & Co Ltd

Farming & Birds by Raymond J. O'Connor and Michael Shrubb
Published by Cambridge University Press

Field and Hedgerow The Last Essays of Richard Jefferies — Collected by his Widow
Published by Oxford University Press, Walton Street, Oxford OX2 6DP

Foresty Commission Booklet no. 15 Conifers by Alan F. Mitchell (Including a revision of some text originally written by the late Herbert L. Edlin)
Published by H.M.S.O. London

Foresty Commission Booklet no. 20 Broadleaves
Text by the late Herbert L. Edlin Revised by Alan F. Mitchell
Published by H.M.S.O. London

Frenchman's Creek by Daphne Du Maurier,
Published by Victor Gollancz Ltd.,

Guide to the Archaeological Sites of Britain by Peter Clayton
Published by B. T. Batsford Ltd, 4 Fitzhardinge Street, London W1H 0AH

Hardy Country by Gordon Beningfield,
Published by Allen Lane, Penguin Books Ltd, 27 Wright Lane, London W8 5TZ

Jefferies' Countryside nature Essays by Richard Jefferies
Published by Constable, London WC2

John Clare — Selected Poems, Edited by J. W. Tibble & Anne Tibble
Published by J. M. Dent & Sons Ltd, Aldine Press, Welbeck St., London

Kidnapped by Robert Louis Stevenson
Published by The Children's Press, London

Kilvert's Diary 1870-1879
Published by Century Publishing, London

Letter From a Far Country by Gillian Clarke
Published by Carcanet New Press Limited

Life before man by Zdenek V. Spinar
Published by Thames and Hudson, London

Lovely Britain edited by S.P.B. Mais and Tom Stephenson
Published by Odhams Press Ltd., Long Acre, London WC2

Mushrooms and other fungi of Great Britain and Europe by Roger

Phillips
Published by Pan Books Ltd., Cavaye Place, London SW10 9PG

Nature Guide to The Lake District Cumbria and N. Lancashire by Cliff Waller
Published by Usborne Publishing Limited, 20 Garrick Street, London WC2

Palgrave's Golden Treasury Compiled by Francis Turner Palgrave
Published by Lamboll House, London

Remains of Elmet by Ted Hughes
Published by Faber and Faber

RSPB Reserves Visiting edited by Anthony Chapman
Published by the Royal Society for the Protection of Birds, The Lodge, Sandy, Bedfordshire SG19 2DL

Shakespeare's Birds by Peter Hayman
Published by Kestrel Books, Penguin Books Ltd, Harmondsworth, Middx.

Shakespeare's Flowers by Jessica Kerr
Published by Longman Group Ltd

Tarka the Otter by Henry Williamson,
Published by Macdonald & Co., (Publishers) Ltd.

The Atlas of Wintering Birds in Britain and Ireland by Peter Lack
Published by T. & A.D. Poyser Ltd., Town Head House, Calton, Staffordshire

The Batsford Book of Country Verses
Published by Batsford Ltd., 8 Hardings Street, London

The BP Guide to Exploring Britain's Wildlife by Ian Beams
Published by David & Charles plc, Brunel House, Newton Abbot, Devon

The Celts by T.G.E. Powell
Published by Thames and Hudson, 30 Bloomsbury Street, London WC18 3QP

The Changing Countryside Edited by John Blunden & Nigel Curry
Published by Croom Helm Ltd., Provident House, Burrell Row, Beckenham, Kent BR3 1AT

The Collected Poems of A. E. Houseman
Published by Jonathan Cape, Thirty Bedford Square, London

The Complete Book of British Birds by RSPB and AA
Published by The Autombile Association Fanum House, Basing View, Basingstoke, Hants RG21 2EA

The Concise British Flora in Colour by W. Keble Martin
Published by Sphere Books (in association with Ebury Press and Michael Joseph)

The Country Life Book of the Natural History of the British Isles.
Consultant Editor Pat Morris,
Published by Country Life Bks (Hamlyn Publishing Group)

The Definitive Edition of Rudyard Kipling's Verse
Published by Hodder and Stoughton Ltd., Mill Road, Dunton Green, Sevenoaks, Kent

The Faber Book of Poems & Places edited with an introduction by Geoffrey Grigson,
Published by Faber & Faber, 3 Queen Square, London WC1N 3AU.

The History of the Countryside by Oliver Rackham
Published by J.M. Dent & Sons Ltd, Aldine House, 33 Welbeck Street, London W1M 8LX

The Macmillan Guide to Britain's Nature Reserves
Forewordby HRH The Prince of Wales,
Published by Macmillan London Ltd.

The Natural History of Selborne and The Naturalist's Calendar by Gilbert White.
Published by Blackie and Son Limited, London

The New Dragon Book Of Verse, Edited by Michael Harrison and Christopher Stuart-Clark
Published by Oxford University Press

The New Naturalist Heathlands by Nigel Webb
Published by Collins, Grafton Street, London

The Oxford Illustrated Literary Guide to Great Britain & Ireland edited by Dorothy Eagle & Hilary Carnell
Published by Peerage Books, 59 Grosvenor Street, London W1

The Oxford Book of English Verse, Chosen and Edited by Sir Arthur Quiller-Couch
Published by Oxford University Press Ltd.

The Poetry of Flowers by Samuel Carr
Published by B.T. Batsford Ltd. London

The RSPCA Book of British Mammals edited by Leofric Boyle
Published by Collins, St James's Place, London

The Shepherd's Calendar by Eric Robinson and Geoffrey Summerfield
Published by Oxford University Press

The South Downs by The Tramp
Published by London, Brighton & South Coast Railway

The Trees of Britain and Northern Europe by Alan Mitchell
Published by Collins, St James's Place, London

Time's Delights chosen by Raymond Wilson
Published by The Hamlyn Publishing Group Ltd.

Trees in Britain Europe and North America by Roger Phillips
Published by Pan Books

Where to Watch Birds in Bedfordshire, Berkshire, Buckinghamshire, Hertfordshire and Oxfordshire by Brian Clews, Andrew Heryet and Paul Trodd,
Published by Christopher Helm Imperial House, 21-25 North Street, Bromley, Kent BR1 1SD

Where to Watch Birds in Devon and Cornwall by David Norman and Vic Tucker
Published by Croom Helm Ltd., Provident House, Burrell Row, Beckenham, Kent BR3 1AT

Where to Watch Birds in Kent, Surrey and Sussex by Don Taylor, Jeffery Wheatly and Tony Prater
Published by Christopher Helm Publishers Ltd., Imperial House, 21-25 North Street, Bromley, Kent BR1 1SD

Where to Watch Birds in Wales by David Saunders,
Published by Christopher Helm Ltd., Imperial House, 21-25 North Street, Bromley, Kent BR1 1SD

Wild Flowers of Britain by Roger Phillips
Published by Pan Books

Wind in the Willows by Kenneth Graham
Published by Methuen, London

Wuthering Heights by Emily Bronte
Published by Nelson Doubleday Inc., Garden City, New York.

LIST OF NATURE CONSERVATION ORGANISATIONS

CC Countryside Commission,
John Dower House, Cresent Place, Cheltenham, Glos, GL50 3RA

NT National Trust
42 Queen Anne's Gate, London SW1H 9AS

NCC Nature Conservancy Council, for England (English Nature)
Northminster House, Peterborough PE1 1UA

RSNC Royal Society for Nature Conservation
The Green, Witham Park, Waterside South Lincoln LN5 7JR

RSPB Royal Society for the Protection of Birds
The Lodge, Sandy, Bedfordshire SG19 2DL

RSPCA Royal Society for the Prevention of Cruelty to Animals,
Causeway, Horsham, West Sussex RH12 1HG

WWT Wildfowl & Wetlands Trust
Slimbridge, Gloucester Gl2 7BT

WdT Woodland Trust
Westgate, Grantham, Lincolnshire NG31 6LL

Avon WT
(0272) 268018/ 265490
Avon Wildlife Trust
The Old Police Station, 32 Jacob's Wells Road, Bristol BS6 6YU

Bristol Naturalists' Society,
c/o Bristol City Museum, Queens Road, Bristol BS1 5AQ

Beds & Cambs WT
(0223) 880788
Bedford & Cambridgeshire Wildlife Trust
5 Fulbourn Manor, Manor Walk, Fulbourne, Cambridge CB1 5BN

Beds & Hunts WT
(0234) 64213
Bedfordshire and Huntingdonshire Wildlife Trust
Priory Country Park, Barkers Lane, Bedford MK41 9SH

Berks Bucks & Oxon NT
(0865 775476)
Berkshire, Buckinghamshire and Oxon Naturalists' Trust 3 Church Cowley Road, Rose Hill, Oxford OX4 3JR

Birmingham UWG
(021) 666 7474
Urban Wildlife Group (Birmingham)
131-133 Sherlock Street, Birmingham B5 6NB

Urban Wildlife Trust
Birmingham Nature Centre, Pershore Road, Edgbaston, Birmingham B15 7RL

Cheshire CT
Cheshire Conservation Trust
c/o Marbury Country Park, Northwich, Cheshire CW9 6AT

Cleveland WT
(0642) 608405
Cleveland Wildlife Trust
The Old Town Hall, Mandale Road, Thornaby, Stockton on Tees, Cleveland TS17 6AW

Cornwall TfNC
(0872) 73939
Cornwall Trust for Nature Conservation,
Five Acres, Allet, Truro, Cornwall TR4 9DJ

Cornwall Bird-Watching and Preservation Society.
Trendian, Perranwell Station, Truro, Cornwall.

Cumbria WT
(0966) 32476
Cumbria Wildlife Trust,
Church Street, Ambleside, Cumbria LA22 0BU

Derbyshire WT
(0332) 756610
Derbyshire Wildlife Trust
Elvaston Castle Country Park, Derby DE7 3EP

Peak Park Joint Planning Board,
Aldern House, Baslow Road, Bakewell, Derbyshire DE4 1AE

Devon WT
(0392) 79244
Devon Wildlife Trust
35 New Bridge Street, Exeter, Devon EX4 3AH

Devon Bird Watching and Preservation Society
Wichmor, Dousland, Yelverton, Devon

Dartmoor National Park Authority
Parke, Haytor Road, Bovey Tracey, Newton Abbot, Devon TQ13 9JQ

Dorset TfNC
(0202) 24241
Dorset Trust for Nature Conservation
39 Christchurch Road, Bournemouth BH1 3NS

Kenneth Allsop Memorial Trust
Knock-na-Cre, Millborne Port, Sherborne, Dorset DT9 5HJ

Durham WT
(091) 386 9797
Durham Wildlife Trust
52 Old Elvet, Durham DH1 3HN

Essex NT
Essex Naturalists' Trust
Fingringhoe Wick Nature Reserve, Fingringhoe, Colchester, Essex CO5 7DN

Basildon Natural History Society
80 Sparrow House, Basildon, Essex SS16 5EN

Gloucester TfNC
(045) 382 2761
Gloucestershire Trust for Nature Conservation
Church House, Standish, Stonehouse, Glos Gl10 3EU

Hants & I.O.W. NT
(0794) 513786
Hampshire and Isle of Wight Naturalists' Trust
71 The Hundred, Romsey, Hampshire SO5 8BZ

I.O.W. Natural History and Archaeological Society.
66 Carisbrooke Road, Newport, Isle of Wight PO30 1BW

Hereford NT
(0432) 56872
Herefordshire Nature Trust
Community House, 25 Castle Street, Hereford HR1 2NW

Herts & Middx WT
(0727) 58901
Hertfordshire and Middlesex Wildlife Trust

Kent TfNC
(0622) 5301/59017

Grebe House, St Michaels Street, St Albans, Herts, AL3 4SN

Kent Trust for Nature Conservation
The Annexe, la Bower Mount Road, Maidstone, Kent ME16 8AX

Jeffrey Harrison Memorial Trust
Sevenoaks Experimental Wildfowl Reserve, Tadorna,
Bradbourne Vale Road, Sevenoaks, Kent TN13 3DH

Lancashire TfNC
(0772) 324129

Lancashire Trust for Nature Conservation
The Pavilion, Cuerden Park Wildlife Centre, Shady Lane, Bamber Bridge, Preston, Lancs PR5 6A

Manchester Ornithological Society
3 Sunnybank Avenue, Manchester M30 9HD

Leics & Rutland TfNC
(0533) 553904

Leicestershire & Rutland Trust for Nature Conservation,
1 West Street, Leicester LE1 6UU

Lincs, S. Humber TfNC
(05212) 3468

Lincs & S. Humberside Trust for Nature Conservation,
The Manor House, Alford, Lincolnshire LN13 9DL

London WI
(071) 278 6612/3

London Wildlife Trust
80 York Way, London N1 9AG

Ecological Parks Trust,
c/o The Linnean Society,
Burlington House, Piccadilly, London W1V OLQ

Landmark Trust, 21 Dean's Yard
Westminster, London SW1 3PA

Ministry of Defence,
Lands Dept, Tolworth Tower, Ewell Road, Surbiton, Surrey KT6 7DR

Selborne Society
7 Glebe Court, Church Road, Hanwell, London W7 3BY

Norfolk NT
(0603) 625540

Norfolk Naturalists' Trust
72 Cathedral Close, Norwich, Norfolk NR1 4DF

Norfolk Ornithologists Association,
Aslack Way, Holme Next Sea, Hunstanton, Norfolk PE36 6LP

Northamptonshire WT
(0604) 405285

Northamptonshire Wildlife Trust
Lings House, Billing Lings, Northampton NN3 4BE

Northumberland WT
(091) 232 0038

Northumberland Wildlife Trust
Hancock Museum, Barras Bridge, Newcastle Upon Tyne NE2 4PT

Borders Natural History Society
The Reenes, Bellingham, Hexham Northumberland NE48 2DU

Nottinghamshire WT
(0602) 588242

Nottingham Wildlife Trust
310 Sneinton Dale, Nottingham NG3 7DN

Shropshire WT
(0743) 241691

Shropshire Wildlife Trust
St Georges Primary School, Frankwell, Shrewsbury, Shropshire SY3 8JP

Shropshire Ornithological Society
13 North Hermitage, Shrewsbury

Somerset TfNC
(082345) 587/8

Somerset Trust for Nature Conservation
Fyne Court, Broomfield, Bridgwater TA5 2EQ

Exmoor National Park Committee,
Exmoor House, Dulverton, Somerset TA22 9HL

Wells Natural History and Archaeological Society
c/o The Museum, Wells, Somerset

Staffordshire NCT

Staffordshire Nature Conservation Trust,
Coutts House, Sandon, Staffordshire ST18 0DN

Suffolk WT
(0728) 3765

Suffolk Wildlife Trust
Park Cottage, Saxmundham, Suffolk IP17 1DQ

Surrey WT
(0483) 797575

Surrey Wildlife Trust
The Old School, School Lane Pirbright, Woking, Surrey GU24 0JN

Horsell Common Preservation Society,
Fairbanks, Pembroke Road, Woking, Surrey GU22 7DP

Sussex WT
(0273) 492630

Sussex Wildlife Trust
Woods Mill, Shoreham Road, Henfield, West Sussex BN5 9SD

Warwickshire TfNC
(0926) 496848

Warwickshire Nature Conservation Trust
Montague Road, Warwick CV34 5LW

Wiltshire TfNC
(0380) 5670

Wiltshire Trust for Nature
19 High Street, Devizes, Wilts SN10 1AT

Worcestershire NCT

Worcestershire Nature Conservation Trust,
Hanbury Road, Droitwich, Worcs WR9 7DU

Yorkshire WT

Yorkshire Wildlife Trust
10 Toft Green, York YO1 1JT

North York Moors National Park Committee,
The Old Vicarage, Bondgate, Helmsley Yorks YO6 5BP

Yorkshire Dales National Park Committee,
Colvend, Hebden Road, Grassington, Skipton, N. Yorks BD23 5lB

WALES

Brecknock WT
(0874) 5708

Brecknoch Wildlife Trust
Lion House, 7 Lion Street, Brecon, Powys LD3 7AY

Clwyd

Deeside Naturalists' Society
Melrose, 38 Kelsterton Road,
Connah's Quay, Deeside, Clwyd

Dyfed

Pembrokeshire Coast National Park Authority,
Dyfed County Council, County Offices, Haverfordwest, Dyfed

West Wales Naturalists' Trust,
7 Market Street, Haverfordwest, Dyfed

Glamorgan WT
(0656) 724100

Glamorgan Wildlife Trust
Nature Centre, Fountain Road, Tondu, Mid Glamorgan CF32 0EF

Gwent WT
(0600) 5501

Gwent Wildlife Trust
16 White Snaw Court, Church Street, Monmouth, Gwent NP5 3BR

Brecon Beacons National Park Committee,
Monk Street, Abergavenny, Gwent NP7 5NA

Gwynedd	Snowdonia National Park Committee Snowdonia National Park, Penrhyn-deudraeth, Gwynedd, LL48 6LS	
Montgomery WT (0686) 24751	Montgomeryshire Wildlife Trust 8 Severn Square, Newtown, Powys SY16 2AG	
Radnorshire WT (0597) 3298	Radnorshire Wildlife Trust 1 Gwalia Annexe, Ithon Road, Lland-rindod Wells, Powys LD1 6AS	
North Wales WT	North Wales Wildlife Trust 376 High Street, Bangor, Gwynedd LL57 1YE	
	Countryside Council for Wales Plas Penrhos, Ffordd, Penrhos Bangor, Gwynedd.	

SCOTLAND

Scotland SWT (031) 226 4602	Scotland Wildlife Trust Headquarters, 25 Johnston Terrace, Edinburgh EH1 2NH
	Scottish Wildlife Trust 30 Woodend Road, Ayr
	Scottish Wildlife Trust 1 Westbank Quadrant, Glasgow W2
	Fair Isle Bird Observatory Trust, 21 Regent Terrace, Edinburgh EH7 5BT
	Forestry Commission, 231 Costorphine Road, Edinburgh EH12 7AT
	National Trust for Scotland Chief Ranger, Suntrap, 43 Gogarbank, Edinburgh EH12 9BY
	National Council for Scotland 12 Hope Terrace, Edinburgh EH9 2HS Tel 031 447-4784

NORTHERN IRELAND

R.S.P.B.	Royal Society for the Protection of Birds, Kebble, Rathin Co, Antrim BT54 6RT
	RSPB Reserves Officer, Belvior Park Forest, Belfast BT8 4QT

	Royal Society for the Protection of Birds, Castiecaldwell, Co, Fermanagh
National Trust	The National Trust Murlough NNR, Dundrum, Co. Down BT33 0NQ
	The National Trust Giant's Causeway Centre, 44 Causeway Road, Bushmills Co, Antrim BT57 8SU
	The Strangeford Lough Warden, The National Trust, Rowallane House Saintfield, Co. Down BT24 7LH
Antrim	Antrim Area Nature Reserves Warden. Department of the Environment for NI, Portrush Countryside Centre, 8 Bath Road, Portrush Co. Antrim B56 8AP
Armagh	Lough Neag / Armagh Nature Reserves Warden, Department of the Environment for NI. Oxford Island Visitor Centre. Craigavon. Co Armagh BT66 6NJ
Down	East Down Area Nature Reserves Warden, Department of the Environment for NI. Quoile Centre, 5 Quay Road, Down-patrick, Co Down BT30 7JB
	Mournes Warden Department of the Environment for NI Mournes Countryside Centre, 91 Central Promenade, Newcastle, Co Down BT33 0NH
Fermanagh	Fermanagh Area Nature Reserves Warden, Department of the Environment for NI. Castle Archdale Country Park, Castle Archdale, Irvinestown, Co Fermanagh
Londonderry	Londonderry/ N. Tyrone Area Reserve Warden, Roe Valley Country Park, 41 Leap Road, Limavady, Co Londonderry
Tyrone	Tyrone Area Nature Reserves Warden, Department of the Environment for NI. Peatlands Park, Parkside Depot, 33 Derryhubbert Road, Dungannon, Co. Tyrone BT71 6NW
	The Head Forester, Department of Agriculture for NI, District Forest Office, Crown Buildings, Mountjoy Road, Co Tyrone BT79 7AY
	Department of the Environment for Northern Ireland. Countryside & Wildlife Branch, Calvert House, 23 Castle Place, Belfast BT1 1FY
	Department of Agriculture for Northern Ireland, Forest Service, Dundonald House, Belfast BT4 3SB
Ulster WT	Ulster Trust for Nature Conservation, Barnett's Cottage, Barnett Demesne, Upper Malone Road, Belfast BT9 5PB

ACKNOWLEDGEMENTS

No book can be the work of one person, and in this case I have been merely an interpreter, assembling the facts that I felt would be of interest to the widest range of people who love the countryside and use it for their work and for recreation. Very many places throughout the country are designated "Nature Reserves", no two are alike and all are of equal value be they 28,000 acres or merely $\frac{1}{2}$ acre in size. It was not easy to single out which reserves to include and no doubt I have missed some outstanding examples — for that I apologise and can say only that this book reflects my personal choice.

Many organisations and individuals have been of immense assistance, providing me with data and it would take another volume to name them all — I thank each and every one of them. However, I must give a special thanks to particular people who smoothed my path — among them the unsung heros of conservation, the local Natural History Societies, without them there would be no conservation movement and few nature reserves. These societies come under the umbrella of The Royal Society for Nature Conservation (RSNC) and I would have found it impossible to unravel the complexities of this organisation were it not for Trina Paskell and her team in the Press and Public Relations Department in Lincolnshire.

The RSPB holds a very special place in my affections, being the springboard for my natural history career in the late 1950's. I'm indebted to Sue Steptoe, Chris Harbard and Anthony Chapman and all my many friends in the regions and various departments at the headquarters at Sandy — and I would like to thank the wardens of the RSPB reserves I visited for their knowledge freely shared.

I am also indebted to the Northern Ireland Tourist Office for opening my eyes to the beauty of the province, and providing such excellent photographs.

During the preparation of this book Sir Peter Scott died. I knew him for many years and owe him a personal debt of gratitude for his encouragement. His banner is now ably carried by the Director General of the Wildfowl and Wetlands Trust, Dr. Brian Bertram. I've always received the information I needed from Jackie le Fevre, the press staff and the people who actually work on the Society's many reserves.

Michael Clarke of Tewin Orchard in Hertfordshire helped me with information and photographs of badgers and foxes, and arranged access to the nature reserve in the orchard ajoining his house, which exists through his enthusiasm, and assistance from the Herts and Middlesex Wildlife Trust.

The Nature Conservancy Council for Great Britain and Northern Ireland were very helpful too and it would be discourteous to name some people while omitting others — both at head office in Peterborough and at the many regional and reserve offices where it was my good fortune to encounter so many experts.

Thanks must go to my publishers, Bishopgate Press and particularly Austen Smith, Publishing Director, who suggested I should write this book in the first place and for his unfailing courtesy and enthusiasm, never did he attempt to drive me along routes I did not wish to follow, and his humour and understanding were necessary when the size of the manuscript exceeed our initial estimates.

One of the joys of a civilised society is the library service. The chief librarian and staff of Hemel Hempstead's library helped me to find, on their crowded shelves and in the stores at County, many of the books on poets and writers I have used in this work.

I regard photography as a vital part of my work, but have to depend upon the skill and dedication of experts when it comes to the mechanical process of turning a hidden image on film into a beautiful slide; for this expertise I turned to the directors and staff of Bushy Colour Laboratories Ltd. The same care and attention to detail was shown by Berkhemsted Photographic who were able to meet impossible deadlines without lowering their high standards. These photographic specialists gave me the facility and time to retake some shots that otherwise I would have missed. I must also thank Margaret Beer and Michael Ricketts for loaning me some of their superb slides.

A complex book requires teamwork, and I'm grateful to Lynn Gold who had no idea what she was letting herself in for when I suggested she type a "few lists" — her care and effort in what turned out to be a mammoth task, made things so much easier.

It would be safe to say that I should have found the task of researching, writing, illustrating and photographing this book impossible had it not been for one person — the sheer effort required to draft and redraft, type and retype, and edit my appalling spelling and page long sentences is mind bending; but twenty-seven years ago I was sensible enough to marry the person to whom this book is dedicated, my wife Ann. Without her organisational skills, attention to detail and inability to tolerate second best, this book would not exist. And all this while running the household and juggling the finances. For these, and for many other things, I thank her with my love and admiration.

Dennis Furnell

Gadebridge
Hertfordshire 1991